1 AND 2 KINGS

NEW INTERNATIONAL BIBLICAL COMMENTARY

1 AND 2 KINGS

IAIN W. PROVAN

Based on the New International Version

© 1995 by Hendrickson Publishers, Inc.
P. O. Box 3473
Peabody, Massachusetts 01961–3473

First published jointly, 1995, in the United States by Hendrickson
Publishers and in the United Kingdom by the Paternoster Press,
P. O. Box 300, Carlisle, Cumbria CA3 0QS.
All rights reserved.

Printed in the United States of America

ISBN 1–56563–053–X

First printing — November 1995

Library of Congress Cataloging-in-Publication Data

Provan, Iain W. (Iain William), 1957–
    1 and 2 Kings   /   Iain Provan.
       (New International biblical commentary)
       Includes bibliographical references and indexes.
    ISBN 1–56563–053–X
       1. Bible.   O.T.   Kings—Commentaries.   2. Bible.   O.T.
Kings.   English.   New International.   1995.   I. Title.
II. Series.
BS1335.3.P77   1995
222′.5077—dc20   95–6225
                                                          CIP

British Library Cataloguing in Publication Data
A catalogue record for this book is available
from the British Library.

ISBN 0–85364–728–3

Scripture taken from the HOLY BIBLE, NEW INTERNATIONAL
VERSION. Copyright © 1973, 1978, 1984 International Bible Society.
Used by permission of Zondervan Bible Publishers.

To the glory of God
For Andrew, Kirsty, Duncan, and Catherine
With the prayer that they may always remember that:

"The fear of the LORD is the beginning of wisdom."
(Proverbs 9:10)

Table of Contents

Foreword
New International Biblical Commentary

As an ancient document, the Old Testament often seems something quite foreign to modern men and women. Opening its pages may feel, to the modern reader, like traversing a kind of literary time warp into a whole other world. In that world sisters and brothers marry, long hair mysteriously makes men superhuman, and temple altars daily smell of savory burning flesh and sweet incense. There, desert bushes burn but leave no ashes, water gushes from rocks, and cities fall because people march around them. A different world, indeed!

Even God, the Old Testament's main character, seems a stranger compared to his more familiar New Testament counterpart. Sometimes the divine is portrayed as a loving father and faithful friend, someone who rescues people from their greatest dangers or generously rewards them for heroic deeds. At other times, however, God resembles more a cruel despot, one furious at human failures, raving against enemies and bloodthirsty for revenge. Thus, skittish about the Old Testament's diverse portrayal of God, some readers carefully select which portions of the text to study, or they avoid the Old Testament altogether.

The purpose of this commentary series is to help readers navigate this strange and sometimes forbidding literary and spiritual terrain. Its goal is to break down the barriers between the ancient and modern worlds so that the power and meaning of these biblical texts become transparent to contemporary readers. How is this to be done? And what sets this series apart from others currently on the market?

This commentary series will bypass several popular approaches to biblical interpretation. It will not follow a *precritical* approach that interprets the text without reference to recent scholarly conversations. Such a commentary contents itself with offering little more than a paraphrase of the text with occasional supplements from archaeology, word studies, and classical theology. It mistakenly believes that there have been few insights into the Bible since Calvin or Luther. Nor will this series pursue an *anticritical* approach whose preoccupation is to defend the Bible against its detractors, especially scholarly ones. Such a commentary has little space left to move beyond showing why the Bible's critics are wrong to explaining what the biblical text means. The result is a paucity of vibrant biblical theology. Again, this series finds inadequate a *critical* approach that seeks to understand the text apart from belief in the meaning it conveys. Though modern readers have been taught to be discerning, they do not want to live in the "desert of criticism" either.

Instead, as its editors, we have sought to align this series with what has been labeled *believing criticism.* This approach marries probing, reflective interpretation of the text to loyal biblical devotion and warm Christian affection. Our contributors tackle the task of interpretation using the full range of critical methodologies and practices. Yet they do so as people of faith who hold the text in the highest regard. The commentators in this series use criticism to bring the message of the biblical texts vividly to life so the minds of modern readers may be illumined and their faith deepened.

The authors in this series combine a firm commitment to modern scholarship with a similar commitment to the Bible's full authority for Christians. They bring to the task the highest technical skills, warm theological commitment, and rich insight from their various communities. In so doing, they hope to enrich the life of the academy as well as the life of the church.

Part of the richness of this commentary series derives from its authors' breadth of experience and ecclesial background. As editors, we have consciously brought together a diverse group of scholars in terms of age, gender, denominational affiliation, and race. We make no claim that they represent the full expression of the people of God, but they do bring fresh, broad perspectives to the interpretive task. But though this series has sought out diversity among its contributors, they also reflect a commitment to a common center. These commentators write as "believing critics"—scholars who desire to speak for church and academy, for academy and church. As editors, we offer this series in devotion to God and for the enrichment of God's people.

Robert L. Hubbard Jr.
Robert K. Johnston
Editors

Preface

Academic man is no more an island than any other kind, and no piece of academic work is ever entirely the product of one person's efforts. This commentary, for example, was largely written during a period of sabbatical leave from the University of Edinburgh in the summer of 1993; and if leave had not been made possible, it would not yet have been written. Thanks are therefore due to my colleagues in the Faculty of Divinity, some of whom bore extra burdens because of my absence. I would like to thank in particular Dr. Graeme Auld, who has proved during my time in Edinburgh to be a most stimulating partner in dialogue about Kings, and who very kindly allowed me to read an advance copy of his interesting new book on textual and compositional matters, *Kings Without Privilege* (Edinburgh: T. & T. Clark, 1994). I am also most grateful to those who created the immediate environment in which I was able to work. I was privileged to hold a Visiting Fellowship at Clare Hall, Cambridge, throughout my time away from Edinburgh, and greatly enjoyed participating in the life of that community. My thanks are due to the President and the Fellows of the college for their invitation to join with them. Tyndale House, Cambridge, provided excellent accommodation and library resources, and—most important of all—a stimulating academic and spiritual context in which to do my daily work. I am deeply grateful to the staff and to my fellow workers for the experience. My family remain, finally, the solid mortal rock upon which all my enterprises are built and the touchstone for their connection with reality. They endured the project bravely and coped particularly well with the discovery that the relationship between the English noun "sabbatical" and the Hebrew verb *šābat* ("cease, desist, rest") is a tenuous one. The book is dedicated to my children, as a token of my love for them and as a witness to my aspirations for their future.

Three people need to be thanked in particular for their efforts in reading the manuscript. As it was being produced, the whole book was read by Dr. Lynette Provan and by Dr. Phil Long.

Both applauded sufficiently to be encouraging, and both offered criticism that has undoubtedly made it a better book than it otherwise would have been. I regard the presence of the Long family at Tyndale House during my time there as, in fact, providential. This is not only because of the benefits that I gained from talking with Phil and reading his excellent new book, *The Art of Biblical History* (FCI; Grand Rapids: Zondervan, 1994). It is also because of the babysitting facilities that they were able (and always willing) to offer. Such things are not unimportant. Towards the end of the process of composition, Dr. Philip Satterthwaite kindly read the introduction and offered helpful comment upon it. To all three, I express my warm appreciation.

A brief word is required about citations. My general policy has been to cite in the additional notes to each section of the commentary only certain very recent books and articles that touch upon what I consider important points of interpretation and that have not been taken into account by previous commentators on Kings. The preface is the place, therefore, where I must make clear how indebted I am to *all* those who have written before me. In this respect, too, the academic is far from being an island. I would like to have some trees left on my bit of land, however; so I cannot possibly mention everyone by name.

Iain Provan
New College, Edinburgh

Abbreviations

AB	Anchor Bible
ANET	J. B. Pritchard, ed., *Ancient Near Eastern Texts*
b.	Babylonian Talmud
BA	*Biblical Archaeologist*
B. Bat.	*Baba Bathra*
Ber.	*Berakot*
Bib	*Biblica*
BHS	*Biblia hebraica stuttgartensia*
B&L	The Bible and Literature Series
BSem	The Biblical Seminar
BZAW	Beihefte zur *ZAW*
CBQ	*Catholic Biblical Quarterly*
CBQMS	Catholic Biblical Quarterly Monograph Series
ConB	Coniectanea Biblica
DSB	Daily Study Bible
EBC	Everyman's Bible Commentary
ExpT	*Expository Times*
FCI	Foundations of Contemporary Interpretation
FOTL	Forms of the Old Testament Literature
Gen. Rab.	*Genesis Rabbah*
Gk.	Greek
GKC	E. Kautzsch, ed., *Gesenius' Hebrew Grammar,* trans. A. E. Cowley
Hb.	Hebrew
HTR	*Harvard Theological Review*
HSM	*Harvard Semitic Monographs*
IBC	Interpretation: A Bible Commentary for Teaching and Preaching
IBD	J. D. Douglas, ed., *The Illustrated Bible Dictionary*
ICC	International Critical Commentary
ICT	Issues in Contemporary Theology

Int	*Interpretation*
ITC	International Theological Commentary
JBL	*Journal of Biblical Literature*
JSOT	*Journal for the Study of the Old Testament*
JSOTSup	Journal for the Study of the Old Testament, Supplement Series
JSS	*Journal of Semitic Studies*
lit.	literally
LXX	Septuagint
MS(MSS)	manuscript(s)
MT	Masoretic Text
NCB	New Century Bible
NIV	New International Version
NT	New Testament
OBS	The Oxford Bible Series
OT	Old Testament
OTL	Old Testament Library
OTS	*Oudtestamentische Studiën*
POS	Pretoria Oriental Series
Proof	*Prooftexts*
RB	*Revue Biblique*
RSV	Revised Standard Version
Sanh.	*Sanhedrin*
SBLDS	Society of Biblical Literature Dissertation Series
SBLMS	Society of Biblical Literature Monograph Series
SHANE	Studies in the History of the Ancient Near East
SJOT	*Scandinavian Journal of the Old Testament*
SJT	*Scottish Journal of Theology*
TC	Tyndale Commentaries
Tg.	Targum
UCOP	University of Cambridge Oriental Publications
VT	*Vetus Testamentum*
VTSup	Vetus Testamentum Supplements
War	*The Jewish War*
WBC	Word Biblical Commentary
WBT	Word Biblical Themes
ZAW	*Zeitschrift für die alttestamentliche Wissenschaft*

Introduction

First and Second Kings represent two parts of what must clearly be thought of as one book.[1] Kings will consequently be referred to throughout this commentary as "the book" rather than "the books" of Kings. That is not to imply, of course, that this "book" is itself a self-contained entity that may be read in splendid isolation from the other books of the OT. On the contrary, it constantly presupposes knowledge of the story of Israel thus far, whether in Samuel (its close connection to which is well captured in the LXX title "1–4 Reigns" for Samuel-Kings); in Joshua and judges (cf. the traditional Jewish designation "The Former Prophets" for Joshua-Kings); or in the Pentateuch (particularly Deuteronomy). It also frequently invites reflection upon itself in the light of the prophetic and other writings of the OT.[2] This is a book that must be read with an eye to all the other books comprising the library that Christians call "the Old Testament." Indeed, a truly Christian reading will involve reflection upon the meaning of Kings in the total canonical context of the Christian Bible. The Book is the environment in which the individual book must be read.

The book of Kings tells us a story; it is *narrative literature*. It is a story that is certainly about the past (whatever else it may also be about); it is literature with *historiographical intent*. It is, finally, *didactic literature*—it seeks to *teach* its readers a number of things about God and the ways of God. By way of introduction we shall explore each of these three aspects of the nature of the book further.[3]

The Book of Kings as Narrative Literature

The book of Kings is *narrative* literature, rather than some other sort. A story is narrated, presenting a number of characters; events follow each other in chronological sequence; and verbal and thematic links bind the whole entity together. The main characters in the story are the LORD God of Israel, various Israelite kings and prophets, and a number of significant foreigners—although it is not always the main characters who are given prominence.[4] The plot is concerned with the attempt that Israel makes (or more often, does not make) under its monarchy to live as the people of God in the promised land and with how God deals with the Israelites in their success and failure. It is a plot worked out gradually, as king succeeds king, from David (1 Kgs. 1:1) to Zedekiah (2 Kgs. 25:7), with an epilog reserved for Jehoiachin (25:27–30), and in an ordered way, as the reign of each king finds its particular place in the book's framework. That framework characteristically tells us when, in relation to another king, a certain monarch came to the throne, how long he reigned, and the name of his capital city. We learn about his death/burial and his successor and about where to look for further information about him. We are offered an evaluation of him in terms of his religious policy. In the case of Judean (rather than northern Israelite) kings, we are told the name of his mother and his age at his accession to the throne. A good example of the full set of these so-called "regnal formulae" occurs in 1 Kings 22:41–43, 45, 50. With their general regularity of expression throughout Kings, the formulae contribute much to the book's sense of coherence—to the sense that it "hangs together" as a single piece of work (compare, e.g., 1 Kgs. 14:22–24 with 2 Kgs. 16:2–4, and both with 2 Kgs. 17:7–11). In fact, ancient tradition ascribed the book to a single author—to the prophet Jeremiah (cf. b. *B. Bat.* 15a).

Modern scholars have, on the whole, doubted the reliability of this tradition. They have generally doubted, indeed, whether a single author could have written the whole book at all. Although they acknowledge a significant degree of coherence within it, they claim to find a greater or lesser degree of incoherence as well—features that are unexpected in the work of a single author (e.g., inconsistencies, repetitions, variations in style and language). This suggests that the person who put Kings together was not able to do just as he wished. He was to a greater or lesser extent constrained by the material available to him, unable or unwilling to impose complete consistency upon it.[5] Alternatively (or in addition), the original work has been expanded by one or more editors.[6] They too were constrained by what lay before them, and they too were able to make the text convey their particular message only to a certain extent. What we have in Kings, then, is a composite work, put together over a period of time by a number of authors or editors, its various parts speaking with more or less conflicting voices.[7] Some voices may be louder than others, but they are still unable entirely to drown out their fellows.

Given this general perception of the nature of Kings, it is hardly surprising that scholarly reading of the book *as a book* in the modern period has generally ceased. It is not difficult at all to find monographs and articles written in the last two centuries that hypothesise about the original source material used by the editors of Kings or about the various levels of editing that might exist in the text.[8] It is not even very difficult to find discussion of the theology or theologies of the various people supposed to have been responsible for the book.[9] What is scarce before the last decade is writing on the book itself in its final form as a piece of narrative. This is also true in the commentaries. Numerous commentaries tell the reader, on the one hand, what individual pieces of Kings might have meant before they were incorporated into the book, or, on the other hand, which pieces are "original" to the book and which are late additions (or worse, "mere glosses"). There is no shortage of discussion of the historical and cultural background of the various parts of Kings, of the likely geographical location of the various cities mentioned in the text, of the obscurities of OT flora and fauna. Of the analysis of bits and pieces there has been (and continues to be) no end. Of the reading of a reconstructed narrative of some kind—the text rearranged to make it more "plausible," and the various "inconsistent" parts filtered out or subordinated to the narrative line being pursued by the commentator—there has been a little. Of the reading of the book as it stands *as a complete story* there has been, until recently, scarcely any.

But is the fundamental assertion of incoherence—which has fixed such a gulf between modern academic reading of Kings and both ancient and modern reading of other kinds—is this assertion well-founded? Repetition can, after all, be an aspect of literary artistry.[10] Variation in style and language can have many explanations other than difference in authorship. "Inconsistent" is a word often used where terms such as "theologically complex" or "ironic" would do just as well.[11] Is there anything that *compels* us to see incoherence in Kings? Or is it simply that OT scholars, often lacking general competence in literary matters and approaching Kings with inherited presuppositions about its incoherent nature, have largely found what they expected to find?

It is certainly the case that more recent work on Hebrew narrative, which has eschewed speculation about the way the biblical texts might have reached their present form and has attempted to understand them just as they are, has been extraordinarily fruitful in its efforts to make sense of them. It has, indeed, revealed the extent of the artistry involved in the construction, not only of individual stories, but also of whole sections of text and entire books. Incoherence tends to dissolve in the course of such analysis. Searching questions tend to be asked about models of composition that presuppose frustrated or reluctant authors, not fully in control of their material, or incompetent editors, intruding their presence sufficiently that we should notice them, but unable fully to impose themselves. The biblical text begins, in fact, to make considerably more sense (and to be a much better read) than many of the books written about it.

Encouraged by recent work of this kind,[12] and by my own reading of Hebrew texts, to believe that the trouble with Kings does indeed lie with the readers and not with the text, I have certainly set out in this commentary to read the book of Kings as a unified whole.[13] By this I do not imply that the book was, after all, produced by a single author at one particular moment in time, never to be touched by human hand again. I am persuaded, rather, that the books of the OT generally grew gradually into their present form in dialogue with each other, each shaping the developing tradition and being shaped by it. Only this explains the high level of intertextuality to be found in the OT—the way in which individual books either share portions of text with other books (e.g., 2 Kgs. 18:17–20:19 and Isa. 36:1–38:8; 38:21–39:8; 2 Kgs. 24:18–25:30 and Jer. 52:1–34), or quote them (e.g., 1 Kgs. 22:28 and Mic. 1:2), or otherwise reveal that they are aware of them (e.g., by narrating stories in such a manner that they evoke other stories with which they might usefully be compared or contrasted: see the commentary).[14]

For this reason I prefer the term "authors" to the term "author" when referring to the human forces responsible for the book's creation. My working assumption, nevertheless, has been that these "authors" have not been the victims either of their sources or of their own incompetence. They have presented the material that they wanted to present, ordered and crafted in the way they wanted to do it—just as the authors of Chronicles or the Gospels have done. They have produced a text that is intended to make sense as it is read cumulatively from beginning to end, each part being seen in the context of the whole. This is, of course, only an assumption. It is a reasonable assumption, nonetheless, corresponding to the assumption with which we approach narrative literature in general and grounded in what has been discovered about individual sections of Hebrew narrative in particular. It is reasonable—and reasonableness is all that can be hoped for where working assumptions are concerned. When such an assumption is brought to the text, together with a commitment to consider it possible that "problems in the text" may actually be "problems with my understanding of the text," I believe that the book of Kings can indeed be seen as a carefully crafted and coherent entity. The story "works." It does not need tinkering to make it do so.[15]

The stakes are high. The modern period has seen the gradual breakdown of the Bible story as the defining story of Western culture.[16] What was once regarded as a unified narrative whole that set the context in which individual human narratives were to be understood and lived out has come to be seen largely as a collection of larger or smaller fragments, unrelated to each other, and requiring recontextualization by the individual reader if they are to be properly understood. The Bible is a kind of primordial chaos, waiting for the reader-as-god to create something out of it. We have seen, in other words, the progressive loss of a sense of Scripture. This is certainly true of the Western world in general; but it is also true—in particular where the OT is concerned—of the church. The OT is a part of the Bible that the church seems increasingly happy to live without, except when it can be plundered for the odd illustration of a NT theme. The idea that it tells a coherent story that itself *defines* the church, although implied in many credal formulations, is not an idea that is in practice always taken very seriously. This is true across the theological spectrum. Even conservative commentaries on the OT narrative books tend to supply coherence to the story from elsewhere, rather than drawing it out of the story itself. They show little interest in reading the text *as a text*—even though they assert most firmly that it is a text inspired by God himself.[17] What is going on *behind* the text is regarded as much more important than what is happening *in* it.

For those who claim to stand in the orthodox Christian tradition, this loss of the OT as Scripture in both church and world cannot be a matter of indifference. Rather, its recovery must be regarded as of the utmost importance. This commentary is intended as a small step in that direction. It is therefore a commentary primarily on the book of Kings as narrative literature.[18]

The Book of Kings as Historiographical Literature

The importance of dealing with the biblical narrative texts on their own terms as literature is gradually becoming more widely acknowledged. It is striking, however, that so many of the authors who write so helpfully in this area at the same time display a marked reluctance to affirm the importance of dealing with these texts as accounts of the past. They acknowledge that a book like Kings gives the impression of speaking about the past. They concede that a history-like element is an obvious and important feature of this kind of book. They emphasize the life-likeness of much of the depiction, the lack of artificiality or heroic elevation in so much of the story. This is "realistic narrative." Yet they resist the idea that the narrative world thus portrayed has anything to do with the "real" world of the past. It is, rather, a "fictive world," entire in itself and referring only to itself. Its integrity must not be compromised by seeking to relate it to anything outside itself. Text and history must be kept apart.[19]

Why has this kind of argument become so popular? One would not wish to oversimplify. Yet it seems clear that its popularity has at least partly to do with a desire for protection. Those who have come to appreciate biblical narrative as narrative—even to rediscover, as they recover from a particularly large dose of historical criticism, the existential power of the biblical story as a story—wish to protect it (and themselves) from harm, to keep the text "safe." Experience has shown that the text is not "safe" in the hands of those concerned with what has happened in the past, wherever they claim to stand in the theological spectrum. These people have characteristically regarded it, not as a story to be read, but as a problem to be solved; not as literature, but as a quarry out of which "facts" may (or may not) be dug and used at will. It is largely those with historical interests, in fact, who have in the past rendered books like Kings unreadable, battling over the bits and pieces and obscuring the whole. This being so, is it not best simply to deny proper access to these Philistines who have no feel for the text and no interest in it for its own sake? And how better to do this than to affirm that the sort of questions that they might ask of it—those questions of historical referentiality— are simply irrelevant? It does not matter whether what Kings says corresponds to what appears to have happened in historical Israel. All that matters is that the story makes sense in itself and when read along with the other OT stories.

Interestingly enough, it is not only those with literary interests who want to keep text and history apart. It is increasingly the historians themselves. It has become fashionable to distinguish quite self-consciously between "biblical Israel" and "historical Israel." "Historical Israel" is the real Israel that occupied the central Palestinian highlands for just over two centuries and has left its traces in Palestinian soil. This Israel is to be studied by looking at the artifacts the people left behind, the buildings they occupied, and the literature they certainly wrote (i.e., datable inscriptions), all within the framework of general theory about such things as social and state formation. "Biblical Israel," on the other hand—the Israel presented to us in the OT—is a literary construct. It has some points of contact with the past, but it is so ideologically slanted that it cannot serve as the starting point for serious historical enquiry. It must be set aside, as we attempt to replace fiction with facts—as a truly critical scholarship takes over from a scholarship compromised by religious sentiment.[20]

Separation of text and history is popular, then, on all sides. Some like it because it offers the prospect of insulating both text and reader against the chilly winds of historical enquiry. Others favor it because it clears the way for the progress of *proper* historical enquiry, as the last demons of religious presupposition are forever cast out. The fact that it is popular, however, does not mean we should accept it as a given. First, it is clear that a book like Kings has historiographical intent. It looks, not only sideways at the other books of the OT but also back to the events and characters of the past. It seeks to tell us, not about a fictive world, but about the real world that God has made and in which God acts. To be sure, it does tell us about this real world in ways that sometimes have a fictive quality about them. There appear to be literary conventions governing the use of names and numbers,[21] for example, that must be taken into consideration when attempting any correlation between text and history where these phenomena are concerned. To fail to take the historiographical impulse seriously overall, however, is to fail to take the book seriously. That failure is as profound as the failure to read the book as a book. It will not do—at least, not if one thinks it important that texts and their authors should be treated with respect. Most scholars regard this as important in relation to their own books. It is only proper that they should treat other people's books in the same way.

Secondly, it is not entirely clear why we should dig the great ditch between biblical Israel and historical Israel that the newer historians demand. It is, after all, the case that all historiography, whether ancient or modern, has a story-like quality—that all writing or speaking about the past involves turning happenings and people into events and characters. All historiography is also in some sense ideological literature. That is, any story about the past involves selection and interpretation by authors intent on persuading their readership in some way.[22] This does not mean that historiographical texts are in general incapable of speaking truly about the past. The historians in question clearly believe that some stories about Israel's past are indeed true. They believe this, for example, of many of the modern stories about it—the stories told by archaeologists, anthropologists, sociologists, and the rest. We assume, in addition, that they wish us to regard their own books as true accounts of Israel's past—and not, for example, as cleverly constructed fictions. There is evidently no difficulty in principle, then, about historiographical texts referring truly to the past. It seems that a decision has simply been made that the biblical witness to Israel's past, in particular, is to be marginalised. A selective skepticism is at work here. The biblical stories about Israel, on the one hand, are approached with the maximum degree of suspicion in regard to the extent to which they truly reflect what happened. There is, on the other hand, a touching degree of (sometimes quite uncritical) faith displayed when it comes to modern narratives about this same entity. Confessionalism of a religious sort is attacked in the name of critical enquiry and objectivity, but the noisy ejection of religious commitment through the front door of the scholarly house is only a cover for the quieter smuggling in (whether conscious or unconscious) of a quite different form of commitment through the rear.

Those who think that selective skepticism in general is a poor foundation upon which to build historical reconstruction are, however, likely to take a very different view about the picture of Israel found in the book of Kings. It will be regarded, certainly, as only one portrait of the past among the many that might have been painted. It is clear on any reading of Kings that its authors do not tell us everything that happened during that part of the Iron Age about which they are writing.[23] They do not even claim to do so.[24] Kings is a highly selective account, in which fairly long periods can be passed over briefly and periods of a year or less can occupy quite a bit of space. It is a particular view of the past, with its own highlights and its own persuasive appeal[25]—only one portrait of what happened, but no less valuable as a witness to the past for that.

The person who views Kings as part of Christian Scripture, however, will want to say more than this. This person will want to say that this portrait is one of two concerning this period of Israelite history that God has given the church for use in "teaching, rebuking, correcting and training in righteousness" (2 Tim. 3:16). It is one of the *authorized* portraits of Israel's past (Chronicles is the other) so far as life and faith are concerned; and other portraits are simply of academic interest. It is this portrait that is to be received and studied. I say "received" quite deliberately. It is no part of the Christian exegete's task to participate in that attempted re-painting of the portrait in the modern colors favored by so many of the commentators on Kings. This exercise has as its premise the idea that it is possible to make Kings "more historical" than we currently find it to be. We do this largely by reinterpreting what the authors of the book tell us about the past in terms, firstly, of a closed system of thought where God does not act in the world and where there can be no appeal to miracle as an explanatory account of events;[26] and in terms, secondly, of what people other than the authors of Kings, both ancient and modern, have to say about what was happening during this time.[27] Why the resulting pictures should be regarded as "more historical" than what we are actually given in Kings is something of a mystery. Their most obvious feature is usually their subjectivity, as each scholar paints the portrait of the past which is right in his or her own eyes, according to various (and extremely varied) notions about what is "probable," and "possible," and so on.

The Christian exegete of Kings who is thinking consistently, however, is not going to view the task of exegesis as involving the progressive expulsion of God from the book and the progressive introduction of other, "more objective," explanations for the course of Israelite history. She or he is certainly not going to view the task as involving the reshaping of the book on the basis of material that was not at first included in it. The portrait as painted will be the object of study. The narrative will be taken seriously as a whole, in its relationship to the past.

In summary, my conviction is that, although it is the *text* that is authoritative for the Church and not the history behind the text—the *portrait* and not the subject painted—the question of historical referentiality cannot be dodged. Kings must be taken seriously as a narrative about Israel's past.[28]

The Book of Kings as Didactic Literature

The book of Kings is not only a narrative about the past. It is also a narrative that seeks to *teach* its readers a number of things about God and his ways. That is, the book of Kings tells us about Israel's past, not so that we should become better informed about it in some abstract, intellectually detached way, but so that we should learn from it (Rom. 15:4; 1 Cor. 10:11). The best way into this subject is probably first of all to summarize the story as a whole, before discussing in a more thematic way its theology.

The book of Kings opens towards the end of David's reign with a struggle over which of his sons should succeed him. Solomon emerges victorious over Adonijah and is given instructions by David about how he should rule (1 Kgs. 1:1–2:11). He should keep the law of Moses, so that the LORD will keep his promise to David of an everlasting dynasty over Israel, and he should act as a man of wisdom. The succeeding narrative is constructed around these two ideas of wisdom and law (2:12–11:43). For much of the time Solomon's wisdom functions in a positive way, as the people of Israel enjoy prosperity and peace and see the temple of the LORD built in their midst. At both the beginning and the end of his reign, however, it operates in a more self-interested way, as Solomon eliminates those who threaten his hold on the throne and accumulates vast wealth. For much of the time, the king is presented as someone committed to the LORD and his ways. Yet there are from the very beginning questions about his complete adherence to the law, and eventually he turns away and worships other gods. Surprisingly, however, his disobedience does not lead to the end of the Davidic dynasty. A prophet announces that punishment will be deferred until the days of his son, who is to lose only part of the kingdom, rather than all of it. This alienation of northern Israel from David will itself not last forever. It is only a temporary phenomenon.

The dissolution of the empire is duly described, as Jeroboam, son of Nebat, leads northern Israel into independence from Rehoboam and Judah (1 Kgs. 12:1–24). It is an exodus into

slavery, however, as the northern kingdom is immediately capti-
vated by other gods and never again succeeds in breaking free of
their influence, whether they be the gods manufactured by Jeroboam (12:25ff.) or those introduced from elsewhere (16:29ff.).
Prophets oppose the apostate kings, whose dynasties come and
go as the judgment of God falls upon them. The most notable of
these prophets are Elijah and Elisha, whose activities take up a
substantial part of the narrative throughout 1 Kings 17–2 Kings
13. They themselves in some respects mitigate the full force of
God's wrath upon Israel, offering salvation in the midst of judgment. Final judgment is in any case slow in coming, because of
God's promises and his compassion for his people (2 Kgs. 10:30;
13:23). Eventually, however, it arrives; northern Israel is sent into
exile in Assyria (2 Kgs. 17).

Although the religious situation in Judah is initially no
better than that in Israel (1 Kgs. 14:22–24; 15:3–5), Judah's story
thereafter is not one of continuous apostasy. Relatively good
kings do rule in the gaps between the wicked kings (1 Kgs.
15:9–22:50; 2 Kgs. 12:1–15:38), and towards the end of the story,
we meet two of the very best kings there ever were (2 Kgs. 18:1ff.;
22:1ff.)—kings who reform Israelite worship and obey and trust
in God. Sin gradually accumulates, nevertheless, and although it
at first appears that, because of a deep commitment to David,
God will treat Judah with less severity than Israel, in the end this
commitment only delays judgment rather than averting it. The
sins of Manasseh are too much to bear (2 Kgs. 21), and Judah is
duly exiled to Babylon (2 Kgs. 24–25). The future of the Davidic
line apparently hangs by the slender thread of a displaced ruler
sitting at the table of the king of Babylon (25:27–30).

Various themes are prominent in the story.[29] First, God is
indeed God. He is not to be confused with the various gods
worshipped within Israel and outside—for these are simply human creations (1 Kgs. 12:25–30; 2 Kgs. 17:16; 19:14–19). They are
part of the created order, like the people who worship them, and
they are powerless, futile entities (1 Kgs. 11:5; 16:13; 18:22–40;
2 Kgs. 17:15; 18:33–35). The LORD, by contrast, is the incomparable Creator of heaven and earth (1 Kgs. 8:23; 2 Kgs. 19:15),
utterly distinct from the world created (1 Kgs. 8:9, 14–21, 27–30;
18:26–38), yet powerfully active within it. It is God, and not any
god, who controls nature (1 Kgs. 17–19; 2 Kgs. 1:2–17; 4:8–37;
5:1–18; 6:1–7, 27). It is God, and neither god, nor king, nor
prophet, who controls history (1 Kgs. 11:14, 23; 14:1–18; 22:1–38;

2 Kgs. 5:1–18; 10:32–33; 18:17–19:37). This latter point is perhaps illustrated most clearly in the way that prophets generally function within the book, describing the future before God brings it about (1 Kgs. 11:29–39; 13:1–32; 16:1–4; 20:13–34; 2 Kgs. 19:6–7, 20–34). Nothing can hinder the fulfilment of this prophetic word—although God in divine freedom can override its fulfilment for divine purposes (1 Kgs. 21:17–29; 2 Kgs. 3:15–27). There is only one living God; it is the LORD (1 Kgs. 18:15; 2 Kgs. 5:15).

Secondly, as the only God there is, the LORD demands exclusive worship. God is not prepared to take a place alongside the gods or to be displaced by them. God is not about to be confused with any part of the created order. God alone will be worshipped, by Israelite and foreigner alike (1 Kgs. 8:41–43, 60; 2 Kgs. 5:15–18; 17:24–41). Much of Kings therefore addresses the problem of illegitimate worship. The main interest is in the *content* of this worship, which must not involve idols or images nor reflect any aspect of the fertility and other cults of "the nations" (1 Kgs. 11:1–40; 12:25–13:34; 14:22–24; 16:29–33; 2 Kgs. 16:1–4; 17:7–23; 21:1–9). There is subsidiary concern about the *place* of worship, which is ideally the Jerusalem temple and not the local "high places" (1 Kgs. 3:2; 5:1–9:9; 15:14; 22:43; 2 Kgs. 18:4; 23:1–20). The book is also concerned to describe the moral wrongs that inevitably accompany false worship. For as the worship of something *other* than God inevitably leads to some kind of mistreatment of fellow-mortals in the *eyes* of God (1 Kgs. 21; 2 Kgs. 16:1–4; 21:1–16), so true worship of God is always bound up with obedience to the law of God. By the same token, true wisdom is defined in terms of true worship and wholehearted obedience. It is not something that can be divorced from either (1 Kgs. 1–11). Worship and ethics are two sides of the same coin, in Kings as elsewhere in the OT.

Thirdly, as the giver of the law that defines true worship and right thinking and behavior generally, the LORD is also the one who executes judgment upon wrongdoers. The world of Kings is a moral world in which wrongdoing is punished, whether the sinner be king (1 Kgs. 11:9–13; 14:1–18), prophet (1 Kgs. 13:7–25; 20:35–36), or ordinary Israelite (2 Kgs. 5:19–27; 7:17–20). It is not a vending-machine world, however, in which every coin of sin that is inserted results in individually packaged retribution. There is no neat correlation between sin and judgment in Kings, even though people are told that they must obey God if they are to be blessed (1 Kgs. 2:1–4; 11:38). This is largely because of the compassionate character of the Judge, who does not desire final judgment to fall upon beloved creatures (2 Kgs. 13:23; 14:27) and is ever ready to find cause why such judgment should be delayed or mitigated (1 Kgs. 21:25–29; 2 Kgs. 22:15–20). God's grace is to be found everywhere in the book of Kings, confounding the expectations that the reader has formed on the basis of law (1 Kgs. 11:9–13; 15:1–5; 2 Kgs. 8:19). Sin can, nevertheless, accumulate to such an extent that judgment falls not only upon individuals but upon whole cultures, sweeping the relatively innocent away with the guilty (2 Kgs. 17:1–23; 23:29–25:26).

This brings us at the last to the theme: promise. It is promise that is usually found at the heart of the LORD's gracious behavior towards the people of God. The most prominent of the promises in Kings is God's promise to David of an eternal dynasty. It appears in a curiously paradoxical form. In much of the narrative it provides us with an explanation as to why the Davidic dynasty survives, when other dynasties do not, *in spite of* the disobedience of David's successors (1 Kgs. 11:36; 15:4; 2 Kgs. 8:19). The promise is viewed, in other words, as unconditional. At other times, however, the continuance of the dynasty *is because of* the obedience of David's successors (1 Kgs. 2:4; 8:25; 9:4–5). The promise is treated as conditional. As the book progresses this latter view seemingly prevails; accumulating sin puts the promise in its unconditional aspect under too much stress and in the end brings God's judgment down upon Judah just as severely as upon Israel (2 Kgs. 16:1–4; 21:1–15; 23:31–25:26). And yet, Jehoiachin lives (2 Kgs. 25:27–30). His survival in the midst of near total disaster, like that of Joash before him (2 Kgs. 11), holds out the possibility of recovery for the Davidic line—the possibility that the promise transcends sin after all and that David will indeed rule again over all Israel, as 1 Kings 11:39 implies. It suggests that grace may triumph over law in the story of Israel's future, as in so much of the story of her past. A similar possibility is clearly in mind with regard to the other great promise in the book—the promise to Abraham, Isaac, and Jacob of descendants and everlasting possession of the land of Canaan. This too is a promise that influences God's treatment of his people in the story (2 Kgs. 13:23, and implicitly in 1 Kgs. 4:20–21, 24; 18:36), and it is a promise that lies in the background of Solomon's prayer in 1 Kings 8:22–53, as he looks forward to the possibility of forgiveness after judgment. Grace may not be presumed upon, but it can be hoped for on the basis of God's character and promises.[30]

The story of Kings, which has these themes at its heart, is not self-contained. It is part of the whole story of the Bible from Genesis to Revelation, and it must be read by the Christian reader with an eye to that total canonical context. The Book, as I asserted towards the beginning of this introduction, is the environment in which the individual book must be read. This does not mean (as it has sometimes been taken to mean in the past) that Kings has no theological significance of its own and that its meaning is entirely bestowed upon it by the NT. That is not to take the OT seriously as Scripture. The OT must be read as speaking to the church on its own terms—as providing the theological (and not simply the historical) context in which the NT is to be understood, as well as being read in the light of the NT.[31] It does mean, however, that Christians must read a book like Kings in the light of the whole biblical story as it has unfolded to its end. We must, in particular, read it in the light of the words and actions of the central character of that story, Jesus Christ. The Bible will be approached, in other words—as it has been throughout the Christian era (although decreasingly so in modern times)—as a ". . . canonically and narrationally unified and internally glossed . . . whole centered in Jesus Christ and telling the story of the dealings of the Triune God with his people and his world . . ."[32]

Read in such a way, one of the things that immediately becomes apparent about the story is its patterning. The biblical story is told in such a way that events and characters in the later chapters recall events and characters in the earlier chapters, by way of comparison or contrast. This is already apparent within the book of Kings. The kings of Judah are compared and contrasted with David; Jeroboam is painted in the colors, first of Moses, and then of Aaron; both Manasseh and Josiah in their own ways remind us of Ahab; and so on. It is also apparent in the NT, whose authors tell the story of Jesus in ways that constantly remind us of Kings, whether at the general thematic level (God; worship and ethics; sin and judgment; grace and promise) or at the level of individual character and event. The story of Kings, in other words, functions typologically in respect of the later NT story, preparing its way and gaining full significance only when read with it in mind. It also functions typologically in respect of the persons addressed by the NT (i.e., us, the readers). It invites us to read our own lives into the lives of its characters—to attach our story to its larger narrative whole—and it gains its full significance for us only as we begin to understand ourselves in its context.[33]

It is naturally impossible in the course of a single book to comment fully on how such patterning works and on how OT and NT are drawn together by it.[34]I have, however, cited NT references where it has seemed to me that reflection on the NT might contribute to the reading of Kings in a particularly significant way (and vice versa). In addition, I have on four occasions departed from straightforward commentary on the text to offer some thoughts on major characters in the book in canonical context (see §§18, 34, 46, 57). Those looking for ideas as to how sections of Kings can be preached or taught in a Christian context might well look at these excursuses and at the scripture index at the end of the commentary, where the other biblical passages mentioned in the commentary are listed. The commentary is designed, however—like the book upon which it comments—to be read all the way through, rather than simply dipped into here and there, and it is only engagement with the whole book of Kings that will truly communicate its distinctive message. It exists not to be *raided* but to be *read!*

Notes

1. The break between the present two "books," right in the midst of the account of Ahaziah's reign in 1 Kgs. 22:51–2 Kgs. 1:18, is evidently artificial. Readers should note at this point that wherever the MT and the NIV differ in their verse numbering, I will follow the NIV. Those wishing to correlate the commentary with the Hb. text need to remember that 1 Kgs. 4:21–34 is 1 Kgs. 5:1–14 in the MT and therefore that the number fourteen has to be added to the verse numbers in the NIV's 5:1–18 to get the Hb. equivalents. They will also need to add the number one to the NIV's verse numbers in 1 Kgs. 22:43b–53 and 2 Kgs. 11:21–12:21, and to remember that there are slight differences in verse division between the MT and the NIV at 1 Kgs. 18:33–34; 20:2–3; and 22:21–22.

2. We may note, for example, the way the Solomon story, as it grapples with the nature and consequences of that king's "wisdom," so frequently echoes themes from the book of Proverbs (see the commentary for details) and the way the closing words of the prophet Micaiah

in 1 Kgs. 22:28 invite us to understand the Ahab story in the light of the book of Mic.

3. The book of Kings is not, of course, unique in having this three-fold nature. Many of the biblical books are like this, as others have pointed out—although not necessarily using the precise terms that I have selected here. Cf., for example, M. Sternberg, *The Poetics of Biblical Narrative: Ideological Literature and the Drama of Reading* (Bloomington: Indiana University Press, 1985), pp. 1–57; and M. Hengel, "Literary, Theological and Historical Problems in the Gospel of Mark," in *Studies in the Gospel of Mark* (London: SCM, 1985), pp. 31–58.

4. It is a recurring feature of the Elisha narratives in 2 Kgs. 3–8, for example, that the humble and lowly are the channels of God's salvation to Israelite and foreigner alike, rather than those of status and importance. The account of the healing of Naaman in 2 Kgs. 5 offers a particularly good example.

5. An influential study along these lines, which takes in all the books from Deut. to Kgs., is Martin Noth's *The Deuteronomistic History* (JSOTSup; Sheffield: JSOT Press, 1981), first published in German in 1943. The tensions within this deuteronomist history are the result of its incorporation of source materials of differing perspectives. Its author, "the Deuteronomist" (because of the centrality of Deuteronomy to his thinking), " . . . did not intend to create something original and of a piece but was at pains to select, compile, arrange and interpret existing traditional material . . . " That is why " . . . the separate parts of the work seem disunited and heterogeneous" (p. 77).

6. Even those who have argued for substantial unity in Kgs. (and in the "Deuteronomistic History" from Deut. to Kgs. as a whole) and have criticised Noth for giving insufficient attention to the author as a genuine author (as opposed to an editor) have generally accepted that the original Deuteronomistic book of Kings has to some extent suffered secondary editing. We may note, for example, J. Van Seters, *In Search of History: Historiography in the Ancient World and the Origins of Biblical History* (New Haven: Yale University Press, 1983), pp. 277–321. For summaries of the main positions with regard to composition and editing, see further I. W. Provan, *Hezekiah and the Books of Kings: A Contribution to the Debate about the Composition of the Deuteronomistic History* (BZAW; Berlin: De Gruyter, 1988), pp. 1–31; and S. L. McKenzie, *The Trouble with Kings: The Composition of the Book of Kings in the Deuteronomistic History* (VTSup; Leiden: Brill, 1991), pp. 1–19. For a brief discussion of such issues in the context of ancient history-writing, see B. O. Long, *1 Kings, with an Introduction to Historical Literature* (FOTL; Grand Rapids: Eerdmans, 1984), pp. 14–21.

7. Some scholars have argued that there was already a substantial and continuous narrative about the Israelite monarchy as early as the 9th century BC. See, for example, A. F. Campbell, *Of Prophets and Kings:*

A Late Ninth-Century Document (1 Samuel 1–2 Kings 10) (CBQMS; Washington: The Catholic Biblical Association of America, 1986). Most doubt, however, that there was any such thing until at least the 7th century (e.g., Provan, *Hezekiah,* 153–55; McKenzie, *Trouble,* pp. 117–34). It is clear, of course, that the book in its present form could not possibly have been written before the 6th century (cf. the description of Jehoiachin's release in 2 Kgs. 25:27–30), which is precisely when some think it was *first* put together (e.g., Noth, *Deuteronomistic History,* pp. 79–83). Others maintain that it is the product of a still later time. See, for example, P. R. Davies, *In Search of "Ancient Israel"* (JSOTSup; Sheffield: JSOT Press, 1992), pp. 75–133.

8. See again Provan, *Hezekiah,* pp. 1–31; McKenzie, *Trouble,* pp. 1–19.

9. We may note, for example, Noth, *Deuteronomistic History,* pp. 89–99; G. von Rad, *Old Testament Theology,* vol. 1 (Edinburgh: Oliver & Boyd, 1962), pp. 334–47; M. Weinfeld, *Deuteronomy and the Deuteronomic School* (Oxford: Oxford University Press, 1972), pp. 191–319; H. W. Wolff, "The Kerygma of the Deuteronomic Historical Work," in *The Vitality of Old Testament Traditions,* ed. W. Brueggemann and H. W. Wolff (Atlanta: John Knox, 1975), pp. 83–100.

10. Cf. J. Licht, *Storytelling in the Bible* (Jerusalem: Magnes, 1978), pp. 51–95; R. Alter, *The Art of Biblical Narrative,* (London: Allen & Unwin, 1981), pp. 88–113.

11. Cf. Sternberg, *Poetics,* pp. 84–152, 186–320; D. M. Gunn and D. N. Fewell, *Narrative in the Hebrew Bible* (OBS; Oxford: Oxford University Press, 1993), pp. 46–89, 147–73.

12. I have been particularly encouraged by the readings of Kgs. offered in the major commentaries of B. O. Long, *1 Kings,* and *2 Kings* (FOTL; Grand Rapids: Eerdmans, 1991); T. R. Hobbs, *2 Kings* (WBC; Waco: Word, 1985)—note especially his excellent introduction "On Reading 2 Kings," pp. xxvi–xxx; and R. D. Nelson, *First and Second Kings* (IBC; Louisville: John Knox, 1987). My debt to these writers will be apparent to all who know their work, although I frequently disagree with them in matters of interpretation.

13. In using the phrase "the book of Kings" in this context, I refer to the literary composition reflected by the MT as it stood at the beginning of the process of copying and textual transmission. In the first instance, our approach to this text is via the Leningrad Codex, as it appears before us on the pages of *BHS.*

14. On inter-textuality, cf., for example, M. Fishbane, *Biblical Interpretation in Ancient Israel* (Oxford: Clarendon, 1985); D. A. Carson and H. G. M. Williamson, eds., *It Is Written: Scripture Citing Scripture: Essays in Honour of Barnabas Lindars* (Cambridge: Cambridge University Press, 1988), pp. 25–83. See further the comments of L. Eslinger, "Inner-Biblical Exegesis and Inner-Biblical Allusion: The Question of Category," *VT* 42 (1992), pp. 47–58.

15. My approach to Kgs. in this commentary is thus rather different from the one adopted in my *Hezekiah* volume. While I would certainly want to stand by much of the detailed exegetical work in that volume, I am no longer convinced that the presuppositions governing the overall analysis are correct. I agree, in fact, with J. G. McConville's criticism of the book, in his *Grace in the End: A Study in Deuteronomic Theology* (Grand Rapids: Zondervan, 1993), p. 81: that the analysis " . . . diverted attention from important features of 1, 2 Kings as narrative." It is this fault that I seek to remedy here.

16. Cf. H. W. Frei, *The Eclipse of Biblical Narrative: A Study in Eighteenth and Nineteenth Century Hermeneutics* (New Haven: Yale University Press, 1974).

17. It is striking that D. J. Wiseman, *1 and 2 Kings* (TC; Downers Grove, Leicester: InterVarsity, 1993), for example, spends much more time relating pieces of text to events outside the text, about many of which the text knows nothing, than he spends explaining the connection of the various pieces of text *to each other*. The nature of the text as continuous narrative is simply not taken seriously when it comes to its interpretation. His comments on 2 Kgs. 8:1–6 offer a particularly good example of this. Apparently we may only say, in spite of its narrative location, that the incident described here *"may* [my italics] have taken place in the reign of Jehoram" (p. 212)!

18. For a brief and accessible introduction to many of the issues raised in this section, cf. T. Longman III, *Literary Approaches to Biblical Interpretation* (FCI; Grand Rapids: Zondervan, 1987).

19. Cf., for example, Frei, *Eclipse,* pp. 1–16, who distinguishes between what is "history-like" and what is truly "historical"; and Nelson, *Kings,* who frequently puts distance between what the canonical text says and what may actually have happened historically (e.g., in regard to Jeroboam, p. 81).

20. The precise way in which the argument is framed here owes much to Davies, *Search.* He is only one of a growing number of OT scholars, however, who adopt this kind of position in relation to text and history. We may note, for example, G. Garbini, *History and Ideology in Ancient Israel* (London: SCM, 1988); N. P. Lemche, *Ancient Israel: A New History of Israelite Society* (BSem; Sheffield: JSOT Press, 1988); T. L. Thompson, *Early History of the Israelite People from the Written and Archaeological Sources* (SHANE; Leiden: Brill, 1992).

21. It has long been recognized by scholars, for example, that certain names in the MT have been deliberately corrupted, apparently in order to express disgust for them (cf., e.g., 2 Sam. 2:8 and 1 Chron. 8:33, where the name of the god Baal in Esh-Baal's name has been replaced by the Hb. noun *bōšet,* "shame") and that the large numbers of the MT are not necessarily to be understood as actual historical numbers. The use of smaller numbers also raises questions, however. The immediate

successors of kings who receive news of impending judgment on their royal house, for example, characteristically reign for "two years" in Kgs. (1 Kgs. 15:25; 16:8; 22:51; 2 Kgs. 21:19). Are we really being told exactly how long they reigned, or are we to see this as an example of narrative art, linking these kings together and inviting reflection upon them as a group? And what are we to make of the highly schematic ending to the book, where the last four kings of Judah are described as reigning successively for three months; eleven years; three months; and eleven years (2 Kgs. 23:31–24:20)? One wonders whether some of the attempts to resolve the enormous problems connected with the chronology of the MT Kgs.—e.g., E. R. Thiele, *The Mysterious Numbers of the Hebrew Kings* (3d ed.; Grand Rapids: Zondervan, 1983)—would have been quite so tortuous if the scholars concerned had paused to ask how the various numbers concerned were *meant* to be taken.

22. On these two points about historiography, see the excellent general discussion in K. L. Younger Jr., *Ancient Conquest Accounts: A Study in Ancient Near Eastern and Biblical History Writing* (JSOTSup; Sheffield: JSOT Press, 1990), pp. 1–58, and the bibliography there. For further illustration of this discussion in terms of modern historiography, see J. Clive, *Not By Fact Alone: Essays on the Writing and Reading of History* (London: Collins Harvill, 1990).

23. Assyria is first mentioned in Kgs., for example, in the description of Menahem's reign in 2 Kgs. 15:17–22. Extrabiblical texts claim, however, that Assyrian kings had been campaigning in the west long before that. Even after 2 Kgs. 15:17–22, Assyria is referred to relatively infrequently, mainly in the story of the siege of Jerusalem (2 Kgs. 18–19, cf. 20:6), otherwise only in 2 Kgs. 15:29; 16:7–10, 18; 17:3–6, 23–27; 23:29. Assyria plays only a minor part in the overall drama of 2 Kgs. 15–23, even though extrabiblical texts report it as engaging in quite a bit of "off-stage" activity throughout this period. For a convenient selection of the extrabiblical material in question, cf. M. Cogan and H. Tadmor, *2 Kings* (AB; Garden City, N.Y.: Doubleday, 1988), pp. 333–40.

24. The regnal formulae continually point us to sources from which, it is implied, the material in Kgs. has been drawn (e.g., 1 Kgs. 11:41; 14:19, 29). It is thus made quite explicit that a substantial amount of the material the authors knew of has been omitted.

25. We may note, for example, that whereas the account of Manasseh's reign of fifty-five years occupies only eighteen verses (2 Kgs. 21:1–18), the account of the religious reform in Josiah's eighteenth year takes up at least forty-one (2 Kgs. 22:3–23:23). Zimri, who ruled for seven days (1 Kgs. 16:15–20), gets almost as much space as Omri (1 Kgs. 16:21–28), who ruled for twelve years, and Azariah (2 Kgs. 15:1–7), who ruled for fifty-two.

26. J. Gray, *1 & 2 Kings* (OTL; 3d ed.; London: SCM, 1977) is perhaps the worst offender where miracle-stories are concerned. He

regularly offers quite ludicrous re-readings of them in order to make them more "believable" (e.g., on 1 Kgs. 17:2–24 and 2 Kgs. 6:1–7), while at the same time accusing certain other commentators, amazingly enough, of being "rationalistic" (e.g., on 1 Kgs. 18:34). His approach to these texts is only a particularly extreme example, however, of the general tendency to explain away miracles.

27. So it is, for example, that although Assyria is given only a small part in the book of Kings, it is one of the central players in many *interpretations* of the book. Cf., for example, R. H. Lowery, *The Reforming Kings: Cults and Society in First Temple Judah* (JSOTSup; Sheffield: JSOT Press, 1991).

28. For an excellent introduction to the subject of historiography, biblical and otherwise, see V. P. Long, *The Art of Biblical History* (FCI; Grand Rapids: Zondervan, 1994).

29. The theology of the book of Kings is often referred to as "Deuteronomistic" (sometimes "Deuteronomic"). This is a helpful label in so far as it calls attention to the very obvious theological links that exist between Deut. and Kgs. It must always be remembered, however, that "Deuteronomic/Deuteronomistic theology" is as much of an abstraction as "Deuteronomistic History"—the construct of scholars theorising about the corporate views of the original authors of Deuteronomy–Kings, rather than the theology of any particular book taken as a whole in its present form. Particular books tend to display a much greater theological subtlety and complexity than the construct does (cf. McConville, *Grace*, for an extended discussion). This is certainly true of Deut., and it is equally true of Kgs. It is a little surprising, therefore, that even among scholars who are interested in reading the OT books in their final form (which is presumably, on any theory of composition, a *post-Deuteronomistic* form), terms like "Deuteronomic/Deuteronomistic theology" and "Deuteronomistic History" should still be so widely used. The construct can, indeed, lead such final-form reading astray, as in the case of R. D. Nelson, "The Anatomy of the Books of Kings," *JSOT* 40 (1988), pp. 39–48, who contrasts the "straight deuteronomistic ideology" of some parts of Kgs. (where is such ideology actually to be found in the OT?) with other material that undermines such ideology (pp. 45–48).

30. For a readable introduction to the themes of the book of Kings, cf. T. R. Hobbs, *1, 2 Kings* (WBT; Dallas: Word, 1989).

31. Cf. B. S. Childs, *Biblical Theology of the Old and New Testaments: Theological Reflection on the Christian Bible* (Minneapolis: Fortress, 1993), pp. 70–79.

32. G. A. Lindbeck, "Scripture, Consensus, and Community," in *Biblical Interpretation in Crisis: The Ratzinger Conference on Bible and Church* (ed. R. J. Neuhaus; Grand Rapids: Eerdmans, 1989), pp. 74–101, on p. 75.

33. See further L. Goppelt, *Typos: The Typological Interpretation of the Old Testament in the New* (Grand Rapids: Eerdmans, 1982).

34. For a recent book that examines the phenomenon in some depth with reference to the OT and the Synoptic Gospels and lists relevant bibliography, see W. M. Swartley, *Israel's Scripture Traditions and the Synoptic Gospels: Story Shaping Story* (Peabody, Mass.: Hendrickson, 1994).

§1 Solomon Becomes King (1 Kgs. 1:1–53)

The narrative that begins our book (1 Kgs. 1–2) is really not a beginning at all, but the last chapter of the larger story of David, which is found in 1–2 Samuel. It is in 2 Samuel 11 that Bathsheba, who plays such a prominent role in 1 Kings 1–2, first appears— possessed by David at the cost of her husband's life (2 Sam. 11:6–27). Later the lives of various of David's sons are recounted (2 Sam. 12–18). The end of 2 Samuel is a sorry tale of wickedness and weakness, which raises a important question in the reader's mind. The prophet Nathan, himself a major player in 1 Kings 1–2, had earlier promised David that his dynasty would last forever (2 Sam. 7:1–17). David's kingship would not be like Saul's, which all but died with him (1 Sam. 31). Instead, God would raise up one of David's sons and establish his kingdom forever (2 Sam. 7:12–13). How is this promise now to be fulfilled, in view of Nathan's later word of judgment to David in 2 Samuel 12 and its outworking? Where is a surviving son to be found now, to sit on David's throne? It is this question that the first two chapters of the book of Kings will resolve. Chapter 1 tells us how it came to pass that it was Solomon, and not someone else, who succeeded David. Chapter 2 reports David's last instructions to Solomon and tells us what Solomon did immediately after David's death to tie up several "loose ends" from the David story and consolidate his position. After this transition from David to Solomon the story of Solomon continues.

1:1–4 / First Kings 1 begins in what at first sight seems a rather puzzling way. The real interest of the authors of the chapter lies in describing, first, Adonijah's abortive attempt, towards the very end of David's life, to seize the kingship; then second, the elevation of Solomon to the throne. Why, then, do they begin their account with this story about the **king** and the **virgin**? What connection is there between these events and the events that follow, particularly those described in 1:5–27? A number of factors combine to imply that the importance of the Abishag incident lies in its indication to the watching court (and to Adonijah in particular) that David has lost his virility and thus his ability to govern. Here is a very beautiful girl. The David of old had not shown himself to be impervious to such women's charms (1 Sam. 25, especially v. 3; 2 Sam. 11, especially v. 2). He had been known to take great trouble to possess a woman he desired. Yet now, with Abishag in bed beside him and fully available to him, we are told that **the king had no intimate relations with her.** The king is, to coin a phrase, "past it"; he is impotent, and Adonijah sees his chance to gain power. That is the significance of the immediate juxtaposition in verses 4 and 5 of **the king had no intimate relations with her** and **Now Adonijah . . . said, "I will be king."** The one event (or non-event) leads to the other.

1:5–6 / **Adonijah** was the fourth of David's sons born in Hebron (2 Sam. 3:2–5). His eldest, Amnon, and his third, Absalom, have died by this point in the story (2 Sam. 13–18). The second, Kileab, is missing (presumed dead) from the narrative after 2 Samuel 3. It is Adonijah, then, who now strides to the center of the stage as the eldest surviving son and gathers the symbols of kingship around him—**chariots, horses,** and a regiment of soldiers (cf. 1 Sam. 8:11). The action reminds us of Absalom (2 Sam. 15:1), with whom he is explicitly associated in verse 6. But the similarity extends yet further than this. Absalom, too, was a **very handsome** man (2 Sam. 14:25–26) and the "beneficiary" of parental negligence and indulgence (cf. the picture throughout 2 Sam. 13–18 of a son out of control, and a father who seems unaware of, or uncaring about, what is happening). In associating Adonijah so clearly with his brother, the authors have already hinted to us that this son, too, is heading for disaster. The succession will not be through any of the sons born in Hebron at all, in fact, but through one of the sons born in Jerusalem (2 Sam. 5:13–16).

1:7–10 / It is, indeed, in the tension between Hebron (representing David's Judean past) and Jerusalem (representing his present in the united kingdom of Judah/Israel) that we are probably to find at least part of the explanation for the way support divides between Adonijah and Solomon. **Joab son of Zeruiah** is an important figure in 2 Samuel, where he appears early on as David's right hand man and the commander of his troops (e.g., 2 Sam. 2–3; 11–12; 14; 18). **Abiathar the priest** is also one of David's oldest associates (1 Sam. 22:20–23). These are men with deep roots in David's Judean past. It seems likely, in view of the fact that the guest list for Adonijah's feast mentions only those **royal officials** who were **men of Judah** (and not also Israel), that their support for Adonijah represents at least in part a commitment to history and tradition and to the continuing influence of Judeans at the centers of power.

By contrast, only **Benaiah the son of Jehoiada** of the individuals named in the opposing group has any claim to such a longstanding association with David (cf. 2 Sam. 20:23; 23:20–23), although we must include here also the men who made up **David's special guard** (the "mighty men" of 2 Sam. 23:8–39). Aside from these men and **Rei** (otherwise unknown), we find mentioned in this group **Shimei,** who does also appear in 2 Samuel (16:5–14) but only as an antagonist of David from the house of Saul, as well as **Nathan the prophet** and **Zadok the priest,** neither of whom appear in the narrative before 2 Samuel 7:2 and 8:17 respectively (i.e., after David's move from Hebron to Jerusalem, 2 Sam. 5:6–10). It seems reasonable to assume that what unites at least these last three around the Jerusalem-born Solomon is a commitment to the present *in contrast to* the past—a commitment to a kingdom in which Jerusalem is centrally important and the northern tribes are more likely to play their full part than if they were under Adonijah. We must understand the events of 1 Kings 1–2, in other words, in the light of the Judah-Israel tensions already evident in Samuel (e.g., 2 Sam. 20) and soon to explode into schism again in 1 Kings 12 (cf., in particular, 2 Sam. 20:1 and 1 Kgs. 12:16)

1:11–27 / Why had Solomon alone of **the king's sons** (v. 9) not been invited to Adonijah's feast? Was this son of the scandalous union with Bathsheba (2 Sam. 12:24–25) not considered to be a serious threat to Adonijah? Or was it precisely because it was well known (though not officially announced, vv. 20, 27) that Solomon had been designated as David's successor and was therefore the heir-designate that had to be opposed? We are not told. Indeed, the precise status of the "oath" of David to Bathsheba, which is described by Nathan in verse 13, is unclear. It is not mentioned in 2 Samuel, and it may be significant that Nathan himself does not mention it to David in verses 24–27. He only questions why *Adonijah* has become king. He does not explicitly promote *Solomon's* claim, restricting his advocacy here

to the rather more subtle **your servant Solomon he did not invite**
(v. 26)—i.e., he is the only one of the king's sons not involved in
the conspiracy and therefore worthy of David's consideration. Is
the "oath" anything more than pillow-talk between David and
Bathsheba? Perhaps not, and perhaps the hitherto loyal Joab and
Abiathar are not so much hostile to David's expressed intent in
the matter of the succession, as simply in despair over his decay-
ing state and the power vacuum that has resulted from his
impotence.

Whatever its precise nature, however, the oath has now
become the slender peg upon which Nathan and Bathsheba have
hung their hopes for the future. Can they push the slowly abdi-
cating David towards the quick decision they need by reminding
him of these few words uttered some time before—this **aged
king** closeted in his **room** (v. 15) with his beautiful nursemaid,
ignorant of what is going on in the outside world (v. 18), this
indecisive man who has, by his failure to announce **who will sit
on the throne** . . . **after him** (vv. 20, 27), allowed the present
situation to develop? Their strategy in making the attempt is to
appear, so far as possible, independent of each other. They enter
David's chamber separately. Both describe what has happened in
language similar enough, yet different enough, to be convincing
as independent testimony (vv. 19, 25). Each adds to this description personal comment that relates only to her/himself and not to
the other. Bathsheba expresses concern (vv. 17, 21) for her son's
rights and safety (as well as her own). She plays on David's sense
of honor and compassion. Nathan simply objects to being kept in
the dark and excluded (vv. 26–27). He invites David to share in
his sense of anger at being marginalized and ignored by the
conspirators. In this way the pair hope to avoid the impression of
collusion, while at the same time provoking the king into decisive action. They are successful.

1:28–40 / The oath is remembered and reinforced by a
second swearing (again in secret, to Bathsheba alone, v. 28), and
the king who has remembered that he still sits on the throne
becomes the man of action. Nathan and the others mentioned by
him in verse 26 are summoned and charged with ensuring that
Solomon is immediately anointed king (vv. 32–35). They accompany him (vv. 38–40), along with **the Kerethites and the Pelethites** (probably the **servants** of v. 33—apparently David's own
personal troops) to **Gihon**, where Zadok duly anoints him with

oil from the sacred tent, and all the people acclaim him king. It
is no doubt significant that this is so obviously described as a
public event (cf. the emphasis on the great noise of the festivities
in vv. 40–41, 45). The contrast with Adonijah's private dinner
party for the few elite is evident. This is the proper way to
become a king, the text tells us: out in the open, with mules, oil,
and music, with popular involvement. Adonijah's attempted
coup, by stealth and patronage, is an aberration.

1:41–53 / The noise of the celebrations reaches the ears
of Adonijah and his guests as they are finishing their meal, and
is followed immediately by its interpretation through the mouth
of **Jonathan son of Abiathar.** This astute young man wastes no
time in declaring where, in view of this fresh turn of events, his
own loyalties lie (***Our* lord King David . . .** , vv. 43, 47). Nor have
others wasted time in doing the same. The **royal officials** have
already been to see David (v. 47)—the very group whose Judean
members Adonijah had been trying to seduce to his cause (1:9).
By the time Jonathan has finished speaking, the guests are in no
mood to linger. They disperse, and Adonijah seeks refuge in the
sanctuary (**took hold of the horns of the altar,** v. 50: compare
2:28–29 for the location of the altar in the sacred tent), apparently
confident that Solomon will not inflict violence upon him there.
A bargain is struck (vv. 52–53): a promise of good behavior (implied) in return for clemency. And so the first chapter of Kings
closes with Solomon on the throne and Adonijah dismissed to his
house.

Additional Notes §1

1:2 / **To attend the king and take care of him . . . lie beside
him:** In view of the likely meaning of vv. 1–4 taken together, it seems
that there is a little more to the wording of v. 2 than the NIV, in common
with most English translations, permits us to see. A rendering that
better brings out the ambiguities of the verse would be: " . . . to serve
(Hb. ʿmd lipnê) the king and be of use to him (skn) . . . lie in his (Hb.
'your') arms (škb bᵉhêq)." ʿmd lipnê, "stand before," is open to a number
of interpretations, but clearly refers to availability for sexual intercourse
in Lev. 18:23. Skn, "be of use or benefit to," similarly leaves the precise
nature of the use and benefit open. The combination škb bᵉhêq, however,
certainly has sexual overtones (e.g., Gen. 16:5; 2 Sam. 12:3, 8; Mic. 7:5).

The courtiers thus seem to have in mind a heat more actively generated than would be the case if Abishag was simply lying beside David. That is why they look so carefully throughout Israel for such a beautiful girl. It will take someone exceptional to sexually arouse such an elderly man.

1:6 / **Very handsome:** In describing Adonijah in terms of his physical appearance alone, and omitting any mention of other attributes, the authors are not only associating him directly with Absalom, but also, and just as significantly, with Saul (1 Sam. 9:2; 10:23–24). Saul and Absalom are both the kind of stereotypical hero-figures considered by the people (or many of them) to be the stuff of kings. The authors of Samuel, however, go out of their way to stress that God looks on the heart and not on the external appearance of things (1 Sam. 16:7, with its sequel in the story in 1 Sam. 17 about giant Saul's impotence against the larger Goliath, in contrast to the small David's striking success). Adonijah, like Absalom and Saul, is an impressive figure with all physical prowess on his side. But it is the enfeebled David who will once again emerge on top, and the eternal throne will once again be won by a person described not merely in terms of his external attributes but also in terms of what is in his heart and mind (cf. 1 Kgs. 3).

1:7–10 / **Nathan the prophet, Shimei:** Commentators have been reluctant to identify the Shimei mentioned here with the man of the same name in 2 Sam. 16:5–14 and 1 Kgs. 2:8–9, 36–46, though why this should be is something of a mystery. The wording of 1 Kgs. 2:8 (" . . . you have *with you* Shimei son of Gera . . . ") clearly implies that it is indeed this same Shimei who has joined Solomon's party, and it is the natural assumption of the reader who has read thus far in Samuel—Kings. His presence in the Solomonic party is sufficiently explained by his likely antipathy to the Judean Adonijah, a king not likely to favor someone from Saul's clan. Solomon is perhaps nothing more to him than the lesser of two evils. On the likelihood that Nathan was a prophet from the pre-David city of Jebus (2 Sam. 5:6–10), concerned to ensure that the old city's traditions maintained their part in Israel's understanding of itself, see most recently G. H. Jones, *The Nathan Narratives*, JSOTSup (Sheffield: JSOT Press, 1990).

1:11–27 / **Why then has Adonijah become king?:** It may be the intention of the authors that we see the strategy of the speeches in these verses as involving selective exaggeration. There is really nothing in 1:9–10 to suggest that Adonijah's meal is the coronation banquet it appears to have become in vv. 13, 18–19, 24–25. Is the hope that David will feel compelled to act if he thinks matters have progressed further than they have? Such a strategy would also help to explain why **Joab the commander of the army** (v. 19) has by v. 25 become **the commanders of the army** in the plural. Large scale desertion requires even more urgent attention by the king than a single defection.

1:18 / **You . . . do not know about it:** There is an interesting play on this idea of "knowing" in 1 Kgs. 1 that is obscured in the NIV's choice of "had no intimate relations" to render Hb. *yd˓*, "know," in 1:4. David was not able to "know" Abishag sexually as he had once "known"

Bathsheba; now he does not know about Adonijah, even though he used to have the reputation of possessing "wisdom like that of an angel of God [to know] everything that happens in the land" (2 Sam. 14:20). A declining king indeed! See further the stimulating article by J. S. Ackerman, "Knowing Good and Evil: A Literary Analysis of the Court History in 2 Samuel 9–20 and 1 Kings 1–2," *JBL* 109 (1990), pp. 41–60.

1:38 / **The Kerethites and the Pelethites:** We deduce from the various contexts in which these troops appear (cf. prior to this 2 Sam. 8:18; 15:18; 20:7, 23) that they were David's own personal guard, probably mercenary troops drawn from among the non-Israelite population of Canaan, most likely (as the names imply) of Cretan and Philistine origin. David had spent some time among the Philistines (1 Sam. 27; 29–30, cf. 30:14, "the Negev of the Kerethites"), and had known their loyalty as soldiers before (2 Sam. 15:19–22).

King David's mule: The mule is significant because it belongs to David and thus marks out the Solomon who rides it as David's favored son. It is possible, however, that it was also regarded as in itself a symbol of kingship and thus that Solomon's procession on the mule was ipso facto making a statement about his status (cf. Zech. 9:9, with its famous application in Matt. 21:1–11 and parallels).

1:39 / **The horn of oil:** The choice of language is again interesting, since Samuel used a horn (Hb. *qeren*) of oil to anoint David (1 Sam. 16:1, 13) but only a smaller flask (Hb. *pak*) of oil to anoint Saul (1 Sam. 10:1). As with the mule, a connection is firmly being made here between David and his heir.

The sacred tent: Hb. simply has "the tent," which in 2:28–30 becomes "the tent of the LORD." It would be natural to assume, without any further clarification being given, that the tabernacle is meant (cf. Exod. 34:26; Num. 12:5, 10)—particularly since the only horned altars (cf. 1 Kgs. 1:50–51; 2:28) mentioned in Gen.–Sam. are located there, and both the ark of the covenant (also located in Jerusalem, 1 Kgs. 3:15) and the tabernacle apparently come up together to the temple in 1 Kgs. 8:3–5. On this view, the tent pitched by David for the ark in 2 Sam. 6:17 is the tabernacle itself (cf. 2 Sam. 7:2, 6), perhaps reconstructed after its destruction at Shiloh (Jer. 7:12–13). The Chronicler, however, is at great pains to stress that David's tent in Jerusalem (the location of the ark) is not the tabernacle and to place the tabernacle (the location of the altar) at Gibeon (2 Chron. 1:1–6). Our assessment of his interpretation of the facts here will depend largely on the view that is taken of his approach to the tradition in general (cf. the commentaries on Chron.).

1:41 / **They were finishing their feast:** It may at first sight seem unimportant that Adonijah spends most of ch. 1 eating, while his world falls apart around him. Certainly there is a neat irony in the fact that, while Adonijah imagines that it is David who lacks the crucial information from "outside" his small bedroom world that would enable him to frustrate his designs, it turns out to be Adonijah who is fatally ignorant, closeted away from political reality, wining and dining his friends. There is probably even more to it than that, however. It is at least a curious coincidence that the name of Adonijah's mother, Haggith, is derived, like several other Hb. names, from the verbal root *ḥgg*, from which we also have the noun *ḥag*, "a feast" (though this is not the word used in this verse). The name Bathsheba, on the other hand, probably means "daughter of the oath." Its second part (*šeḇa*) is connected with the verbal root *šḇ*ᶜ, which in the Niphᶜal means "to swear an oath"—the very verb that is found throughout 1:13–30 and that reappears in 1:51. While the son of the feast-lady eats, the daughter-of-the-oath reminds the king of what he has sworn and so ensures that Adonijah is dependent for his life upon Solomon's own oath. The story is constructed quite deliberately so as to make these connections between the mothers and their sons clear and to invest the characters with a sense of predestination. See further M. Garsiel, "Puns upon Names as a Literary Device in 1 Kings 1–2," *Bib* 72 (1991), pp. 379–86.

1:42 / **A worthy man:** The Hb. is *ʾîš ḥayil*, which can be taken as referring to moral worth. The similar phrase *ben-ḥayil* in v. 52 does refer to this. It is also possible, however, that it is Jonathan's prowess as a warrior to which Adonijah is alluding (cf. *ʾîš ḥayil* in 2 Sam. 11:16; 23:20; 24:9).

1:49–53 / **Clinging to the horns of the altar:** It is apparent that Adonijah believes that the altar as a holy place provides him with some protection from Solomon's vengeance. Joab later gives evidence of believing the same (2:28), daring Solomon to have him killed while he is there (2:30). There is evidence within the OT that the Israelites shared the common ancient Near Eastern custom in regard to asylum at shrines (Exod. 21:12–14). As Joab will discover, however, Solomon is not beyond ignoring convention if it suits his purposes.

§2 David's Charge to Solomon (1 Kgs. 2:1–11)

Chapter 1 anticipated David's death. Chapter 2 will describe it. First, however, David has a few things to say to Solomon about his conduct as king (2:1–4). Then there are certain "loose ends" to be tied up (2:5–9). Only after he has seen to the good of the kingdom in this way will he be able to die in peace (2:10–11).

2:1–4 / Like God's words to Joshua upon his "succession" to the leadership of Israel after Moses' death (Josh. 1:6–9), David's parting words to Solomon open with an injunction to **be strong** (the language of warriorship, cf. 1 Sam. 4:9 for the conjunction of **be strong** and **show yourself** [be] **a man**), before moving on immediately to define the framework within which that strength must be exercised (obedience to God). The exercise of royal power is not to be arbitrary, for the king is not a law unto himself. It is rather to be in accordance with **the Law of Moses** (2:3, cf. Josh. 1:7, "all the law my servant Moses gave you"). Particularly in view here (as in Joshua) is the law code of Deuteronomy. That is the text to which the language of verses 3–4 taken cumulatively points us (e.g., **observe what the LORD your God requires,** cf. Deut. 11:1; **walk in his ways,** cf. Deut. 8:6; **keep his decrees and commands,** cf. Deut. 6:2; **that you may prosper in all you do,** cf. Deut. 29:9; **that the LORD may keep his promise,** cf. Deut. 9:5; **with all their heart and soul,** cf. Deut. 4:29). It is deuteronomic language such as this that we shall find recurring throughout Kings, as first Solomon himself (1 Kgs. 11) and then all the succeeding kings of Israel and Judah are weighed in relation to the Mosaic law code and found wanting.

Their deficiencies in this respect, of course, are not unimportant. For as David makes clear to Solomon in verse 4, the continuance of the dynasty depends upon obedience. Those are the terms of God's **promise** to David. The reference here is apparently to 2 Samuel 7:11b–16, although it is noteworthy that this passage has, in fact, no explicit mention of any conditions being attached to the promise. Indeed, it is plainly stated (7:14–15) that wrongdoing on the part of David's successors will not lead to the end of the dynasty, but only to corrective, parental discipline from God. These verses seem to give the Davidic promise a somewhat unconditional ring, and a few passages in Kings also sound this note (1 Kgs. 11:36; 15:4; 2 Kgs. 8:19). There is thus a degree of tension in Kings as to precisely what the implications of the Davidic promise are. In 1 Kings 2, David himself lends his authority to the view that obedience is crucial—and he, the reader assumes, should know what the terms of the promise are. The subsequent history of the nation then seems to confirm that this interpretation of the promise is correct. By the end of Kings, both Israel and Judah are in exile (as Deut. 4:25–28 had foretold) and the monarchy is no more. Yet there are counter-indications in the text as well, and although the monarchy is gone by 2 Kings 25, yet there is still a king in Babylon (25:27–30). Is the promise really dead and God's grace wholly constrained by law? Or is there yet hope that grace will triumph over human sin and folly? Has David told Solomon everything he knows? We shall explore such issues further as we move through the commentary.

2:5–9 / David's attention now turns from the future to the past. "Wrongs" have to be punished and kindnesses rewarded. **Barzillai of Gilead** appears in 2 Samuel 17:27–29 as one of those who provided for David while he was in Mahanaim. Later (19:31–39), the king tried to return the compliment, but Barzillai declined his offer on the grounds of old age. His family is now commended to Solomon's care: he is to provide for them as they had provided for David.

Shimei's crimes are more fully described in 2 Samuel 16:5–14, and his repentance is told of in 19:16–23. It is of little credit to David that he is apparently prepared now for the second time in his old age (cf. 1:13) to sit lightly to an oath, or at least to evade its force through pedantic interpretation (even though he promised not to kill Shimei, he is now telling his son to do so). Possibly David wants vengeance on Shimei, because he suspects that Shimei's faithfulness to Solomon (1:8) will earn him a comfortable old age.

Before we make a final decision on this point, however, we need to consider also the case of **Joab son of Zeruiah.** Why does David sign *his* death-warrant? It is, of course, quite true that Joab had killed both Abner (2 Sam. 3:22–30) and Amasa (2 Sam.

20:4–10), and the suggestion has already been made (2 Sam. 3:28–29) that, in the case of the former, Joab had brought the danger of divine retribution on David and his house through association with the awful deed. Certainly that is how Solomon interprets the situation to Benaiah in 1 Kings 2:31–33. Joab is to be killed so as to **clear me and my father's house of the guilt of the innocent blood that Joab shed** (v. 31), both Abner's and Amasa's. This is all well and good; but there are some questions to be asked.

Hitherto, David has apparently never felt compelled to take any action of the sort he is now contemplating. He has been content simply to state his own innocence and to leave the rest to God (2 Sam. 3:28–29). How seriously concerned can he have been, then, about this blood-guilt? Apparently not concerned enough to rid himself of someone utterly loyal to him, someone who frequently took the initiative on his behalf and for his good (e.g., 2 Sam. 14; 19:1–8). Joab was, after all, a very useful person to have around, especially when David wanted someone killed without any blame being attached to the king (2 Sam. 11:15— another instance when David does not seem to have been too concerned about blood-guilt). We may wonder, then, about the sincerity of what he has to say to Solomon, particularly when we remember that the circumstances in which Abner and Amasa died were not quite so unambiguous as David makes them appear. In one sense Joab's killing of Abner was itself blood-vengeance for the death of Joab's brother. It is also possible that Joab sincerely believed that Abner had come to Hebron to spy (2 Sam. 3:25), thus committing an act of war. The circumstances in which Amasa, so recently the commander of the rebel forces (2 Sam. 17:25), mysteriously fails to collect the men of Judah in time to pursue the rebel Sheba (2 Sam. 20:4–5) are even less clear. Is he simply incompetent, or is his delay deliberate? And is Joab really to blame, in view of what he knows of David's character, if he interprets David's implicitly critical words as signalling his desire that Amasa should disappear? He had, after all, built a career on having people killed for David's benefit, whether at his express command or not (2 Sam. 18:14–15), and there is certainly no mention of any Davidic concern over Amasa's death before we reach 1 Kings 2:5. All in all, then, it is difficult to believe that blood-guilt is the real reason why loyal Joab is now, at this late date, to be done away with.

Why, then, is he to be killed? The clue is perhaps to be found, not so much in the *religious* significance of the actions that are described, as in their *political* significance. We are reminded in 1 Kings 2:5–6 of two occasions when Joab's independent activity undermined David's attempts at reconciliation between warring factions within Israel. Is the real issue here, then, simply that Joab is too dangerous to be allowed to live in Solomon's united kingdom once David is gone? That is the real reason for the timing of the action. He is too much a man of the Judean past; he has already shown this through his allegiance to Adonijah. He is not a man who will be content with Solomon's kingship; nor will he make the government of a united Israel easy. He must therefore be removed, and the issue of blood-guilt becomes simply a convenient justification for his death.

If it is indeed concern for "the good of the state" that lies behind David's words in 2:5–6, then there may be more to the appearance of Shimei in 2:8–9 than first meets the eye. Indeed, this could provide the explanation for why these three men—Joab, Barzillai, and Shimei—have been selected for consideration at all, and placed in this order. For Shimei, too, has been from the very first a partisan—though this time of the north and not the south (2 Sam. 16:5–14; 19:20). It is, indeed, in the context of a (failed) attempt at national reconciliation (2 Sam. 19:9–20:22)—to which neither of the sons of Zeruiah are apparently sympathetic (19:21–23; 20:8–10)—that David spares his life. Shimei, then, like Joab, represents an element likely to be hostile to a united kingdom under a Davidic king (his temporary allegiance to Solomon in opposition to Adonijah notwithstanding). Between these two disruptive elements from Judah and Israel (2:5–6; 2:8–9) stands Barzillai from Gilead in Transjordan (2:7): a model of dutiful service to his king, who is rewarded by peaceful fellowship around the king's table. The passage is thus most carefully structured so as to present Solomon with an ideal (peaceful community) and to suggest to him what kind of people from David's past must be removed (those likely to disrupt peaceful community) if this ideal is to be attained. As we shall see, he is not slow to understand.

2:10–11 / A death and burial notice concludes the account of the king's reign; this will be the pattern throughout Kings (e.g., in the case of Solomon, 1 Kgs. 11:41–43). The notice about the length of the king's reign is, however, usually to be found as part of the introduction to each king, rather than as part of his obituary.

Additional Notes §2

2:3 / **That you may prosper:** David himself had "prospered" because God was with him (*śkl:* 1 Sam. 18:5, 14, 15, 30). Now he passes the secret of his success on to his son.

2:4 / **That the LORD may keep his promise to me:** The nature of the Davidic promise in Kings has been much discussed, and the tension between its conditional and unconditional aspects has often been exploited in redactional studies of the book. R. D. Nelson, *The Double Redaction of the Deuteronomistic History,* JSOTSup (Sheffield: JSOT Press, 1981), pp. 99–118, has sought to resolve the tension by suggesting that "Israel" in 2:4, 8:25, and 9:4–5 refers only to the northern kingdom and not to Israel/Judah combined. The promise mentioned here is a conditional promise about the northern kingdom alone, which is unrelated to the promise described in 2 Sam. 7. This is an unlikely hypothesis, however, since it requires us to believe in a second Davidic promise that has not yet been described and since the phrase "throne of Israel" clearly refers to the throne of the united kingdom in 1 Kgs. 8:20 and 10:9 (see further Provan, *Hezekiah,* pp. 106–10). It seems that we must simply live with the tension and seek to understand what the final form of the text, which has both these conditional and unconditional elements in it, has to say to us.

2:6 / **Deal with him according to your wisdom:** The emphasis is upon subtlety. Solomon must not act rashly, but use his brain and find some justification for removing Joab from the scene (cf. also v. 9). There will be great emphasis on Solomon's wisdom (*ḥokmâ*) in the following chs. (3; 4:29–34; 10:1–13), but it will never again be used to such ruthless effect as it is in ch. 2.
Do not let his grey head go down to the grave in peace: That is, do not let him die a peaceful and natural death in old age (cf. v. 9). The Hb. behind the NIV's **grave** is *šeʾōl,* strictly the proper name (Sheol) of the underworld.

2:7 / **Those who eat at your table:** In view of my interpretation of Barzillai, it is of some significance that it is *Solomon's* table that stands at the center of the account of his glorious and peaceful rule over Judah/Israel and the nations in 1 Kgs. 4 (cf. esp. 4:27). Along the same lines, the apparent final end of Davidic rule over Judah/Israel is symbolized by the sitting of King Jehoiachin at the king of Babylon's table (2 Kgs. 25:29).

2:10 /   David appears in the NT, of course, as both ancestor and type of Jesus Christ. Thus, it is no surprise that we find references back to this death-notice in Acts 2:29; 13:36, where it is played off in particular against Ps. 16:12 ("nor will you let your Holy One see decay") in order to show that David's hopes were not fulfilled in reference to himself, but have now (as the resurrection proves) been realized in Christ.

§3 Solomon Consolidates His Position
(1 Kgs. 2:12–46)

David has gone, and Solomon has been left to fend for himself. **His rule was firmly established,** 2:12 tells us. This is clearly an allusion to 2 Samuel 7:11b–16, where the verb _kwn_ (**established**) appears on three occasions (vv. 12, 13, 16; cf. also v. 26) of God's action in ensuring for David an everlasting dynasty. In 1 Kings 2:12–46, this same verb appears on four occasions, strategically positioned at the beginning and end of the section (vv. 12, 45–46) and halfway through (v. 24). God has done for Solomon what he had done before for David (2 Sam. 5:12), in accordance with his promise (1 Kgs. 2:24). He has established Solomon as king. And everything that happens in 2:12–46, our authors tell us by structuring their account around _kwn_, must be understood in this context. Solomon may only have acceded to the throne in the most desperate of circumstances (ch. 1). The main focal point of that abortive coup (Adonijah) may still be at large, thanks to Solomon's generosity. And it may well be the case, as David has suggested to his son, that obedience to Moses' law must be accompanied by ruthless politics, if fragile peace is to become a lasting harmony. Nevertheless, God has ordained that Solomon should be king, as Adonijah himself acknowledges in 2:15. While in one sense, then, these verses concern the consolidation of Solomon's position, and he can be completely secure only by their end (after the necessary executions have taken place), in another sense his security is never in doubt. He is predestined to succeed by the God who is "sovereign over the kingdoms of men and gives them to anyone he wishes" (Dan. 4:25), "who sets up kings and deposes them" (Dan. 2:21). That is the ultimate reality, no matter what the human players in this drama may think.

2:12–25 / David had urged Solomon to use wisdom in removing Joab and Shimei—to find suitable occasions for it. He will himself create the occasion for Shimei's downfall (2:36–46), but in the case of Joab the occasion simply presents itself to him. Adonijah approaches Bathsheba with a request, presumably thinking that she will have decisive influence over her son, even though he is now king. His request is couched in terms of compensation for loss. Only a short time before, **All Israel looked** to him **as their king** (a massive exaggeration, so far as we can tell from ch. 1). Now **the kingdom has gone,** as a result of divine providence, to Solomon. All he asks for now is Abishag.

The significance of this request is not clear. Is it quite innocent, or does it represent a calculated attempt to revive Adonijah's claim to the throne? Second Samuel 16:20–22 might suggest that sexual liaison with the king's concubines amounted to such a claim and even if Abishag was not strictly a concubine, she was intimately associated in people's minds with David. Then again, how are we to understand Bathsheba's response to this request? Is she simply naive? Or is she shrewd, calculating that onward transmission of the request is likely to lead to Adonijah's death, and thus greater safety for both herself and Solomon? The ambiguity is never resolved, but if Bathsheba has calculated, she has done so with accuracy. Solomon chooses to see in Adonijah's action exactly the "evil" that he had warned him against in 1:52. Interpreting his request as a revival of the conspiracy of chapter 1 (2:22), he orders execution. The first casualty of Solomon's "wisdom" is thus, paradoxically, someone that David had not even mentioned to him and, if past events are any guide, would certainly not have wanted dead. David was never one to take firm action against his sons. Solomon, however, has come to the conclusion that his earlier leniency with Adonijah was a mistake—that he is too great a threat to be allowed to live. He becomes only the first casualty of this somewhat chilling chapter.

2:26–35 / There is no evidence at all, of course, that Abiathar and Joab had anything to do with Adonijah's initiative. We do not know whether they did or not. We do know, however, that Solomon has been waiting for the right moment to kill Joab, and Adonijah gives him his opportunity. Joab and Abiathar are pronounced guilty by association. The latter is simply banished to his family estate in Anathoth and **removed . . . from the priesthood of the Lord** (v. 27), to be replaced as chief priest by his long-time companion Zadok (v. 35). The reason found for such leniency (v. 26) is not a very convincing one, particularly when it is realized that Abiathar is, in fact, never described in the books of Samuel as carrying **the ark** before David. Joab could also have cited a long history with David in mitigation of his crimes, had anyone been concerned to listen. The authors, indeed, themselves remind us of this history with that curious phrase **though not with Absalom** in v. 28. Why mention Absalom here at all, if not to help us recall that this is Joab's "first offence" in an otherwise blameless career, from the point of view of loyalty to David? What really differentiates Joab from Abiathar is not his history, but his importance in Solomon's mind. He is uninterested in Abiathar, whereas he is utterly determined to settle with Joab. No doubt that is why Joab flees **to the tent of the LORD and** takes **hold of the horns of the altar** (v. 28), refusing to come out (v. 30). He knows that he can expect no mercy. Perhaps he does not count on Solomon being just as ruthless as he himself is, prepared even to have someone killed in the place of sanctuary. If so, he has miscalculated. Benaiah is dispatched to the tent, and with a cool obedience worthy of Joab at his best (or worst), he strikes him down at the altar (v. 34).

There is, in truth, poetic justice in all of this. Joab had lived by the sword, killing (among others) two army commanders who happened to be his professional rivals. Now he dies by the sword and is immediately replaced by his killer as commander of the army (v. 35). Yet obviously we must take Solomon's rhetoric in verses 31–33 with a pinch of salt. Joab is not being killed because of Solomon's overwhelming desire to clear David's house of **the guilt of innocent blood** (v. 31, cf. §2 above). He is being killed because he is a threat to Solomon and the united kingdom. And there is something rather repellent about a king born of a union forged in innocent blood (2 Sam. 11–12)—a union made possible through the obedience of the very man pursued in this passage—now claiming to occupy the high moral ground and waxing lyrical about the difference between Joab's house and his own. But *Realpolitik* is, of course, often dressed up in respectable clothing and presented as something better than it is.

2:36–46 / Adonijah had presented Solomon with his first opportunity to act on David's advice. For his second, he has to work a little harder. Shimei is summoned and instructed to **build . . . a house in Jerusalem and live there.** He is forbidden to **go anywhere else** on pain of death. We may perhaps assume that this is in part an attempt by Solomon to prevent a potential troublemaker from operating within his own power-base in Benjamin: that appears to be the implication of the mention of **Kidron** in 2:37, which Shimei would naturally cross if on his way home. Whether he interpreted Solomon's instructions to mean that he must *never* under any circumstances leave Jerusalem is not clear. All we are told is that after three years of perfect compliance (v. 39) Shimei leaves Jerusalem for a while to retrieve some slaves from Gath. He does not, in fact, **cross the Kidron valley** on his way—the silence of the text on this point (v. 40) is deafening. He is going westward to Gath, not eastward to Bahurim. But Solomon takes the opportunity to have him executed anyway (v. 46). David's instructions have been carried out; Solomon has proved himself to be a "wise" king. And his kingdom remains, inevitably, **firmly established** in his hands.

As we look back over 1 Kings 1–2, what do we see? We see, first, a dying king, now out of touch with reality, now fully in control, with a selective memory and a curiously ambivalent attitude to oaths. His oath to Bathsheba he stands by; his oath to Shimei he chooses to "interpret." The loyalty of Barzillai he remembers, for it costs him nothing to do so; the loyalty of Joab he chooses to forget, because to remember would be to make evident that his conscience about blood-guilt has been found late and conveniently. David is a man who, once persuaded that action is needed, is willing to follow it through ruthlessly so that his kingdom should survive him. Solomon, the new king, is no different. He, too, takes oaths seriously when it suits him to do so, and "interprets" them in ungenerous fashion otherwise (2:23, 36–46). He, too, has a selective memory, as both his treatment of Abiathar and Joab and his speech in 2:31–33 reveal. He too is a man of ruthless action, pursuing power by all means at his disposal. What we have here, in fact, is a fairly sordid story of power-politics thinly disguised as a morality tale. So tortured are the attempts to convince us that the men who died did so because they deserved it, however, that we cannot but be aware of their speciousness. Technically they may be guilty: but is morality entirely a matter of technicalities? Surely not. And we are thus faced with the question as to whether David's dynasty is really any more "innocent" of blood now than it has been in the past or will be in the future (2 Kgs. 21:16; 24:3–4). If God has truly ordained that Solomon should be king and have a dynasty, then it is not (as Solomon implies in 2:31–33) because David's house is innocent (cf. Prov. 16:12), but rather (the authors seem to be telling us) because God's grace is sufficient to deal with their guilt. God works his purposes out through this house (he has **established** it), not because even its first two members are perfectly good (these opening chapters of Kings provide quite sufficient evidence that they are not), but because David's house is the subject of his election. The conditionality of the Davidic promise, then, is only part of the story (see §2 above); its unconditional aspects are also crucially important. And that will remain true throughout the book of Kings. For without grace, law can ever lead mortal beings, be they kings or not, only to disaster.

Additional Notes §3

2:12 / **His rule was firmly established:** Since this is clearly something that the authors regard as already a reality (cf. also 2:24), it is misleading of the NIV to head 2:13–46 with the title **Solomon's Throne Established,** as if this establishment was a consequence of the events described rather than their presupposition. This in turn has led the NIV into a misleading translation of v. 46b: **The kingdom was now firmly established in Solomon's hands.** There is no **now** in the Hb. text. Verse 46b is simply a restatement of the God-ordained reality (Solomon's grip on the throne is firm) that has just been illustrated by the events described.

2:19 / **Bathsheba went to King Solomon:** If we were to regard Bathsheba as a calculating woman, then we could also consider that she may have had personal reasons (if she knew the facts) for wanting revenge on Adonijah's associate Joab, who was the effective killer of her husband Uriah. See further J. W. Wesselius, "Joab's Death and the Central Theme of the Succession Narrative (2 Samuel 9–1 Kings 2)," *VT* 40 (1990), pp. 336–51, for an interpretation of 1 Kgs. 1–2 that is similar in some ways to the interpretation offered here, but also strikes out in different directions.

He had a throne brought for the king's mother: It is perfectly possible that it was indeed a **throne** (that is, a seat with some official significance, like Solomon's), rather than simply a "seat," although much depends here upon whether we think the queen-mother had any official political status in the Israelite or Judean court (see most recently Z. Ben-Barak, "The Status and Right of the *Gᵉbîrâ*," *JBL* 110 [1991], pp. 23–34). Certainly Bathsheba is positioned in a place of honor, **at his right hand.**

2:22 / **He is my older brother:** It is not clear how customary it was for the eldest son to succeed his father to the Israelite throne. Even in the later monarchy (2 Kgs. 23:31–37), we find Josiah being succeeded by Jehoahaz rather than the older Eliakim (presumably, as in 1 Kgs. 1–2, for political reasons). At least some Israelites, however, may have regarded the eldest son as having a particular claim on the throne, as is seen in Adonijah's threat to Solomon's position.

2:27 / **Fulfilling the word the LORD had spoken at Shiloh:** The reference is to 1 Sam. 2:27–36, where Eli is told that his priestly house is to be rejected and the house of a "faithful priest" established by God. Abiathar is identified as a member of Eli's house in 1 Sam. 22:20; he is described as the grandson of Ahitub, the grandson of Eli (1 Sam. 14:2–3). The "faithful priest" who will "minister before my anointed one always" (1 Sam. 2:35), then, is Zadok (1 Kgs. 2:35). Kings is very interested in this idea of prophecy and fulfillment—one of the themes that binds the book together and gives it its distinctive atmosphere (see further on 1 Kgs. 13).

2:31 / **Strike him down and bury him:** See the additional note on 1:49–53. Joab's "guilt" may or may not be regarded as having been established. What is certain, however, is that in ordering his execution beside the altar, Solomon himself is guilty of breaking the law. Exodus 21:12–14 quite clearly states that a murderer is to be *taken away* from the altar and put to death, and Benaiah certainly seems to be aware of this (cf. his instinctive interpretation of Solomon's first command in v. 29 as implying execution *outside* the sanctuary, v. 30). Solomon's willingness to ignore the letter of the law when it suits him only throws into sharper relief his vindictive treatment of Shimei in 2:36ff., where the letter of the law is crucial.

§4 More on Solomon and Wisdom (1 Kgs. 3:1–15)

Wisdom (Hb. *ḥokmâ*) has already played an important role in the narrative, guiding Solomon in his treatment of those who were a threat to him (1 Kgs. 2:6, 9). It will play an even more central role now in 1 Kings 3. Solomon has a dream wherein he confesses a lack of discernment before God and is promised (among other things) a "wise and discerning heart" (3:4–15). He then hands down a legal judgment in which his use of this new gift is of crucial importance (3:16–28). The major question of interpretation is how to understand this new material on Solomon and wisdom in the light of both the general context provided by 1 Kings 1–2 and the more specific context provided by 1 Kings 3:1–3. How does 1 Kings 3 function to carry the Solomon story forward, particularly in its characterization of the king?

We shall come to 1 Kings 3:1–3 in a moment. We must first reflect critically, however, on the fact that Solomon's story has so often in the past been divided into two fairly self-contained parts: an earlier period, in which he was obedient to God and was consequently (along with Israel) blessed; and a later period, in which he was disobedient to God and was consequently (with Israel) judged by God, and the kingdom was "torn away" (cf. 11:11). This is undoubtedly a neat scheme, but it represents a massive over-simplification. It arises in large measure from reading the story, in practice if not in theory, as beginning in 1 Kings 3:4, with 3:3a perhaps slotted in beforehand. But before 3:4–15 we have read, not just 3:3a, or even 3:1–3 together, but 1:1–3:3. And that narrative—also about Solomon's early days—is far from unambiguous in its assessment of the king's actions after his accession to the throne and is quite unwilling to allow any easy correlation between the "obedience" of the house of David and the fact that David's son now rules. **The kingdom** is **firmly established in Solomon's hands** (2:46), but this, our authors suggest, has to do more with God's sovereignty than with royal righteousness (Prov. 16:12).

3:1–3 / It is not just 1:1–2:46 that undermines the simplistic view of Solomon's reign, however. Before we ever get to the new "wisdom material" in 3:4ff. (the seed-bed for so much of the tradition that has grown up about the early and "good" Solomon), we must first read 1 Kings 3:1–3. And these are verses that provide us with a number of further grounds for questioning the notion that Solomon is presented in the early chapters of Kings as an unambiguously virtuous character. "The kingdom" is "firmly established." What is the first thing that the new king does, after the dubious acts of 2:13–46? He makes **an alliance with Pharaoh** by marrying **his daughter** (3:1)—another dubious act! **Egypt** is, of course, a name that resonates throughout OT tradition with negative connotations: oppressor, arch-enemy of old, source of temptation (e.g., Exod. 1–15, esp. 13:17–18). Deuteronomy, in particular, had warned against "a return to Egypt" (Deut. 17:16) in terms of too-close relations with that nation, and it had explicitly forbidden intermarriage with foreigners, lest Israelites be led into apostasy (Deut. 7:3–4: the verb is *ḥtn*, as in 1 Kgs. 3:1; 2 Kgs. 8:18). First Kings 3:1a cannot, therefore, represent anything other than a criticism of Solomon, particularly in view of what David has said in 2:1–4 about keeping the law of Moses (cf. §2 above for the links between this passage and Deuteronomy) and in view of what happens to Solomon in chapter 11. We are shown right at the beginning of Solomon's reign what the authors perceive to be the very root of his later apostasy (cf. 11:1–8; cf. also the fate of Jehoram in 2 Kgs. 8:18).

The same is probably true of 1 Kings 3:2–3. Much, however, depends on how we read 3:1b. Is it simply descriptive, with no implications in terms of the portrayal of Solomon in chapter 3? It has often been taken as such. This seems very unlikely, however; once more, what we find later in the Solomon account helps us to gain a clearer perspective. For there (1 Kgs. 6:38–7:1) we find authors who are determined to emphasize that Solomon spent almost twice as much time building the palace (*his* house, Hb. *bêtô*) as he did building the temple (the house of *the* LORD, Hb. *bêt yhwh*) and who, by the positioning of the account of building the palace, imply that it interfered with and delayed the completion of the other project. The order in which the projects are mentioned in 1 Kings 3:1b (**he finished building his palace** [*bêtô*] **and**

the temple of the LORD [*bêt yhwh*])—which is not their chronological order in the narrative (cf. 1 Kgs. 6–7; 9:1, 10)—is likely to be significant, preparing us (as 3:1a does) for later parts of the story. It is likely to represent a comment on the ordering of Solomon's priorities; the palace was more important to him than the temple. Indeed, we cannot help but ask whether the authors do not also intend us to see the influence of his foreign wife in this. For the question of divided loyalties has already been raised by the *ḥtn* of 3:1a (foreign wives lead Israelites to apostasy), and this particular foreign wife, living in temporary accommodation while her new palace is being built, has a particular vested interest in the progress of the building program.

If blame is being attached to Solomon in all of 3:1, and not just in 3:1a, then it also seems likely that the critique is continued in 3:2. This verse is usually read in such a way that the emphasis falls upon exonerating the people; it was all right for them to sacrifice **at the high places** because **a temple had not yet been built.** However, it is much more probable in view of 3:1 that we should place the emphasis upon the second part of the verse, i.e., Solomon was to blame for the people's continued worship at these places because of his delay in building the temple. And again, we should see here the influence of his foreign wife: for it is precisely the influence of the foreign wives in 1 Kings 11 that dulls the edge of Solomon's concern about **high places** and indeed involves him in proliferating them and following after other gods (11:7–8). Deuteronomy 12—the text lying in the background here—explicitly associates purity of worship around the one sanctuary with the removal of those foreign influences that would tempt Israel in different directions. There is, of course, nothing in 1 Kings 3:2 to suggest that the people have already succumbed to temptation. The implication is that they do worship **the Name,** even if is not in the ideal place. But the potential for disaster is clear enough, and 11:33 will tell us of a people who eventually follow Solomon into sin.

All of this must influence our reading of 1 Kings 3:3. Here we are for the first time told something about Solomon that seems unquestionably positive: he displayed **love for the** LORD. The point about this rather positive looking statement is, however, precisely that it is so heavily qualified by the two surrounding statements regarding worship at the **high places**—the second of which now implicates not just the people but Solomon himself in this worship (3:3b). At the very least, then, the authors are again asking us to see (as in 3:1a) that Solomon's love for God, even at this early stage in his career, was not entirely whole-hearted. He does not keep the law of Moses; he does not take action quickly enough with regard to this matter of worship. As in 3:2, there is no hint yet of apostasy. His worship at Gibeon (3:4ff.) is worship of the LORD. Yet we are bound to ask: what kind of "love" is this, that does not issue in the keeping of the Law? Certainly not a love that involves all of Solomon's heart and soul and strength (Deut. 6:4). As in 3:1–2, the atmosphere is rather that of divided loyalties. And in a way the choice of the word **love** (*ʾhb*) itself reflects that—at least within the context of the book of Kings. It is certainly a word that has been carefully chosen; Solomon is the only king in Kings, in fact, who is said to have "loved" the LORD. It is not a verb used in relation to other kings' religious orientation. And it is difficult to avoid the impression that its use here has quite a bit to do with the fact that it reappears twice in 1 Kings 11 (vv. 1 and 2) in relation to Solomon's other great "loves"—the foreign women, of whom Pharaoh's daughter is one. The questions that are raised in chapter 3 about the completeness of Solomon's love for God, in other words, are compounded if one is aware of the end of his story and knows how fragile this love did indeed turn out to be.

First Kings 3:1–3 presents us, then, with a Solomon who loves God—who does share his father David's basic commitment to God (3:3)—but who right at the beginning of his reign also carries with him the seeds of his own destruction. His lack of wholeheartedness, already outlined here, will eventually become fully evident (11:4), and in the end his lack of personal unity or integrity will be the catalyst, not only for his own apostasy but also for the fracturing of Israelite unity that we shall read about in chapters 11–12.

3:4–15 / We are now in a better position to approach the story of Solomon's request for wisdom. For it is the Solomon we have met in 1:1–3:3—a divided, conflicted, sinful Solomon, with only a very partial grasp of God's dealings with his house—who comes now to the **high place** in **Gibeon** to make his **burnt offerings** to God and to whom God appears **in a dream**, inviting him to make his request. As Solomon makes this request, it is that same limited grasp of theology that first comes to expression. The basic covenant position as he understands it is that God has **shown great kindness** to David because he was **faithful** and

righteous and upright in heart (3:6)—that is why Solomon sits on the **throne** (3:6). Not for the first time, however, what Solomon has to say is undermined for the reader who knows the story, by aspects of the way in which he says it. It is, of course, quite true that David's basic orientation was towards God. Both the narrator of Kings (e.g., in 3:2) and God himself (e.g., in 3:14) will often confirm this, portraying David as a model against which other kings can be measured. Yet it is equally clear from both Samuel (cf. the discussion of 2:13–46 above) and Kings (e.g., 1 Kgs. 15:5) that even David's righteousness is regarded as only relative. Royal righteousness alone (even David's) cannot be the explanation for Solomon's occupation of the throne. It is significant, then, that even in Solomon's own words to God in verse 6, we find that double use of the word *ḥesed*, **kindness.** A much better translation of this noun is "covenant love," as in 1 Kings 8:23 and, more to the point, 2 Samuel 7:15. For it is here that God promises David that he will never take away his love from David's successor *even if he does wrong*. The noun *ḥesed*, therefore, reminds us that even though Solomon is focusing upon conditionality, the nature of God's dealings with the Davidic dynasty is unconditional. It reminds us that God has already treated David as he promises to treat David's descendants (2 Sam. 7). He has treated him differently from Saul—even though both sinned.

Of this truth Solomon himself shows no conscious knowledge. His grasp of reality where David is concerned seems entirely the same as in chapter 2. Yet what is equally striking in 3:4–15 is the very fact that, confronted by God in this dream, he *is* apparently prepared to admit that *his* kingship thus far has not been without flaws. He has used wisdom before in dealing with affairs of state, seemingly with great competence, yet now he confesses ignorance (3:7) in the face of a task that is too great for him (3:8) and asks for **a discerning heart to govern your people and to distinguish between right and wrong** (3:9). Is this to be seen as a confession of the inadequacies and sinfulness of his behavior up to this point? Is he saying that he has not done very well up till now and that he wishes to make a fresh start? Certainly God is **pleased** with his request precisely because Solomon has not sought in making it to confirm his own position in life (3:10–11). He has not asked for **long life** or **wealth;** nor has he sought (as in ch. 2) **the death** of his **enemies.** What is more, when God then promises to give Solomon the things for which he had *not* asked (3:13–14), the death of enemies is not mentioned (although long life and wealth are). The whole implication of all this is that Solomon has recognized and God is confirming that the "wisdom" of chapter 2 was of a highly unenlightened, self-serving sort, which must now be replaced with a higher sort, in order that the king may rule justly and well over his subjects (3:9, 11). An important theme of the OT is brought to mind by such a reading: it is the fear of the LORD that is truly the beginning of wisdom (Job 28:28; Ps. 111:10; Prov. 15:33). Solomon has apparently only just learned this. Because he has learned it, however, and has now placed himself in a humble and submissive position in relation to God, seeking the common good rather than simply his own, the blessings of God are now to follow. Much of the succeeding narrative about Solomon will, in fact, be concerned to describe the **riches and honor** (3:13) that he accumulated in the course of his **long life** (3:14). Before that, however, we read of an occasion when Solomon's new God-given wisdom in relation to his subjects was amply illustrated and Israel first came to perceive Solomon as the wise king *par excellence.*

Additional Notes §4

3:2 / **The high places:** The term refers to local places of worship, as opposed to the one place of worship described in Deut. 12 and taken in the book of Kgs. to be the temple. The continuation and proliferation of worship at these shrines, unchecked by royal intervention, is one of the main concerns of Kgs. It is always wrong to worship at them, so far as the authors of Kgs. are concerned; it is particularly wrong when this worship becomes idolatrous. In this respect Solomon's own life sets the pattern for what happens in the life of Judah later in the narrative. He begins by sitting lightly to God's law, tolerating worship of the LORD at the high places (3:2; cf. 1 Kgs. 22:43; 2 Kgs. 12:3; 14:4; 15:4, 35), and he ends up being drawn into full-blown apostasy at them (11:7–8; cf. 2 Kgs. 18:4; 21:3–9).

3:7 / **I am only a little child:** Rehoboam must have been born right at the very beginning (or shortly before the beginning) of Solomon's reign (cf. 1 Kgs. 11:42 with 1 Kgs. 14:21). Solomon must therefore have been old enough to procreate. The statement does not, of course, concern biology, any more than does Luke 18:17, with its concern that we should enter the kingdom of God "like a little child." It is a statement about how inadequate Solomon feels in view of his great task (cf. also Jer. 1:6). Yet we should not dismiss the idea of youthfulness entirely from our minds, since the Hb. word pair *yṣ*ᵓ/*bw*ᵓ (lit. "to go out—to come in") that lies behind the NIV's **to carry out my duties** probably has a military connotation, and may imply here lack of military experience. See further A. van der Lingen, "*Bw*ᵓ-*yṣ*ᵓ ('To Go Out and To Come In') as a Military Term," *VT* 42 (1992), pp. 59–66.

3:12 / **I will give you a wise and discerning heart:** The emphasis of the line, and indeed of the whole section 3:4–15, is that this wisdom comes as a supernatural gift from God. It is not innate (as it is implicitly in 2:1–4); it is not acquired by patient hard work, utilizing careful observation and self-discipline (as it is explicitly in much of Prov. and in 1 Kgs. 4:29–34). This is wisdom from above, not below. See further R.E. Clements, *Wisdom in Theology* (Grand Rapids: Eerdmans, 1992), esp. pp. 94–122.

It is of some interest to note the similarity in theme between 3:11–13 and both Matt. 6:25–34 and Luke 12:13–21, the first of which explicitly mentions Solomon as an archetypal figure of **riches and honor.** The essential element of these NT passages is that people ought to seek God and the kingdom of God first of all, rather than the things of this world. If they do, Matt. 6:25–34 tells us, then these other things will follow. In the same way, Solomon's seeking of God's kingdom rather than self-aggrandisement will bring in its train material blessings. See further D. McL. Carr, *From D to Q: A Study of Early Jewish Interpretations of Solomon's Dream at Gibeon,* SBLMS (Atlanta: Scholars, 1991), pp. 164–70.

3:14 / **If you walk . . . I will give you a long life:** The language again has the atmosphere of the promise to David as it is described in 2:4. It is conditional in nature. Yet we shall see that Solomon apparently goes on to have a long life even though aspects of it are no more in conformity to God's **ways** and **statutes** after this dream than they were beforehand. Once again, then, a question is asked about the relationship between law and grace. Fulfillment of the promise *involves* the active and obedient participation of the human party, but does it really *depend* on it? God demands obedience and sets out terms, but will he necessarily bring down the full penalty of the law if the terms are not met?

3:15 / **He returned to Jerusalem . . . sacrificed:** The significance of this second set of sacrifices is unclear. Does Solomon now realize where he should have been worshiping all along (**before the ark,** rather than at the high place)? If so, the first effect of his newly received wisdom is to help him to distinguish in *himself* between right and wrong (3:9).

§5 A Wise Ruling (1 Kgs. 3:16–28)

"The lips of a king speak as an oracle," Proverbs 16:10 tells us, "and his mouth should not betray (or 'act treacherously against') justice." Quite so. For the king is the hub around which the whole legal process revolves. He is the highest court of appeal and the foundation of all administration and justice. To invent a proverb: if the core is rotten, then there is no hope for the apple (cf. Prov. 28:15–16; 29:2). Yet the picture that we have of Solomon in 1 Kings 1–2 has indeed raised the question of whether he has not hitherto "betrayed" justice in his dealings with certain of his subjects, and our reading of 3:1–15 has also suggested it. First Kings 3:16–28 now wishes us to see how the new wisdom he has just received from God makes all the difference in his ability to "distinguish between right and wrong" (3:9) and to administer justice (3:11). In this passage Solomon is much more a wise king than he was before, "winnowing out all evil with his eyes" (Prov. 20:8, 26) and searching out things that are concealed (Prov. 25:2)—the model king, in fact, who is described by so many of the OT texts that talk about wisdom and politics.

3:16–22 / The occasion of Solomon's famous demonstration of discernment is a legal case involving **two prostitutes** living **in the same house** who both claim a particular newborn **child** as their own. It is probably not insignificant in the context that they are prostitutes (Hb. *zōnôt*). Prostitutes appear in Proverbs 1–9 as one category of women that men do well to avoid, setting their heart instead on a relationship with Lady Wisdom (6:26; 7:10; cf. also 23:27; 29:3). With Wisdom's help they will be able to see through the seductive and misleading words of these other women (e.g., Prov. 2:16–19; 5; 6:20–29), and so avoid disaster. The language of prostitution also appears in numerous texts that concern idolatrous worship (e.g., Deut. 31:16; Judg. 2:17) or improper relationships with foreign nations (e.g., Ezek. 16:26–28). All these ideas are, of course, important in the context of the

Solomon story. Solomon has already entered an improper relationship with a foreign nation (3:1) and will enter several more
(11:1–2). This in due course leads to idolatrous worship (11:7–8).
For the moment, however, he is on honeymoon with his new
wife, Wisdom, and remains faithful to her. He will thus have no
difficulty in seeing through the words spoken to him by the
two women who stand before him. He will be able to "discern"
(Hb. *byn*, 3:9, 11–12) in the midst of their testimony what is
actually true.

The testimony that he hears comes mainly from one side
(cf. vv. 17–21, 22b), the side of the person we may term "the
complainant." The other person, "the respondent," speaks only
in verse 22a. No one else is involved—which is perhaps why we
find the case before the king at all. There is no second witness to
corroborate the testimony (Deut. 19:15) and allow the legal process to take its normal course. From this complainant Solomon
hears about the death of the respondent's child during the night
and her own discovery in the morning that this dead child had
been exchanged for her own living one. The respondent answers
this charge with a flat denial. Impasse. What is the king to do?

3:23–28 / The resolution of the story is well-known.
Faced with claim and counter claim, Solomon gives instructions
that the child be cut in two. The true mother is willing to give
her child up alive to another rather than see him die; the other
woman is happy to have death deprive the first of her son, as it
did her. The identity of the true mother, the one who gives up her
child out of love, is thus revealed to Solomon, and Solomon is
revealed to his subjects as one who has **wisdom from God to
administer justice** (v. 28).

So far so good. But while this may be the end of the story
for Solomon and his subjects, it is not the end of the story for the
reader. For we have not been let in on the secret as to *which* of the
speakers in verses 16–22 is the mother who cries **Don't kill him**
in verse 26. The NIV has the potential to mislead on this point; it
has Solomon say in verse 27, **Give the living baby to the first
woman.** The wording might well make us think that the woman
in question is not simply the first speaker in verse 26 (which is
certainly correct) but also the first speaker in verses 16–22 (cf.
v. 22, **the first one,** the complainant). It has certainly been the
assumption of the majority of exegetes that the complainant has
been telling the truth. There is nothing in the Hebrew text of 3:27,

however, that implies this. This text reads simply "Give the living baby to *her*," not strictly specifying which woman is in view at all. Perhaps Solomon was pointing when he spoke, but we, unlike those present, cannot see him. And we are consequently in the dark about which of the two speakers in 3:16–22 is the true mother, and which was lying.

An interesting question is whether this darkness has been deliberately created for our benefit. Are the authors trying to put us in the same position as Solomon was in, denying us a neat resolution to the story so that we too may grapple with the problem he faced and come to realize how wise he really was? Certainly the focus of the narrative's conclusion is not on what has happened to the women, but on what has happened to Solomon. The transformation of the king is by the end of the story complete. His old "wisdom" had led to the use of the **sword** for executions whose justice is questionable. His new wisdom leads him in more constructive paths. He still uses the sword, but in a more positive way, threatening execution only to achieve justice. The sword is functioning in the service, not of the ruthless self, but of the kingdom as a whole. Solomon's sword has become what it is elsewhere in the hands of God (e.g., Ps. 17:13): the instrument of right judgment, of kingly "truth, humility and righteousness" (Ps. 45:2–4).

Additional Notes §5

3:27 / **Give the living baby to the first woman:** For an interesting exploration of the issues raised by the ambiguity of this instruction in the Hb. text and some of its other features, see S. Lasine, "The Riddle of Solomon's Judgment and the Riddle of Human Nature in the Hebrew Bible," *JSOT* 45 (1989), pp. 61–86.

§6 Solomon's Rule over Israel (1 Kgs. 4:1–20)

The NIV divides the text into sections in such a way that v. 20 is divorced from v. 19 and forms the introduction to the next section, which is headed *Solomon's Daily Provisions.* It is the case, however, that the Hebrew text treats verses 1–20 as a single unit—as a single chapter in fact (Hb. ch. 4)—with our English 4:21–5:18 being treated as Hebrew chapter 5. Certainly it makes much better sense to take all of 4:1–20 together. First Kings 4:1 indicates that the following verses will concern the king's rule over all Israel, and 4:20 provides a fitting climax to this initial description of his reign by telling us what the consequences of his organizing abilities were (**Judah and Israel . . . were happy**). Verses 21–34 then go on to speak about Solomon's rule over "all the kingdoms from the River to the land of the Philistines" and his impact on the world more generally. Israel is seen in these verses in a much broader context. Accordingly, 4:1–20 is treated here as a unit *(Solomon's Rule over Israel),* and 4:21–34 is dealt with separately *(Solomon and the Nations).*

Wise king Solomon sits on the throne of Israel, then, enabled by God to rule in justice (1 Kgs. 3:4–28). What kind of kingdom results? First Kings 4:1–20 begins to describe it. It is a well-ordered place (4:1–19); it is a happy, prosperous place (4:20). It is the sort of kingdom one would expect, when a king has been gifted by God to rule (cf. Ps. 72, "Of Solomon").

4:1–6 / The **chief officials** are first described to us: those at the very top of the hierarchy, just one step down from the king himself. **Azariah son of Zadok—the priest** (v. 2) comes as something of a surprise. In this context, at the head of such a list, **the priest** most naturally refers to *The* Priest, i.e., the chief priest, in distinction to mere (though still important) **priests**, without the definite article, in verse 4. Apparently we are meant to understand (although we have nowhere been told) that **Zadok** (v. 4) has stepped (or been pushed) aside into a lesser position, to be succeeded by his son. What of **Abiathar** (v. 4)? We last met him in 2:27, where he was deposed from the priesthood by Solomon. His apparent reinstatement here is unsurprising, if the king's change of heart in 1 Kings 3 is taken seriously. This is a new order, an order devised out of God-given wisdom. It stands apart from the order based on the old wisdom of chapter 2. Nothing could symbolize this more clearly than the restoration of the banished Abiathar to the royal court and the nullification Zadok's consequent promotion. Both Zadok and Abiathar now stand as equals once again—though with Zadok's son in charge.

Benaiah (v. 4) we have also met already. The other characters are, however, entirely new to us. **Elihoreph and Ahijah** (v. 3) hold the office of **secretaries** in this new adminstration. Precisely what their function was is unclear: did they have a general managerial responsibility, or was their task a more limited one to do with writing (annals, letters)? **Jehoshaphat** (v. 3) is the **recorder** or "herald" or perhaps even "state prosecutor"—again, the nature of the office is unclear. **Azariah** and **Zabud** (v. 5), sons of **Nathan** (who is surely meant to be taken as the well-known prophet of chs. 1–2), are respectively **in charge of the district officers** of verses 7–19 and **priest and personal adviser to the king** (lit. "friend of the king," cf. Hushai in 2 Sam. 15:37; 16:16; and esp. 17:5ff. for the basis upon which the NIV, no doubt correctly, arrived at the function of the "friend"). **Ahishar** (v. 6) is **in charge of the palace,** i.e., the royal steward (cf. 1 Kgs. 16:9; 18:3; etc.). Finally, **Adoniram** is **in charge of forced labor** (cf. 1 Kgs. 5:13–18; 9:15–22).

4:7–19 / Next we are told about Solomon's representatives in the *regions:* the **twelve district governors** whose job it was to provide **for the king and the royal household** throughout the twelve months of the year. The NIV appears to be following a minority Hebrew reading here, $n^e s\hat{\imath}b\hat{\imath}m$, **district governors,** instead of $niss\bar{a}b\hat{\imath}m$, "district officers." We are surely not to understand, however, that the men in 4:7 are different from those in 4:5 (Hb. $niss\bar{a}b\hat{\imath}m$) and 4:27 ($niss\bar{a}b\hat{\imath}m$, in all but one Hb. MS). It is much the better course of action to read $niss\bar{a}b\hat{\imath}m$, "district officers," in all three places. As to the precise role that these men played, we cannot be entirely sure. Were they simply tax supervisors whose job was to ensure that local government (however we conceive of this) paid its dues to the center? Or did they have a broader administrative role?

It is, of course, not only the months of the year that number **twelve;** this is also the traditional number of the Israelite tribes. The casual reader might well assume, therefore, that we have here a tribal system of support for central government. But this is not so. It is true that some of the tribal names known to us from elsewhere in the OT do appear here (**Ephraim,** v. 8; **Naphtali, Asher, Issachar, Benjamin, vv.** 15–18). **Naphtali, Issachar,** and **Benjamin** may well have been districts based entirely on tribal areas. **The hill country of Ephraim** is not, however, to be understood as corresponding to the tribal area "Ephraim," but as including at least part of Manasseh as well (Josh. 17:14ff.), and **Asher** is not a district by itself, but only in conjunction with the unknown **Aloth.** Other districts are either named after towns that presumably gave their names to regions (e.g., vv. 9, 12), or by regional name (v. 19), not after Israelite tribes. Here traditional tribal boundaries have had no defining impact upon the new system (e.g., v. 9, where the second district comprises both **Shaalbim,** assigned to Dan in Josh. 19:42 and Judg. 1:34–35, and **Beth Shemesh,** assigned to Naphtali in Josh. 19:38 and Judg. 1:33). Solomon's arrangements thus move beyond the tribal system, while having points of contact with it. They represent a new order.

It has often been asserted, in spite of the claim in verse 7 that the district officers were **over all Israel**, that the authors did not mean us to understand these arrangements as involving Judah. As a corollary to this argument, it has usually been maintained that **all Israel** does not necessarily imply "all twelve tribes" in Kings, but can refer simply to the northern tribes, "Israel." For all its popularity, however, the position is not strong. We shall return to the general claim about the meaning of **all Israel** in Kings when we discuss 1 Kings 12. So far as 1 Kings 4:7 in particular is concerned, the phrase is unlikely to be referring to the northern tribes alone. Its scope is sufficiently defined by the opening and closing verses of the Hebrew chapter: "Solomon ruled over all Israel" (v. 1) . . . "the people of Judah and Israel were happy" (v. 20). But the broader context is also important. On the one hand, there is no case in 1 Kings 1–11 where the phrase cannot refer to the whole united kingdom (or representatives from all its tribes) once ruled by David (1:20; 11:16) and now by Solomon (3:28; 8:62, 65; 11:42). In several cases, on the other hand, it is simply implausible or impossible that the northern tribes alone are meant (3:28; 8:65; 11:42). The authors clearly meant *all* **Israel** when they used the phrase in these chapters, and they meant this also in 4:7.

The reason why readers have had so much difficulty with this most natural reading of our verse, it seems, is that they have doubted whether there is any reference to Judean territory in the list of districts itself. The difficulty is more perceived than real. Verse 10 is the crucial verse. The name **Hepher** certainly has mainly non-Judean associations in the OT (Num. 26:32–33; 27:1; Josh. 17:2–3) even though it does appear in the list of clans of Judah in 1 Chronicles 4:1–23 (v. 6). **Socoh,** however, is known in the OT only as the name of a Judean town (either in the Shephelah, Josh. 15:35; 1 Sam. 17:1, or in the hill-country, Josh. 15:48). There is no northern Socoh known within the biblical tradition. This leaves us with **Arubboth,** which is otherwise entirely unknown in the OT. Joshua 15:52 lists a town named "Arab," however, whose root consonants are identical with our Arubboth; this is a Judean town. We thus have one Judean town mentioned along with another that could be Judean, in a district whose name can plausibly be connected with a third. It therefore seems apparent that the **twelve district governors** represented Solomon in all of **Israel,** including Judah.

4:20 / The consequence of the new system of organization is that **Judah and Israel . . . ate . . . drank . . . were happy.** Solomon's concern in 3:8–9 had been that he would not be able to govern so many people. Even though **the people** are **as numerous as the sand on the seashore** (a fulfillment of the Abrahamic promise in Gen. 22:17), he has proved equal to the task, for his wisdom is of equal measure (as 4:29 will make explicit). He has devised an economic system that, while it ensures the royal household has enough to eat and drink, does not oppress or deprive the king's subjects of what they need. It is government by the righteous person; when he thrives (lit. "grows great") the people rejoice (Prov. 29:2). It is not government by the wicked person who makes the people groan (Prov. 29:2; cf. 1 Sam. 8:10–18). This picture of harmony in Israel is, of course, implied by 1 Kings 2:5–9—all tribal dissension is banished, and Israel and Judah are united around the king's table as the symbol of their unity (cf. also 4:27).

Additional Notes §6

4:4 / It is astonishing how much difficulty this mention of **Zadok and Abiathar** has occasioned commentators. The phrase is often simply regarded as an addition to the "original" text. No one seems interested in the question of *why* it should have been added, in what is (to the commentators concerned) such an evidently inappropriate position.

4:7 / **Twelve district governors:** The complexities of Solomon's twelve-district system have been elaborated elsewhere, and there is little point in rehearsing the arguments here. For a discussion see T. N. D. Mettinger, *Solomonic State Officials: A Study of the Civil Government Officials of the Israelite Monarchy* ConB (Lund: Gleerup, 1971), pp. 111–27. For a visual reconstruction, see J. Bimson et al., eds., *New Bible Atlas* (Leicester: InterVarsity, 1985), p. 43—although I disagree with the positioning of the third district.

4:19 / **He was the only governor over the district:** The NIV is somewhat obscure. We have been told in v. 7 that there are twelve district governors over all Israel, only to be told now in v. 19 that Geber was the only governor over the twelfth district. Is this meant to imply that the others had more than one? Why would we be told this now? A different interpretation surely has to be sought. The Hb. text is lit. "And one governor who was over the land." It has sometimes been argued that this implies a reference to Judah (the LXX explicitly provides one), "land" being taken as "homeland" and Judean authorship of the list being presupposed. This would, however, increase the number of officials mentioned in this list covering "all Israel" to thirteen, rather than twelve, creating a conflict between the numbers in v. 7 and in vv. 8–19. A more fruitful line of interpretation begins with the observation that Hb. $n^e\hat{sib}$, "governor," in v. 19 is, in fact, a different word from Hb. $ni\underline{ss}\bar{a}b$, "district officer," in vv. 5, 7, 27. This implies that we are to differentiate between this one person "over the land" and the others who are in charge of districts. It seems best, therefore, to take the last part of v. 19 as a reference to the Azariah of v. 5: there was one governor ($n^e\hat{sib}$) over the whole land of Israel, to whom the twelve district officers just listed ($ni\underline{ss}\bar{a}\underline{b}\hat{im}$) were responsible.

§7 Solomon and the Nations (1 Kgs. 4:21–34)

The previous section, 4:1–20, was clearly defined by its beginning and ending ("all Israel . . . Judah and Israel"). It was a passage about Solomon's rule over Israel. With 4:21 we begin a new section concerning Solomon's rule over other kingdoms and his impact on the world more generally. It is revealed that Israel's peace and prosperity are related to Solomon's dominion over the surrounding kingdoms (they contribute to the prosperity and represent no threat to the peace, vv. 21–28). It is further revealed just how great Solomon's wisdom is: it is unsurpassed (vv. 29–34).

4:21–28 / Solomon not only ruled over Israel (4:1)—he also **ruled over all the kingdoms from the River** (that is, the Euphrates) **to the land of the Philistines, as far as the border of Egypt.** This area is further defined in verse 24 as extending from **Tiphsah** (on the Euphrates, east of Aleppo in Syria) to **Gaza** (on the western coast, in the far south of Philistia). It is a large area, corresponding to the ideal extent of Israel's dominion as promised in Genesis 15:18 (cf. 1 Kgs. 4:20 for another aspect of the Abrahamic promise picked up in reference to Solomon) and overlapping quite a bit with the area of David's dominion as deduced from texts such as 2 Samuel 8:1–14 and 2 Samuel 10. The countries in this region, we are told, **brought tribute and were Solomon's subjects all his life.** So it is that an enormous quantity of food flows into the kingdom from outside, with the result that all Israel, from very north to very south (**Dan to Beersheba**) lived **each man under his own vine and fig tree.** That is to say, they lived under God's blessing (Joel 2:22; Mic. 4:4; contrast Ps. 105:33; Jer. 5:17), having a degree of economic independence (cf. 2 Kgs. 18:31 for an explicit threat to such independence). This fits in very much with the thrust of 4:7–20 (that Solomon's economic arrangements were not oppressive and that his subjects were happy and prosperous under his rule); indeed, it gives us the broader context in which to comprehend these verses. It is at least partly because of the flow of goods into Israel that the system of districts described in 4:7–19 does not create economic difficulties for the people (4:20). If this is indeed the line of argument then it is no surprise that, having described the broader economic picture, the authors should return to the local scene in verses 27–28. It is because of Solomon's international position that the **district officers** are able to do their job.

The picture is a glorious one. It is very much the picture that the book of Micah paints of the kingdom of the "last days," in which swords are beaten into plowshares, in which everyone sits without fear under vine and fig tree, in which the nations come in pilgrimage to Zion (Mic. 4:1–5). The gathering around Solomon's **table** described in 1 Kings 4 represents in essence a kind of proto-messianic banquet (cf. Matt. 8:11), with Solomon as the ideal king!

But what about the **horses** referred to in verses 26 and 28? Do they merely attest to Solomon's great wealth? This seems unlikely. We noted in chapter 3 how the authors are intent, even in a passage that is otherwise very positive about Solomon, to make us see his darker side—that Solomon, in breaking God's law early in his reign (and particularly the law as it is found in Deuteronomy), was storing up trouble for himself in the future. Aware of this precedent, we need also to be aware of Deuteronomy 17:16, which forbids the king from acquiring "great numbers of horses for himself" and further forbids him from making the people "return to Egypt to get more of them." Solomon clearly infringes the first part of this prohibition in 1 Kings 4:26; he will infringe the second in 1 Kings 10:26–29, just before we hear again of Pharaoh's daughter (11:1; cf. 3:1) and of Solomon's apostasy. Once more, as if to bring us down to earth in the midst of this heavenly picture of the great king and his kingdom, the authors drop into the text (in a curious place, as if to catch our attention—why not place vv. 26 and 28 together?) something of a time bomb. It is a bomb that will tick away quietly, along with all the others in 1 Kings 1–11, until the combined explosion occurs in chapters 11–12.

4:29–34 / This negative note notwithstanding, we proceed now with an exultant passage about the wisdom of Solomon, which seeks to exalt him above all others who have ever claimed to be wise. His **wisdom** was certainly great enough (v. 29) to govern the numberless people of verse 20. It was greater, even,

than the wisdom of any of those folk from places (v. 30) proverbial for their wisdom (**the East,** cf. Matt. 2:1–12; **Egypt,** cf. Acts
7:22). It was greater than named individuals (v. 31) famous for
their wisdom (**Ethan, Heman, Calcol,** and **Darda;** cf. 1 Chron. 2:6;
6:33ff.; and the headings to Pss. 88:1; 89:1). So wise was Solomon,
indeed, that he was actually famous all over the world (v. 31),
attracting visitors to Israel **to listen** to what he had to say (cf.
1 Kgs. 10:1–13), whether in **proverb** (v. 32; e.g., Prov. 10:1) or **song**
(v. 32; e.g., Song Sol. 1:1), whether about flora or fauna (v. 33). The
gift of chapter 3 has truly produced the glory of chapter 4.

Additional Notes §7

4:21 / **Solomon ruled:** The Hb. verb is *mšl*. The Hb. word for
"proverb" (v. 32) is *māšāl* and its associated verb also *mšl* ("to use a
proverb"). Since the passage is about the wise rule of proverb-speaking
Solomon over the kingdoms and about Israel's consequent exaltation
among the nations, we are surely justified in seeing a play on words
here. It is equally interesting that the penalty for royal disobedience
to God in 1 Kgs. 9:6ff. is that Israel will become a "byword" (*mašal*,
"proverb") and an object of ridicule among all peoples, reversing the
picture in ch. 4. Literary concerns evidently contributed to the choice of
mšl in 1 Kgs. 4:21. The authors want to associate "rule" with "wisdom"
and "subjection to enemies" with the "foolishness" of disobedience
to God.

4:26 / **Four thousand stalls for chariot horses:** The **stalls** may
well be "teams" (of horses) for chariots. See G. I. Davies, "ʾUrwōt in
1 Kgs. 5:6 (EVV. 4:26) and the Assyrian Horse Lists," *JSS* 34 (1989), pp.
25–38. Chariots, of course, do not conjure up any better associations in
the OT, when linked with kings, than do multitudes of horses (e.g.,
1 Sam. 8:10–18). It will be noted that the NIV prefers the minority Gk.
reading **four thousand** to the MT's "forty thousand" here. One wonders
why. We find equally fantastic numbers at precisely those other points
in the Solomon story where Deut. 17:16–17 is most obviously the text
in the background—where Solomon is accumulating both gold (e.g.,
1 Kgs. 10:14) and wives (1 Kgs. 11:3). The extremely large number in the
Hb. text of 4:26 is to be expected in view of what the text is trying to say
about Solomon as the archetypal multiplier of horses—and numbers in
the OT characteristically do aim to do much more than simply communicate facts (see the introduction).

4:33 / **He described plant life . . . animals:** Careful observation of the natural world and how it works is one of the "normal" ways

people gain wisdom in the OT (cf., for example, Job 38–41; Prov. 30:15–31), as in the NT (e.g., Matt. 6:25–34). Here Solomon himself is characterized as someone concerned with the natural world, from the largest tree (the proverbially high **cedar of Lebanon**) to the smallest plant (the small wall-plant **hyssop**), from **birds** to **fish.** Wisdom "from below" (as here) and wisdom "from above" (as received in ch. 3) are thus combined in this one person, the wisest of all Israel's kings.

§8 Preparations for Building the Temple (1 Kgs. 5:1–18)

In the MT, the material in these eighteen verses form part of chapter 4; that is, they are part of the same unit as the material on Solomon's rule over the surrounding kingdoms and his immense wisdom. This has the effect, much more explicitly than would otherwise be the case, of making the events concerning the preparation for the building of the temple a part of the discourse about Solomon and the nations. It is implied that Hiram, king of Tyre, was simply one of those who were "Solomon's subjects all his life" (4:21)—something that is much more explicitly affirmed in 9:19, where we are told that Solomon "ruled" over Lebanon (the Hb. root *mšl*: see the additional note on 4:21). At first sight, this seems to create something of a difficulty for the reader of 5:1–18. Undoubtedly Hiram acknowledges, as all other people have acknowledged (4:34), that Solomon is wise (5:7). Goods arrive in Israel from Tyre (5:8–18) in the same way that they have arrived from places that are subject to Solomon (4:21–22). Yet at first it appears that Hiram is more an equal of Solomon than his vassal and that his goods flow into Solomon's kingdom more as a matter of trade than of tribute. What is the truth of the matter? Does Solomon really "rule" over Lebanon?

5:1–7 / **Hiram, king of Tyre** had been, as the text says, **on friendly terms with David** (2 Sam. 5:11–12), sending him materials and men to help build his palace. Solomon's response to his greetings takes Hiram back to that important moment in David's life (2 Sam. 7:1–17) when he was addressed by God, not only about the succession (which has just happened) but also about the temple (which has not yet been built). David had not been able to build a temple because his was a time of war rather than of peace (2 Sam. 7:10–11; cf. 8:1–14; 10–11; 12:26–31; 15–20). Now, however, God has given Solomon the peace (lit. **rest**, as in 2 Sam. 7:11) on every side that he had promised David and has

put his enemies under his feet (cf. Ps. 110:1). The time is right for the commencement of the temple building project, divinely ordained as the task for David's successor (2 Sam. 7:12–13). Accordingly, Solomon asks for the same kind of help (men and materials, specifically **cedars**) that David received from Hiram in building his palace.

This is an interesting scene, not only because Hiram is presented in 5:6 as someone who has a certain right to set his own terms and conditions (a point to which we shall return in a moment) but also precisely because of the links between palace building and temple building that are are evoked. Although Solomon does not mention it, it was precisely the fact that David felt guilty about his palace of cedar that put the idea of building a temple into his head in the first place (2 Sam. 5:11; 7:2). David recognized that something was wrong if a king was living in better accommodation than his God (cf. Hag. 1:2–11 for a similar message). Solomon seems to have the same perception, as we would expect of a **wise son** (v. 7). He is determined to build God's house, and in his message there is no mention of any house for himself. Surely this is a king who has his priorities exactly right! Having contemplated the **cedars of Lebanon** (1 Kgs. 4:33), he knows, in his wisdom, what they are to be used for (5:6; cf. 6:9, 10, 15, 16, 18, 20, 36). Yet it will only be a little while (as 3:2 has already hinted) until Solomon, having started so well, apparently loses his vision and turns his attention prematurely to his palace. Not for the first time, we are prepared for the future by the way in which the present is described and the past evoked.

5:8–12 / Solomon had suggested to Hiram a co-operative venture ("my men will work with yours," v. 6) and, possibly (although the Hb. is ambiguous), that Hiram should set the level of wages to be paid to his men. Hiram responds with proposals of his own. He suggests that his own men alone should deal with the cutting and the transporting of the wood down the coast to Israel and that Solomon's men should be involved only after this has been done (v. 9). The "wages," moreover, are to be paid not to the laborers, but to *his* **royal household** in the form of food supplies (v. 9). It is this second proposal upon which the narrative focuses in the first instance, describing Solomon's compliance with it (v. 11). Solomon thus gets what he wanted (Hb. *ḥepeṣ*, vv. 8, 10) in the shape of the materials for the temple, but so too Hiram has his **wish** (Hb. *ḥepeṣ*, v. 9) for provisions granted. For the first time we hear of goods leaving rather than entering Israel, of another king besides Solomon having his household well catered for. It is a happy arrangement, sealed by a **treaty** (v. 12): an arrangement that is testimony to the **wisdom** God has given to Solomon (v. 12).

What are the implications? Is the treaty between equals? It is certainly true that Solomon *treats* Hiram, not as a vassal who is *required* to supply goods and men to his overlord, but rather as someone who is to be worked with cooperatively. It is also true that Solomon is prepared to enter into a degree of *negotiation* on the matter. Does this imply equality, or is it merely that Solomon in his wisdom has chosen to "rule" in a way least likely to cause himself trouble? We must read the end of the story for the answer.

5:13–18 / It is often overlooked that by verse 13 we have heard nothing more about Hiram's *first* counter proposal to Solomon about work methods (v. 9). Yet this issue, picked up now in verses 13–18, is crucial to a proper understanding of the relationship between the two kings as it is presented in 5:1–18. The point is this: the narrative proceeds as if Hiram had said nothing about work methods at all! In spite of his attempt to avoid cooperation of the sort that Solomon sought in verse 6, it is *exactly* such cooperation that we find described in verses 14 and 18. A task force was dispatched to Lebanon **in shifts** to help with the timber (vv. 13–14), the Israelites spending **one month** working in Lebanon and then **two months at home.** At the same time another group was working **in the hills** (lit. "on the mountain," we know not where), cutting and collecting the **stone** for the **foundation** (vv. 15–17). The whole venture involved not only the **craftsmen** of Solomon and Hiram but also the men of **Gebal** (Byblos), on the coast to the north of Tyre. Solomon has had his own way— although he is happy to negotiate with Hiram to a certain extent, he is also prepared to ignore terms that do not suit him. It seems, then, that Solomon's "rule" over the kingdoms mentioned in 4:21 is real enough, even if he chooses (in his wisdom) to deal in friendly ways with some of the kings over whom he is dominant. Cooperation there may be, but it is cooperation between a senior partner and a junior who ultimately has no ability to resist his will. This becomes even more apparent in 1 Kings 9:10–10:29, where it also becomes obvious who is the real beneficiary of the "treaty" between the two kings (cf. the commentary on 7:13–14; 9:10–14, 26–28; 10:11–12, 22).

Additional Notes §8

5:6 / **The Sidonians:** A general term in this context, apparently, for Phoenicians, who were indeed famous for their expertise in **timber.** Sidon, like Tyre, was a city on the Phoenician coast, south of what is now Beirut.

5:10 / **Hiram kept Solomon supplied:** The NIV slightly obscures the links between vv. 10, 11, and 12 by its choice of words here. Lit. the Hb. reads "Hiram gave (*ntn*) Solomon . . . Solomon gave (*ntn*) Hiram . . . the LORD gave (*ntn*) wisdom to Solomon . . . and there was peace . . ." The friendly, reciprocal relationship between the two kings (already indicated by the use of *ḥepeṣ* in vv. 8–10) is a relationship made possible by the prior gift of God. Solomon is someone who knows how to deal with people.

5:13 / **Solomon conscripted laborers:** The description of the task force is often taken as implying that Solomon conscripted *Israelites* **(from all Israel,** v. 13) to work abroad; 1 Kgs. 11:28 and 12:3–4, 18 are drawn into the discussion to provide support for this view. Yet 9:15–23 go out of their way to deny that this is so, explicitly stating that he conscripted workers only from the *Canaanite* population of Israel. This is exactly what the Hb. word *mas* (**[he] conscripted laborers,** is in Hb. *yaʿal mas;* cf. also **forced labor,** *mas,* in v. 14) itself implies to the reader who knows the story of Israel up to this point (cf. Josh. 16:10; 17:13; Judg. 1:28, 30, 33, 35, where the Canaanite population becomes a labor force for the Israelite settlers). It seems clear that two quite distinct groups are intended in 5:13–18 and 9:15–23. One comprises 30,000 Canaanites drawn from throughout Israel (**from all Israel**), and is supervised by 550 officials (5:13–14; 9:15–23, esp. v. 23). The other comprises 150,000 Israelites, and is supervised by 3,300 foremen (5:15–18). It is the latter group that is viewed in 1 Kgs. 11:28 and 12:3–4, a group that is never described by the word *mas* (cf. the commentary on these verses and on 12:18).

5:14 / **At home:** It is just about possible to take Hb. *bêtô,* "in his house," in this way. The most natural referent for the suffix, however, is not the individual worker (whose conditions of work would then be remarkably pleasant for a forced laborer) but Solomon himself. If so, this must be another allusion to the royal palace (cf. 3:2). Even at this stage, the authors hint, Solomon is spending twice as much time on his palace as on the temple (cf. the commentary on *bêtô* in 7:1), while appearing to press ahead quickly with the latter.

§9 Solomon Builds the Temple (1 Kgs. 6:1–38)

The preparations for building the temple are complete, and we now move on to a detailed description of the building itself. Much is obscure to us as readers who stand at such a distance from the authors of the text, and we shall not pause at any length to puzzle over the architectural detail or marvel at all the glitter and the gold. Little that is important for interpreting the book of Kings hangs on any such detail.

6:1–13 / After a notice about the dates involved (v. 1), the description begins, as we might expect, with the external structure of the temple. We are told of its overall proportions (v. 2) and its basic form (a tripartite arrangement, comprising the **portico** or entrance hall, **main hall,** and **inner sanctuary,** vv. 3–5). We hear of its **windows** (v. 4) and of the strange structure around it with its **side rooms** (vv. 5–6, 8, 10). We are assured that the work was carried out with reverence, avoiding the use of iron tools at the temple site (v. 7; cf. Exod. 20:25; Deut. 27:5–6 for the prohibitions that seem to be in mind here). And finally we hear of a **word** from God (vv. 11–13) that placed the temple very firmly in its proper theological context. God will certainly **live among** his people once it is built. But this "dwelling" will be on the same condition as before, namely obedience to the Law (cf. Lev. 26:11–12). For all its splendor, the temple does not change anything about the nature of the divine-human relationship (or, indeed, about the nature of God, cf. 1 Kgs. 8:27–30). This was something the Israelites were apt to forget after the temple became a centrally important aspect of national life (e.g., Jer. 7:1–34).

6:14–35 / The repetition of verse 9a in verse 14 indicates both a return to the main story line of verses 1–10 after the digression of verses 11–13 and a change of focus. Now we are to hear about the *inside* of the temple. Most attention is paid to the **inner sanctuary** (vv. 16, 19–32). We read of its separation from the larger **main hall** (v. 16), its measurements (v. 20), its decor (vv. 20,

29–30), and its **doors** (vv. 30–32). We read of its **altar** (vv. 20, 22), and its **cherubim** (vv. 23–28): large, winged creatures that dominated the sanctuary, reaching half way up to its ceiling and all the way across from wall to wall. It is not surprising, of course, that the **inner sanctuary** should attract such attention; this was the **Most Holy Place** (or Holy of Holies, v. 16) where the **ark of the covenant** was to be placed (v. 19). It was the very dwelling place of God (cf. 1 Kgs. 8:1–13)—insofar as God had an earthly dwelling place. Here the LORD sat, enthroned on the **cherubim** (cf. 1 Sam. 4:4; Ps. 80:1; 99:1). In comparison to this place, the other parts of the temple were relatively insignificant, and they receive only the attention due to them (the **walls** and **floor,** v. 15; the **main hall,** vv. 17, 29–30, 33–35), although there is much interest in the splendor of the decoration in general. The predominant word is **gold** (vv. 20–22, 28, 30, 32, 35), and there is reference to carvings of more **cherubim** (vv. 29, 32, 35) and to carvings of **gourds** (vv. 18, a wild fruit; cf. 2 Kgs. 4:39), **open flowers** (vv. 18, 29, 32, 35), and **palm trees** (vv. 29, 32, 35)—symbols, perhaps, of God's gift of fertility.

6:36–38 / Having quickly toured the interior of the temple and passed through the "two pine doors" that stand at its entrance, we discover ourselves once more outside, in the **inner courtyard** (v. 36) that stands before it. The description is complete; there remains only to hear from our guide that the building took seven years to complete (vv. 37–38)—or more precisely, seven years and six months, given that **Ziv** is the second month (April-May) and **Bul** the eighth month (October-November) of the Israelite year.

Additional Notes §9

6:1 / **He began to build the temple:** The rather complicated architecture of the temple, and all the uncertainties that surround it and its furnishings (cf. 1 Kgs. 7:13–51), have been more than amply discussed elsewhere. See the commentaries and *IBD,* pp. 1506–1511, 1522–1532. A recent book that deals particularly with the relationship of our biblical narrative to other temple-building narratives from the ancient Near East is V. A. Hurowitz, *I Have Built You An Exalted House:*

Temple Building in the Bible in Light of Mesopotamian and Northwest Semitic Writings, JSOT (Sheffield: JSOT Press, 1992).

6:18 / **Gourds and open flowers:** The symbolism of the temple has suggested to some scholars that the pre-exilic Israelite worship centered there was not very different from the kind of worship condemned by various OT authors as "Canaanite" (e.g., in Deut. 12 and 2 Kgs. 17:7–20). That *popular* Israelite religion was indeed deeply influenced (the authors of Kings would say corrupted) by Canaanite religion is beyond doubt. It is also clear that these authors believed that the temple contained certain cult items later regarded as idolatrous (cf. the commentary on 2 Kgs. 18:4). What is not clear, however, is that the symbolism of the temple in general implies that it was from the start self-consciously syncretistic. Even if we wished to interpret some of this symbolism in terms of "Canaanite" religion (and 1 Kgs. 6–7 give us no obvious warrant for doing so), the real question is whether these symbols were not *from the start* re-contextualized so that they embodied the claim that in fact it was the LORD, and not the god Baal, who was the giver of fertility (the point at issue in 1 Kgs. 18); the LORD, and not the king, who was the establisher and maintainer of the cosmic order. Much depends here on the extent to which we are prepared to trust the witness of the OT texts to Israel's history, rather than peering distrustfully behind them through reductionist spectacles.

§10 Solomon Builds His Palace (1 Kgs. 7:1–12)

The building of the temple structure is finished, and perhaps we expect to hear next how the whole project was brought
to completion through its furnishing. Not so! The description of
the temple is not picked up again until 7:13. Instead, we find
ourselves reading of the royal palace complex. Why do the
authors delay their account of the completion of the temple? Did
they wish simply to describe all the *building* work together, before
moving on? Did they want to subordinate the secular to the
sacred by "losing" the account of the palace building in the midst
of the temple building account? Or did they want to suggest that
Solomon's priorities were not in such good order as his words in
5:3–6 might have led us to believe? The way 6:38 leads into 7:1
suggests that it is this last alternative that we should favor.

7:1–5 / The NIV suggests the nature of the connection
between 6:38 and 7:1 and the force of the transition from one to
the other, but it does not fully capture it. A translation that better
brings out the relationship between them, and particularly the
significance of the word order, runs as follows: "He completed
(*klh*) the temple (*bayit*) . . . he spent seven years building it (*bnh*).
But his own house (*bêtô*) Solomon spent thirteen years building
(*bnh*), and he completed (*klh*) the whole of his house (*kol-bêtô*)."
There are two "houses" in view, and an emphatic contrast is
made between them.

The more obvious point of contrast centers on the verb *bnh*.
Solomon spent much more time building his own house (**palace,**
v. 1, referring here to the whole palace complex of several halls
and buildings described in vv. 2–12) than he did building God's
house. This is not surprising, because just the first of its several
buildings was much bigger than the temple (v. 2, cf. 6:2). The
temple had quite a bit of **cedar** of Lebanon in it (6:9–10, 15–16,
18, 20, 36); this building, however, is packed with so many **cedars**
(7:2–3, 7, 11, 12) that it is called **the Palace of the Forest of**

Lebanon—and this for a building apparently designed only as a treasury or armory (cf. 1 Kgs. 10:17, 21; Isa. 22:8)! The suggestion is that the king was much more concerned about his palace than about the LORD's temple.

It seems likely, however—since otherwise the second part of 7:1, with its repetition of *bêtô*, becomes somewhat redundant—that we are also to see a contrast implied in the double use of the verb *klh*. The key here lies in noting that the extra element in 7:1, when compared with 6:38, is the curious *kol* before *bêtô*: "He completed the temple . . . he completed *the whole of* his house." The implication is that Solomon not only spent more time on the palace project, but also pushed it through to completion before fully finishing his work on the temple. This explains why the account of the palace-building has been inserted between 6:38 and 7:13. The positioning is itself intended to indicate how Solomon's energies were diverted from temple- to palace-building, to the detriment of the former (cf. the commentary on 3:1–3). It is significant, then, that *klh* will be used again in 7:40, when Hiram "completes" all the work undertaken for Solomon within the temple. The temple is not really "complete" until all the work on its interior is finished and it is being *worshiped in*. This does not happen until 7:51, when Solomon's own contribution to the interior is "finished" (Hb. *šlm;* cf. the additional comment on 9:25). Until this point, the temple is little more than an empty shell.

We should understand 7:1, then, in the following way: "But his *own* house Solomon spent thirteen years building, and he completed the *whole* of *his* house!"

7:6–12 / The remaining buildings that formed part of the complex are now described. There was a **colonnade** ("hall of pillars," v. 6), almost as large as the temple, but of uncertain use; a **throne hall,** also called **Hall of Justice,** the use of which is at least partly self-evident (the dispensing of justice); and then two palaces, one for Solomon and one for his Egyptian wife. **Stone** was an important component in the construction of these buildings (vv. 9–11), as in the construction of the **great courtyard** associated with them. The precise layout of all these buildings in relation to each other has been much debated, but remains obscure.

§11 The Temple's Furnishings (1 Kgs. 7:13–51)

After the important digression of 7:1–12 we return now to the temple, to hear how that project was completed and the "house of the LORD" made ready for his occupation in chapter 8. The narrative introduces a new character, whom the NIV calls **Huram** (vv. 13, 40, 45), but whom the MT calls by the same name as the king of chapter 5 ("Hiram"). He is brought from Tyre by Solomon to make the temple furnishings that are to be fashioned from bronze (vv. 15–47). Solomon himself, however, is described as making the furnishings of gold (vv. 48–50).

7:13–14 / Although Hiram is summoned from **Tyre**, the authors are most careful to point out that it is only his **father**, from whom he had learned his trade, who is a native of that city. His **mother** is an Israelite **widow** from **the tribe of Naphtali** in the far north of the country, near the Phoenician coast. The detail may well have been provided to reassure us that Hiram was not simply a Gentile with no Israelite roots. The fact that his mother was a widow, indeed, leaves open the possibility that he was a child of her first marriage, and therefore *completely* Israelite (cf. Ezra 4 for similar sensitivity to the question of Gentile involvement in temple building). Be that as it may, he is certainly *described* in a way that reminds us of another famous Israelite with a similar job to do—Bezalel, son of Uri, the chief craftsman involved in the construction of the tabernacle (Exod. 31:1–11; 35:30–35). Both men are said to be "full of wisdom and understanding and knowledge" (the NIV's **highly skilled and experienced**) with regard to **bronze work** (1 Kgs. 7:14; Exod. 31:3–4).

7:15–22 / Hiram's work in bronze is described in detail. We hear first of the two massive and free standing **pillars, Jakin and Boaz** (vv. 15–22), positioned at the temple entrance, which along with their **capitals,** stood almost as high as the temple itself (23 cubits). The capitals were **in the shape of lilies** (v. 22) and decorated with **chains** (plaited, interwoven art work, v. 17) and

pomegranates (possibly a symbol of fertility, vv. 18, 20). The names of the pillars are intriguing. The precise derivation of **Boaz** (Hb. *bōˁaz*) is uncertain. It has sometimes been explained with reference to Psalm 21, which begins "O LORD, the king rejoices in your strength" (Hb. *bᵉˁozzᵉkā*) and ends "Be exalted, O LORD, in your strength" (Hb. *bᵉˁuzzekā*), describing what divine strength has done for the king. The name would then embody the hope that God will act in a similar way on behalf of the king who has built the temple. Certainly this interpretation of **Boaz** fits well with the likely interpretation of **Jakin,** which is by form a Hiphˁil imperfect from the verb *kwn,* "to be firm, established." This is the verb used in 2:12, 24, 45, 46 of God "establishing" David's throne and Solomon upon it. A pillar named "he will establish" clearly implies that hopes for the future of the dynasty are now bound up with the temple. God will establish the throne of the temple builder, as he had promised (cf. 2 Sam. 7:13).

7:23–47 / We hear next of the **Sea,** the **gourds** that decorated it (cf. 6:18), and the **twelve bulls** upon which it stood (vv. 23–26). As the name suggests, the **Sea,** a large metal basin, would have held water—a lot of water (see the NIV footnote)! It is not made clear in this passage whether its function was purely symbolic, representing the forces of chaos that have been subdued and brought to order by the LORD, who is creator of the world (cf. Gen. 1:1–23; Pss. 74:12–17; 89:5–11; 93), or also practical. Certainly 2 Chronicles 4:6 tells us that the priests used the water for washing, and Exodus 30:18–21 and 40:30–32 tell us of such a bronze basin for priestly washing in the tabernacle. The **bulls** have also attracted much interest in terms of their possible symbolism, but again, the text itself gives us no help. Next described are the **ten movable stands** (vv. 27–37), decorated with **lions, bulls,** and **cherubim** (cf. 6:23–29), each designed to hold a **basin** smaller than the Sea (vv. 30, 38). Five stands with their basins were placed on the south side of the temple along with the Sea and five on the north (v. 39). We assume that they, too, had a practical function (cf. 2 Chron. 4:6 again). Lastly we are told (v. 40) that Hiram made **basins, shovels,** and **sprinkling bowls.** In view of verse 45 (**pots, shovels,** and **sprinkling bowls**), we are probably to understand that these **basins** are not those of verses 38–39 but are different utensils used in cleaning out the altar (cf. Exod. 27:3). The close association in both 1 Kings 7:45 and Exodus 27:3 between the **pots** and the **shovels** suggests that the latter were also used for this purpose, while the **sprinkling bowls** would have been used for applying the blood of the sacrifices (cf. Exod. 27:3 again, and the associated verbal form *zrq* in Exod. 24:6). The production of these last items brought Hiram's work for Solomon to completion (Hb. *ḵlh*, cf. the commentary on 7:1–2). He had made so much that it could not be weighed (v. 47).

7:48–51 / Bezalel, son of Uri, had been "full of wisdom and understanding and knowledge" to such an extent that he could work (among other things) in gold, silver, *and* bronze (Exod. 31:3–4). Silver is not mentioned in relationship to craftmanship in 1 Kings 6–7, and the authors tell us in 10:21 why this is (it was not valuable enough). What is most interesting, however, is the way in which 7:13–51 makes a clear distinction between Solomon and Hiram where work in the other two metals are concerned. Hiram takes responsibility only for the work in bronze; it is Solomon who has charge of the work in **gold** (vv. 48–50). Hiram may himself be "full of wisdom and understanding and knowledge" and a worthy successor to Bezalel, but the authors are anxious that we should remember who is the preeminent embodiment of these qualities (cf. 1 Kgs. 3:4–15; 4:29). At the close of the narrative about the temple project—as at its beginning—the spotlight falls upon Solomon. We are reminded of one thing that we know already (about the **altar** of 6:20, 22), but we are also given new information. We are told about the **table** for the **bread of the Presence** (cf. Exod. 25:23–30, where the bread signifies the presence of God with God's people). The **lampstands . . . in front of the inner sanctuary** are mentioned, with their floral embellishments, their **lamps,** and their **tongs** (cf. Isa. 6:6), along with other associated items. The mention of the **gold sockets** for the doors brings our description of the building and furnishing of the temple finally to its end. Solomon brings the items **dedicated** by David into the **treasuries** (2 Sam. 8:10–12), and the temple is ready for worship.

Our reading of the narrative of 1 Kings 6–7 has taken some time. It would have taken longer if we had paused to consider the many obscurities in the Hebrew text, which our English translations disguise for the sake of a coherent reading. Arriving at a precise mental picture of Solomon's temple has always required a certain amount of educated guesswork. At least one thing, however, is clear. This is a building that to the authors is one of famous complexity and splendor—a building designed to impress.

Even the sockets for the doors were made of gold! Yet that
ominous word in 6:11–13 should prevent us from getting too
carried away with the beauty of what we have seen. It reminds
us that God is not half so impressed with structures as with
obedience. This is a point made much later by Stephen in Acts 7
(cf. particularly vv. 44–53, where the story in 1 Kgs. 6–8 is centrally important). It is a point, however, that the book of Kings
will itself work out at some length, as the glory that is the
Solomonic temple is gradually deconstructed in the midst of
gross disobedience (1 Kgs. 14:26; 2 Kgs. 16:17; 18:16; 24:13; 25:9,
13–17) and we are finally tempted to wonder whether the Glory
that is the LORD has departed with it forever (Ezek. 10–11)—
whether God has indeed "abandoned" the people of Israel
(1 Kgs. 6:13). In the Bible the beauty of temples is never any
guarantee that God will not leave them or bring judgment upon
them (cf. Luke 21:5–6).

§12 The Ark Brought to the Temple (1 Kgs. 8:1–21)

The ark of God, the great symbol of the LORD's presence with the people and the receptacle for the tablets of the law (Exod. 25:10–22; Deut. 10:1–5; Josh. 3–6), had hitherto remained in a tent sanctuary somewhere in the old city of David (2 Sam. 6:16–17; 7:2; 1 Kgs. 3:15)—except for the brief trip described in 2 Samuel 15:24–29. First Kings 8:1–21 recounts the circumstances of its relocation and Solomon's speech about the significance of the event.

8:1–2 / It is interesting, in view of the discussion in §10 about the temple's delayed completion, just how vague the dating in verses 1–2 is when compared with the precision of 6:1, 37–38. We are, in fact, given no indication of how many years have elapsed between 6:38 and 8:1. We are told only that when the ark was eventually moved, the event took place in **the seventh month, at the time of the festival** of Tabernacles (cf. vv. 65–66; Lev. 23:33–43). The association with Tabernacles is significant, given that the Israelites are instructed in Leviticus 23:42–43 to live in temporary shelters during this feast as a reminder of the exodus. For the moving of the ark, along with the moving of the **Tent of Meeting** (i.e., tabernacle; cf. the commentary on 1:39), symbolizes the moving of the God of the exodus from a temporary to a more permanent dwelling (cf. 2 Sam. 7:6). Later generations of Israelites certainly misunderstood the significance of this symbolism. Rather than seeing it as implying *continuity* between the new order and the old, they imagined that God had left the past behind—that the LORD was now a static deity tied to city and temple, bound to legitimate the status quo, rather than a dynamic deity free to move, bringing judgment upon sinfulness and oppression in all its forms (e.g., Jer. 7:1–29). The authors will themselves in verse 9 undermine such a mistaken view of the event, and Solomon will join forces with them in the course of his blessing (vv. 14–21) and prayer (vv. 22ff.).

8:3–13 / **The priests** carry the ark (v. 3), for not even the **elders of Israel** are safe in its immediate proximity (cf. Josh. 3:1–4; 2 Sam. 6:1–7), and only priests can take it right into the **inner sanctuary** (v. 6). Awareness of the potential for disaster that accompanies the ark may, indeed, lie behind the very large number of (precautionary) sacrifices described in verse 5 (cf. 2 Sam. 6:1–19, esp. vv. 13, 17). **The priests and Levites** carry the **Tent** and its **sacred furnishings** (v. 4; cf. Num. 4 for the regulations about who can touch these). We are not told what becomes of these after their journey. The ark, however, is duly placed beneath the **cherubim** (1 Kgs. 6:23–28), and we are assured that its **poles** are **still there today** (v. 8), which was no doubt true for some earlier recipients of the tradition in a way that it cannot be true for us. We are further assured (v. 9) that **there was nothing in the ark except the two stone tablets** of Deuteronomy 10:1–5. In view of the emphases of verses 14–21 and 22–66 (see below), we are surely to take this as applying not only to other physical items, but also to God. The ark is witness to his covenant and symbol of his real presence. It cannot capture or define him.

No sooner have the priests withdrawn from the inner sanctuary than another well-known symbol of God's presence appears: **the cloud** that is so often associated with his appearing in the OT (e.g., Exod. 13:21–22; 16:10; 19:9) and that covers the tabernacle upon its completion in Exodus 40:34–38. Like Moses, the **priests could not perform their service** because of the **glory of the LORD** (Exod. 40:35; 1 Kgs. 8:11; cf. Rev. 15:8). It is a sure sign that the new arrangements for worship have the divine blessing (vv. 12–13; cf. **dark cloud**, Hb. *ᶜᵃrāpel*, in Exod. 20:21; Deut. 4:11; 5:22). The God of Exodus and Sinai has come **to dwell** in this temple.

8:14–21 / Having seen what has happened within the temple, Solomon now turns to the people to address them. His focus is on God's **promise** to David recorded in 2 Samuel 7:1–17. He, Solomon, is the son whom God had told David would **sit** on his **throne** (2 Sam. 7:12); he is the son who was to **build the temple** (2 Sam. 7:13a). He will address the third part of the promise (an eternal dynasty, 2 Sam. 7:13b–16) in verses 22–26. One important feature of this speech (vv. 16–20), and also of the prayer that follows in verses 22–53, is the way in which the word

Name is used as a way of avoiding saying that God actually dwells in the temple (cf. also 3:2; 5:3, 5). God's presence in the temple is real enough, and people will get God's attention by calling the name, but God is not to be thought of as "living" there in any sense that detracts from the reality of God's transcendence. This is one way of overcoming the problem language presents us with when we want to talk of a God who is both immanent (with us) and transcendent (beyond us; cf. further Matt. 23:21–22).

Additional Notes §12

8:8 / **They are still there today:** The Hb. is ʿad hayyōm hazzeh, "until this day"—a phrase we shall find a number of times in Kings when connections are being made between past and present (1 Kgs. 9:13, 21; 10:12; 12:19; 2 Kgs. 2:22; 8:22; 14:7; 16:6; 17:23, 34, 41; cf. also 2 Kgs. 10:27). Since the ark of the covenant had disappeared long before the period in which the book of Kings reached its final form, however (cf. Jer. 3:16, which anticipates its absence; Josephus, *War* 5.219; and the dispute in b. *Yoma* 53b–54a), the "present" that is in view is evidently an earlier one. The phrase must therefore represent in this instance a survival either from the source documents used when the book was put together or from an earlier (preexilic) version of them that has later been expanded. The extent to which this is the case elsewhere in Kings is not clear (except perhaps in 1 Kgs. 9:21, which is equally problematic in terms of a postexilic context); caution is therefore required in the interpretation of such texts. Sometimes the phrase may not be intended by the final producers of Kings so much to make a claim about their present, as to make a claim about the trustworthiness of the earlier traditions that they are presenting to their readers—"the people who passed these stories on had evidence of their truth before them."

§13 Solomon's Prayer (1 Kgs. 8:22–53)

Solomon now turns to address God in a prayer that is of great importance for our understanding of the book of Kings as a whole. After further attention to the link between temple-building and Davidic promise (vv. 22–26), he offers us significant reflections on the nature of God's "dwelling" in the temple (vv. 27–30; cf. v. 13), followed by a seven-fold petitionary prayer about the response of God to those who will approach through this new medium (vv. 31–51), and a brief summarizing tailpiece (vv. 52–53).

8:22–26 / The main concern of the first part of the prayer is to pick up the third part of the divine promise to David that has already been alluded to in verses 15–21: the promise of an eternal dynasty. The incomparable God (**there is no God like you;** cf. Exod. 15:11) has thus far kept covenant with David (vv. 23–24), and Solomon asks that God would now fulfill the promise about the dynasty: **You shall never fail to have a man to sit before me on the throne of Israel.** We last came across this promise, with its conditional form, in 1 Kings 2:4, and we noted there the curious way in which its terms do not, in fact, match up with the terms as described in 2 Samuel 7:11–16. By this point in the story the reader has had several hints that Solomon himself sits on the throne by grace and not because he has continued **wholeheartedly** in God's **way** (v. 23; cf. 3:1–3; 4:26; 6:38–7:1). The repetition in 8:25, then, of the Davidic promise as phrased in 1 Kings 2:4, serves only to heighten the tension between its conditional and unconditional aspects that we first noted in 2:4. The basis upon which God deals with the Davidic dynasty seems at one level clear enough, and God will emphasize the importance of obedience in 9:3–9. Yet God's graciousness is as incomparable as any of God's other attributes. Thus, we shall hear in passages such as 2 Kings 8:19 of the Davidic promise *delaying* God's judgment and in this prayer (vv. 31–51) of the possibility of forgiveness *after* judgment. God's choices are always in the end more important than the choices made by mere mortals, in all their frailty and sinfulness.

8:27–30 / Having completed the line of thought begun in 8:15, Solomon now turns his attention to the temple's broader significance as a focal point for prayer. Verses 27–30 help us with the transition in thought, in advance of the petitions that the king will make in verses 31–51, each with their plea that God should "hear from heaven" (vv. 32, 34, 36, 39, 43, 45, 49). The main purpose of 8:27–30, indeed, is to emphasize that this *is* (if anywhere is) the "place" from which God hears. God cannot **dwell** on earth (v. 27). The temple—in spite of the statement of verse 13—is not to be thought of as a place where *God* is but only as a place where God's *Name* is, a place towards which God's **eyes** are **open** (v. 29; cf. Isa. 66:1–3). The hearing of prayer is done **from heaven** (v. 30). This is (if anywhere is) the **dwelling place** of God. Even then, however, God cannot, strictly speaking, dwell in **even the highest heaven** (v. 27). Being utterly transcendent, God cannot be "placed" at all; all human language about **dwelling** must be qualified constantly, so that attempts to describe do not in fact minimize. One consequence of divine transcendence, of course, is that people do not have to be in one designated place in order to pray. As God's eyes are open **toward** the temple rather than *in* it (v. 29), it is sufficient for people to pray **toward** the temple rather than be physically in it (vv. 29–30; cf. John 4:21–24).

8:31–51 / With these explanatory words about God, temple, and prayer ringing in our ears, we come to the seven specific petitions. The first (vv. 31–32) concerns a legal case where difficulties over evidence or witnesses make resolution in any normal way impossible (cf. 1 Kgs. 3:16–28). A priestly ritual is in view (cf. Num. 5:11–31); God is invoked as a judge to condemn the **guilty** and clear the **innocent** individual.

The second, third, and fourth petitions concern various disasters that might befall the people of Israel more generally: defeat in battle and subsequent exile from the **land** (vv. 33–34); drought (vv. 35–36); and assorted perils such as **famine, plague,** and siege (vv. 37–40). In each case the cause of the problem is sin, and the main requirement of the situation is forgiveness, although divine instruction is also requested (v. 36).

From the Israelites we move next (vv. 41–43), to the foreigner who has heard of the LORD's **great name . . . mighty hand . . . outstretched arm** (Deut. 4:34; 5:15) and prays towards the temple. Solomon is concerned that this person, too, would know answered prayer and that **all the peoples of the earth** would **know** God's **name and fear him** (cf. Isa. 2:1–4; 56:6–8; Luke 7:1–10). The sixth petition (vv. 44–45) is, like the second, concerned with war. However, this time the focus is not upon defeat as a result of sin but upon victory in God's cause (**wherever** *you* **send them**, v. 44)—the army fighting as the executive arm of God's justice on the earth. The seventh petition (vv. 46–51) returns to the question of defeat and exile. Its length, and the fact that it returns to a topic already dealt with, identifies this as the major concern of the prayer. If exile should take place, and if the people should **repent** and pray towards **land, city,** and **temple** (vv. 47–48; cf. Dan. 6:10 for the practice), then God is asked to regard them once more as God's people and **uphold their cause** (v. 49, cf. v. 45). They are, after all, the LORD's **inheritance** (vv. 51), the people **brought out of Egypt, out of that iron-smelting furnace** (vv. 51; cf. Deut. 4:20). Surely a second Exodus, from a different land, is not beyond the bounds of possibility!

What is striking about these seven petitions is how different they are in atmosphere from the first part of the prayer in verses 23–26. There the stress was upon the necessity of obedience. Here, however, human disobedience is simply presupposed (esp. in v. 46: **there is no one who does not sin**), and the prayer moves beyond God's judgment to dependence upon divine forgiveness and grace. It does so hinting that it is God's choices, and not Israel's, that are the crucial element in the God-Israel relationship. The **land** is the land given to the **fathers** (i.e., the patriarchs, vv. 34, 40), the land given as an **inheritance** (v. 36; cf. Deut. 4:37–38)—statements that remind us, like the case of the foreign worshiper in verses 41–43, of the divine promise to Abraham in Genesis 12:1–3; 17:1–8. The **people . . . brought out of Egypt** are Abraham's descendants, delivered from oppression not because of their ability to keep the law but simply because of the promise.

8:52–53 / It is to this question of gracious election that Solomon returns as he brings his prayer to a close, again emphasizing the choice of Israel as the LORD's **inheritance,** the people **brought . . . out of Egypt.** The repetition simply underlines the reality of the way in which grace always underpins law and provides it with its broader context.

Solomon's prayer is of the utmost importance, for it places both the temple and the law in wider perspective. The temple is an important building, to be sure. For much of the remainder of Kings it will play a central role in Israel's story, as bad kings corrupt its worship and good kings seek to reform it. But God, who is not confined by a building and who is certainly not dependent upon it, will survive even its destruction and hear the people's prayers in exile. Likewise, obedience to the law is very important. In Kings, monarchs are judged good or bad in terms of their adherence to the law, particularly on matters of worship. Yet Solomon holds out hope for restoration beyond failure, for he holds out hope that grace will have the last word. It is a prayer upon which we shall have cause to reflect further before the story is finished.

Additional Notes §13

8:33 / Defeated by an enemy: It seems certain that the woes in Solomon's seven petitions have been chosen because they appear in the list of covenant curses for disobedience in Deut. 28:15–68 (cf. esp. 28:21–25, 36–37). Our Kgs. passage looks for a removal of these curses after repentance. What is particularly striking, however, is the way in which 1 Kgs. 8:46–53 quite consciously uses the language and ideas of Deut. 29:17–27 to evoke this idea of reversal of fortunes in the case of exile in particular. See further J. G. McConville, "1 Kings 8:46–53 and the Deuteronomic Hope," *VT* 42 (1992), pp. 67–79, although his assertion that the Kgs. passage and Deut. 30:1–10 differ in their view of Israel's future must surely be modified if 1 Kgs. 8:33–34 and 46–53 are read as part of the same text. First Kings 8:34 is quite explicit about Israel's restoration to the land.

§14 The Temple Narrative Ended (1 Kgs. 8:54–9:9)

We are not yet finished with the temple! We have still to hear of Solomon's second address to the people (8:54–61) and of the conclusion of the festivities associated with its dedication (8:62–66). Most importantly, we have still to read of God's grave words to Solomon about dynasty and temple, people and land (9:1–9). Only then shall we be able to think again of other things—albeit with a more sober attitude than before.

8:54–61 / His prayer completed, Solomon now stands (he has apparently changed his posture at the altar in the course of his prayer, cf. v. 22) to address the people once more. He again celebrates the fulfillment of God's promises, though this time more broadly than in verses 15–21, referring to the promises given through **Moses** (**rest** being an allusion to the establishment of Israel within the land of Canaan). His desire is that God would be with Israel and cause them to walk in his ways, so that **all the peoples of the earth may know that the LORD is God and that there is no other** (Deut. 4:35). Here again we see a rather universalistic idea of Israel's role in the world (cf. vv. 41–43). Israel is to be "a kingdom of priests," mediating God to the Gentiles and bringing God's salvation to the ends of the earth (cf. Gen. 12:1–3; Exod. 19:6; Isa. 49:6).

8:62–66 / First Kings 8 finally closes with an account of the **sacrifices** offered in the course of the dedication of the temple—so many that the **bronze altar** outside the temple was not sufficient for the task! Part of the **courtyard in front of the temple** had to be **consecrated** for use as well. A **vast assembly** was involved in the celebrations, including people from the far north (the **Hamath** region) and the far south (the **Wadi of Egypt**). Afterwards they **went home** (lit. "to their tents," v. 66), **joyful and glad in heart.** This picture of a happy, unified kingdom stretching from Egypt to the Euphrates very much corresponds to the picture in chapter 4. It will not be so very long now, however, before Israelites will be found going "to their tents" for a very different reason and in a very different mood (12:16). The days of joy are strictly numbered—as 9:1–9 will now suggest.

9:1–9 / The first occasion upon which God appeared to Solomon (1 Kgs. 3:4–15) marked the beginning of Solomon's rise to greatness; he was endowed with the heavenly wisdom that enabled him to govern his empire well, to build the temple and the palace, and to achieve everything he **desired to do** (9:1)— probably a reference to other building work, as in 10:19. This second appearance of God marks the endpoint of Solomon's upward mobility and points us ahead to disaster. The place of the temple as a focal point for prayer is certainly assured, as Solomon had asked (v. 3; cf. 8:27–53), and there is a favorable response to his request about the future of the dynasty (vv. 4–5; cf. 8:25–26). The future of the temple and the dynasty, however—as well as possession of the very land itself (v. 7)—is made dependent upon obedience: the obedience of Solomon (9:4) and the obedience of future generations of Israelites (note the plural **you** in v. 6 and the inclusion of **your sons**). The particular focus here is on idolatry; the people must not **go off to serve other gods and worship them** (vv. 6, 9). If they do, the magnificent temple will become a ruin (v. 8; cf. Deut. 29:22–28; Lam. 1:12; 2:15), and Israel will be **cut off** from the land, transformed from a nation renowned for its wisdom (1 Kgs. 4:21–34) into a nation that is a **byword** (i.e., "proverb"; cf. the additional note on 4:21) **and an object of ridicule.** This last word pair comes directly from the list of covenant curses in Deuteronomy 28 (cf. v. 37)—the list that lies behind so much of the prayer of 8:22–53 with its straightforward assumptions about the inevitability of sin (cf. esp. v. 46). To read 9:1–9 in the light of 8:22–53 is to see immediately, then, the inevitability of disaster. The **if** of verse 6 cannot in reality be anything other than a **when** (8:46). Obedience will inevitably give way to apostasy. If this is truly the basis of God's dealings with Israel, there can be no other outcome but tears. A dark cloud now looms quite visibly over the Solomonic empire, for all the glory of 1 Kings 3–8. The temple is no sooner built than we hear of its inevitable end; the empire is no sooner created than we hear of its inevitable destruction.

§15 Glory under a Cloud (1 Kgs. 9:10–10:29)

It was Solomon's rule over the surrounding kingdoms, combined with his status in the world in general (4:21–34), that put him in a position to be able to plan, build, and dedicate the temple (5:1–8:66). First Kings 9:10–10:29 brings us back to consider the glory of this empire. It is glory that must now be seen with respect to 8:22–53 and 9:1–9. It is therefore glory under a cloud, destined to fade away.

This of itself would affect our view of what we read in 9:10–10:29, even if we were to find here only repetition of the material of chapters 4–5. It is not, however, merely the new *context* in which Solomon's glory is described that lends the account in 9:10–10:29 its air of impending doom. It is also the way the account itself is written. Themes from chapters 4–5 are picked up now in a way that hints, not of wisdom, but of foolishness (Solomon's dealings with Hiram, 9:10–14 etc.; his use of forced labor, 9:15–23; foreigners coming to listen to his wisdom, 10:1–13). Other material (e.g., 9:24; 10:26) reminds us of foolishness already revealed in 1 Kings 1–8. All in all we are forced to be aware, even as we hear of accumulating gold and proverbial splendor (cf. Matt. 6:29), that we are reading the last chapter of the story of Solomon's "golden age"—that he is heading very shortly for a fall.

9:10–14 / We first came across **Hiram, king of Tyre** in 5:1–18. It was he who had supplied Solomon with **cedar and pine** for the temple (5:10). In one sense 9:10–14 simply confirms the impression gained from that passage that Hiram is very much the "junior partner" in his relationship with Solomon. The **gold** that is now introduced into the narrative is not the subject of any agreement so far as we can tell; there was, of course, no mention of any gold in the agreement struck between the two kings in 5:1–18. Hiram simply supplies Solomon with as much gold as **he wanted** (cf. 5:8, 10). Solomon in turn "rewards" him with **twenty**

towns in Galilee of dubious worth. He is clearly the only real beneficiary in this relationship; yet Hiram's displeasure (v. 13) does not affect his "willingness" to send men to sea to bring back more gold (vv. 26–28; 10:11–12, 22)—for Solomon! Truly Solomon does rule over Lebanon (9:19), and here, as in 5:1–18, Hiram cannot ultimately resist his will.

The significance of the introduction of gold as part of the "Hiram theme" is, however, much greater than this; for this is only the first mention of this metal in a section of Kings littered with such references (9:28; 10:2, 10–11, 14, 16–18, 21–22, 25). In 1 Kings 9:10–10:29 Solomon is a king who accumulates gold in extraordinarily large amounts—amounts that increase as we read (120 talents in 9:14; 420 in 9:28; 666 in 10:14—for the significant exception in 10:10 see the additional note on 10:11) and that are collected from more and more exotic places (9:28; 10:22). Commentators have generally regarded this as a positive thing, reminding the reader that God had promised Solomon riches (1 Kgs. 3:13; cf. 10:23). Yet it is not so simple as all that. Why, we must ask ourselves, have we not been told about Hiram's gold before, especially when it was presumably the very gold that Solomon used in the temple (1 Kgs. 6:20–22, 28, 30, 32, 35; 7:48–51)? Why, indeed, is there no mention of gold at all in the description of Solomon's glory in chapters 4–5, where prosperity is described rather in terms of *food?* And why does gold appear in such abundance here, after the solemn warning of 9:6–9 about "turning away from God," and in company with other material that leads us to expect just this "turning away" of Solomon (cf. the commentary on 9:15–25; 10:26–29)? These are interesting questions, particularly in view of texts like Proverbs 30:8 and Deuteronomy 17:17. Excessive wealth brings with it the danger of apostasy.

We have grounds for suspecting, then, that all this gold is not necessarily meant to attract our unqualified approval. What is particularly striking about 1 Kings 9:10–10:29 when compared with 1 Kings 4–5 is the manner in which the authors go out of their way in 4–5 to emphasize that the prosperity of the king was shared with his subjects (cf. 4:20, 25). This is a theme that is notable for its absence in 9:10–10:29, where all the emphasis lies upon the luxury of the royal court (cf. the commentary on 10:14–29 in particular). God may well have given Solomon riches, but has he used them wisely (cf. Luke 12:13–34)?

9:15–25 / First Kings 9:15–23 is another section that refers us back to 5:1–18, where we were told of the **forced labor**
(Hb. *mas*) that Solomon **conscripted** to build his temple. Again, it
is the additions that are significant. At one level, the purpose of
these additions seems to be that of clarification. First, Solomon
did not use this 30,000-strong taskforce only for the temple but
also for his other building operations (vv. 15–19), especially his
new fortifications in strategically important cities. Secondly, it
did not include his Israelite subjects (who had other jobs to do,
vv. 22–23) but only the descendants of those Canaanite peoples
whom the Israelites could not exterminate (v. 21) when they
settled in the land. But why delay this clarification until now? If
we need to be clear that Israelites were not involved in the *mas*,
why were we not told at precisely the point (5:13) where confusion might (and often has) arisen?

The significance of the delay becomes clearer when we
notice the way the authors have associated the Canaanite laborers with **Pharaoh's daughter** (v. 24). She was first introduced
(waiting for her **palace**) in 3:1, in language that reminded us of
the deuteronomic warnings about intermarriage with foreigners
(Deut. 7:1–6)—precisely those **Amorites, Hittites, Perizzites,
Hivites,** and **Jebusites** mentioned in 1 Kings 9:20. These people
were to be exterminated (Hb. *ḥrm,* Deut. 7:2; 20:17; as in 1 Kgs.
9:21) precisely so that they could not lead Israel into apostasy.
Their appearance (very much alive) along with Pharaoh's daughter in 1 Kings 9 again serves to prepare us for Solomon's downfall. Like later kings (cf. 2 Kgs. 17:7–8), he will indeed be seduced
by the other gods (11:4). It is of little comfort to read, in the sure
knowledge of this future reality, that Solomon is for the time
being an orthodox worshiper in the temple (v. 25; cf. Exod.
23:14–17).

9:26–10:13 / The supply of gold pouring into Solomon's
coffers continues, with the assistance of hapless Hiram, as his
ships sail to **Ophir** in Arabia (Gen. 10:29; cf. Ps. 45:9; Isa. 13:12
for its fame). It is not merely gold that arrives at Solomon's court
from that region, however. A queen now travels from **Sheba** (cf.
Gen. 10:28) to see him and **to test him with hard questions**
("riddles," 1 Kgs. 10:1; cf. Judg. 14:12–19). Here again a theme is
picked up from earlier in the narrative: the worldwide fame of
Solomon, which attracts foreigners to his court (4:29–34). The
ease with which he answers her questions combined with her

own observation of his wealth leaves this queen of the south breathless (rather than **overwhelmed,** v. 5), if not speechless. Her words (vv. 6–9) largely confirm what our authors have already told us elsewhere. Yet her emphasis is slightly different from theirs. They had stressed the practical benefits of Solomon's **wisdom** (v. 4) for all his subjects (4:20, 25). She, however, refers in the first instance much more narrowly to the blessing Solomon must be to his **men,** his court **officials** (v. 8), focusing on their appreciation of his wise *words.* This is consistent with the whole atmosphere of chapter 10, where the focus is very much upon the benefit that wisdom brings to the royal court and particularly to Solomon himself rather than upon any benefit that might flow out to the people. The influx of food described in chapters 4–5 has been replaced by an influx of luxury goods (vv. 2, 10–12, 22, 25), and Solomon's use of all this wealth is entirely self-indulgent (vv. 14–29). We are reminded of Samuel's warnings about kingship (1 Sam. 8:10–18). We wonder, in the midst of the silence of 1 Kings 10 about happenings elsewhere in the land, whether this particular king is also now living in luxury (cf. 1 Sam. 8:13) at the expense of his subjects. Do the Queen of Sheba's fine words about **justice and righteousness** (v. 9) have any relation to social reality outside the court? Solomon clearly knows all the answers (1 Kgs. 10:3), but is he any longer asking the right questions? Have "wise words" playfully exchanged with visiting dignitaries entirely displaced wise *action* on behalf of his people?

10:14–29 / The closing verses of the chapter press this issue upon us still more forcefully. The accumulation of **gold** continues. It is mentioned no fewer than ten times in verses 14–29 (vv. 14, 16–18, 21–22, 25). What does Solomon use it for? He decorates his palace (v. 16) with it; he overlays the finest **throne** ever seen with it (vv. 18–20); he makes household items with it (v. 21). If he does not bother much with **silver** (Deut. 17:17), it is only because it was **of little value in Solomon's days** (v. 21). This does not, however, prevent him from accumulating it anyway (vv. 22, 27), along with **chariots and horses** (v. 26). We have discussed the accumulation of horses before (cf. the commentary on 4:26). Again, it is the addition to the theme which is significant: **Solomon's horses were imported** *from Egypt* (v. 28). All but one of the instructions about kingship in Deuteronomy 17:16–17 are thus seen to have been abrogated by Solomon in these verses. That remaining one ("he must not take many wives") we shall be told about in chapter 11. Is this a wise way for any Israelite king to behave?

Additional Notes §15

9:13 / **Cabul:** The NIV footnote, in common with many modern commentators, apparently wishes us to explain this name in terms of the Hb. root *blh*, "to waste away." It is much more likely, however, that the root is *kbl*, from which we get the noun *kebel*, "fetters" that is found in Ps. 149:8—a psalm that celebrates the supremacy of Israel over the nations! It would not be surprising, if our interpretation of 9:10–14 is correct, to find Hiram calling the region in question "fettered"; for this is a word that reflects what is essentially the nature of his relationship with Solomon. This is not the only time in the Bible, of course, that we find evidence of towns in Galilee being undervalued (John 1:46).

9:16 / **Pharaoh . . . captured Gezer:** It is interesting that the same passage that tells us (v. 21) of Israelite inability to exterminate the Canaanites also tells us that their enemy of old, the Egyptian Pharaoh, has recently captured Gezer and killed all its Canaanite inhabitants—a city that had hitherto provided forced labor, according to Josh. 16:10. Why are we told of these Joshua-like exploits just at this point? Perhaps for this reason: that it helps us to see clearly just how easily *Solomon*, in all his glory and power, *could* have dealt with the Canaanites in the way deuteronomic law had commanded—if he had wished to. It points to the conclusion, in other words, that he continued to use them as labor *out of choice*, rather than out of necessity, because of his enthusiasm for building—and so willingly put himself at risk of their baneful influence. It should not pass unnoticed, either, that some of the building is of a highly questionable sort (v. 19; cf. the commentary on 4:26).

9:22 / **Government officials:** The NIV's translation obscures an important point, which a more literal translation brings out: "From among the Israelites, Solomon did not make any servant; they were his fighting men, his servants . . ." There is something of a play on the concept of "servant" going on here. Given that the point at issue is the composition of the *mas* in 5:13–14, we do well to remember that "servants" in 5:6, 9 (Hb. *ʿăḇāḏîm*, which the NIV renders "men") refers, not to **government officials,** but to those who will do the work, to those in 5:13–18 (both in the *mas* and not). It is much more likely that the distinction in 9:22, then, is precisely that implied in 5:13–18 between Canaanite "servants" (5:13–14) and other "servants," now identified as

Israelites. A translation that would better bring out the point is: "Solomon did not make any slaves; they were . . . his workers."

9:25 / **Fulfilled the temple obligations:** The Hb. is lit. "finished the house." The same verb (Hb. *šlm*) was found in 7:51, and its use here underlines the point that the temple was not truly regarded as "finished" by the authors of Kings until it was ready for worship (cf. the commentary on 7:1–5).

10:1 / **The queen of Sheba:** The visit of the Queen of Sheba to Solomon's court is also referred to in Matt. 12:42 and Luke 11:31, as Jesus addresses the "wicked generation" who will not recognize that "one greater than Solomon is here."

10:11 / **Hiram's ships brought gold:** Why, we may ask, does this note about Hiram appear here? It seems even more out of place than the story in 9:10–14, for it not only partly concerns (like 9:10–14) materials used in the construction of the temple but also interrupts the account about the Queen of Sheba. Yet the interruption is not without point. We have just been told that the queen herself brought gold and precious stones to Solomon, as well as an unparalleled amount of spices (v. 10). The authors want to set this gift very firmly in context. Solomon was already receiving precious stones from the Arabian region and much more gold than the Queen of Sheba had brought with her (the **gold from Ophir** of v. 28—note that her gift is exactly the same size as Hiram's *first* installment in 9:14, now superceded by his second in 9:28). Moreover, he was already importing unparalleled amounts of almug wood (evidently a wood whose value was equivalent to or greater than that of the spices, although we cannot identify it). Solomon was, in short, a vastly wealthier person than the queen—something that is underlined in v. 13. She cannot eclipse him.

10:15 / **The Arabian kings:** The NIV takes its cue here from the parallel passage in 2 Chron. 9:14. The MT actually reads "kings of the evening" (Hb. *ʿereḇ*), which is somewhat obscure. It seems possible, however, that it is a poetic reference to kings of the *west* (where the sun sets), and that we are meant to understand this, along with **governors of the land,** as a reference to the rulers of the various kingdoms within the Solomonic empire, which was located to the *west* of the Euphrates river (4:24). Certainly **governors of the land** is best understood in the light of the organization of the later Persian empire, when the land described in 4:24 as lit. "Across-The-River" (often "Trans-Euphrates" in the NIV) was indeed administered on behalf of the Persian emperor by **governors** (Hb. *paḥôṯ;* cf. Ezra 8:36; Neh. 2:7, 9). Solomon's wealth, then, comes not only from explorers (better than the NIV's **merchants;** cf. Hb. *twr* in Num. 13:2ff.) and **traders,** perhaps working outside the empire, but also from revenue deriving from within.

10:22 / **Trading ships:** Lit. "ships of Tarshish." Tarshish often appears in the OT as a distant port, far to the west (cf. Isa. 66:19; Ezek. 27:12–15; 38:13; Jonah 1:3; Ps. 72:10), a place that, like Ophir and Sheba, has exotic overtones. A "ship of Tarshish" is a ship capable of a journey

to such a faraway place. This second Solomonic fleet (not to be confused
with that of 9:26–28) sails to lands so distant, indeed, that it takes three
years to return with its extraordinary cargo. The whole world, throughout its entire extent, contributes to Solomon's wealth—a point that
vv. 24–25 underline, with their picture of the **whole world** flocking to
Jerusalem, each person bringing "tribute" (NIV **gift;** but cf. the translation of this same Hb. *minḥâ* in 4:21).

§16 Solomon's Apostasy (1 Kgs. 11:1–13)

While stopping short of questioning his basic commitment, and certainly allowing that he was blessed by God in a tremendous way, our authors have hinted throughout 1 Kings 1–10 that all is not well with Solomon's heart (e.g., 3:1–3; 4:26, 28; 5:14; 6:38–7:1). The prayer of 8:22–53 and God's response in 9:1–9 have, however, made clear both the importance of keeping the law and the consequences of disobedience; read in this context, 9:10–10:29 have sounded ominously like the climbing of the mountain just before the fall. That fall is now reported as the authors, returning to the marriage/worship theme of 3:1–3, come out in open critique of Solomon and describe the inevitable consequences of all that has gone before. His sins have found him out, and they have led him to apostasy.

11:1–8 / Solomon loved the LORD (3:3). In spite of the LORD's own warning about the dangers of intermarriage with foreigners (Deut. 7:3–4), however, he also **loved . . . Pharaoh's daughter** (Hb. ʾhb, v. 1–2) and many other women besides: he **held fast to them** (dbq, v. 2). The use of both verbs is to be understood in terms of their appearance in Deuteronomy (6:5; 10:12, 20; 11:1, 22; 13:4; 30:20), where they speak of unswerving human loyalty to God. The Israelite was to love the LORD wholeheartedly (Deut. 6:5). But Solomon's **heart** was divided (v. 4); he was a man unable to practice his own advice to his subjects (8:61). And in spite of his pious hope that God would always turn Israelite hearts towards God (1 Kgs. 8:58), we read that in his old age, the king's wives **turned** *his* **heart** in the opposite direction—**after other gods** (v. 4). The threat implied in much of Solomon's life story to this point now becomes a full-blown reality, and hints of impropriety become direct accusation: **Solomon did evil in the eyes of the LORD** (v. 6). He has ceased to be like **David his father** (vv. 4, 6) who, whatever his other faults may have been, certainly never worshiped other gods. Solomon not only worships them, he builds sanctuaries for them on the Mount of Olives (the **hill east of Jerusalem,** v. 7) and elsewhere that rival the temple (**He did the same for all,** v. 8). His "turning away" is truly spectacular.

11:9–13 / It comes as no surprise to readers of Kings to find God becoming **angry** with Solomon because of his apostasy (v. 9) or announcing that **the kingdom** is going to be torn **away** from him (v. 11). That is what 2:4, 8:25, and 9:4–5 have led us to expect. Those who have read Samuel before Kings, on the other hand, have long been living with something of a tension in regard to these descriptions of the divine promise to David. Is the continuance of the Davidic dynasty really conditional upon obedience? Or rather, will the wrongs of David's successors in the end be punished with measures other than the deprivation of dominion suffered by Saul (cf. 2 Sam. 7:11–16)? First Kings 11:11 only adds to this second reader's sense of puzzlement, because it so obviously recalls Samuel's words to Saul in 1 Samuel 15:28, thus correlating Saul with Solomon. First Kings 11:12 does little to help, except for the solace it offers in drawing the first reader now into the sense of confusion. The implicit threat of 2:4, etc., is unexpectedly mitigated: **I will not do it during your lifetime.** And what of verse 13? Here it is no longer the **whole kingdom** that is jeopardized by disobedience but only eleven of its tribes. **One tribe** remains out of grace, **for the sake of David and for the sake of Jerusalem, which I have chosen.** This is more than readers of Kings (or indeed Solomon), with their knowledge only of law, had any right to expect; but it is certainly less than the readers of 2 Samuel 7, with their deeper convictions about grace, might have anticipated. Everyone ends up surprised, standing unexpectedly on middle ground somewhere between rigid law and boundless grace. This is, indeed, where we shall be standing for much of the remainder of the book: one tribe (Judah) will remain due to God's grace, "for the sake of David," for a very long time (cf. 1 Kgs. 15:4; 2 Kgs. 8:19). Eventually, law will appear to prevail (2 Kgs. 24–25); but we shall return to this topic in a moment.

Additional Notes §16

11:3 / **Seven hundred wives . . . three hundred concubines:** Not for the first time in the Solomon story (cf., e.g., 4:26), we may suspect that the number (a round 1000) is not meant to be taken literally. The point is that everything Solomon did, he did in a big way! Song Sol. 6:8–9 contrasts the one true love of the king (Pharaoh's daughter? cf. V. Sasson, "King Solomon and the Dark Lady in the Song of Songs," VT 39 [1989], pp. 407–14) with his 60 queens and 80 concubines—a more modest number, though not in itself unimpressive, particularly when combined with "virgins beyond number."

11:5 / **Molech:** The NIV changes the MT's *milkôm* here and in 11:33 and 2 Kgs. 23:13 so as to make the text refer instead to the **Molech** of 11:7 and 2 Kgs. 23:10. This is an unusual and implausible variation on a popular scholarly theme, which is that **Molech** is a corrupt form of Milcom—itself an argument with little to commend it (how is it that both forms are found in the text of Kings on two separate occasions?). We certainly cannot assume that the same god is meant just because the same people worship him. Two different gods are, in fact, described; or, as the text puts it, two "detested things" (Hb. *šiqquṣ*), avoiding even the word "god" lest they be thought to have anything in common with Israel's God. See further J. Day, *Molech: A God of Sacrifice in the Old Testament*, UCOP (Cambridge: Cambridge University Press, 1989), esp. pp. 31–33.

11:6 / **Solomon did evil:** Solomon's apostasy is only the first of many in Kings, and we find in this text many themes that recur throughout the book. Individual kings are characteristically assessed in the story that follows in terms of whether they "did what was right" or **did evil** in the eyes of the LORD (e.g., 1 Kgs. 15:11, 26, 34); and Judean kings are said to be like **David** or not (e.g., 1 Kgs. 15:3, 11). The worship of other gods and the existence of high places lie at the very heart of the authors' concern (e.g., 1 Kgs. 14:23; 15:14; 16:31–33; 22:43).

A divided heart will lead to a divided kingdom: that was effectively God's promise to Solomon in 11:9–13. This last section on the great king pursues this theme of division. It tells us of still further seeds of destruction that were planted in the earlier part of his reign and have now grown into plants whose shadow looms darkly over the kingdom. It tells of opposition on the edges of the empire, and it introduces for the first time the man who will be the focal point of that same opposition within Israel itself—the man who will eventually become king of the northern tribes in place of Solomon's son. He is Jeroboam son of Nebat; his name will later echo throughout the book as that of the arch-idolater.

11:14–22 / "When a man's ways are pleasing to the LORD, he makes even his enemies live at peace with him" (Prov. 16:7). Thus Solomon had claimed in 1 Kings 5:4 that he was without **adversary.** Now the blessing has departed and the peace is fractured. We hear of two adversaries, enemies who had hitherto not caused significant problems but are now **raised up** by God to oppose the apostate king in his old age. The first is **Hadad,** a victim of David's wars (2 Sam. 8:13–14). In a story strangely reminiscent of Israel's own, he finds favor in Egypt (v. 19; cf. Gen. 39:4). He prospers, marrying an Egyptian woman (cf. Gen. 41:45) and fathering a son, **Genubath.** We do not need the hint from his son's name (cf. Hb. *gnb,* "to steal") to realize, however, that this is a man likely to be very angry indeed about the "stolen" lives of his countrymen and unlikely to want to stay forever in Egypt. It is therefore no surprise to find him later pleading with Pharaoh to **Let** him **go** (Hb. *šlḥ,* vv. 21–22). The plea is well-remembered from Israel's past (cf. Exod. 5:1; 7:16; 8:1 etc.), but on this occasion Pharaoh fails to harden his heart, and Hadad (the narrative implies, without being specific about the circumstances) is allowed to leave for Edom. Solomon's first adversary is thus, ironically, set upon him by an old enemy of Israel whom he had unwisely treated as a friend (1 Kgs. 3:1).

11:23–25 / **Rezon son of Eliada** had apparently either escaped from the battle described in 2 Samuel 8:3–4 or flown from **Hadadezer** later, unwilling to submit to imperial rule from Jerusalem. He had formed a bandit group that late in Solomon's reign took control of **Damascus** (garrisoned by David in 2 Sam. 8:6 and clearly part of the territory ruled by Solomon in 1 Kgs. 4:24), the capital of the new state of **Aram,** which plays such an important part in Israel's subsequent history (e.g., 1 Kgs. 15:18–20). Rezon opposes the king from the north, Hadad from the south. Where there was peace on all sides, now there are only enemies.

11:26–33 / Solomon's most important enemy, however, is to be found right on his doorstep: **Jeroboam son of Nebat,** erstwhile superintendent of the **labor force of the house of Joseph** that had been helping with the construction work in Jerusalem (vv. 27–28). It is outside Jerusalem that he is approached by **Ahijah the prophet of Shiloh** (v. 29). This scene is clearly reminiscent of the passage about the rejection of Saul in 1 Samuel 15, where we also find an outer garment torn as a symbol of the fact that God is tearing (Hb. *qrᶜ*) the kingdom away from the reigning king (1 Sam. 15:27–28; cf. 1 Kgs. 11:11). On this occasion, however, it is only *division* of the kingdom that will take place, and so the **cloak** is divided into twelve pieces, of which **ten,** symbolizing ten tribes, are given to Jeroboam (vv. 30–31). **One tribe** is to remain for the sake of **David** and **Jerusalem.** The mathematics are strange, since ten plus one does not equal twelve. It is clear from chapter 12, in fact, that two tribes actually remained under Davidic control (Judah and Benjamin, 12:21; cf. also 15:22). Benjamin, for some reason, is not highlighted in 11:30–39; its possession by Solomon is simply presupposed. The emphasis here (and indeed most of the emphasis in 12:1–24, cf. vv. 17, 20) falls upon Judah. Because of his apostasy, this is all the territory that Solomon will retain (v. 33). Solomon's abandonment of God, it should be noted, is also the people's abandonment of God. This is demonstrated in the plural phrase, **they have forsaken me,** which reflects the way that in the book of Kings, kings are characteristically models for and representative of the behavior of their subjects.

11:34–39 / The mitigation of 11:12–13 is repeated, although in a slightly different way. Solomon will not lose any tribes during his lifetime, and even his son is to retain one tribe so that David will always have a **lamp . . . in Jerusalem** (v. 36). God's grace to Solomon and to Solomon's successors is reaffirmed. And indeed, there is just a hint of a resolution here to that tension between law and grace that we noted again in 11:11–13. Jeroboam is promised that he, too, can have a dynasty like David's in the north, if he is obedient (v. 38), but there is already concealed in this promise the expectation of failure. For the division of the kingdom, verse 39 implies, is **not forever**. There will be a reunion. Even such punishment as has been meted out to David is not, it turns out, eternal punishment. Though it appears that God has treated Solomon very much like Saul (in spite of 2 Sam. 7:15), in reality he is merely handing down fatherly discipline (2 Sam. 7:14). Here is a glimmer of hope to hold on to as the story that follows unfolds. Law does indeed appear to prevail in the last Judean king's loss of his throne at the end of Kings. But law is not in the end more powerful than grace, and grace, 11:39 implies, does not function only to mitigate judgment, but ultimately to transform it into blessing. God's anger (11:9) will not last forever.

11:40–43 / We are not told exactly what happened after Jeroboam received Ahijah's message. We are told simply that Solomon, aware of the threat, sought Jeroboam's death only to find his own. Jeroboam escaped to Egypt, and from there he will shortly re-emerge with hostile intent (ch. 12). Like Hadad, he will use the liberation language of Exodus. Jeroboam, however, will be intent on liberating Israel, not from Egypt, but from Judah.

Additional Notes §17

11:14 / **An adversary:** The Hb. here is *śāṭān*, which in other OT texts refers to the great adversary, Satan (e.g., Job 1:6; 2:1). It is this latter opponent who is normally in view when "satan" appears in the NT (e.g., Matt. 12:22–37), although the human contribution to "opposition" is certainly prominent in Matt. 16:21–28.

11:25 / **As long as Solomon lived:** This is lit. "all the days of Solomon." It has sometimes been argued either that the authors are now telling us that Solomon was troubled by adversaries throughout his entire reign or that this was what their sources here said, and they have, in trying to make them say something different (that there was only opposition to Solomon in his *later* years), simply failed to remove the "contradiction." The latter view implies editorial ineptitude so colossal as to be unbelievable, especially in literature that gives evidence of being as carefully crafted as does 1 Kgs. 1–11. The former view is equally implausible, given how much trouble the authors have otherwise taken to convince us that adversaries only became a problem late in Solomon's life. We must remember that it has been part of the strategy throughout 1 Kgs. 1–11 to suggest that the *seeds* of what occurred later in Solomon's reign were already present earlier. The fact that Rezon and Hadad (and indeed Jeroboam) may have been Solomon's adversaries from early on (if "all his days" does not simply mean "all the *remaining* days of his old age," cf. 11:34) does not logically entail that they were a *problem* to him as such ("adversaries" worthy of the name) or that their activities were so significant in Solomon's earlier period that the general state of affairs could not be described as "peace" (5:4). It is noteworthy that we are not told when, exactly, Hadad was allowed to leave Egypt or when, exactly, Rezon took control of Damascus and "ruled in Aram."

11:26 / **One of Solomon's officials:** The Hb. is once again *ʿebed*, which is the same word as in 11:11 (the NIV's "subordinate"). It is a very general term, which may refer not to Jeroboam's job after his elevation in v. 28 but rather to his job before this as a "worker" (cf. the commentary on 9:22). Given that the emphasis in v. 28 is, in addition, upon the quality of his work, Hb. *gibbor ḥayil* in that verse is much better understood in terms, not of his social status (**a man of standing**), but of his physique—he had the physical attributes of a warrior (cf. *gibbôr ḥayil* in Josh. 1:14; 6:2; 8:3; Judg. 11:1; etc.). It is such attributes that mark men out for leadership in the OT, and indeed for kingship (see 1 Sam. 9:1–2, where *gibbor ḥayil* is also best understood in these terms; cf. 10:23–24). Solomon advances a man eminently suited to be, and certainly destined to be, his successor. Not for the only time in this narrative, echoes of the earlier Saul/David story are audible (cf. 1 Sam. 16:18, where David is also *gibbôr ḥayil*, advanced by the king he will replace).

11:28 / **Labor force:** Hitherto in the narrative we have met only the *mas,* comprising 30,000 Canaanite forced-laborers (1 Kgs. 5:13–14; 9:15–23) and a larger number of other laborers who worked on the temple (5:15–18). The labor force in 11:28 is said to have worked, like the *mas* (9:15), on some of Solomon's building projects in Jerusalem (11:27), though it is called not *mas,* but *sēbel.* The obvious implication of the choice of a different term is that this is an Israelite, and not a Canaanite, group; this is borne out by the fact that Jeroboam, an Ephraimite worker, is elevated from among its number to supervise the work (the *mas* being overseen by Adoniram, 5:14). The neatest solution in the light of all the evidence is to regard the *sēbel* as the northern component of the labor force of 5:15–18, kept on in Jerusalem after the temple-building for further work. The only other occurrence of the root *sbl* in Kgs. is, in fact, to be found in 5:15 (70,000 *carriers,* Hb. *nōśēʾ sabbāl*). What kind of group was this? We must certainly imagine, given the insistence of 9:15–23 that no Israelite was the same sort of "servant" as any Canaanite, that the authors do not wish us to regard the *sēbel* as forced labor in the same sense as the *mas;* and indeed, the difference can be seen in Neh. 4:17, where we are again told of the building of Jerusalem's wall. That is not to say, of course, that many *Israelites* did not see it as a harsh regime (cf. ch. 12). To them, *sēbel* undoubtedly has much more the atmosphere of the Egyptian oppression (cf. Ps. 81:6).

11:30 / **The new cloak:** It comes as no surprise to the reader who has begun to appreciate the artistry of 1 Kgs. 1–11 to discover that **cloak,** Hb. *śalmâ,* has almost exactly the same consonants as the name Solomon (Hb. *šᵉlōmōh*). The division of the cloak thus speaks particularly forcefully of the division of Solomon's kingdom.

11:32 / **He will have one tribe:** It is difficult to know why the authors felt that Davidic rule over Benjamin could be presupposed and not explicitly mentioned. One possibility is that they regarded Benjamin simply as Jerusalem's own territory, on the analogy of the Canaanite city-state: this territory came with the city, as it were, and needed no special mention. Certainly Jerusalem is regarded as belonging to Benjamin in Josh. 18:21–28. What is really important here, however, is Judah—the tribe that gives the whole southern kingdom its name (e.g., 1 Kgs. 14:21), even though Benjamin is incorporated into it.

§18 Excursus: Solomon in Canonical Context

The story of Solomon is ended. He was for the most part a wise king, although his wisdom was not always used for honorable ends (1 Kgs. 2:13–46), and towards the end of his reign it had degenerated into a self-indulgent playing of games with words (1 Kgs. 10:1–13). He was for the most part a king who was committed to his God. Yet even from the start there were question marks about his integrity (1 Kgs. 3:1–3, etc.) and signs of a wayward heart. Eventually his accumulated individual indiscretions turned to outright apostasy, as he turned away from God (1 Kgs. 11:1–8). He was in many ways an ideal king ruling over an ideal kingdom, but ideal and reality were always in some degree of tension, and eventually the reality was much less than ideal. He was, most of all, a king blessed by God. Solomon consistently believed that the blessing of God, and particularly the blessing of an eternal dynasty, was in the first instance tied up with moral virtue—his father's and his own. That is what his father had himself told him (1 Kgs. 2:2–4), and that is what God had seemingly confirmed to him (1 Kgs. 9:3–9). Blessing in fact continued even through indiscretion, however, and eventually it appeared (1 Kgs. 11), as readers of 2 Samuel 7 would suspect it might, that there was more to God's dealings with David's house than David had told his son. Eventually it appeared that God's punishment of this house would not be as bad, initially, as might have been expected (1 Kgs. 11:12–13, 32, 34, 36) and that even such punishment as had befallen was not eternal (1 Kgs. 11:39). *God's* choice was in the end indeed to be more important than *human* choices, even if mortals could never presume on grace in order to evade the demands of law. Such a hopeful ending to the Solomon story carries with it the implication that there can also be hope (the hope expressed in Solomon's own prayer of 1 Kgs. 8:22–53) at the end of Israel's story, when the as yet unfulfilled threats of 1 Kings 9:6–9 finally become realities (2 Kgs. 24–25). For if David's son is always to sit on the throne, God must forgive; a throne must be

restored upon which he may sit; and a people must be reconstituted over which he may rule.

The idea of an eternal throne for the son of David is, of
course, very much an idea that the NT picks up and develops.
Here Jesus is identified as *the* Son of David towards whom the
Davidic promise ultimately points (Matt. 1:1–16; 21:1–11; 22:41–46),
the king who sits upon David's throne (Luke 1:32–33; John
18:28–40; Acts 2:29–36). He is the one greater than Solomon,
fulfilling the messianic promise of Isaiah 11:1–9 (with its back-
ward glance at Solomon in vv. 2–3) to whose wisdom people
should listen as the Queen of Sheba had listened to Solomon
(Matt. 12:42; Luke 11:31; cf. also Matt. 13:54; Luke 2:40, 52). Like
the wisdom teachers of the OT, Jesus is often to be found in the
Gospels encouraging his hearers to learn about God by observing
how God's world works (e.g., Matt. 6:25–34; Luke 12:22–34).
More than that, however, the NT presents him to us as himself the
incarnation of wisdom, the very Wisdom of God (1 Cor. 1:24),
present with the Father from the very beginning of creation
(John 1:1–18; Col. 1:15–20; cf. Prov. 3:19–20; 8:22–31). Jesus super-
sedes Solomon—not least in the fact that in Jesus wisdom and
obedience to law are perfectly integrated (Rom. 5:19; Heb. 5:8),
whereas in Solomon they were always in tension and ultimately
divorced. At the same time, Solomon points forward typologically to Jesus. Once this is seen, it is impossible to read the
Solomon story without echoes of the Jesus story constantly sounding in our ears (e.g., in the "coronation" scene of 1 Kgs. 1:38–40;
cf. Matt. 21:1–11).

All the OT characters who prefigure Jesus are, of course,
less than the ideal towards whom they point. Even David had
deficiencies, as Matthew's genealogy of Jesus somewhat brutally
reminds us (Matt. 1:6) in referring to Bathsheba, not by name, but
as "Uriah's wife." We have seen plenty of evidence of Solomon's
deficiencies in our reading of 1 Kings 1–11. Towards the end of
our reading, I was pointing out what seemed to be a degree of
ambivalence in the text about Solomon's wealth. It is therefore
interesting to note that the only reference to Solomon's "splendor" in the NT occurs in a section of Jesus' teaching (recorded in
slightly differing forms in Matt. 6:25–34 and Luke 12:22–31) that
seeks to encourage believers not to allow concern about material
needs to interfere with the seeking of God's kingdom. Both
Gospels associate this teaching, in fact, with other teaching about
"not storing up treasures on earth" but in heaven, lest the heart

go astray (Matt. 6:19–21; Luke 12:32–34). Luke makes the issue doubly clear by associating the teaching also with the parable of the rich fool (Luke 12:13–21) and with the injunction to "sell your possessions and give to the poor" (Luke 12:33). The emphasis in these texts on God's provision of the *necessities* of life and on the imperative to *share* wealth are particularly interesting when one considers the emphasis in 1 Kings 9:10–10:29 on Solomon's *extravagance* and apparent *self-absorption*. We even have a token pagan "running after these things" (Matt. 6:32; Luke 12:30) in the shape of the Queen of Sheba!

In this example Solomon functions, then, less as a type of Christ than as a warning and example to the NT believer. He is "one of us," one of the people of God, and a theme from his story can therefore be picked up and used in relation to later generations. With this example of intracanonical interpretation before us, it would be possible to pick up other themes and pursue them in the same way. The "wisdom of Solomon" theme is another that could usefully be pursued in relation to the followers of Christ, since the very exploration of the nature of wisdom that we noted in 1 Kings 1–11 is also found in the NT. As pointed out already, Jesus himself exhorted people to "read nature" as a way of finding out about God and his ways (cf. 1 Kgs. 4:33–34). Jesus was also known to commend a worldly-wise attitude to the world, as in Matthew 10:16, "be as shrewd as snakes and as innocent as doves." Solomon, it will be recalled, was quite good at playing the snake, if not quite so convincing as the dove (1 Kgs. 2). As far as wisdom in administration is concerned (1 Kgs. 4–5), the NT is plainly in favor of it (e.g., Acts 6:3). Yet the NT is, like the Solomon story, keenly aware of the inadequacies of and dangers inherent in a wisdom that is simply "from below." The NT authors know that it can express itself as idle words and empty philosophy, if not as outright apostasy and "freedom" from God's law (e.g., Rom. 1:21–25; Col. 2:8; Jas. 3:13–18). And there is a very strong line of thought running throughout the NT that concerns the inability of the "wise" themselves to hear the Gospel (e.g., 1 Cor. 1:18–25). True wisdom must be revealed "from above"; and it is characteristically revealed to "children" (Luke 10:21)—to those who are not wise by worldly standards at all (e.g., 1 Cor. 1:26–31). Wisdom "from above" is thus given the same central place in the NT as it is in the Solomon story (1 Kgs. 3), where it, too, is wisdom that is revealed to "a little child" who knows his need

(3:7)—wisdom that leads on to wise judgment (cf. the expectation of 1 Cor. 6:5).

A few words, finally, about the Solomonic temple. We have already noted the importance of the temple building narrative in 1 Kings 6–8 to Stephen's speech in Acts 7 (esp. vv. 44–53)—a speech that leads to the dispersion of the early church from Jerusalem and from the temple (with its Solomonic "Colonnade," Acts 3:11; 5:12) where they had continued to worship. "The Most High does not live in houses made by men," he affirms, and other NT writers develop the thought, describing the church (or the individual believer as part of the church) as the temple of God (e.g., 1 Cor. 6:19; 2 Cor. 6:16; Eph. 2:19–22), a temple that is "not made by man" (cf. Mark 14:58; John 2:18–22) but is Christ's own body. The temple, like Solomon, has been superseded. Precisely because this is the case, however, a knowledge of OT texts about the temple and its worship is important if we are to understand much of what the NT has to say about Christ and his church, particularly in both Hebrews and Revelation, which develop the idea of the heavenly temple that is both prototype of the earthly temple (e.g., Heb. 8:3–5) and its eschatological fulfillment (Rev. 3:12; 7:9–11; 11:19; 15:5–8; 21:22).

The king is dead. Long live the king! Well, not quite. We are now to read of the tearing away of the kingdom that has been threatened in chapter 11. As Moses led his people out from slavery under the house of the Egyptian Pharaoh, so Jeroboam will lead Israel out from "slavery" under the house of David; as God hardened Pharaoh's heart in order to accomplish all his will, so the hardness of Rehoboam's heart will precipitate this schism also. The exodus will take Israel towards a new promised land, but they will soon be led off their path, as "Jeroboam as Moses" is transformed into "Jeroboam as Aaron," who fashions golden calves for them to worship. Eventually the result will be ejection from their land and exile in another.

12:1–4 / **Rehoboam went to Shechem** so that he could be crowned **king** by "all Israel" (NIV **all the Israelites**). We had reason to discuss the phrase "all Israel" in 4:7, where I argued that it was best taken in 1 Kings 1–11 as referring to the whole united kingdom or representatives from all its tribes. Certainly that is the most natural reading of 11:42, which is part of the concluding statement about the whole of Solomon's reign. He is the only king in Kings who is described as ruling over "all Israel," because he was, of course, the only king who did! In view of 11:42 in particular, "all Israel" in 12:1 must also refer to all the tribes. Rehoboam now comes to inherit the kingdom that his father had ruled.

We are not explicitly told why he comes to **Shechem**. Shechem does not appear in the narrative in relation to the kingship of David and Solomon. It is, however, a name that strikes a number of chords with those who know the story of Israel *prior* to the monarchy. It seems likely, given the dialog that follows, that this is significant. It is a place of covenant renewal (Josh. 24:1–27)—a place where the Israelites, having entered the land, first took stock of themselves and reflected upon their identity and direction. It is the place where Joseph's bones are buried (Josh. 24:32), bringing the exodus story to its final conclusion (cf. Gen. 50:22–26). It is also the place where kingship first, if briefly, intruded itself into the tribal life of Israel, a mortal being (and a wicked one at that) taking the place of God as ruler over God's people (Judg. 8:22–23; 9). Shechem is an ideal place, therefore, to which a prospective king might be invited if you wished to ask him (as the Israelites do) how his kingship was going to be exercised so as to be consonant with the nature of the covenant people of God—if you wished to ask him to reflect on the identity of Israel and her future direction.

The people's complaint is precisely that their identity has, under Solomon, become confused. They are no longer the people set free to live in the promised land. They have become once more a people under **harsh labor,** as they were in Egypt (Exod. 1:14; 2:23), toiling as oxen would under a **heavy yoke. Jeroboam** appears as a kind of second Moses, implicitly taking a leading role in the approach to Rehoboam. The similarity even extends in the MT (cf. the NIV footnote to v. 2) to a certain reluctance to take on such a role (cf. Exod. 4:1–17). He remains in Egypt, we are told, and has to be sent for.

12:5–15 / As Jeroboam is Moses in this replay of the exodus story, so Rehoboam is Pharaoh. The **elders**—who had, no doubt, had the benefit of Solomon's own wisdom (cf. 1 Kgs. 10:8) and had little hope of or desire for further advancement from his son—give Rehoboam wise advice: that effective leadership comes from below and not from above (12:7). But he chooses instead to accept the foolish advice of his younger contemporaries (v. 8). They, of course, owe their position in life to him, and they give him advice that he evidently wishes to hear. He should take a hard line (vv. 8–11), substituting **scorpions** (perhaps a particularly vicious form of whip) for mere **whips.** When he does so (vv. 12–14), of course, he is behaving exactly as Pharaoh had behaved before him, reacting to the words of "Moses" by increasing the oppression (cf. Exod. 5:1–21). He is bound to act thus, however, for the LORD has ordained that his **word** to **Jeroboam** through **Ahijah** should come to pass (v. 15). In the midst of all the human decisions that are described to us, God's decision is being carried through. We have heard it all before: "Pharaoh's heart became hard and he would not listen to them, just as the LORD had said" (Exod. 7:13; cf. 4:21; 7:3–4; etc.). Nor did this **king . . . listen to the people, for this turn of events was from the** LORD.

12:16–20 / Rehoboam's bluff, if bluff it was, is called. **All Israel** reacts by making it clear that kingship cannot be imposed upon the people but must have their consent. They take upon their lips a cry (v. 16) that is very similar to Sheba's in 2 Samuel 20:1, and they leave for their **tents.** They do so, not this time in postassembly joy and gladness of heart, happy under a Davidic king (1 Kgs. 8:66), but in the grim determination of those who will appoint a king of their own choosing. They leave David's **house** to fend for itself. This choice, too, is of course preordained (11:31, 35, 37–38), and Jeroboam, God's choice, duly becomes king after Rehoboam fails to impose his will on the people through Adoram (NIV's **Adoniram,** v. 18; see the additional notes).

He becomes king, it should be noted, **over all Israel** (v. 20). Commentators have often argued that, since we are also told in verses 17 and 20 that Judah remained under the control of Rehoboam, **all Israel** must refer here only to the northern tribes. Given that up to this point in 1 Kings the phrase is used only in reference to the whole united kingdom, however, it is difficult to believe that this is all that is meant. The wording of verse 17 is itself curious: **Rehoboam still ruled over** all those **Israelites who were living in the towns of Judah.** If a straightforward distinction between the southern and northern kingdoms is indeed intended in this passage, it is not immediately clear why the authors do not simply say "Judah" in verse 17 and "Israel" in verse 20, adopting the language that is common later in the story (e.g., 15:1, 9, 25). Taking everything together, it seems much more likely that we are not being told here simply that the northern tribes seceded from the house of David whereas Judah did not. We are also being told something about the *legitimacy* of the two new spheres of rule, from a human and political point of view (if not the divine). There was, on the one hand, an official decision by all the tribes gathered in council (Jeroboam shall have the whole kingdom), and there was, on the other hand, a de facto reality after the event (Rehoboam retained control over some of the people *in* the kingdom). The very same **all Israel** that Solomon had reigned over (11:42) and that had gathered to crown Rehoboam only then to reject him as king (12:1, 16)—this same entity has decreed that the kingdom is Jeroboam's, yet one tribe has, nevertheless, remained with Rehoboam in partial contradiction to this corporate ruling. The language of politics at this point parallels the language of theology in a highly significant way: "I will tear the kingdom away . . . yet I will not tear the whole kingdom" (11:11–13). Politically and theoretically speaking, Jeroboam is the legitimate ruler of the whole kingdom and Rehoboam has no legitimacy at all—for **all Israel** has turned away from him and left his "Egypt" for a better country. Nevertheless, in his sovereign grace God has decreed that Rehoboam should hold Judah and that Jeroboam should have ten tribes rather than twelve. So that is what happens. Political theory and political reality are not permitted to match up.

12:21–24 / Persistent to the last, however, Rehoboam again tries to impose his will upon **the kingdom** through force, mustering both **Judah** and **Benjamin** (cf. the additional note on 11:32), as well as some mysterious other **people** (v. 23), to fight against the **house of Israel** (the northern tribes). It requires a prophetic oracle from **Shemaiah** to prevent war by convincing the people that what has happened is indeed of God. But this situation does not last long; there will be a continuous war between north and south throughout the period after the schism (1 Kgs. 14:30; 15:6, 16). Perhaps Rehoboam was untimately unwilling to give up his own view of reality in favor of God's. Perhaps the northern tribes (in spite of Jeroboam's own knowledge of God's will) were unwilling to accept the continuing contradiction to the corporate decision of all Israel that Rehoboam's kingship over Judah and Benjamin represented. We do know of at least one other case where the de facto contradiction of a decision of the whole nation gathered together "from Dan to Beersheba" was resolved by war (Judg. 20). In that case, of course, God was firmly on the side of the tribal assembly, and they succeeded. In this case, he is firmly on his own side, a third party in a conflict between two factions who cannot accept his decision. All the wars will therefore come to nothing, until the two sides come to see that they are indeed **brothers** (v. 24; cf. 1 Kgs. 22, esp. v. 44) and should live in peace. There is much to happen in 1 Kings, however, before we get to that point.

Additional Notes §19

12:4 / **Your father put a heavy yoke on us:** It is the claim of "all Israel" that Solomon's regime in part or as a whole has been unduly harsh. The authors do not commit themselves on the point. They do want us to think differently about the *mas* (forced labor) that the Canaanite population carried out and the *sēbel* that at least the house of Israel performed (see the additional note on 11:28), and they have certainly not described most of Solomon's reign (1 Kgs. 3–8) in a way that would make us think it oppressive. There are perhaps hints in 9:10–10:29, however, that they are preparing us for Israel's speech here (see the commentary).

12:7 / **If today you will be a servant:** There is a play on the Hb. root *ᶜbd*, "to serve," throughout 12:1–15 that is not transparent in the NIV translation. It appears twice in v. 4 (labor, serve) and three times in v. 7 (servant, serve, servants). The king has the Israelites as servants, to which they do not in principle object; but if he really wants them as servants, he must be a servant to them and demand less service.

12:10 / **My little finger is thicker than my father's waist:** The Hb. here is lit. "my little one is thicker than my father's loins." If the "little one" is a finger, this is the only place in the OT where it is so. Given the location of the loins in the lower part of the body, and the fact that power and sexual potency were very much associated in the ancient Near East (cf. the commentary on 1 Kgs. 1:1–4), it may well be that the "little one" is in fact the male sexual organ. It is certainly not beyond the bounds of possibility that young men might respond to a challenge by using language containing fairly basic sexual imagery. Whatever is the case, the claim is that Rehoboam is a bigger man than his father—a power to be reckoned with.

12:18 / **Adoniram, who was in charge of forced labor:** The Hb. here is Adoram, a name that also appears in 2 Sam. 20:24. It is not clear whether the same person is meant as in 1 Kgs. 4:6 and 5:14, and it is not explicitly said what his mission is, as the person in charge of forced labor (Hb. *mas*). It cannot be to re-impose conditions of *mas* on Israel, since Israel has not yet been under such conditions (cf. 1 Kgs. 9:15–23). The exodus narrative again gives us our clue (Exod. 1:11). Rehoboam is intent, as "Pharaoh," on regarding Israel as if they were still in Egypt, putting them now under conditions of forced labor. If they think that their experience under Solomon was the "hard labor" of Egypt, they are shortly to discover that this was nothing compared to life under the new regime. The sending of **Adoniram,** in other words, represents the first move in the direction of trying to deal harshly with Israel (cf. 1 Kgs. 12:13–14). The Israelites are to be treated under the new regime as if they were Canaanites.

12:20   /   **The tribe of Judah remained loyal:** The translation is misleading and may well derive from the common assumption among commentators that Judean representatives were not present at the assembly and were not party to its decisions. We are not told this in the text; nor are we told whether or not Judah remained under Rehoboam's control out of loyalty. We are simply told that Rehoboam did in fact retain control of Judah (that this tribe "went after" him, Hb. *hāyāh ʾaḥarê*) despite the decisions of vv. 16 and 20.

§20 Jeroboam's Sin (1 Kgs. 12:25–33)

Israel has once again broken free from slavery in "Egypt"; a new "Moses" is leading the way. It is not long, however, before this new exodus leads, as the first had done, to the worship of golden calves. It is Jeroboam's action in facilitating such worship that will constantly be referred to in the narrative about the northern kingdom that follows (e.g., 15:26, 34) as Israel's characteristic sin that leads eventually to exile in a foreign land (2 Kgs. 17:20–23).

12:25–30 / The first task undertaken by Jeroboam is the obvious one of defence (v. 25). He evidently does not trust Rehoboam to remain in Jerusalem very long. In fact, he does not seem to trust anyone. He is not convinced, in spite of the events of 12:1–20, that his newfound subjects have really given him their total commitment and would not **kill** him if circumstances demanded it (v. 27). He is not even convinced—in spite of these same events—of the legitimacy of his own kingship; he refers to Rehoboam as **their lord** (i.e., Israel's lord) despite the fact that he is self-evidently (and not merely de facto) the only **king of Judah.** Most of all, he does not trust God. In spite of the clear prophetic word of Ahijah in 11:31–39, he is not prepared to leave it to God to maintain his hold over the northern tribes. He fears that the presence of the **temple of the LORD** in Jerusalem (12:27) will be a more decisive factor in this matter than his own obedience (11:38). It is this inability to trust that is his downfall, for he must now strive for security by himself. In his thinking, religion becomes simply an aspect of political control; such faulty thinking about the place of God in the universe, combined with **advice** (v. 28) just as flawed as that given to Rehoboam, inevitably leads him to sinful actions. Because he thinks the solution is to put religion in the service of the state, he builds centers of worship within his own territory, in the far north (**Dan**) and south (**Bethel**).

This is bad enough, for it represents the proliferation of "high places" rivalling the temple—something about which the authors of Kings are deeply concerned (cf. the additional note on 1 Kgs. 3:2). What is worse, though, is the construction of the **two golden calves** as focal points for worship at these sanctuaries. Jeroboam/Moses is transformed into Jeroboam/Aaron (Exod. 32:1–35), making **gods** for the people to worship in defiance of the LORD's words at Mount Sinai (Exod. 20:4). His words to them in 1 Kings 12:28 (**Here are your gods, O Israel, who brought you up out of Egypt**) are, indeed, almost exactly the words with which the people greet the construction of the first calf (Exod. 32:4). Jeroboam has followed Solomon into sin, and as readers of both the exodus and Solomon stories know, this can bring only God's judgment. For the LORD is in fact the living God who controls history. The LORD is not simply a convenient symbol that human rulers may adopt to further their *own* control of history. God cannot be captured in an image any more than be confined in a temple. And all moves designed to produce human security that fail to take this into account are doomed to failure. Trusting obedience is, after all, the only fruitful path.

12:31–33 / Having described the calves and their locations, the authors now turn their attention to Bethel in particular, for it is at Bethel that Jeroboam invests the major part of his effort to set up worship arrangements to rival those in Jerusalem. Unfortunately, the NIV partially obscures this fact by translating Hebrew *bêṯ bāmôṯ* in verse 31 as **shrines on high places.** This fails to reflect its clear connection with *bêṯ yhwh*, "house of the LORD" in verse 27, and leaves the hitherto unmentioned **altar** of verse 32 with no temple (and no context in which to make sense of it). Rehoboam has a "house" in Jerusalem; Jeroboam needs a "house" to compete with it. So he builds a "house of high places" (i.e., an illegitimate temple in the singular) with its own **altar** in Bethel (v. 32). He appoints **priests** to service this temple (v. 31) and installs these "priests of the high places" (i.e., an illegitimate priesthood) there. Finally, he needs a central festival to celebrate, **like the festival in held in Judah** (v. 32). So he creates one, as he has created both temple and priesthood. It is, however, an illegitimate festival, which takes place in the **eighth month—a month of his own choosing** (v. 33). We assume that this is Jeroboam's version of the Feast of Tabernacles, celebrated in Jerusalem in the seventh month (cf. 1 Kgs. 8:2; cf. Lev. 23:33–43).

The new king has built a temple outside Jerusalem that infringes the prohibition in Deuteronomy 12; created a priest-hood that has blurred the important distinction between those set apart by God for priestly service (here **Levites**) and those simply of the **people** (cf. Num. 3–4); and invented a festival celebrated on a date with no divine significance whatsoever. The story is still evoking memories of Aaron; he, too, made his golden calf, built an altar, and announced a festival on a date **of his own choosing** (cf. Exod. 32:5). And on that occasion it was the **Levites** who were distanced from the celebrations (Exod. 32:26).

We are also being invited to read Jeroboam against the background of Solomon. The mention of the festival in particular reminds us of the previous occasion upon which we heard tell of a celebration of Tabernacles—the dedication of the Jerusalem temple, when the ark of the covenant was brought up and God met with his people in his new house. It suggests to us that we read Jeroboam's first festival celebration (v. 33) as a self-conscious attempt to rival that great occasion—to "dedicate" his new house and its priesthood. Since God is not with him in the venture, however, nothing good can come of it—as we shall shortly dis-cover (13:1–10; 14:1–20). For the moment we are left with a question: if Solomon's eventual apostasy lost him the kingdom, what will Jeroboam's much quicker departure from the LORD's commandments cost *him?*

Additional Notes §20

12:28 / **Here are your gods:** It is often held that Jeroboam has had a raw deal from the authors of Kings and that he did not in fact initiate idolatrous worship in Israel at all but, in effect, only substituted calves for ark and cherubim, in a slightly different version of the wor-ship of the LORD in Jerusalem. He is not so much wicked, it is claimed, as misunderstood, even misrepresented; what he really wanted was for Israel to worship the LORD *through the medium of* the calves. Such is the dogmatism with which this position is sometimes asserted that it is difficult to keep clearly in view the extent to which its basis lies in speculation rather than in evidence. The opposite position has, in fact, been asserted with equal force—that Jeroboam deliberately set out to lead his people (back) into Canaanite worship, and chose his symbols carefully with that end in mind. See most recently N. Wyatt, "Of Calves and Kings: The Canaanite Dimension in the Religion of Israel," *SJOT* 6

(1992), pp. 68–91. The real curiosity of the first position, however, lies in its claim that what "actually happened" (Jeroboam encouraging worship of the LORD via the calves, on this view) is not "actually" idolatry at all. From whose point of view? It is certainly idolatry so far as passages like Deut. 4:15–24 are concerned. You cannot worship the LORD using representations of him, for then you are not worshiping him at all but "other gods" (1 Kgs. 14:9). Whatever Jeroboam *thinks* he is doing with his calves, it is idolatry from the point of view of these passages; and it is already clearly associated with the worship of Canaanite deities in 1 Kgs. 14:15. Sincerity—if that is what it is—is not enough.

12:29 / **One he set up in Bethel:** Although two sanctuaries are mentioned initially, it is the sanctuary at Bethel that is clearly the more important of the two to the authors. This is the place where Jeroboam builds the focal point for his new religious arrangements. Bethel also appears in the book of Amos, of course, as the royal sanctuary of the northern kingdom (Amos 7:10–17); there the issue of using religion as a means of political control again surfaces. Amaziah suggests that Amos has no right to preach against the king at Bethel because he is not an official prophet of the kingdom. Amos' response is to assert God's freedom to speak wherever and however God chooses. The true prophet is beyond human control—as Jeroboam son of Nebat will shortly discover for himself.

12:31 / **Even though they were not Levites:** It is often argued that this implies that only Levites, and no one else, could be priests. This is in spite of passages like Num. 3–4 and in spite of the connection between 1 Kgs. 12:25–33 and 1 Kgs. 8, where (in the only other place in Kings where Levites appear, 8:4) a distinction between priests (i.e., descendants of Aaron) and Levites (i.e., priests who are not descended from Aaron) is clearly in view. The background to the assertion is an ongoing debate among OT scholars about the nature of the OT priesthood throughout Israel's history, a debate in which it is certainly impossible to participate fully here. It is sufficient simply to note, in relation to 1 Kgs. 12:31 in particular, that to affirm that priests were appointed who were not Levites is not the same thing as affirming that only Levites could be appointed priests. There are other reasons why the Levites might have been singled out for mention here, with no reference being made at the same time to others who could legitimately be priests. Not the least of these is the fact that the Levites are singled out for mention in Exod. 32—a passage constantly in view in 1 Kgs. 12. For a brief discussion of the wider debate, see *IBD*, pp. 1266–71.

§21 The Man of God from Judah (1 Kgs. 13:1–34)

Jeroboam stands, like Solomon (1 Kgs. 8:22), at the altar of his new temple, ready to dedicate it to his gods. He does not, however, get his chance to speak, for this temple has no legitimacy. And so, as Solomon's temple was built in fulfillment of a prophetic promise about both temple and dynasty (2 Sam. 7:1–17), the building of Jeroboam's temple evokes prophetic threats (1 Kgs. 13:2–3; 14:7–13), which in due course will come to fulfillment in the destruction of both dynasty and temple. The LORD is the God of history, whose word must be obeyed—even by the very prophets who deliver it—if blessing is to follow (13:11–32).

13:1–6 / Jeroboam had been promised a dynasty as enduring as David's, if only he would obey God (1 Kgs. 11:38). He had not, however, been promised a temple and temple worship, and his moves to acquire these now elicit prophetic opposition in the shape of a **man of God** from **Judah**. His focus is in the first instance upon the **altar** and not the dynasty, which will come under consideration in 14:7–13. Yet his words already assume the end of the dynasty (even before it has begun), for they point forward to a time when all northern dynasties have come to an end and only the **house of David** remains to take action against Bethel (cf. **Josiah**'s desecration of the altar through the burning of **human bones** and his slaughter of the illegitimate **priests** who service it, in 2 Kgs. 23:15–20). These events are still a long way off, and so a **sign** is also described and then enacted, which indicates that the prophecy is true (vv. 3, 5). The **altar** is **split apart and its ashes poured out.** The God who can ensure that prophecy comes to pass in the short term can surely do so over the longer term. The splitting of the altar is a graphic illustration of the truth that God is not and cannot be under Jeroboam's control. No less graphic is what happens to the king's **hand** when he stretches it out to give the command that the prophet should be arrested

(v. 4). He has no more power over God's prophet than he has over God. He is, in fact, entirely dependent upon him for the healing of his **shriveled** digits (v. 6).

13:7–30 / The sequel to this story is also the introduction to the next part of the narrative, for it is in the sequel that we discover the man of God himself to be under the strictest of divine commands. He **must not eat bread or drink water or return by the way** he came (v. 9). The reason for the prohibition, and for the seemingly related desire of the other characters to offer their hospitality, is never explicitly given. Elsewhere in the OT, however, we do find texts that characterize true prophets of the LORD as free from obligation to other mortals and thus able to speak God's word without fear or favor (e.g., Amos 7:10–17). False prophets are those beholden to other mortals in some way, speaking only what people wish to hear (e.g., Mic. 3:5–7; cf. 1 Kgs. 22). We may be intended to read Jeroboam's invitation to dine and receive a **gift** (v. 7), then, as an attempt to buy the Judean's loyalty. If the prophet can reverse God's judgment in the small matter of the hand, perhaps he can also exchange the curse on the altar for a blessing. The invitation from the **old prophet living in Bethel** (a false prophet who later spoke truly) can be understood in the same way (vv. 11, 15)—as an attempt to stave off the destruction of Bethel, and the desecration of his own tomb, which he knows must follow the Judean's words of verse 2 (v. 32). It is concern about the possibility of corruption, then, that may lie behind the instructions given to the Judean about his journey. He is to go directly to Bethel and come directly back. He is not even to stop for refreshment, and he is to vary his route so that he cannot easily be found and prevented from completing his mission (cf. Matt. 2:12). It is when he does stop (v. 14) that his troubles begin.

Whatever the reason for both the prohibition and the committed attempts to persuade the man to disregard it, it is clear that God requires complete and radical obedience to this command. The man of God starts out well, resisting the king's invitation and setting out on **another road** (v. 10) so as not to **return by the way he had come.** Later, however, when he is overtaken on his journey, he is persuaded by the old **prophet** to accept hospitality in his house by the (false) claim that he too has had a prophecy from God (vv. 11–19). While sitting at table, the Bethel prophet then receives a *true* prophecy condemning the man of

God because he has **defied the word of the LORD** (v. 21) that he first received. The Judean will not make it home, he says, to be **buried in the tomb of** his **fathers** (v. 22). The man of God duly meets his fate, as a **lion** meets him on the road and kills him (vv. 23–25). He is subsequently buried in the Bethel prophet's **own tomb** (vv. 26–30). The point is thus forcefully made that he ought to have followed through the word of the LORD that *he* had received (**the command . . . God** *gave you,* v. 21) rather than being led off his path by another's prophetic claim (v. 18). It is further made clear that God's law stands over everyone—that even prophets must obey it, or face judgment—and that God can use even false prophets occasionally to speak the truth.

13:31–34 / The closing verses of the chapter tie the story of the prophets back to the Jeroboam narrative. True prophecy will bring forth the judgment it promises; even prophets cannot escape if they are disobedient. And if prophets cannot escape, neither can kings. **Bethel,** and by extension all the other **shrines on the high places** that center around Bethel's cult, will indeed be destroyed (v. 32). Even in face of all that has just happened, however, Jeroboam continues in his **evil ways** (v. 33), appointing illegitimate **priests for** the **high places** just mentioned. That is to say, he proliferates his new cult, extending it beyond Bethel and Dan into the rest of his kingdom. And because all the warnings of chapter 13 have led him, not to repentance (like Ahab in 1 Kgs. 21:28–29), but to a hardening of heart, the **destruction** of his house is now assured (v. 34). **This was the sin**—this persistence in idolatry—that led him to disaster. His adherence to his religious reforms has put the prize of an everlasting dynasty out of reach; his attempt to make his own "house" secure, by building a "house" for his gods at Bethel and lesser shrines for them elsewhere, has failed.

Additional Notes §21

13:28 / **Neither eaten . . . nor mauled:** The point is that what happened is miraculous, divinely initiated. Lions would not normally kill a man and then stand over the body with an uneaten donkey for company (cf. also v. 24) while ignoring the meals passing by (v. 25).

13:31 / **Lay my bones beside his bones:** It has sometimes been suggested that the old prophet simply desires to be remembered *in* the grave along with the man who spoke what was true. This view of the request tends to be allied to a view of the prophet as basically benevolent—a view that is difficult to square with the fact that he knowingly lied. Given the context, it is much more likely that his concern is not so much to be *remembered* in the grave as to be allowed to *remain* in the grave. Thus, this is his alternative plan (after his hospitality stratagem failed) to avoid the desecration of his bones that he knows will otherwise take place (v. 32; cf. v. 2). As it turns out, this second plan is one that works (2 Kgs. 23:17–18).

13:32 / **Samaria:** As a city, Samaria became the capital of the northern kingdom under Omri, the father of Ahab (1 Kgs. 16:24). The name is used here by extension for the territory of which Samaria is the capital (cf. 2 Kgs. 23:15–20)

13:33 / **Did not change his evil ways, but once more appointed:** The Hb. is lit. "did not return from his evil way, but returned and made." There is an evident play on the verb *šwb* "to return" here (cf. 13:16, 18, 19, 20, 22, 23, 26, 29), and in particular on the phrase "return by the way" (13:9, 10, 17). The man of God was told not to retrace his steps at any point on his journey, but he did so in order to return to the prophet's house (vv. 19, 22). Because he allowed himself to be brought back alive ("returned") by this prophet (vv. 18, 20, 23, 26), he was eventually brought back dead (v. 29), since God's judgment fell upon him. In spite of this, Jeroboam also "retraces his steps"—and this too will bring downfall and destruction. There is an interesting parallel here, of course, between Jeroboam's construction of his altar, in order to prevent the kingdom "returning to the house of David," and his attempts to prevent the man of God from returning to Judah. The failure of the second hints at the failure of the first, already alluded to in 11:39—although the hope enshrined there is hope for a future that, in the context of the book as a whole, must lie beyond the time when Judah too has been led astray and "buried in the grave" beside its northern neighbor (2 Kgs. 17:18–20).

Jeroboam had been promised a dynasty like David's (1 Kgs. 11:38). His desire to have also a temple like David's, however, has led him into disobedience—and we have seen in chapter 13 what happens to the disobedient. First Kings 14:1–20 now describes to us the consequences of Jeroboam's attempt to possess the two "houses" he wanted instead of the one he was promised, and they do so in a way that makes clear the essential differences between the two kings.

14:1–5 / We begin on familiar territory. In spite of the events of chapter 13, Jeroboam apparently still thinks he can control his own destiny—that he can manipulate a prophet of God into giving him a positive message about his son. He appears to believe still that only human actors participate in this drama—albeit some of these actors have special powers and can speak words that count (cf. Acts 8:9–25). His plan is, of course, flawed, for it has been devised in ignorance of reality. He is ignorant even of **Ahijah**'s human condition. There is little point in disguising yourself to visit a blind man (v. 4)! He is also ignorant, however, of his spiritual condition. There is no point in disguise when the blind man is so in touch with God that he can see through deception with ease (v. 5). God cannot be frustrated by human stratagems; God's ways cannot be diverted by **cakes** and **honey** (v. 3).

14:6–11 / So it is that although Jeroboam's wife thinks she has been sent to Ahijah to find out about her sick child, she discovers that in fact *he* has been **sent** to *her* with a message about the kingship (v. 6). Jeroboam has failed to be like David (14:8; cf. 11:38); he has, like Solomon, worshiped **other gods** (v. 9). Because he has **done . . . evil** (Hb. r^{cc}) in this way (v. 9), God is **going to bring disaster** ($rā^c â$) **on the house of Jeroboam** (v. 10). **Every last male** will be **cut off,** bringing the dynasty inevitably to an end, and it will be a dishonorable end, since the bodies will not be buried, but eaten by **dogs** and **birds** (vv. 10–11; cf. 1 Sam. 31:8–13 for evidence of the importance of proper burial). This prophetic "promise" thus stands in stark contrast to the promise of 2 Samuel 7. David will always have a descendant (cf. Hb. *lōʾ krt,* "never fail," in 1 Kgs. 2:4; 8:25; 9:5), but Jeroboam will be harshly deprived of descendants (Hb. *krt,* **cut off**). This is, of course, why God deals so much more leniently with Solomon (and Rehoboam, as we shall see) than he does with Jeroboam.

14:12–13 / It is in this context that we are to understand the reference to Jeroboam's son. **The boy will die.** This is a tragedy in any circumstances. Yet in the context of what will happen to all the other males in Jeroboam's house, his death can be seen as a blessing—for he, at least, **will be buried.** The real tragedy is what will happen to the **house of Jeroboam** as a whole. There are further echoes here, of course, of David's story. David, too, lost a sick child (2 Sam. 12:15–23) because of sin; his sin also affected his whole house, as God brought calamity (Hb. *rāʿâh*) upon him (2 Sam. 12:10–12). Yet there was never any suggestion that his house would be destroyed. The death of his first son by Bathsheba was immediately followed by the birth of his second, Solomon—the one who would succeed him (2 Sam. 12:24–25). Sin cannot subvert David's promise, as it can and does Jeroboam's. We are reminded of this in a context where David's righteousness is once again stressed (v. 8); for David certainly did not do **only what was right in** God's **eyes** in the matter of Uriah the Hittite (cf. 1 Kgs. 15:5). Not for the first time in 1 Kings we are being invited to ponder on the real reason why a distinction has been made between David and other kings (Saul, Jeroboam). His relative righteousness cannot be the entire explanation.

14:14–16 / Ahijah's prophetic gaze turns finally to the distant future. He restates what the fate of the house will be, now describing the precise means by which judgment will fall (a new **king over Israel,** v. 14), but he looks also to the fate of the northern kingdom as a whole. In the absence of a strong dynasty to rule them, they are destined to know only the instability of **a reed swaying in the water** (cf. Matt. 11:7; Luke 7:24) and eventual exile in a land beyond the **River** Euphrates. That is where persistence in the **sins** of **Jeroboam** will lead. The instability of which Ahijah speaks is well described in the account of the northern kingdom, which follows; the land beyond the river, it turns out, is Assyria (2 Kgs. 17:1–6, 21–23). Jeroboam's disobedience affects not just his own destiny (as the Judean prophet's had done), nor just that of his house; it affects the destiny of the whole kingdom.

14:17–20 / The **boy** duly dies as Jeroboam's **wife** returns to her **house** in **Tirzah,** to which Jeroboam has apparently moved his court. Like the splitting of the altar in 13:5, the fulfillment of this immediate prophecy functions as a sign that everything else will also come to pass. We cannot regard the succession of **Nadab,** then, as anything other than temporary; for we know that Jeroboam's house is doomed, just as surely as we know that David's is secure.

Additional Notes §22

14:2 / **Disguise yourself:** The theme of royal disguise appears in other places in the OT where the point is made that, whatever the king may think, it is God and not the king who determines the course of events (e.g., 1 Sam. 28; 2 Chron. 35:20–27). We shall come across the theme twice more in 1 Kgs. (20:35–43; 22:29–38). See further R. Coggins, "On Kings and Disguises," *JSOT* 50 (1991), pp. 55–62.

14:10 / **Every last male:** Lit. "he who urinates against a wall." The NIV's desire for discretion obscures the obvious connection between the urine and the **dung** or excrement that God uses as fuel for the fire of destruction. Jeroboam's house smells; radical action is needed to deal with this sanitation problem.

Slave or free: The Hb. is *ʿāṣûr weʿāzûb,* which appears on four other occasions in the OT (Deut. 32:36; 1 Kgs. 21:21; 2 Kgs. 9:8; and in a slightly different form, 2 Kgs. 14:26). It is a notoriously difficult phrase, but it does seem most unlikely, in a context that has to do with succession to the throne from within Jeroboam's "house," that a distinction between **slave** and **free** is intended. In both Deut. 32:36 and 2 Kgs. 14:26 it appears in association with the idea of powerlessness: the people of Israel have no strength after God's judgment, there is no one to help them in face of their enemies. It is in this situation that there has ceased to be *ʿāṣûr weʿāzûb.* Whatever the phrase means precisely, it seems probable that when used of the males of the royal house, it is their nature as sources of "power" and "help" to the king that is in view (cf. the analogous "cutting off" of "every horn of Israel" in Lam. 2:3, with its associated "no one to help her" in Lam. 1:7).

14:14 / **This is the day! What? Yes, even now:** A better translation is: "This is the day! What more can there be now?" It is a strange line, but it evidently functions to lead us from a description of what will happen in the short term (beginning on the same **day,** cf. v. 17), which might be thought bad enough, to a description of what will happen in the longer term, which is catastrophic. Surely there can be no news worse than the news about son and house—but there is (vv. 15–16)!

14:15 / **Asherah poles:** The goddess Asherah was the consort of the Canaanite god Baal, and Asherah poles (Hb. *ʾašērîm*) are wooden objects used in her worship. The golden calves are thus already being associated with the worship of foreign deities that will break out in Israel with a vengeance during the reign of Ahab (1 Kgs. 16:29ff.).

14:16 / **He will give Israel up:** The translation has connotations of abandonment that the Hb. verb (*ntn,* "to give") does not necessarily have. It would be better to translate "he will deal with Israel" (particularly in view of 8:22ff. and 2 Kgs. 13:23; 14:27).

§23 The End of Rehoboam (1 Kgs. 14:21–31)

Rehoboam's story, begun in chapter 12, has been delayed until Jeroboam's is over. We now return to find out what has happened in Judah in the meantime, and we shall, in fact, hear of three kings of Judah (1 Kgs. 14:21–15:24) before we are told again of Jeroboam's son Nadab (1 Kgs. 15:25–32). The way in which *their* story is told before we read of *his* will make quite apparent the different ways the kings of Israel and Judah are being treated by God.

14:21–24 / It is a feature of the regnal formulas of Kings (cf. the introduction) that each king is evaluated in terms of his commitment to the LORD as evidenced by his religious policies. The case of Rehoboam is, however, unusual; for here we are told (v. 22), not that Rehoboam **did evil in the eyes of the LORD**, but that **Judah** did so. The emphasis falls upon the nation as a whole, rather than simply upon the king himself (cf. 15:3), although it is presumably his role in instigating the **evil** that is indicated by the interesting repetition of the information about his mother in verses 21 and 31. What else would we expect from the son of an **Ammonite** woman (cf. 11:1–6)? Nevertheless, it was the whole nation that became involved in setting up **high places** at which idolatrous worship could take place, that engaged in those **practices** that had been current in the land before God had **driven out** its previous inhabitants. The threat is implicit rather than explicit—sinning in the same way will lead to Judah being "driven out" of the land as well, just as following the sin of Jeroboam will lead the people of the northern kingdom into exile (14:15–16). We are reminded of those as yet unfulfilled threats of 1 Kings 6:11–13 and 9:6–9. Right at the beginning of their account of the divided kingdom, in other words, the authors are hinting to us that both north and south are equally sinful (Judah **also** did these things) and thus heading for the same fate. It is no surprise, then, that in the summary account of the reasons for the exile of Israel in

2 Kings 17:7–17 we should find the language of 1 Kings 14:22–24 so plainly reflected (cf. 2 Kgs. 17:8–11).

14:25–31 / Yet what is noticeable in this brief account of Rehoboam's reign is that there is no prophetic oracle about the end of David's house to match the oracle of 14:7–16 about the end of Jeroboam's. Rehoboam *does* suffer a reverse at the hands of **Shishak king of Egypt,** losing the treasure that his father had so carefully stockpiled in both **temple** and **palace** (v. 26; cf. 1 Kgs. 7:51; 10:14ff.). The golden age of Solomon *is* replaced by the rather grubbier **bronze** age of Rehoboam (vv. 27–28), and the peace that Solomon had known *is* replaced by **continual warfare** (v. 30; cf. 1 Kgs. 5:4). All this, however, is little more than the fatherly discipline of 2 Samuel 7:14. It is not without significance, then, that the authors' introduction to Rehoboam's reign juxtaposes the information about his Ammonite mother with a reminder that Jerusalem is the chosen city (v. 21). For it is, of course, God's choice of David and Jerusalem (cf. 11:31–39) that is the only explanation for the difference in the treatment of David and Jeroboam. And what symbolizes this difference more than anything is that Jeroboam's son Abijah dies, even though there is some good in him (14:13), whereas Rehoboam's son Abijam (the NIV's **Abijah,** in line with some Hb. MSS) lives to succeed him, even though he is just as bad as his father (14:31; 15:3). Judah will, in fact, have a stable dynasty throughout the period when Israel is "like a reed swaying in the water"; and Asa, the descendant of two wicked Judean kings, will be sitting comfortably on the Judean throne at the very point when Nadab, the descendant of one wicked Israelite king, loses the Israelite throne.

Additional Notes §23

14:23–24 / **Sacred stones:** Deut. 12:3 lists these among Canaanite cult objects that the people must destroy upon entry to the land. Given that we are dealing with a fertility cult, these "pillars" may well have been phallic symbols. **Shrine prostitutes** are associated with such a fertility cult in Hos. 4:14, although there they are female, whereas here they are either **male** or of both genders (cf. Deut. 23:17–18). Their precise function in the context of this cult is never made clear in the OT. On

Asherah poles see the additional note on 14:15. Judah has abandoned its first lover for others and made him "jealous" (v. 22).

14:26 / **He took everything:** This the first of a series of notices in Kings about the loss of treasure from the temple and the palace (15:18; 2 Kgs. 14:14; 16:8; 18:15–16; 24:13), the culmination of which will come in 2 Kgs. 25. The **everything**, as the comparison of all the texts concerned reveals, is not to be taken literally. Hebrew *kōl*, "all, everything," is often used hyperbolically in the OT, in the same way that numbers are (cf., for example, Josh. 10:40–42; 2 Kgs. 11:1–2). See further M. Brettler, "2 Kings 24:13–14 as History," *CBQ* 53 (1991), pp. 541–52.

§24 Abijam and Asa (1 Kgs. 15:1–24)

We remain for the moment in Judah, with Rehoboam's immediate successors. Abijam is the characteristically bad Judean king, indulging in the idolatry of Solomon's later years and of Rehoboam. Asa is the characteristically good Judean king, behaving relatively faithfully like David and the younger Solomon. These two between them set the pattern for all subsequent Judean kings, who are measured in terms of whether they have been "like David" or not.

15:1–8 / **Abijam** was just as bad as his father and, indeed, his grandfather in his later years: **his heart was not fully devoted to the LORD his God** (cf. 11:3). Because of the special place held by David and Jerusalem in God's affections, however (11:11–13, 31–39; 14:21), the idolatry of Solomon and Rehoboam had not brought upon them the judgment of God that had been expected. It is no different with Abijam. **For David's sake the LORD his God gave him a lamp in Jerusalem** (v. 4; cf. 11:36). *This* dynasty, unlike Jeroboam's, is secure; sin cannot affect *its* fortunes in any ultimate sense. Why is this? Not for the first time the authors suggest a reason that does not seem entirely adequate. **David had done what was right in the eyes of the LORD** (v. 5). He was basically committed to God—he had been a faithful king. Yet even David sinned, **in the case of Uriah the Hittite.** He had, in fact, been the subject of God's grace every bit as much as his successors. David's piety is indeed a model for other kings; but it cannot be the complete explanation for the favor shown by God to the Davidic line.

15:9–15 / By contrast with his immediately preceding ancestors, **Asa** was a good king—someone who **did what was right in the eyes of the LORD** (v. 11), whose **heart was fully committed to the LORD all his life** (v. 14). We are to understand by this, not that he was perfect, but that he followed the Davidic pattern and eschewed idolatry. He took action against the **shrine prostitutes** mentioned in 14:24 (v. 12), "removed" the idols made in previous reigns, and **deposed** his own idolatrous mother (cf. the additional note on 15:10) who had made a **repulsive** object of uncertain character for **Asherah** (v. 13) He did not **remove** (Hb. *swr*) **the high places** and focus his reformed worship only on the temple in Jerusalem, but otherwise he was exemplary in his religious policy. He reminds us of Solomon in his earlier period, unwisely failing to intervene to end worship at the local sanctuaries (3:2–3), yet faithful enough to **bring into the temple of the LORD the silver and gold and the articles that he and his father had dedicated** (7:51). At the same time he points us forward to kings who will be still more faithful than he is: to Hezekiah, who will eventually "remove" (Hb. *swr*) the high places (2 Kgs. 18:4); and to Josiah, who will burn much more than a single repulsive object for Asherah in the **Kidron Valley** (v. 13; cf. 2 Kgs. 23:4, 6). He is a good king—but he is not the best king Judah will have.

15:16–24 / Asa's reign in Judah was a long one and he saw five Israelite kings rise and fall (15:25–16:28) before Ahab began to rule in the north (16:29ff.). **Baasha** was the second of these (cf. 1 Kgs. 15:33–16:7). Why has this particular story been selected by the authors for inclusion at this point? The answer may well lie in the further parallels between Asa and Solomon that it accentuates. Even though Asa was like the early Solomon, he did not know the kind of peace that Solomon knew: **there was war between Asa and Baasha king of Israel throughout their reigns** (15:16, repeated in 15:32 for emphasis). So precarious was Asa's position as Baasha pushed into Benjamin and **fortified Ramah,** only a few miles north of Jerusalem, that instead of receiving treasures flowing into the city *from* places like **Aram,** Asa was forced to send a substantial **gift** (strictly a "bribe," Hb. *šōḥad*) *to* **Aram** to try to buy a new friend (vv. 18–19). This was a "wise" thing to do (Prov. 17:8). Yet one cannot help but notice that whereas Solomon very much had the upper hand in his **treaty** with Hiram of Tyre (1 Kgs. 5; 9:10–14), Asa is quite clearly the suppliant in regard to **Ben-Hadad** of **Aram.** He does not even receive any help with the **stones and timber** for the building work that results from the treaty (v. 22; cf. 5:18)—he has to resort to the imposition of forced labor upon his Judean citizens. Nor can it escape our attention that, whereas Solomon's political arrangements contributed to the *maintenance* of the empire, Asa's strategy results in the *loss* of parts of Israel to a foreign king (v. 20). Faithfulness like Solomon's no longer brings Solomon's glory in its wake. These are different times—times of humbling for David's descendants (11:39). Solomon held his head high while he obeyed his God; Asa's ultimate reward is **diseased feet** (15:23)—or is there just a hint here that Asa, too, departed from God in his **old age** (cf. 11:4) and was punished for doing so?

Additional Notes §24

15:6 / **There was war between Rehoboam and Jeroboam:** It is curious that a reference to *Rehoboam* should appear here, particularly in view of the reference to *Abijam* and Jeroboam in v. 7. Presumably the point is to stress the continuity between the two "wars." It is not just that Abijam has picked his own quarrel with Jeroboam (or vice versa); the feud between the houses of Rehoboam and Jeroboam (cf. ch. 12) is itself still rumbling on.

15:10 / **His grandmother's name was Maacah:** It is, strictly speaking, possible that the Hb. *ʾēm* refers, not to Asa's female parent, but to someone further up the family tree (possibly his **grandmother**, as the NIV translates it). We have an analogy in the use of *ʾāb,* **father,** in v. 11, to refer to Asa's great-grandfather David. It is certainly not the natural way in which to take *ʾēm,* however, given that in all the other occurrences of the word in the introductions to the reigns of the Judean kings (1 Kgs. 14:21, 31; 22:42; 2 Kgs. 8:26; 12:1; 14:2; 15:2, 33; 18:2; 21:1, 19; 22:1; 23:31, 36; 24:8, 18) it seems to mean (and is translated by the NIV as) "mother." We should consider the possibility, therefore, that the authors of Kings mean to say that Asa was the product of an incestuous relationship between Abijam and Maacah (cf. 15:2). It would be only one evil among the many that Abijam perpetrated, and certainly not beyond imagining (cf. Lev. 18:6ff.)

15:12 / **He expelled . . . prostitutes . . . got rid of all the idols:** the NIV obscures the word plays in vv. 12–14 that tie the three verses together. Asa begins by removing the shrine prostitutes (Hb. *qᵉdēšîm*) and ends by bringing "dedicated things" (Hb. *qodšîm*) into the temple. He removes (Hb. *swr*) the idols and his mother; but the high places are not removed (Hb. *swr*). It is hard to imagine a neater way in which to describe both the radical nature of the reform and its limitations. Exactly what Asa did to the prostitutes, the idols, and his mother is not clear, but **expelled . . . got rid of . . . deposed** may be too benign. The later Josiah certainly destroyed both human life and inanimate material in his reform (2 Kgs. 23:4–20).

15:19 / **As there was between my father and your father:** We are not told elsewhere of any treaty between Abijam and Tabrimmon king of Aram, presumably because that story, unlike the present story, served no useful purpose in the authors' development of their theme. We met a king of Aram before, of course, in 1 Kgs. 11:23–25. The adversary raised up there against Solomon in his apostasy now opposes Asa in his faithfulness—another sure sign that the times have changed.

§25 From Nadab to Ahab (1 Kgs. 15:25–16:34)

The fulfillment of the prophecy against the house of Jeroboam has been delayed until it has been made clear how different God's treatment of the house of David is. Now, however, we shall hear that it all turned out as Ahijah had said; as king succeeds king in this fast-moving tale of northern intrigue and violence, we shall also begin to see what he meant by describing Israel as a "reed swaying in water" (14:15). Political stability is certainly not the order of the day.

15:25–32 / The reign of **Nadab son of Jeroboam** is short lived (**two years,** v. 25). He walks **in the ways of his father,** doing **evil in the eyes of the LORD,** and is murdered by the very **Baasha** to whom we have been introduced in 15:16ff. Baasha in turn kills all the other members of Jeroboam's **family,** just as Ahijah had said he would (14:10–11). The house of Jeroboam is no more; the **house of Issachar** rules (v. 27).

15:33–16:7 / We are not told whether Baasha knew about Ahijah's prophecy. He certainly shows no sign of understanding that it is God who has placed him on the throne. For he, too, walks **in the ways of Jeroboam and in his sin,** with predictable consequences. A prophet appears—**Jehu son of Hanani**—to announce that the fate of his house will be the same as Jeroboam's (16:3–4). Baasha no doubt had many other **achievements** (16:5) of which to boast. They are, however, unimportant in comparison to his failure to remove idolatry in Israel. That is why the authors allow only one more verse to the description of his reign of **twenty-four years** (15:33) than they do to the two-year reign of Nadab.

16:8–14 / Like Jeroboam, Baasha does have a son succeed him, but **Elah** lasts no longer than Nadab (**two years**). He, too, is the subject of a conspiracy, though he is murdered, not in battle, but at home (v. 9). The assassin is **Zimri,** whose butchery on this occasion is not restricted to the family of Baasha only, but extends to friends (v. 11). The devotion of the house of Issachar to **worthless idols** (lit. "insubstantial things") has led it to destruction.

16:15–22 / Zimri is the most spectacularly unsuccessful king of all. Not only does he fail to put a son on the throne of Israel (however briefly)—he himself also fails to reign for more than a week. When the **army** (seemingly still involved in the endless siege of **Gibbethon,** cf. 15:27) hears what has happened, it takes action as "all Israel" (the tribal assembly, vv. 16–17; cf. 12:1ff.) to oppose him. **Omri** is proclaimed king, and the army marches on **Tirzah.** Zimri's suicide brings the seven-day "reign" to its end, and after a lengthy power struggle (cf. 16:15, 23), **Omri** fights off the challenge of **Tibni** and rules over Israel unopposed.

16:23–28 / The only event of Omri's reign that is described is his purchase of **the hill of Samaria** and his building of the new northern capital there. His life as king, too, is simply subsumed under the heading "idolater" (vv. 25–26). He took the throne; he sinned; he died. Almost everything else (and extrabiblical evidence suggests there was quite a bit) is unimportant. **Samaria,** it should be noted, appears in the succeeding narrative in reference both to the city founded by Omri and to the kingdom of which it is capital (=Israel). It is not always easy to distinguish which is meant.

16:29–34 / The last Israelite king to gain the throne during Asa's reign in Judah is **Ahab son of Omri,** and the last is also the worst. He too walks in the **sins of Jeroboam son of Nebat,** but he adds to this iniquity marriage to a foreign woman, **Jezebel** (cf. the commentary on 3:1–3), who inevitably leads him into the worship of **Baal** (cf. the Sidonian woman/women of 11:1 who lead(s) Solomon to the worship of a Sidonian deity in 11:5). In addition to the temple and altar for the calf at Bethel there is now a **temple** and an **altar for Baal** in **Samaria.** The sins of the northern kingdom have multiplied.

As we look back over 1 Kings 12–16, it seems evident that their major theme is "God's control over history." Monarchs may think that the LORD is not or should not be involved in politics, but the LORD *is* involved, directing their affairs in ways that make the ultimate kingship over the world absolutely obvious. Everything comes to pass just as the prophets say it will. David's house stands firm even as God's judgment falls upon Solomon, just as Nathan has said (2 Sam. 7:1–17); Jeroboam's house is destroyed, just as Ahijah has predicted (1 Kgs. 14:7–13). Judah knows political stability, as the prophets have prophesied (2 Sam. 7:1–17; 1 Kgs. 11:31–39); Israel's royal houses come and go, as prophets announce their doom (1 Kgs. 14:7–13; 16:1–4). Beyond human control—even prophetic control (1 Kgs. 13)—what God wills comes to pass, whether in the short term (13:3, 5; 14:12–13, 17–18) or in the long term (13:2; 2 Kgs. 23:15–20). It is no coincidence that the close of 1 Kings 16 (16:34; cf. Josh. 6:26) reminds us of the fulfillment of prophecy over the longer term. For it is noticeable that Omri, unlike Jeroboam and Baasha, has not received any word of the fall of his house; his son is to reign for twenty years more than theirs. Has this most sinful of Israel's royal houses confounded the prophecy about Israel's fate as a "reed"? By no means. Judgment will eventually be spoken and enacted, even though Omri's house in the end holds the throne for over a hundred years. Its first channel will be the most significant prophetic figure so far in northern Israel's history. The most sinful of Israel's kings, Ahab, will have to reckon with the most powerful of prophetic interventions, in the shape of Elijah. God will certainly act, even if on a timescale that is slightly different than hitherto. This is a message that the NT also picks up in relation to God and history. We should never confuse God's long-term planning with an unwillingness or inability to communicate and to act in human history. Prophets will eventually speak, and the prophetic word will always come to pass (e.g., John 1:19–28; 6:1–15; Acts 3:17–26; 2 Pet. 3:3–13; Rev. 22:7–20). God's silences are not long when seen in the context of eternity; God's inactivity is really patience in disguise.

Additional Notes §25

16:7 / **Also because he destroyed it:** The fact that the destruction of Jeroboam's house was ordained by God did not mean that Baasha bore no moral responsibility for his actions. We find a similar duality of perspective when we compare Hos. 1:4 and 1 Kgs. 21:21–24 (cf. 2 Kgs. 9:14–10:17). Both these texts raise in a very sharp way the mystery at the heart of God's dealings with mortal beings. Christian theologians have long grappled with this mystery using the categories of predestination and free will (cf. Matt. 26:24; Mark 14:21; Luke 22:22).

16:19 / **The sins he had committed:** Zimri had, of course, ruled for only seven days and would not have been able to indulge in or encourage very much idolatrous worship in that time. It is, however, not so much the length of time as the nature of the action that is important to the authors. He is an idolater—and so he does not hold on to the throne.

16:34 / **Hiel . . . rebuilt Jericho:** Joshua's curse on the man who rebuilt Jericho (Josh. 6:26) is evidently understood here as akin to a prophecy (**the word of the Lord**). Its enactment against **Hiel** reminds us that mortals cannot escape judgment against their house (although the details in this case are obscure), even if much time elapses between a prophecy and its fulfillment. The fact that Hiel is from **Bethel** reminds us, not only that Bethel is now a thoroughly impious place—its residents treat prophecy with contempt—but also that it, too, has a prophetic threat hanging over it that will become a reality in due course (1 Kgs. 13:2; 2 Kgs. 23:15–20). His rebuilding of **Jericho** reminds us, finally, of the difference between Israel's past under Joshua and its present under the apostate monarchy. Israel no longer conquers the Canaanites but instead embraces their religion and courts their fate (1 Kgs. 9:6–9; 14:24).

§26 Elijah and the Drought (1 Kgs. 17:1–24)

We have lacked a prophet to address the house of Omri, but now a prophet bursts onto the scene with a vengeance. His announcement of doom on this house will, however, be delayed until 1 Kings 21:21–24. His first task is to tackle the problem of the Baal-worship that Ahab has introduced into Israel (16:31–32), so as to demonstrate beyond all doubt that Baal is no more a god in any real sense than Jeroboam's calves are. Chapter 17 provides the context in which the climactic demonstration of this truth will take place (18:16–40): the divinely ordained drought of 17:1. It also prepares us for the demonstration by showing us that it is the LORD, and not Baal (nor any other "god"), who controls both life and death, both fertility and infertility. It is thus the LORD, and not any other, who is God—as Elijah's name (Hb. *ʾēlîyāhû*, "the LORD is God") itself proclaims.

17:1–6 / In Canaanite religion it was Baal who had authority over the **rain**. Its absence meant the absence of Baal, who must periodically submit to the god Mot (death), only to be revived at a later date and once again water the earth. It is this polytheistic view of reality that Elijah now challenges. He worships a single God who **lives** (cf. the oath taken in the name of the living God also in 1 Kgs. 1:29; 2:24; 18:10; 22:14; etc.) and yet, while living, can deny both **dew** and **rain** to the land. It is the LORD, and not Baal, who brings fertility; it is the LORD's *presence in judgment* that leads to infertility, rather than his *absence in death* (cf. the echoes of these verses in Rev. 11:6; 12:6). That he is indeed the living and ever-present God who is sovereign over creation is, in fact, revealed in the story that follows in which he is able to sustain and even to restore life *in the midst of* death. We receive our first indication of this in verses 2–6. Elijah leaves Ahab's presence to hide in an inhospitable area **east of the Jordan** where, we deduce, there is no normal food supply. God has saved him from Ahab and Jezebel, it is implied (v. 3, cf. 18:4; 19:1–2), but under normal circumstances he will now die of hunger. God is, however, able to provide for him; God controls not just the rain but the whole natural order, including the **ravens** (v. 4). God is ever present to speak the **word** (v. 2)—and the word brings life. And so, as the Israelites had once been the beneficiaries of God's provision of **bread and meat** in the wilderness (Exod. 16, esp. vv. 8, 12–13), now Elijah also eats **bread and meat**—even more liberally than they (each sort of food twice a day).

17:7–16 / The theme of miraculous provision in the midst of life-threatening circumstances is developed further. The drought takes effect and **the brook** dries up; Elijah must move on. But that "must" is far from indicating constraint on God. The reader of Exodus knows very well that the LORD can just as easily provide water by miraculous means as bread and meat (Exod. 17:1–7). The "must" is simply divine imperative. God has decided to display power in a different way—in what 1 Kings 16:31 implies is the very heartland of the worship of Baal, the region of **Sidon.** Here is a region, some might have thought, over which Israel's God could have no authority. It is nonetheless an area badly affected by the drought announced in 17:1 (cf. v. 12). The LORD can bring drought to all and can disarm death and sustain life in even this area, as well as in Israel. So Elijah is sent to **Zarephath of Sidon,** to meet a **widow** (v. 9) whom God has **commanded,** as he had previously "ordered" the ravens, to **supply** Elijah **with food.** Her situation seems hopeless. The LORD **lives** (v. 12)—the woman is ready to acknowledge that; but she is preparing to **die,** for his living makes no practical difference to hers. How, then, can she provide for Elijah? Yet the word of the LORD has come to pass once already (vv. 2–4), against all natural odds, and Elijah is certainly prepared to trust it a second time (vv. 8–9). He persuades the woman to take a mighty step of faith to join him. Against all parental instinct, she is to feed him **first** (v. 13), before her **son.** She does so (v. 15), and she and her son are blessed (cf. Matt. 10:41) as she discovers that Elijah's God is *alive* and *gives* life. **There was food every day for Elijah and for the woman and her family.**

17:17–24 / The threat of death has twice been overcome. The LORD has proved to be sovereign over all the world, controlling both life and death. Elijah and the widow seem convinced; for when death does eventually catch up with the family, both know that it must be the LORD's doing. The **woman** speaks of it obliquely, blaming God's prophet for reminding God of her **sin** (v. 18; cf. the additional note). **Elijah,** on the other hand, speaks directly of the LORD's action against the family (**causing her son to die,** v. 20). The essential difference is that the woman apparently thinks this the end of the matter (v. 18), while **Elijah** is not content to let it rest (vv. 19ff.). Here is the ultimate test of the LORD's authority. It is one thing to rescue people from the jaws of death, but can he do anything when death has clamped tight its jaws and swallowed the victim up? He can act across the border from Israel in Sidon, but is there a "border" that he ultimately *cannot* cross, a kingdom in which he has no power? When faced by "Mot," must the LORD, like Baal, bow the knee? Elijah knows the answer, even if the woman does not, and so he prays and **the boy's life** is restored (v. 22). Even the underworld is not a place from which the LORD can be barred (Ps. 139:7–12). Life can storm even death's strongest towers and rescue those imprisoned there (cf. the further echoes of the story in Luke 7:11–17; Acts 9:32–43; 20:7–12; Heb. 11:35).

In a way the story has a strange ending. The widow's response to this raising of her son from the dead is faith—but faith that is focused upon Elijah rather than upon God himself. It is Elijah's credentials as a **man of God** (v. 24) that have been validated by the miracle, rather than God's ability to act. Was there reason to doubt these credentials? She had called Elijah **man of God** already (v. 18), and he had already proved himself to her as one who speaks **the word of the LORD** truly (vv. 14–16, 24). In one sense she already believed it, but now that she has seen death transformed into life, she knows. She is the first to know what will soon be public knowledge when Elijah's credentials are put to the test in confrontation with hundreds of others who claim to be "prophets" of a living god, but who are found wanting.

Additional Notes §26

17:9 / **Go . . . to Zarephath:** The incident is referred to by Jesus in Luke 4:25–26. Like Elijah, he implies, he has been sent, not (only) to Jews, but to Gentiles. This theme of Jesus and the Gentiles is also picked up, with echoes of 1 Kgs. 17 still sounding, in Matt. 15:21–28 and

Mark 7:24–30 (the healing of the daughter of a Canaanite/ Phoenician woman).

I have commanded a widow: The widow shows no awareness of having been directly "commanded" by God, and we are perhaps to understand the verb here and in v. 4 (Hb. *ṣwh*) in a more indirectly causative way ("I have ordained that . . .").

17:18 / **To remind me of my sin and kill my son:** The Hb. is lit. "to bring to remembrance my sin and kill my son." In the context a causative *connection* between sin and death is probably in view: "to bring my sin to *God's* notice and cause my son to die." Just by being there, Elijah has focused God's attention on the household in an unhelpful way (cf. Mark 1:24; Luke 4:34). Elijah picks up the exact wording of the second part of the complaint ("causing her son to die") in his prayer, while refraining from any comment on the question of the *cause* of the tragedy. He is more interested in action than in speculation (cf. John 9:1–12).

17:21 / **He stretched himself out on the boy:** The purpose of the action is not made clear. What *is* certain is that it is the prayer that is the crucial element in the whole scene ("he **cried to the** LORD . . . the LORD heard Elijah's cry," v. 22).

§27 Elijah and the Prophets of Baal (1 Kgs. 18:1–46)

Chapter 17 launched Elijah suddenly into the public arena of Israel's politics (v. 1) only to whisk him away again into the privacy of the Transjordanian wilderness and a Sidonian home. There he has contributed in a small way to the war that the LORD is now waging upon the worship of Baal, while leaving the drought to do most of the damage. The time has now come for his reappearance on the main stage—for the great battle of the war, indeed. The drought is to end, but before it does it must be indisputable, not only to the widow of Zarephath but also to "all Israel," who is God. There must be a public test of strength—a face-to-face confrontation between the prophet of the LORD and the prophets of Baal.

18:1–15 / We assume that Elijah has been living quietly and well-provided for in Zarephath. The day for rain, however, has now arrived (17:14; 18:1); Elijah is to **present himself to Ahab**—for Ahab will surely never find him, no matter how much he looks (v. 10)! Even though Elijah has been living only a few miles from Jezebel's home town, he has not been discovered. Ahab, like Baal, is impotent. He can do nothing. He cannot **find** (Hb. *mṣ'*) Elijah (v. 10); he is hard pressed, indeed, to **find** (Hb. *mṣ'*) **grass to keep the horses and mules alive** (v. 5). All the initiative must come from God and God's prophet. And even when initiative has been taken and Elijah is on his way, it is noteworthy that it is Ahab, of the two people wandering the countryside (v. 6), who fails to come across him.

This pleasure belongs to **Obadiah.** He is a **devout believer** (v. 3), a "servant of the LORD" (the meaning of the name "Obadiah") and also of Elijah as God's prophet (cf. v. 7, **my lord Elijah;** v. 9, **your servant**). At the same time, he is a high official of the royal court and Ahab is his **master** (v. 10). He is caught in the middle—between the LORD and Baal, between Ahab and Elijah—

and he needs to be sure that Elijah's intentions are honorable. He is, in fact, not quite prepared to believe that it is truly the prophet's intention to present himself to Ahab (vv. 11–14). It would, he feels, be a poor reward for saving so many other prophets—doing the work of God by supplying (Hb. kwl) God's servants with **food and water** (vv. 4, 13; cf. kwl of the ravens "feeding" and the woman "supplying" in 17:4, 9)—if he should now be killed for the sake of one prophet who cannot stand still. It is only Elijah's solemn oath (v. 15) that persuades him that he means business.

18:16–19 / Ahab is duly retrieved from his search for fodder to meet the man he holds responsible for what has happened—this **troubler** (Hb. ʿkr) **of Israel** (v. 17). The epithet perhaps explains why he wanted to find him: for Israel had once before escaped God's curse by finding and killing a man who was bringing "trouble" upon them (cf. Josh. 6–7, esp. Hb. ʿkr used generally in 6:18 and of Achan in 7:25). At the same time it betrays, of course—as Ahab's frantic search for Elijah has also betrayed—Ahab's fundamental misunderstanding about the source of his problem. It does not lie in the prophet at all, but in himself (**I have not made trouble . . . you and your father's family have,** v. 18). Possession of Elijah would not, therefore, have meant possession of a solution (cf. Jeroboam's similar misunderstanding in 1 Kgs. 13:1–10). The **trouble** has religious roots—the abandonment of **the LORD's commands** and the worship of the **Baals** (the various local manifestations of Baal; cf. 2 Kgs. 1). And it is Ahab, not Elijah, who is (ominously for him) the Achan of this narrative.

18:20–24 / The identity of the "troubler of Israel" in Joshua 7 had been settled in public before "all Israel"; and it is before "all Israel" (the NIV's "people from all over Israel" in v. 19), gathered on **Mount Carmel** (on the coast, about 17 miles northwest of Jezreel) that the issue is to be settled now as well. Who is responsible for the disaster—the worshipers of Baal or the worshipers of the LORD? That question is bound up with another: who is really God (v. 21)? The people are not as neutral as the NIV's translation of verse 21 implies (see the additional note). They may **waver between two opinions,** but while they are weighing up the odds in their heads they are in practice worshiping Baal as their **god** (v. 24) and neglecting the worship of **the LORD** (note the dilapidated state of the altar in v. 30). This is a people whose hearts have strayed; the ordeal of fire is devised to draw them back. **The god who answers by fire—he is God** (v. 24), and the people will be expected to **follow him.** For Elijah will have defied the overwhelming odds against him (v. 22)

18:25–29 / The prophets of Baal make the first attempt at getting a god to "answer" them (Hb. ʿnh—a key word throughout the story; cf. vv. 26, 29, 37), dancing **around** their **altar** and calling **on the name of Baal** (v. 26). After several hours Elijah begins to taunt them, and they redouble their efforts, shouting and slashing themselves with **swords and spears** and **prophesying** (vv. 27–29). They continue **until the time for the . . . sacrifice** (the precise timing is more uncertain than the NIV's **evening** implies), but all that results is—"no voice; no answer; no attentiveness" (vv. 26, 29).

Hitherto in Kings, when prophecy has been spoken of the emphasis has fallen upon the act of communication: a word from the LORD comes to those who need to hear it (e.g., 11:29–39; 12:22–24). In 18:29, however, no specific divine-human communication is in view. The focus of attention is on a kind of supranormal *state* (the Baalists are "behaving like prophets"). This is not the only place in the OT where this is so. Numbers 11:16–30 and 1 Samuel 10:5–6, 10–11 come to mind. Even more striking are 1 Samuel 18:10–11 and 19:18–24, where we find precisely the bizarre sort of behavior evidenced in 1 Kings 18. The condition is commonly referred to as "ecstatic," because the person involved "stands outside himself" (Gk. *ekstatis*) in a state of spirit possession. In OT thinking this possession can be by good influences or by bad (cf. the Spirit of God in Num. 11:16–30; the "evil spirit" in 1 Sam. 16:14; 18:10), although whichever is involved, it is always liable to be interpreted by others as equivalent to madness (cf. 2 Kgs. 9:11; Jer. 29:26). In the present passage, of course, it is certainly not a good influence that is in view: these men "prophesy by Baal" (Jer. 23:13; cf. further the "lying spirits" of 1 Kgs. 22:1–28). Elijah, on the other hand, is one empowered by the Spirit of the LORD (vv. 12, 46; cf. Acts 8:26–40, esp. v. 39).

18:30–40 / And now it is Elijah's turn. He rebuilds the **altar of the LORD.** He uses **twelve stones,** reminding the people of their true identity as the LORD's people (vv. 30–31; cf. Gen. 35:10). Having placed on this altar *his* **bull,** he saturates the whole area with water. There is so much water that it **even filled the trench** that he had dug (v. 35). No possibility of spontaneous

combustion here! If *this* offering is consumed in fire, it *must* be the
LORD! Having done all this, Elijah simply prays. No dancing, or
shouting, or self-mutilation—simply a prayer. No all-day ritual to
manipulate the deity into action—simply a few words over a
speedily-prepared offering **at the time of sacrifice** (vv. 29, 36),
requesting an "answer" (Hb. ʿ*nh,* twice for emphasis in v. 37). But
Elijah has the ear of a living God—the **God of Abraham, Isaac
and Israel** (Jacob), who has responded to Elijah's prayers before
(17:17–24). The **fire of the LORD** falls—and it consumes not only
the **sacrifice** but everything else around it, whether inflammable
stones or soaking **soil** (v. 38). **The LORD— he is God!** And many
of those who have truly been "troubling" Israel are duly executed, so as to remove their baneful influence (v. 40; cf. Josh.
7:25–26).

18:41–46 / Ahab survives, for the moment, to join in the
post-sacrificial meal (v. 41). He has watched the construction of
the twelve-stone altar; he has "seen God"; now he is to **eat and
drink** (cf. the parallels in Exod. 24, esp. vv. 4 and 11). Elijah,
however, climbs to the very top of the mountain, to wait for the
rain that God has promised (v. 42, cf. 18:1) and that, in his prophetic imagination, he can now hear. It is a long wait, but at last
a cloud as small as a man's hand is seen **rising from the sea.**
Though small, it is enough to assure Elijah that the drought is
over (cf. Luke 12:54), and after warning Ahab to leave or get wet,
he races him to Jezreel **in the power of the LORD.** As we might
expect, in view of the story so far, he wins. It is a fitting conclusion
to the chapter. For although Obadiah builds Ahab up as someone
to be feared (18:9–14), from the moment Elijah meets the king he
dominates him. Ahab speaks but once in the entire story (18:17),
and having been silenced by Elijah's aggressive and fearless
response (18:18), he spends the rest of the time either doing what
the prophet tells him (18:19–20, 41–42, 44–45) or watching from
the sidelines so quietly as to be invisible (18:21–40). He is as
impotent as the god he worships. Elijah's "win" over him is as
comprehensive as his "win" over the prophets of Baal.

Additional Notes §27

18:3 / **A devout believer in the** LORD: Lit. "feared the LORD greatly." Like the widow of Zarephath, however, Obadiah is not entirely convinced that the fact that the LORD lives (17:12; 18:10) is of any special relevance to the question of his own grasp on life. He hangs a question mark over God's ability or willingness to intervene. He has seen most of the LORD's prophets killed, and those who were saved were rescued, not by God's special intervention, but by his own more humble efforts involving the cave (cf. Heb. 11:32–38 for a description of the normal lot of prophets, with several allusions back to the Elijah stories).

18:17 / **You troubler of Israel:** It is interesting, in view of the way the figure of Saul was already lurking in the background of the portrayal of Jeroboam (a king from whom God withdrew love, in contrast to God's treatment of David's descendants, 2 Sam. 7:15), that the relatively rare verb *ʿkr*, "to trouble," is also found in 1 Sam. 14:24–46. Here, too, there is a dispute about who is really the troubler of Israel—is it Saul, who has bound the people under a foolish oath (cf. Judg. 11:29–40, esp. *ʿkr* in v. 35), as Jonathan claims (1 Sam. 14:29); or is it Jonathan himself? This is not the only time we shall detect the Saul story influencing the telling of the Ahab story (cf., for example, 1 Kgs. 20:35–43; 22:29–38).

18:19 / **The four hundred prophets of Asherah:** Elijah's hope is that he will be able to gather all the prophets, both of Baal and of his consort Asherah, in one place and deal with them all at one time, but apparently only the prophets of Baal turn up at Mount Carmel (18:22–29, 40). In view of the general characterization of Ahab in 1 Kgs. 18 and the emphasis placed in 18:19 on the queen's table as the eating place of the prophets, it is tempting to see Ahab's failure to obey Elijah's command here as further testifying to his impotence—this time in relation to his wife! These are *her* prophets, and he cannot gather them to himself at will. Certainly we must see the absence of the prophets of Asherah from the proceedings on Mount Carmel as linked to the absence of Jezebel herself. For both represent the absent threat that will still remain (although grossly underestimated by Elijah) at the end of ch. 18. Elijah has dealt decisively with the men on the mountain; but what of the women, who were never involved in the proceedings? Ahab has been brought to submission, Baal shown to be no god; but what of Jezebel and Asherah?

18:21 / **How long will you waver between two opinions?:** The problem with NIV's translation is that it obscures the connection (in the form of the rare Hb. *psḥ*, "to limp, hobble") between this question and the description of the prophets of Baal in v. 26. It thereby gives the impression (in contradiction to what he says in v. 24) that Elijah does not think that the people are committed worshipers of Baal. The Hb. of the question is, however, lit. either "How long will you hobble at the crossroads?" or "How long will you hobble on two crutches?" The Hb. at the end of v. 26 is lit. "they hobbled around the altar they had made." The worship of the people is connected with the worship of the prophets, and it is not something with which either Elijah (v. 21) or the authors (v. 26) are impressed. The joyful dance of faith (2 Sam. 6:14; Pss. 149:3; 150:4) has given way to the weary shuffle of idolatry.

18:22 / **I am the only one . . . left:** It is, of course, part of Elijah's strategy to make the odds against his success seem overwhelming—that is why he emphasizes the numbers again in v. 25, allows the Baal prophets first choice of bull and first "shot" at evoking divine reaction in vv. 25–29, and douses his own sacrifice so thoroughly with water in vv. 33–35. Whether the odds quoted here in v. 22 (450 to 1!) are entirely accurate, or simply part of this strategy, is unclear. He is certainly the only prophet of the LORD *present*, but is he the only prophet of the LORD **left** (cf. 18:4, 13; 20:35–43; 22:1–28)?

18:24 / **The god who answers by fire:** The LORD's association with "fire" (perhaps "lightning" here) is well-attested in the OT (cf. Lev. 9:24; 10:2; Num. 16:35). There is also some evidence from extrabiblical sources that Baal was thought of as a god who controls fire and lightning; cf. L. Bronner, *The Stories of Elijah and Elisha as Polemics against Baal Worship*, POS (Leiden: Brill, 1968), pp. 54–65. The question in 1 Kgs. 18 is: which of these claims about control over "fire" is true? The false god in this story will be unable to deliver; although it is interesting that this is not the case in Rev. 13:13, which echoes this verse.

18:27 / **Deep in thought, or busy, or travelling . . . sleeping:** A real god, of course, would be able to respond to shouts, no matter what he was doing. But he would be most unlikely in any event to be **travelling** or **busy** (i.e., attending to bodily functions, relieving himself), much less having a lunchtime snooze. The humor is keen, if basic.

18:29 / **Their frantic prophesying:** The kind of condition apparently in view is also well-attested outside Palestine. The most interesting example from the point of view of this passage is given by the Egyptian traveller Wen-Amon (around 1100 B.C.), who has left us an account of a violent prophetic frenzy in the midst of a sacrificial temple ritual in Byblos, a city on the Phoenician coast to the north of Jezebel's home town of Sidon (cf. *ANET*, pp. 25–29). The NT, of course, also knows of spirit possession by malevolent rather than beneficent forces, often involving violence and self-abuse (e.g., Matt. 15:21–28; Luke 8:26–39; 9:37–43), and Jesus' own prophetic ministry was, indeed, seen as "madness" by some (e.g., John 7:14–20; 8:48–59; 10:1–21).

18:30 / **He repaired the altar of the LORD:** Strictly speaking, this represents the restoration of a "high place"; and the authors of Kings are generally opposed to worship at such local shrines (cf. the commentary on 3:2–3). They are even more opposed to idolatry, however, and it is unlikely that in a context where Israel has given itself over to idolatry, they intend us to think critically of Elijah for acting thus. Centralization of the worship of the LORD is the ideal (cf. Deut. 12), but any worship of the LORD is better than worship of Baal. And the LORD removes the altar, of course, after it has served its purpose (v. 38)!

It is interesting to note that "all Israel" is conceived in this passage, as earlier in Kings, to consist of twelve tribes and not ten. Israel is still Israel, whatever the de facto political situation with regard to its mode of government may be (cf. the commentary on 1 Kgs. 12:1–24); thus, **twelve stones** make up the altar (v. 31; cf. the echoes of Exod. 24 and Josh. 4) and it is doused *twelve* times with water (four jars, emptied three times each, vv. 33–34).

18:35 / Filled the trench: Much has been made of the presence of "so much water" in the midst of drought. Are we being asked to see this as another example of God's miraculous provision for Elijah (cf. 1 Kgs. 17)? Or is the assumption simply that a general state of drought does not necessarily imply an absolute absence of water? The authors clearly do not elsewhere in the narrative presuppose an absolute absence of water throughout the land (cf. 18:4–5, 13, 41–42), and they are certainly aware that there is water in the sea (18:43ff.).

18:42 / Bent down . . . face between his knees: The significance of the action is not made clear in the text. Is Elijah simply exhausted? Or is he praying for rain (as Jas. 5:13–18 might imply, in its exhortation to Christians to pray, like Elijah, with faith)?

18:45 / Jezreel: We are not explicitly told why Ahab rather unexpectedly left for Jezreel. The implication of 19:1–2 is, however, that this is where Jezebel is, and 21:1 will make clear that the king and his consort had a palace there. The fact that Elijah heads for Ahab's home territory is suggestive of the extent to which he thinks the war is now over. The fact that he remains there for only two verses (19:1–2) before leaving again is testimony to the enormity of his misjudgment.

§28 Elijah and the LORD (1 Kgs. 19:1–21)

Elijah has been involved in a mighty battle. He seems to think it decisive and so he has left the battlefield for Jezreel. Yet there have been several hints in the narrative thus far that it is the queen, and not the king, who is the real general of the opposing forces. She will not be so easily cowed as her husband, and Elijah is now to see that to win a battle is not necessarily to win the war. That realization will send him into retreat, both physical and mental, as victory becomes defeat. Retreat will in turn lead him to another mountain, to confront, not Baal, but the LORD himself—whom Elijah serves, but whose ways he only partly understands and accepts.

19:1–2 / Thus far in the story **Jezebel** has remained in the background. Elijah has been dealing entirely with Ahab (17:1; 18:1ff.). Yet it was Jezebel who took initiatives and got things done in chapter 18, in marked contrast to her passive and impotent husband. It was she who rounded up the LORD's prophets and killed them (Hb. _krt,_ 18:4), leaving her husband, unable to find even the one prophet _he_ was looking for (18:10), to worry only about whether he might have to kill his animals (Hb. _krt,_ 18:5). It was she, and not Ahab, whom Elijah himself identified as the focal point of the opposition in 18:19—it was her "table" around which the prophets gathered to eat. So we are not surprised that chapter 19 opens with a bedraggled Ahab reporting to his queen what Elijah has done to him and passing the responsibility over to her. Nor are we surprised to find Jezebel, once told the tale of Carmel, offering the kind of immediate and decisive response of which Ahab was so patently incapable. She solemnly promises that she will make Elijah's **life like that of one of** the prophets he has **killed.** Given her track record (18:4, 13), she is to be taken seriously.

19:3–5 / Elijah is **afraid,** or "sees how things are" (Hb. *rᵊʾh,* in the majority of Hb. MSS)—and he retreats. It is an unexpected response. Elijah has shown himself to be a man of faith and courage (18:15), who trusts God for miracles. He will certainly hide when God tells him to (17:3–5); but the "word of the LORD" is, in fact, conspicuous by its absence here (contrast 17:2, 8; 18:1). It will not reappear until verse 9. There it will take the form of a question that makes it clear that, although the LORD has helped Elijah along the way, the journey was not of divine initiative. That "word" will be followed very shortly, in fact, by a command to "go back" north (v. 15). The journey south was certainly not on God's agenda.

Elijah apparently retreats, then, of his own volition. But then, this is doubtless an unexpected happening. Here is a woman who still swears by her gods (19:2), even after all that has happened—a believer who is impervious to evidence. It is not going to be as straightforward as Elijah thought. In the shock of this realization, he forgets to think theologically and simply reacts (for the first time) to circumstances. He travels a long way, from Jezreel in the north to **Beersheba** in the far south of the promised land (v. 3; cf. 4:25): as far away from Jezebel as he can get. Having reached Beersheba he heads alone, without his **servant** (cf. 18:43ff.), for the **desert.** He seeks a lonely place in which to **die,** an isolated man (or so he feels) under an isolated **broom tree;** he has **had enough** (v. 4).

19:5–9 / Thus far Elijah has been responding only to Jezebel's "messenger" (Hb. *malʾāk,* v. 2); God has been excluded from the arithmetic. And he has been behaving somewhat like the anti-hero Jonah—travelling to a far-flung place without a divine travel permit (Jonah 1:1–3); attempting to write his own contract for the job of prophet (Jonah 4). Now, however, it is God's turn to take the initiative with a messenger of his own (Hb. *malʾāk,* vv. 5, 7; the NIV's **angel**). It is his first move in trying to lead Elijah, as he tried to lead Jonah, back on to the path of faith from which he has strayed. His treatment of Elijah is, however, noticeably gentler than his treatment of Jonah (Jonah 1:4ff., though contrast 4:6ff.)! So softly does he creep back into Elijah's life, indeed, that it is not at first clear that the messenger is God's (v. 5). Only the unexpectedness of the provision in such a place suggests the identity of the donor (cf. 17:1–6). We are not told plainly that the **angel** is **of the LORD,** in fact, until the second occasion upon which Elijah is woken to **eat** (v. 7)—and now it becomes clear also that there is more to the divine plan than food and sleep. Elijah thought his journey was over; he had had **enough** (Hb. *rab*, v. 4). But now he is to fortify himself for a further journey, that will be **too much** (Hb. *rab*, v. 7) for him if he does not eat. Food was God's response when, at the end (as he thought) of his journey, Elijah cried "Enough!"; now food is provided **a second time** so that he will genuinely have enough— to complete his journey! He seems to know what the angel means. He sets out for **Horeb, the mountain of God** (v. 8; cf. Exod. 3:1). The **forty days and forty nights** of his travels recall Israel's own wilderness wandering (Num. 14:33–34) almost as much as Moses' first sojourn on the mountain (Exod. 24:18). Is he to be servant Moses or stubborn Israel when he gets there, this run-away, self-pitying prophet? Will he, like Moses, see God (Exod. 33:12–23), and will it make any difference to his attitude?

19:9–12 / The food in the wilderness was a gentle re-minder of the past, for Elijah seems to have forgotten the past— miraculous provision, resurrection, mighty acts of God on moun-taintops. When invited by God to speak in verse 9, he mentions none of these, but talks only of Israelite apostasy and prophetic casualties (v. 10). **The Israelites have rejected** (Hb. ʿ*zb*) takes us back to 18:18 ("you have abandoned," Hb. ʿ*zb*); **broken down** (Hb. *hrs*) **your altars** reminds us of 18:30 ("in ruins," Hb. *hrs*); and **put your prophets to death** (Hb. *hrg*) evokes 18:13 ("Jezebel was killing the prophets," Hb. *hrg*). But what of the Israelites restored to faith (18:39); the altar rebuilt (18:30–32); the prophets of *Baal* killed (Hb. *hrg*) **with the sword** (19:1)? Elijah's memory is selec-tive indeed. The resistance of one woman has in Elijah's mind turned massive victory into overwhelming defeat, and the one woman **trying to kill** him has now become a plural **they** (i.e., the **Israelites**)! He *needs* to be reminded of the past in order to remember who God is and what God has done. He needs, in remembering, to regain his sense of perspective, particularly about himself. For he *has* done considerably better than many of his ancestors (v. 4), and he is far from being **the only one left** (v. 10). Somewhere between exaggerated self-loathing and exag-gerated self-importance—both partly the product of selective memory—there is a quiet place where Elijah must rest content with who he is and what he has done. The key is to remember his past with the LORD. And so the LORD has fed him and now brought him to Horeb for another mountaintop experience. He needs to see once again the God of **wind . . . earthquake . . . fire** (vv. 11–12) and to remember Carmel.

But that is not all there is to it, for Horeb (also known as Sinai) is not just any mountain. It is the "mountain of God" (v. 8)—the place where Israel herself, having been sustained in the wilderness (Exod. 16:1–17:7), met with the LORD and discovered in some detail what sort of God he served (Exod. 19–20 etc.). This is significant; it appears that the LORD is intent here, not only on reminding Elijah of his recent history but also on teaching him something new. The emphasis at Carmel had been on God's spectacular ways and particularly on his use of **fire**. The emphasis in verses 11–12, however, is upon God's quiet ways. He is not to be found in the spectacular elements of the storm outside the cave (**wind . . . earthquake . . . fire**). He reveals himself on this occasion in a **gentle whisper.** Elijah needs to remember the past, but he also needs to realize that there is more to the LORD than fire.

19:13–18 / It is not immediately clear to us why it is important for Elijah to realize this, and there is no evidence that Elijah himself understands. Indeed, even the attempt to jog his memory appears to fail. For when he is asked a second time the question of verse 9 (**What are you doing here, Elijah?**, v. 13), his answer is exactly the same as before (vv. 10, 14). The entire point of the demonstration appears, like the LORD himself (v. 11), to have passed him by. Privileged like Moses to see (Exod. 33:12–23), he remains steadfastly like Jonah: slow to understand. There is, indeed, just a suggestion that he does not particularly *wish* to understand. He has always claimed to "stand before the LORD" (Hb. ʿmd lipnê YHWH; cf. the NIV's "whom I serve" in 17:1; 18:15). Yet now, in spite of the command of verse 11 ("Go out and stand . . . in the presence of the LORD," ʿmd lipnê YHWH), he apparently stays in the cave until the storm is over (v. 13). When he does go out it is with his **cloak over his face.** He seems as committed to "not seeing" as Jezebel was in 19:1–2. And so his perspective is still the one that she has inspired in him: "all is lost; and I am feeling very sorry for myself."

It is the LORD's response on this second occasion that suggests what the point of the "gentle whisper" really was. He gives Elijah new instructions: **anoint Hazael . . . Jehu . . . Elisha.** A new order is to succeed the old, and it is this order that will bring about the final victory over Baal-worship. Victory will come, in other words, as a result of political process—not through obviously spectacular demonstrations of divine power. It will arrive, not as a result of Elijah's efforts, but through the efforts of others. Elijah's role in the overall strategy is now clear. It is partly to fight, and he has done that well. But it is also partly (and now more importantly) to prepare the way for others. The Carmel event is only one event in a series that will stretch beyond his lifetime (cf. 2 Kgs. 8:7–15; 9–10). God has other ways of working—some of which make Elijah's God seem almost as nonexistent as Baal (a still small "voice" being only marginally noisier than no "voice" at all, cf. Hb. *qôl* in 18:26, 29). The LORD also has servants other than Elijah (not least the **seven thousand in Israel** who have **not bowed down to Baal** or **kissed him** in veneration, v. 18; cf. Rom. 11:1–6). If the spectacular has not produced final victory, that is no reason for despair. For the overall strategy was always more long term and more subtly conceived than Elijah imagined. From the beginning it had involved the gentle but devastating whisper as well as the all-consuming fire, the quiet ways of God's normal providence as well as the noiser ways of miraculous intervention. Elijah must be content with being *part* of the plan and not *the plan itself.* Where he has run south in despair to the desert of Beersheba, he must now go north in obedience to the **Desert of Damascus** (v. 15).

19:19–21 / The chapter's opening scenes raised the question: will Elijah get back on track as a result of his trip to Horeb? He has not shown evidence of being much affected by his experience. He has been disobedient and uncomprehending of God throughout (and thus exactly like Jonah). It is unsurprising, therefore, to discover at this juncture that his response to God's new commands is less than wholehearted. He finds **Elisha** and enlists him as his **attendant** (v. 21). There is, however, no mention of any "anointing" of Elisha as his prophetic *successor.* Nor will there be in the chapters to come. We would also search in vain for any mention of Elijah ever meeting (or trying to meet) Hazael and Jehu. We shall *never* read of the anointing of the former—Elisha will arrange the anointing of the latter (2 Kgs. 9:1–13). We are entitled to ask whether Elijah has really adjusted himself to God's plans at all.

His seeming lack of enthusiasm for going along with God stands in sharp contrast to Elisha's enthusiasm for going along with Elijah. The prophetic mantle having been cast over his shoulders (and thus put to considerably more use than in v. 13), he immediately leaves his normal employment to follow his new mentor (v. 20). A slight delay admittedly ensues—but only so that (after receiving Elijah's assurance that "No one is preventing you," v. 20) he may properly cut his ties with his old life, kissing his parents **goodbye** and burning his bridges (as it were) by destroying his old means of sustenance (**yoke of oxen . . . plowing equipment,** v. 21). Here is someone who leaps at the chance to be a prophet, soon to succeed someone who has tried to lay down his prophetic office. Here is someone who "runs," as Elijah did (18:46) before he became suddenly weary. A promising apprentice indeed, cutting loose from human securities and placing himself in God's hands—and someone whose very name points to the future era of complete victory. Elijah has all but had his day—the day when it was established that "the LORD is God" (18:39). The new era belongs to Elisha: "God saves."

Additional Notes §28

19:4 / **I am no better than my ancestors:** This may simply mean "I am no better off than my ancestors, who are dead," i.e., "Take my life; I am as good as dead already." But it is consistent with the fairly pronounced egocentricity that Elijah displays throughout the story that he should have thought himself much better than his ancestors up until this point, only now to be reduced to the self-loathing of the high achiever who thinks he has failed.

19:5 / **An angel touched him:** Hb. *malʾāk* is an ambiguous term. It can mean simply a human messenger, as in 19:2. Frequently, however, it refers to beings who are clearly not of this world (e.g., Gen. 21:8–21, with the very theme of miraculous provision in the desert of Beersheba that we find here). The first occurrence of *malʾāk* in v. 5, after its appearance in v. 2, leaves the identity of this "messenger" uncertain, although the reader of 1 Kgs. 17–18 (not to mention Gen. 21:8) is already clear that he brings life from God rather than death from Jezebel. For angels attending NT prophets in the desert, cf. Matt. 4:1–11.

19:9 / **He went into a cave:** The cave is, of course, not a good place for someone to sit who has a selective memory—even if he is a hero of the faith (cf. Heb. 11:37–38). For like the words that Elijah speaks in its midst, the cave harks back to the situation of oppression under Jezebel when other prophets were hidden in a cave (18:4, 13). It is a dark place for someone in a dark mood, and it is significant that God's attempt to change Elijah's thinking is closely tied to an attempt to get him out of the cave (v. 11). It is also significant that Elijah is so reluctant to come out and face God (vv. 11–13)—does he fear that reality will interfere with conviction?

19:12 / **A gentle whisper:** The Hb. is lit. "a voice/sound, a barely audible whisper" (*qôl dᵉmāmâh daqqâh*). For a summary of views on the meaning and import of this phrase, see B. P. Robinson, "Elijah at Horeb, 1 Kings 19:1–18: A Coherent Narrative?" *RB* 98 (1991), pp. 513–36 (esp. pp. 522–27). We are not explicitly told, of course, that the LORD is "in" the whisper, but it is clearly implied in the way the sequence is structured (wind . . . not in the wind; earthquake . . . not in the earthquake; fire . . . not in the fire; gentle whisper . . .). It is also implied in the fact that it is not "the word of the LORD" that comes to Elijah in v. 13 (contrast v. 9), but a "voice" (Hb. *qôl*—the same word as in v. 12). This "voice" is not explicitly associated with God either, but it is clearly God who is speaking. We often find such indirectness of speech in the OT when God is described, lest the outward manifestations of the divine reality should be confused by the reader with its actuality. In one sense, of course, God can no more "have" a voice than be "in" wind, earthquake, and fire. Yet the OT describes God as speaking to mortals with a voice (e.g., *qôl* in Gen. 3:8) and as appearing in the midst of natural cataclysm (e.g., Nah. 1:3–5; Isa. 30:27). Insofar as God reveals Godself in such ways at all, the text tells us, on this occasion it is done in the quietness and not in the noise.

19:16 / **Anoint Elisha:** The idea that Elijah prepares the way for God's kingdom rather than bringing it in himself is picked up in the NT in reference to John the Baptist (Matt. 11:1–19; 17:1–13; Mark 9:2–13; Luke 1:11–17; cf. the OT development of the Elijah theme in Mal. 4:5 and the NT uncertainty about identity in Matt. 16:13–16; 27:45–49; Mark 6:14–16; 8:27–30; 15:33–36; Luke 9:7–9, 18–20). John himself designates Jesus as his "successor" in such passages as Matt. 3:1–17; John 1:19–34 (where he denies being Elijah, v. 21); and the name Jesus means, of course, "the LORD saves," as Elisha means "God saves."

19:20 / **Let me kiss my father and mother:** Hb. *nšq*, **kiss,** is an uncommon verb, and it occurs in Kings only here and in v. 18. We assume that some connection is being made between the two kisses. They both say something, of course, about allegiance. The worshipers of Baal kiss him, symbolizing that they have abandoned (Hb. ʿzb; cf. 18:18; 19:10, 14) the LORD. Elisha wants to kiss his parents, symbolizing that he has abandoned home and livelihood (Hb. ʿzb; cf. 19:20) *for* the LORD. There is an unmistakable allusion to this episode in Luke 9:57–62 (cf. Matt. 8:18–22), where the point appears at first to be that would-be disciples of Jesus must have a greater commitment to service in God's kingdom than Elisha had. Yet the mention there of the plow reminds us of Elisha's decisiveness in leaving his home (he burned the plowing equipment)—which in some ways represents greater commitment than Jesus' disciples actually showed (they only "left" their nets, Mark 1:14–20, later to return to them, John 21:1–14). This is a good example of the way in which taking the OT seriously on its own terms can lead us to ask deeper questions about a particular NT passage, prompting us to relate it to others (e.g., Matt. 21:28–32; Luke 14:25–35).

19:21 / **His attendant:** The Hb. verb behind this translation is *šrt*, "to minister, to serve." It is an ambiguous verb in this context. It is used in some OT texts, on the one hand, of Joshua's relationship with Moses (cf. Exod. 24:13; 33:11; Num. 11:28); and we know that Joshua did indeed go on to become Moses' successor. It has already been used in Kings, on the other hand, of Abishag the Shunammite (1 Kgs. 1:4, 15; cf. also its appearance in 8:11; 10:5); and it will later be used of Elisha's servant (2 Kgs. 4:43; 6:15). In neither of these cases is succession in view. The authors leave us guessing, therefore, about what is going to happen. There is uncertainty about Elisha's precise status.

§29 Ahab's War against Aram (1 Kgs. 20:1–43)

Elijah has recruited Elisha, and we expect to read now, perhaps, of his anointing of Hazael as king over Aram and of Jehu as king over Israel (19:15–18). Instead, we find a story in which a different prophet takes up the running (Elijah does not appear at all) and in which a different king of Aram (Ben-Hadad) loses a war with Ahab. The message of chapter 19 is thus underlined. Elijah is not the only servant of God left, in spite of what he has claimed (19:10, 14), and the quiet ways of God must take their course yet a while before the events that 19:17 speaks of come to pass. At the same time, chapter 20 picks up themes from chapter 18. Ahab is the "troubler of Israel," the Achan and the Saul of the northern monarchy. He knows that the LORD is God, but he acts in ways that belie this. The Jericho-like victory at Aphek (cf. Josh. 6) leads on to an aftermath of Achan-like (and Saul-like) actions that bring prophetic judgment. The threat to Ahab, as a character of this sort, was in chapter 18 only implicit. In chapter 20 it becomes explicit, and we are thus prepared for the king's death in chapter 22.

20:1–12 / Asa, king of Judah, had first involved Aram in the affairs of Israel, inviting a previous **Ben-Hadad, king of Aram** (presumably the "father" of this man, cf. v. 34) to attack Baasha, king of Israel, and so relieve pressure on Judah (15:16–22). On that occasion the Arameans had taken control of a significant proportion of Israelite territory in the north. It is not clear from the present narrative whether it is that campaign that is in view in 20:34 or not, for Ahab's "father" was not strictly Baasha, but Omri. Whatever is the case, the king of Aram has now moved at the head of a powerful alliance (**thirty-two kings**) to put pressure on **Samaria.** He seeks to reduce Israel to vassal status. His terms are at first accepted by Ahab (**Just as you say, my lord the king,** v. 4), but after Ben-Hadad revises them, making them more extensive (**everything you value**), intrusive (**search your palace**), and immediate (**this time tomorrow**), Ahab rejects them (vv. 5–9). Refusal elicits threat (cf. 19:2), followed by taunt (vv. 10–11). Battle becomes the only option (v. 12).

20:13–21 / The mystery of God's quiet ways, in guiding human affairs through politics, war, and the rest, is well illustrated in what happens next. So far, Ahab has known only prophetic *opposition*. Now, at the very point when (we know) the future holds only death and destruction for Ahab's house (19:15–17), he receives from a prophet, for the first time, good news. The superior Aramean forces will be given into his **hand** (v. 13). The atmosphere is that of Israel's past, both in terms of the promise (cf. Judg. 1:2; 4:7; 1 Sam. 23:1–5; 2 Sam. 5:19) and in terms of the tactics (cf. the additional note to v. 14). This is holy war in which God commands the army. God's purpose also echoes of the past and particularly of the exodus: **then you will know that I am the LORD** (cf. Exod. 6:7; 7:5; 10:2; 14:4; 16:12; etc.). As in chapter 18 (cf. vv. 30–39), the past is recalled to remind Israel that the LORD is still the same God and Israel still the same people. Reality has not changed simply because Israel has sought to define it differently by worshiping other gods.

Ever ready to do as he is told (cf. 1 Kgs. 18:19–20, 41–42, 44–45), Ahab sends out his forces to make a preemptive strike (vv. 15–17). The plan benefits from Ben-Hadad's drunkeness (vv. 12, 16) and apparent inability to utter coherent or sensible instructions (v. 18). It is a tricky enterprise, when an army is approaching with hostile intent, to **take** people **alive**. While attempting to put this impractical plan into practice, the Arameans in the front line are **struck down**. The remainder flee (vv. 19–21), along with their **king**.

20:22–25 / The battle over, both sides make preparations for the following **spring** (v. 22)—a characteristic time for kings to go to war (cf. 2 Sam. 11:1). The Arameans reorganize their empire (see the additional note on 20:24), raising a new army to replace the one destroyed in 20:21. They plan next time to **fight** the Israelites **on the plains** (v. 23) This is sound military strategy. The advantage of having the larger of two armies, particularly if it has numerous horses and chariots, is much better pressed **on the plains** than in the **hills** (cf. Judg. 1:19). The theological reasoning that underlies the military strategy is, however, faulty. The king's **officials** argue that the failure of their "gods" (v. 10) in the previous encounter had to do partly with geography (v. 23), because the Israelite gods are **gods of the hills.** The reader of Kings knows, of course, that this is not true: the LORD is the only real God there is, and can be active both in the hills (1 Kgs. 18) and anywhere else (1 Kgs. 17). In a world with no gods or many, the strategy would have had a fair chance of success. The world that the Arameans actually inhabit, however, is not such a world, and military planning will not make it so. "Other things" are not equal—and the Arameans have to learn this (like the Egyptians before them) as much as the Israelites need to be reminded of it.

20:26–34 / The **vast army** of the Arameans marches up a second time against Israel, whose forces are by comparison but **two small flocks of goats** (vv. 26–28). On this occasion the Israelites, better prepared (v. 22), meet the hostile force further north at **Aphek** (v. 26). The result, however, is the same. To show that he is truly God, the LORD delivers the Aramean army into Israel's **hands** a second time (vv. 28–30). Extraordinary casualties are inflicted both by the Israelites themselves and by the **wall** of Aphek, which falls, Jericho-like, on those who have sought refuge in the city (cf. Josh. 6, esp. 6:15 for **seventh day** upon which battle was joined). Ben-Hadad's **officials** produce a second plan (v. 31): surrender! Doubtless more because he has no alternatives rather than because he still trusts their judgment (cf. the origin of "plan A" in vv. 23ff.), Ben-Hadad allows them to proceed (vv. 32–33), clothed to signify penitence (**sackcloth,** cf. 21:27) and submissiveness (**ropes round their heads**—by which they may be led?). A deal is struck that involves the reversal of previous arrangements. The Israelite **cities** taken in an earlier period are returned, and Ahab is given trading privileges in Damascus. Ben-Hadad is set free (v. 34).

20:35–43 / The LORD has been with Israel as of old—so that Israel may know anew who is truly the LORD. But the sequel to the fall of Aphek will begin alarm bells ringing in the mind of the reader who remembers Elijah's accusation of 18:18 and the sequel to the fall of Jericho in Joshua 7. Ahab, said Elijah, was the troubler of Israel (Hb. *ʿkr*), and it was in the aftermath of the fall of Jericho that Achan similarly "troubled" Israel (Hb. *ʿkr*, Josh. 7:25), by making improper use of the booty set apart for destruction as "devoted things" (Hb. *ḥrm*). Is Ahab's sparing of Ben-Hadad for profit a similar kind of action? Will it lead Ahab to Achan's fate? The answer to both questions is "yes." Prophetic encouragement turns once again to prophetic opposition, as Ahab is confronted by **one of the sons of the prophets** (i.e., a member of a prophetic group, v. 35; cf. 2 Kgs. 4:1; 6:1). In a scene reminiscent of 2 Samuel 12:1–4, the king is tricked into pronouncing judgment upon himself, albeit with a disguise whose purpose is obscure (did some prophets have distinguishing marks about the face? did Ahab know this man?). Like Saul, Ahab has released a king whom God **had determined should die** (Hb. ḥrm, v. 42; cf. 1 Sam. 15:17–24). His **life** is therefore forfeit—like the lives of Achan (Josh. 7:25) and of the hypothetical guard of verses 39–40. Bound up with this, of course, is also the loss of the kingship (cf. 1 Sam. 15:26–29). Ahab should have read the past in the present. He ought to have known the implications of holy war. His failure to grasp them means death—both for himself and for his **people.**

The people's death will be a long time coming yet (2 Kgs. 17). Ahab's death is closer; and it is strangely prefigured in the manner in which he hears about it. A prophet has disguised himself (Hb. ḥpś) as a soldier fresh from fighting the Arameans, in order to trick the king. In 22:29ff., *Ahab* will disguise himself (Hb. ḥpś) as a soldier when going *out* to fight the Arameans, in order to foil a prophet (and his God). His strategy will fail as spectacularly as the prophet's has succeeded (cf. 1 Kgs. 14:1ff.). For God is the prime mover behind all that happens to mortal beings, and disguises only succeed when God ordains it so.

Additional Notes §29

20:1 / **Besieged Samaria and attacked it:** It is clear from what follows that Ben-Hadad is some way from the city, perhaps even in Succoth in Transjordan, if the Hb. behind the NIV's "tents" in vv. 12 and 16 means to refer to the town of 1 Kgs. 7:46. Messengers travel back and forth from the Aramean camp to Samaria (vv. 2ff.), which is accessible to the "elders of the land" (v. 7). The army that leaves the city (vv. 15–17) is confronted only after Ben-Hadad receives reports of their movements. The "siege" is evidently from a distance, the "attack" more generalized (on Samaria's territory) than specific (on Samaria itself). A more general translation of Hb. ṣrr therefore seems appropriate (e.g., "put pressure on" Samaria).

20:6 / **To search:** The Hb. is *ḥpś*, the same verbal root as in 20:38, "disguised himself." From the use of this verb elsewhere in the OT, we deduce that Ben-Hadad believes Ahab is concealing something: see further C. Begg, "'This Thing I Cannot Do' (1 Kgs 20:9)," *SJOT* 2 (1989), pp. 23–27. Our chapter begins, then, with Aramean inability to see through Ahab's "disguise." It ends with Ahab's inability to see through a prophetic disguise (20:35ff., esp. *ḥpś* in v. 38), pointing forward to his end, when God will all too easily see through his disguise and the threat of death will become reality (cf. 22:29ff., esp. *ḥpś* in 22:30).

20:11 / **One who puts on his armor . . . :** It is unwise to boast about one's exploits before the battle has even begun—there is time enough for that, if one can, when it is over.

20:14 / **The young officers:** Given the connection between this story and earlier narratives in which the LORD proves to be God by bringing victory against overwhelming odds, it seems unlikely that Hb. *na'ar* here is meant to refer to trained military personnel, especially the elite soldiers of whom some commentators speak. The involvement of such men would introduce exactly that element of doubt about who had achieved the victory that in other narratives of this sort is so deliberately avoided (cf., for example, the complete helplessness of Israel in the exodus story, and esp. Exod. 14:14; and the requirement that Gideon should divest himself of warriors before the battle of Judg. 7). It is, moreover, the case that *na'ar* elsewhere in Kings never requires such a military sense and is, in fact, never translated in such a way by the NIV. Thus far in the narrative of 1 Kings, for example, it has been rendered as "child/boy" (3:7; 11:17; 14:3, 17), "young man" (11:28), or "servant" (18:43; 19:3).

It seems more likely, then, that we are to understand *na'ar* here as a reference to "servants" in a very generalized sense, taking our lead from 1 Sam. 17:33, where the contrast (in a narrative where the theme is also that "the battle is the LORD's," 17:47) is between the young, untrained David (*na'ar*) and the warrior Goliath. It is remarkable that it is said of these "servants" that "each one struck down (Hb. *nkh*) his opponent" (1 Kgs. 20:20; cf. *nkh* in 1 Sam. 17:49–50)—remarkable that they caused panic in the Aramean ranks similar to that of the Philistines of 1 Sam. 17 (1 Kgs. 20:20–21, cf. 1 Sam. 17:51–52). Untrained lads strike the first blow; the Israelite army, following behind, is then involved simply in a mopping-up operation. The NIV's **who will start the battle?** is, in fact, much better translated as "who will *finish* (lit. 'tie up') the battle?": cf. also 2 Chron. 13:2–19, where Abijah "brings to an end" the war with Jeroboam.

20:15 / **The rest of the Israelites:** We confront again the mystery of Hb. numbers, which are evidently used in line with literary conventions that we often do not fully understand (cf. the additional note on 11:3). The Hb. is lit. "all the people, all the Israelites, 7,000." As the number of "all the Israelites" this seems as implausibly low as the numbers of the Arameans in vv. 29–30 seem impossibly high. It is, of course, a curious coincidence that 7,000 is the number of the "remnant" destined to survive the onslaught described in 19:15–18; it may be that it is this "remnant" idea that is being communicated in 20:15. The Israelites are in desperate straits and are reaching deep into their resources. See further the additional note to 22:30.

20:24 / **Other officers:** The NIV interprets the Hb. as speaking of changes in battlefield command. The Hb. behind the very loose **other officers,** however, is simply *paḥôt,* "governors" (as in 10:15). It is apparently centralization of power that is in view here—the replacement of vassal kings with officials directly accountable to Ben-Hadad. The royal advisors seek greater military cohesion through a greater degree of political control.

20:26 / **Aphek:** The precise location is uncertain, but of the various places called Aphek in the OT, it seems most likely in the circumstances described here to be the city in Asher (cf. Josh. 19:30 and Judg. 1:31). If so, the second battle is considerably further north than the first.

20:30 / **The wall collapsed:** It is difficult to imagine any ancient city wall large enough to have literally collapsed on 27,000 people (v. 30). The parallel being drawn with Jericho may be playing its part in the presentation here: this was a great disaster for Israel's enemies, Jericho-like in its proportions. It is interesting that the rebuilding of Jericho has itself been narrated in 16:34 (cf. the additional note), where we were reminded of the *difference* between Israel's apostate present and her more faithful past. This only makes the manner of Ahab's success the more surprising—although the twist in the tale (20:35–43) resolves the tension that this success brings to the Ahab story, by putting the king firmly back under God's judgment.

20:36 / **A lion:** The scene is reminiscent of 1 Kgs. 13, where the same point is made (even prophets must obey) and the same punishment pronounced (**a lion will kill you**). As there, the implication is clear: if disobedient prophets cannot escape God's judgment, then disobedient kings certainly will not. The politeness of the prophetic request has, of course, no bearing on the matter, although the NIV invites misunderstanding on this point by representing the request as being phrased differently on the two occasions it was made (vv. 35, 37).

20:39 / **A talent of silver:** The intriguing thing about the **silver** is that the possibility of an alternative to death is not picked up in 20:41–42. It seems to be taken for granted that **a talent of silver** is simply an impossible amount to raise—which it would have been, of course, for the ordinary soldier. Death is the only option that can realistically be considered. A similar scenario is painted in the parable of the unmerciful servant in Matt. 18:23–34. The servant is put in prison until he pays back what he owes; but he owes such a fabulous sum of money that it is inconceivable that he will ever be able to raise it.

§30 Naboth's Vineyard (1 Kgs. 21:1–29)

We have heard of Ahab's death (20:41–42). We await still the announcement of judgment on his house, delayed since chapter 16 (cf. the commentary on 15:25–16:34). It is of such matters that we shall read in the current chapter, as a reinvigorated Elijah appears again in Jezreel to denounce a new and heinous crime and finally to foretell the destruction of Ahab's family.

21:1–3 / The occasion for Elijah's reappearance is a battle over a **vineyard**. Ahab wants it (v. 2) but **Naboth** (the owner) refuses to give it up, because it is the **inheritance** of his **fathers** (v. 3). It is fundamental to the OT understanding of land that it belonged, not to the families who technically "owned" it, but to God (Lev. 25:23). God had brought Israel into the land in fulfillment of the Abrahamic promise (Gen. 17:8), driving out the previous inhabitants (cf. 1 Kgs. 21:26); and he had, through Joshua, allocated it to the tribes as their **inheritance** (Josh. 13:1ff., esp. v. 7). It was therefore not open to individuals to sell land in perpetuity, and complicated laws existed that were designed to keep land in the family and to prevent its accumulation in the hands of a few (e.g., Lev. 25:8ff.; Deut. 25:5–10). Naboth is obligated to refuse Ahab's offer, then, and in making it Ahab has disregarded Israelite law.

The fact that he desires a **vegetable garden** (Hb. *gan-yārāq*) in particular is significant. The phrase occurs elsewhere in the OT only in Deuteronomy 11:10, where a contrast is offered between Egypt (a vegetable garden requiring human care) and the promised land (which "the LORD your God cares for"). When one realizes that Israel is sometimes portrayed in the OT as a vine under God's special care (e.g., Isa. 3:13–15; cf. Mark 12:1–12 and parallels; John 15:1–17), then it becomes clear that Ahab's desire to replace a vineyard with a vegetable garden is meant to be seen as symbolic of a deeper desire. This is a king who wants to make

Israel like Egypt, as did that earlier king with his foreign wives (cf. the commentary on 3:1; 4:21–28; 9:10–14; 10:14–29). It is not surprising that such a king holds lightly the laws that the God of the exodus has revealed—particularly when he has already turned away to worship other gods. Worship and ethics are but two sides of the same coin, so far as the OT is concerned (cf. Exod. 20:1–17). Abandonment of God (Exod. 20:1–6) inevitably leads to abandonment of righteousness; we see the reality of this in 1 Kings 21—in this society given over to idol-worship, covetousness (21:1–6; cf. Exod. 20:17) leads on to false testimony, murder, and theft (1 Kgs. 21:13–19; cf. Exod. 20:13, 15–16).

21:4–14 / We have already seen hints that it is **Jezebel,** and not the rather passive Ahab, who is the real driving force in the kingdom of Israel (1 Kgs. 18; 19:1–2). It is consistent with this picture that Ahab should now retire to bed **sullen and angry** (in Samaria, we assume; cf. his reaction in 20:43), unwilling to take the matter further, and that Jezebel, contemptuous of her husband's unwillingness to be **king** (v. 7), should be the one to take decisive action by sending letters to Jezreel. Her plan is devastatingly simple: to have Naboth executed on false charges. Every legal system can become the tool of politicians, if the values of those responsible for it have been sufficiently corrupted. In Ahab's Israel this is evidently the case; for **letters** in his **name** can persuade the **elders and nobles** of Jezreel (**Naboth's city,** v. 8— implied rather than explicitly stated), who should be the guardians of justice (cf. Deut. 19:11–14; 21:1–9, 18–21; etc.), to enter into conspiracy. With judges such as these and **scoundrels** as the two witnesses required by OT law (v. 10; cf. Deut. 19:15–21; Matt. 26:59–61), Naboth has no chance. He is duly taken **outside the city** and **stoned** to **death** (v. 13; cf. Exod. 22:28; Lev. 24:14–16).

21:15–24 / Ahab has spent most of his time doing what others tell him (e.g., 18:19–20, 41–42; 20:14–17), and that is what we find him doing again here (vv. 15–16) as he travels from Samaria to **take possession** of the vineyard. As in 18:16–19, however, he is confronted in his travels by Elijah, and once again, he hardly gets a chance to speak. The word of the LORD that Elijah brings concerns both the immediate crime Ahab has committed (vv. 17–19; note that he is as much to blame in his passivity as is Jezebel in her activity) and also the general religious context in which the vile deed has been done (vv. 20–24). We are presumably to take it that Ahab hears both aspects of the message, even though it is the judicial murder that is highlighted when the LORD is speaking to Elijah and the idolatry when the LORD is speaking to Ahab through Elijah. **Dogs** feature prominently throughout: licking up Ahab's **blood** instead of Naboth's (v. 19); devouring Jezebel **by the wall of Jezreel** (v. 23); eating Ahab's family (with the **birds**, v. 24). Ahab's house is to suffer the same fate as the houses of **Jeroboam** and **Baasha** (v. 22; cf. 1 Kgs. 14:10–11; 16:3–4), because Ahab has, like them, **provoked** the LORD to **anger** and **caused Israel to sin** (cf. 14:9, 15–16; 16:2; etc.).

21:25–29 / The chapter closes in a surprising way. On the one hand, we are told that Ahab was the worst of kings (vv. 25–26). This is quite consistent with what we have read thus far; we know that he added to Jeroboam's sin the sin of the Baal-worship (16:30–33). On the other hand, we read that in immediate response to Elijah's words the great sinner demonstrates penitence (**When Ahab heard,** v. 27, paralleling v. 16; he is still only reacting to the words of others). The consequence is that God delays the disaster that will fall on his house (v. 29). This is curious, because the reader did not necessarily expect disaster to fall during Ahab's lifetime in any case. It has *always* been the case thus far in Kings that the sort of prophecy of which we have just read comes to pass, not in the reign of the king addressed, but **in the days of his son** (v. 29; cf. 15:25ff.; 16:8ff.). Presumably we are to take it that Ahab's sins were so very bad that *he could* have expected judgment on his house in his lifetime. Now, however, he has **humbled himself,** and thus he is to be treated as a normal, rather than a spectacular, sinner.

Additional Notes §30

21:3 / **The inheritance of my fathers:** The book of Ruth provides us with further narrative evidence of the concern that existed in Israel about the inheritance of land, and passages such as Isa. 5:8 (interestingly juxtaposed with another passage about Israel as vineyard in 5:1–7) and Mic. 2:1–2 inform us about prophetic attitudes to breaches of the laws. On this whole topic, see further C. J. H. Wright, *God's People in God's Land: Family, Land, and Property in the Old Testament* (Eerdmans: Grand Rapids, 1990).

21:15 / **Take possession of the vineyard:** The implication appears to be that the king may confiscate the property of an executed criminal—we do have a couple of examples of this custom in extrabiblical texts. The fact that there is no provision for such a move in Israelite law serves to emphasize the extent to which Ahab and Jezebel are moving outside this sphere, as does the choice of the verb *yrš*, which reminds us of God's giving of the land to Israel to "possess" as an inheritance (cf., for example, Deut. 4:1; 6:18; 8:1; 11:10; 15:4).

21:19 / **In the place where dogs licked up Naboth's blood:** It has often been noted how Elijah's prophecy, thus translated, creates a difficulty when we reach 22:38 and read that it was fulfilled, not outside Jezreel (21:13), but at a pool in Samaria. See, for example, P. D. Miscall, "Elijah, Ahab and Jehu: A Prophecy Fulfilled," *Proof* 9 (1989), pp. 73–83. There is, however, no need to translate it in this way. Hb. *māqôm* in the construct state can mean simply "in place of, instead of" (e.g., Isa. 33:21; Ezek. 6:13; Eccl. 3:16; and esp. Hos. 1:10 for the precise construction here: *bimqôm ʾăšer* followed by a verb). We should translate: "Instead of dogs licking up Naboth's blood, dogs will lick up your blood—yes, yours!"

§31 Ahab Dispatched (1 Kgs. 22:1–40)

The house of Ahab stands under the prophetic curse. The full outworking of God's wrath is to be delayed until the reign of Ahab's son, because of the king's response to Elijah (21:27–29). Ahab's own death, however, has now been foretold by two different prophets, with no delay in prospect (20:41–42; 21:19), and we thus anticipate an early fulfillment of their prophecy. The appearance now of a third prophet brings us to that fulfillment, as Ahab marches out to meet the Arameans at Ramoth Gilead and falls in battle.

22:1–5 / The peace that followed the battle of Aphek (20:26–34) lasted **three years** (v. 1). Even after such a crushing defeat, however, the **king of Aram** was still able to hold on to the strategically important city of **Ramoth Gilead** in Transjordan (v. 3). Ahab now wishes to take this city back, with the help of **Jehoshaphat king of Judah.** The story of Judah has been suspended for some time now, as we have followed the course of northern history from Nadab through to Ahab (15:25–21:29), and we shall find out more about Jehoshaphat shortly (22:41–50). From these few verses, however, two things are already apparent. First, he is at peace with Ahab (cf. 22:44). The precise circumstances in which peace was re-established between Judah and Israel after the long war described in 14:30; 15:6–7, 16–22 are not described, but given the internal conflict in Israel after Baasha's reign (16:8–22) and the threat of Aram on Israel's northern border from his reign onwards, peace with Judah in the south would have been a political necessity. Secondly, Jehoshaphat is a devout man. He is happy to go with Ahab to **fight against Ramoth Gilead,** but first he wants to **seek the counsel of the LORD** (vv. 4–5). We shall hear more of this commitment to the LORD in 22:43, 46.

22:6–8 / Ahab's response to Jehoshaphat is to gather together **the prophets** to ask for their counsel. The Hebrew here is *wayyiqḇôṣ . . . ʾeṯ-hannᵉḇîʾîm*, which is rendered by the NIV in 18:20 as he "assembled the prophets"—this is the only other place in the OT (apart from 2 Chron. 18:5, which is parallel to 1 Kgs. 22:6) where the same phrase occurs. This is very interesting, in view of the fact that 400 prophets are missing from the assembly on Mount Carmel (cf. the additional note on 18:19) and **about four hundred** turn up here (v. 6). Just as interesting is the way in which verses 6–7 are worded. Jehoshaphat seeks "the word of the LORD," so Ahab summons "the prophets," whose precise relationship to the LORD is left unstated. Jehoshaphat's response to them is to ask if there is not **a prophet of the LORD** (relationship made explicit) who might be now be consulted. Whether *he* is implying that the others are not prophets *of the LORD* is unclear. The difference in nomenclature, however, taken with everything else, does suggest that the *authors* are implying this and inviting us to read the story against the background of 1 Kings 18. Once again a single true prophet is set against a large number of false prophets—by implication the very prophets "left over" from that Carmel narrative. We already suspect, therefore, that this majority is not speaking the truth—that it is the one man who **never prophesies anything good** (v. 8) whose word will prove trustworthy. Whether Ahab also sees it this way is not evident. He has previous experience with prophetic words of victory over the Arameans that subsequently came true (20:13, 28). He has no grounds for suspecting that the words he is now hearing from these prophets are any different. Why listen to a prophet such as **Micaiah,** who is so prejudiced that he will not take each case on its own merits?

22:9–14 / Persuaded by the devout Jehoshaphat, however, that a prophet of the LORD should not be sidelined in the present simply because of what has happened in the past ("The king should not say that," v. 8), Ahab sends for **Micaiah.** As we await his arrival we are given a graphic description of the antics of "the prophets" **at the threshing-floor** (an open space created for agricultural purposes, cf. Ruth 3) that further recalls the scene on Mount Carmel. They "prophesy" as a group before the two kings (vv. 10, 12). Hebrew *nḇʾ* certainly signifies at least a claim to divine-human communication on this occasion (v. 12), but it also signifies prophetic action (as in 18:29, cf. the additional note). **Zedekiah** uses **iron horns** to act out symbolically the role of Ahab as he "gores" **the Arameans** like an ox (v. 11; cf. Ezek. 4:1–5:4;

etc.). **As one man** (v. 13), the prophets encourage Ahab by their prophetic word to **attack . . . and be victorious** (v. 12). The **messenger** who has been sent to fetch Micaiah feels that Micaiah would be wise to do the same. Micaiah, however, resists his view that prophecy is under human control: **I can tell him only what the LORD tells me** (v. 14).

22:15–25 / It comes as something of a surprise that Micaiah's first words to Ahab are exactly those of the other prophets (compare vv. 12 and 15). If he can tell the king only what the LORD tells him, why is he confirming the message of prophets who are (we suspect) false? Something is not quite right—and Ahab himself perceives this (v. 16). His request for **truth,** in fact, elicits a quite different message (vv. 17, 19–23). **The LORD has decreed disaster** for Ahab at Ramoth Gilead (v. 23), and his plan to **entice** the king to his **death** there (v. 20) involves precisely those prophets whom Ahab first summoned into his presence (cf. Ezek. 14:1–11). They are being influenced by **a lying spirit** (vv. 21–23; note again the echoes of the Saul story in this spirit from God, 1 Sam. 16:14–15). All will become clear, Micaiah claims, when the disaster that he is predicting does eventually fall (vv. 25, 28; cf. the **inner room** as Ben-Hadad's hiding place after the disaster at Aphek, 20:30). The people will return **in peace** (Hb. *bᵉšālôm,* v. 17), but Ahab, whatever he thinks, will not return **safely** (Hb. *bᵉšālôm,* v. 27). The **sheep** will be **without a shepherd** (cf. Zech. 13:7–9; Matt. 9:36).

22:26–30 / The appeal to verification in the future (Zedekiah will "see" [NIV has "find out"], v. 25, as Micaiah has "seen," vv. 17, 19) is of little help to Ahab as he seeks to make a decision about what to do in the present. There is an overwhelming prophetic majority in favor of military action. These prophets are said by a single opponent to be lying, but that opponent has himself clearly lied, since one of his two "messages from God" (vv. 15 and 17, 19–23) must be false. Given that Israel has known God's help in fighting the Arameans already and that Micaiah is well-known for his negativity in relation to Ahab, it is perhaps not surprising that Ahab (and devout Jehoshaphat, v. 29) should side with the 400 (cf. v. 27, **until I return safely**). It is a perfectly rational choice. What is not quite so rational is Ahab's decision to enter the battle **in disguise** (v. 30). If Micaiah has truly been lying, what is the danger? And if he has been telling the truth, Ahab will die whatever he does. So what is the point of the disguise?

22:29–36 / The reader suspects that it is Micaiah who is speaking the truth. Ahab is therefore predestined to listen to the false prophets; the LORD has decreed it (v. 22). He is also predestined to die, no matter what measures he takes to avoid this fate, for the LORD is intent on judgment, rather than salvation. The donning of disguise is no more than a harbinger of disaster; it recalls the actions of Jeroboam and Saul (1 Sam. 28) just before their own deaths (cf. 1 Kgs. 14:1–18, esp. the additional note to 14:2). Disguise cannot possibly thwart the purposes of God. Jehoshaphat, though wearing **royal robes** (v. 30), is saved from death because his Judean shout (in form or content) reveals that he is not the man Ben-Hadad is after (vv. 31–33). Ahab, however—playing the commoner—is struck down. An arrow shot **at random** flies unerringly to its divinely ordained target (v. 34)—to a single figure in the vast crowd, to one of the few undefended spots on his body. He stays on the battlefield **all day long,** perhaps to encourage his troops, but at sunset he dies and the **army** withdraws leaderless (vv. 35–36, cf. v. 17). The LORD's deception of Ahab has succeeded; Ahab's attempted deception of the LORD has failed. It was the only possible outcome.

22:37–40 / Two of the prophecies of 1 Kings 20–22 have come to pass (20:41–42; 22:17, 19–23). It remains only to hear about the **dogs** and the **blood** they **licked up,** as Ahab's **chariot** is **washed** at a **pool in Samaria** (v. 38; see the additional note on 21:19). The NIV's translation here is strange, and its footnote unhelpful. The Hebrew is lit. "He (possibly the chariot driver of v. 34) washed the chariot by the pool of Samaria, and the dogs licked up his (Ahab's) blood while the prostitutes bathed . . ." The difficulty that some have felt with regard to the **prostitutes** (reflected in the NIV's suggestion that we render Hb. zōnôṯ, uniquely in the OT, as "weapons") is resolved as soon as we recall Deuteronomy 23:17–18. Here the Israelite is enjoined never to become a temple prostitute (Hb. qᵉḏēšâ or qāḏēš) or to bring into the temple the earnings of a female prostitute (Hb. zônâ) or a male prostitute (keleḇ, lit. "dog"). To mention **prostitutes** alongside **dogs** in 1 Kings 22:38 is not only to raise the question as to what kind of **dogs** these were (canine? human?); it is to remind the reader, by association of ideas, of the whole idolatrous career that has brought Ahab to this ignominious end (cf. the association of prostitutes with the fertility cult in 1 Kgs. 14:24; 15:12). He has fed the people idolatry, and now he is consumed by it. It is poetic justice, not just in relation to the murder of Naboth, but also in relation to all his other iniquitous acts.

Ahab has met his destiny. Like Solomon, he married un- wisely. He was led further astray even than Jeroboam. Like Jero- boam, he was not of David's house and he was not, therefore, exempt from being treated like Saul (2 Sam. 7:14–16). Indeed, the echoes of the story of Saul (among those of many other stories) are everywhere to be heard in Ahab's tale: he was a troubler of Israel; he was opposed (generally speaking) by the LORD's prophets; he was rejected because he would not kill an enemy "devoted to the LORD"; he was troubled by a spirit from God; he resorted finally to disguise, a fruitless effort that only further emphasized his failure to evade his fate at God's hands. With Ahab's death and with the Elijah prophecy of chapter 21 now partially fulfilled, we are back on the prophetic track after an unexpected delay. Ahab is Saul and not David. Ahab's dynasty must therefore fall like all the others (Jeroboam's, Baasha's) of the northern kingdom, the reed that sways in the water (cf. 1 Kgs. 14:14–16). We look ahead now to the reign of his son to see how this is to be accomplished.

Additional Notes §31

22:7 / **Is there not a prophet of the LORD here?:** The Hb. is lit. "Is there not here a prophet of the LORD still?", which is ambiguous. It could mean either "Is there no *other* prophet of the LORD here [whom we may consult]?" (cf. RSV) or "Does no prophet of *the* LORD remain here [whom we may consult]?" (NIV). The ambiguity is consonant with the atmosphere of the whole narrative. Are the other prophets truly "of the LORD" (as they claim, vv. 6, 11–12, 24) or are they not (as the links between 1 Kgs. 18 and 22 imply)? Is Micaiah a prophet of the LORD, even though he has apparently lied in v. 14 and uttered a false "prophecy" in v. 15 (cf. 13:18)? The ambiguity cannot finally be resolved until near the end of the story—although the reader's suspicions about the prophets are aroused early on.

22:21 / **A spirit came forward:** The imagery is that of a council of war, with the heavenly king sitting on his throne surrounded by his army (Hb. ṣābāʾ, v. 19, as in 1 Kgs. 1:19, 25 etc.; the NIV's **host**), making plans to defeat Ahab in battle. A volunteer steps forward with a plan, and is sent out as *agent provocateur*. The divine army has, in fact, been lurking in the background of the whole Ahab story, awaiting its moment, under its commander, "the LORD of armies/hosts" (cf. 18:15; 19:10, 14). It will inevitably win the victory.

22:24 / Which way did the spirit from the LORD go?: The NIV's footnote gives the better translation: "Which way did the Spirit of the LORD go . . ." Micaiah's claim is that Zedekiah and his colleagues have a lying spirit (lit. "spirit of falsehood"). Zedekiah's response is to claim that he has been influenced rather by the "Spirit of the LORD"—who cannot have been speaking to both him and Micaiah. He maintains that it is Micaiah, therefore, who is lying.

22:26 / Amon . . . Joash: Amon is evidently one of Ahab's high officials (the NIV's **ruler** is potentially confusing in this respect), entrusted with control of city affairs in Samaria. **The king's son** is responsible for the confinement of prisoners also in Jer. 36:26 and 38:6. Whether this office requires that its holder is literally the son of the king is unclear.

22:28 / Mark my words, all you people: These closing words from Micaiah are the same as the opening words of the prophet Micah (Mic. 1:2). This invites us (at the very least) to consider the book of Micah and this story in 1 Kgs. 22 in relation to each other. It is, indeed, an interesting book to read against the background of the whole Ahab story. It looks forward to the destruction of Samaria because of idolatry and prostitution (1:2–7) and it condemns both social injustice (2:1–5) and false prophecy (2:6–11; 3:1–12).

22:30 / The king of Israel disguised himself: Ahab's surprising—in view of his passivity hitherto—display of initiative in ch. 22 (cf. vv. 3–4) takes on the appearance at this point of dependence on the ideas of others. As he learned about repentance from Ben-Hadad's servants (cf. 20:32; 21:27), so he has learned about disguise from the wounded prophet (cf. Hb. *ḥpś* here and in 20:38). Such thematic and verbal links serve an important function in binding the various chapters of the Ahab story together into a unified whole. The various numerical links perform the same function (400 prophets in 18:19 and about 400 in 22:6; 7,000 Israelites in 19:18 and 20:15; 32 kings in 20:1 and 32 chariot commanders in 22:31).

§32 Jehoshaphat and Ahaziah
(1 Kgs. 22:41–2 Kgs. 1:18)

Jehoshaphat and Ahaziah, already characters in Ahab's story (1 Kgs. 22:2 etc.; 22:40), now find a place of their own. Our expectations differ with respect to each. Jehoshaphat is a Davidic king, so we anticipate no major disasters in his reign (cf. 1 Kgs. 11:36), particularly since he is evidently pious (cf. 1 Kgs. 22:5). Ahaziah, on the other hand, is an Israelite and a son of Ahab. We anticipate wickedness, and disaster of the sort that has fallen upon all the successors of northern kings who receive negative oracles about their house (cf. 1 Kgs. 14:1–18 with 15:29–30; 16:1–4 with 16:11–13; 21:21–24, 27–29). These expectations are largely fulfilled, but there is a surprise in store for us as well, as we discover that Ahaziah is not the only "son of Ahab" whose existence is important for the way in which our story proceeds.

22:41–46 / It is a long time since we last had word of events in Judah (1 Kgs. 15:9–24); but then, compared to Israel, little has been happening! Revolution and war, apostasy and prophetic intervention—all this has passed the southern kingdom by. Stability is the order of the day, as Asa's reign of forty-one years has led into the twenty-five year reign of his son. The religious policy is the same: Jehoshaphat **did what was right in the eyes of the LORD** (v. 43; cf. 15:11). Like his father, he has nothing to do with **shrine prostitutes** (v. 46; cf. 15:12)—a sign of commitment to the LORD just as much as Ahab's association with prostitutes and dogs in verse 38 is a "sign" of the opposite. Admittedly, the **high places** have still not been **removed** (v. 43; cf. 15:14), and this is not good since the focus of the people's worship should be the Jerusalem temple (cf. the additional note on 1 Kgs. 3:2 and the commentary on 1 Kgs. 15:9–15). But fundamentally Jehoshaphat is a good king, and he is **at peace with the king of Israel** (v. 44). In this respect he is even more like the early

Solomon than Asa was, since Asa never knew the peace that Solomon knew (cf. 1 Kgs. 15:16, 32).

22:47–50 / We noted in the commentary on 1 Kings 15:16–24 how, after drawing parallels between the reigns of Asa and Solomon, the authors of Kings then went on to emphasize contrasts. We find the same strategy at work here. A description of Jehoshaphat's and Solomon's similarities is followed by a description of their striking differences. At first we read of peace and think we may soon be seeing the recovery of the empire. Jehoshaphat apparently rules over **Edom,** just like Solomon (see the additional note on 22:47); he is therefore able, like Solomon, to build **ships** at **Ezion Geber** (near Elath in Edom; cf. 1 Kgs. 9:26–28). Being "ships of Tarshish," they recall the Solomonic expeditions to Ophir and other, far-flung places (1 Kgs. 10:22; cf. the additional note to that verse). They remind us, then, of Solomon in all his glory, of the days when the whole world contributed to the king of Israel's wealth. But these are days of humbling (1 Kgs. 11:39), not glory. And having built up our expectations through comparison, our authors immediately bring them crashing down. *These* ships never went to **Ophir** (contrast 1 Kgs. 9:28; 10:11–12); **they were wrecked** as they lay in port (22:48). *This* peace was sometimes simply absence of hostility, rather than real unity within the Solomonic empire: Solomon took foreigners on board *his* ships (1 Kgs. 9:27), but Jehoshaphat **refused** to have even Israelites along (22:49). He is like the early Solomon then, but this is not the Solomonic empire, whatever the achievements (and pretensions) of the Judean kings who are Solomon's successors.

22:51–53 / Nothing in this summary of **Ahaziah**'s reign is surprising. Its length is exactly what we expect of the son of an oracle-receiving Israelite king: **two years** (v. 51; cf. 15:25; 16:8). His religious commitments are also entirely predictable. Like his father, **he walked in the ways of Jeroboam** (16:31) and **served and worshiped Baal** (16:31–32). We await only an account of his downfall and of the slaughter of Ahab's house (21:21–24, 29).

2 Kings 1:1–17 / Like his father, Ahaziah meets Elijah. The occasion for their confrontation is an injury sustained by the king when falling out of the window (probably, although **lattice** is obscure) of **his upper room** (v. 2). His reaction is to send **messengers** (Hb. *malᵃkîm*) to consult one of the many local manifestations of Baal (cf. 1 Kgs. 18:18) about his fate: **Baal-Zebub, the god of Ekron** (a Philistine city about twenty-five miles west of Jerusalem). In response, the LORD also sends a messenger (Hb. *mal'āk,* **angel;** cf. 1 Kgs. 19:5–7), with the result that Elijah intercepts the king's men on the road with a prophecy about Ahaziah's death. Not for the first time in Kings, a negative oracle addressed to a king elicits an attempt to capture the prophet who delivered it (cf. 1 Kgs. 13:1–7; 17:1–4; 18:9–10; 22:1–28). The prophetic word, however, cannot be brought under human control. A **man of God,** precisely because he is a man *of God,* cannot be coerced by a mere king. The peremptory instructions of verses 9 and 11, therefore, meet with a fierce response, as Ahaziah comes to terms with the reality of the God of Carmel, who can send **fire** from **heaven** to **consume** his captains (vv. 10 and 12; cf. 1 Kgs. 18:38). The **third captain** accords Elijah the respect he is due as a prophet of the LORD and escapes with his life. Ahaziah meets with Elijah as he had wanted, but it changes nothing. The oracle stands as first spoken by the angel (vv. 3–4, 6, 16); the king dies (v. 17).

1:17–18 / The manner of Ahaziah's end is unexpected. He has died, we assume, in his bed. There has been no revolution; the house has not been destroyed "in the days of Ahab's son." Ahaziah, it is true, has himself **no son;** so it appears that the dynasty of Ahab is indeed at an end. But has prophecy partly failed? Is there to be no bloodshed of the kind we read about in 1 Kings 15:25ff. and 16:8ff.? At first it seems so. We lack, however, a crucial piece of information. It turns out (cf. 2 Kgs. 3:1) that the Jehoram who succeeds Ahaziah is his brother. There is *another* son of Ahab, and it is this "son" whose reign will see the true fulfillment of Elijah's prophecy. We are dealing, then, not with failure of prophecy, but with another delay. It is unexpected, but as the Ahaziah narrative reminds us, the LORD *is* God.

Additional Notes §32

22:47 / **There was then no king in Edom; a deputy ruled:** The Hb. for **deputy** is *niṣṣāb,* otherwise used in Kings only of Solomon's officials (1 Kgs. 4:5, 27; 5:16; 9:23). Jehoshaphat controls Edom as

Solomon had controlled his districts, and that is why the "king" of Edom (Hb. *melek*, the same word that lies behind the NIV's **ruled** here) turns up in alliance with Judah in 2 Kgs. 3, in what is noticeably a supporting role. Judah's control of Edom is not, in fact, challenged until the reign of Jehoshaphat's son, Jehoram (2 Kgs. 8:20–22).

22:50 / **Jehoshaphat rested with his fathers:** We shall hear of Jehoshaphat again in 2 Kgs. 3, in a "flashback" to the first seven years of Jehoram of Israel's reign, when Jehoshaphat was still on the Judean throne (cf. 1 Kgs. 22:42 and 2 Kgs. 3:1). He thus appears in the narrative both before and after his reign is formally described in toto.

1:1 / **Moab rebelled:** It is at first surprising to find information about Moab's rebellion (Hb. *pšᶜ*) here, since it disturbs the flow of the narrative about Ahaziah and Baal, and nothing is made of it until 2 Kgs. 3:4ff. Presumably the point is that Asa's relatively righteous successor Jehoshaphat maintains suzerainty over other nations (Edom, 1 Kgs. 22:47), whereas Ahab's Baal-worshiping son loses it. It is significant that it is under Jehoshaphat's Baal-worshiping son Jehoram (2 Kgs. 8:16–24) that Edom rebels (Hb. *pšᶜ*) against Judah.

1:2 / **Baal-Zebub:** Lit. "Baal/lord of the flies." There is some manuscript evidence of a version of this name ("Beelzebub") in a few Gospel texts that refer to Satan (Matt. 10:25; 12:24, 27; Mark 3:22; Luke 11:15, 18, 19). This is interesting in view of the links between OT spirit possession and NT demon possession that have been noted in our discussion of 1 Kgs. 18 (cf. the commentary on 18:15–29 and the additional note on 18:29). The OT figure of Baal stands explicitly behind the NT figure of Satan in these MSS, as it implicitly does even in those better NT MSS that read "Beelzebul" instead of "Beelzebub." It may well be, in fact, that **Baal-Zebub** is itself a deliberate corruption of "Baal-Zebul" ("Baal the exalted"), intended to express the authors' scorn of or hostility towards this "deity." We may note here the analogous substitution of Hb. *bōšet*, "shame," for Baal in 2 Sam. 2:8 (cf. 1 Chron. 8:33) and 2 Sam. 11:21 (cf. Judg. 6:32); and the substitution of Hb. *šiqquṣ*, "detested thing," for "god" in 1 Kgs. 11:5. On the NT material see further W. D. Davies and D. C. Allison, *The Gospel According to Saint Matthew*, ICC, vol. 2 (Edinburgh: T. & T. Clark, 1991), pp. 195–96.

1:8 / **A man with a garment of hair:** The Hb. is lit. "a man who was a lord/owner of hair"—possibly a play on words with "lord of the flies" in v. 2. The "hair" could be either animal or human, which is why translations have varied between **garment of hair** and "hairy" (i.e., long-haired, bearded). Both Matt. (3:4) and Mark (1:6) portray John the Baptist (as "Elijah") wearing both this kind of garment and **a leather belt** (cf. the additional note to 1 Kgs. 19:16).

1:10 / **Fire fell from heaven:** The figure of Elijah appears to stand behind the representation of the two prophets in Rev. 11:1–6, who stop the rain and kill with fire those who try to harm them (cf. also the allusions to Moses here, and the connections between Elijah and Moses in the commentary on 1 Kgs. 19 in particular). Fire is a well-known vehicle of God's judgment in the Bible (cf. Gen. 19:24; Exod. 9:23–24; Num. 11:1–3; Luke 9:54; Rev. 20:7–10).

1:17 / **In the second year of Jehoram:** If Jehoram of Israel did indeed succeed Ahaziah only after **Jehoram son of Jehoshaphat** had properly succeeded his father (cf. 1 Kgs. 22:50), then 2 Kgs. 3 (**Jehoshaphat** goes to war with Jehoram of Israel) presents us with something of a difficulty. The problem may be resolved only if we assume that there was a coregency between **Jehoshaphat** and his son towards the end of the former's reign.

§33 Elijah Gives Way to Elisha (2 Kgs. 2:1–25)

Elijah's days have been numbered ever since 1 Kings 19:15–18. The end of the war with Baal-worship will not come about, we know from that passage, until Elisha has succeeded his mentor and Hazael and Jehu have appeared on the scene. We are now to hear of the first of these events, as the prophetic mantle passes from Elijah to Elisha. As Elijah has called fire down from heaven in chapter 1, so in chapter 2 he will be lifted in fire up to heaven, and Elisha will be authenticated as one who stands in true succession to him as a prophet of the LORD.

2:1–6 / The narrative about the ascension of Elijah is in some ways very puzzling. The first puzzle confronts us in verses 1–6. Why does Elijah, in the course of the journey described here, repeatedly try to leave Elisha behind? He has been told to make Elisha his successor (1 Kgs. 19:15–18), and the succession is to take place, as everyone knows, **today** (vv. 3, 5; for Elijah's knowledge of this see v. 9). It is "today" that the LORD will release Elisha from Elijah's tutelage (cf. the NIV's **take . . . from you,** more accurately translated as "take . . . from over you"). Why, at this moment, does Elijah try to escape? We are not explicitly told. Yet it is clear from the story that follows that he believes Elisha's presence with him at his point of departure to be necessary if he is to receive his "inheritance" of the spirit (cf. the commentary on vv. 9–12). Is this further testimony of Elijah's reluctance to adopt God's plans for the future (cf. 1 Kgs. 19:13–21)? Is he trying to shake Elisha off his tail, so as to subvert these plans? It is certainly not his leadership that is the decisive factor in the way things work out in this chapter. It is, rather, Elisha's commitment to his calling— and possibly also his personal loyalty to Elijah. He sticks with Elijah in spite of all attempts to persuade him to do otherwise.

2:7–15 / Both prophets thus arrive at the **Jordan,** where the main action is to take place. In a scene reminiscent of Moses at the Sea of Reeds, they cross over on dry land (vv. 7–8; cf. Exod. 14:15–31, esp. vv. 21–2). Elisha then requests what an eldest son would expect of a **father** (cf. v. 12) as his inheritance: **a double portion** (cf. Deut. 21:15–17). In this case it is not land that he has in mind, but **spirit**, for Elisha has already left normal life and normal rules of inheritance behind (cf. 1 Kgs. 19:19–21). Elijah promises that Elisha will indeed receive this gift if he sees his departure—which Elisha duly does (vv. 11–12). He is consequently able to repeat Elijah's parting of the waters (vv. 13–14), proving himself to be Joshua to Elijah's Moses (cf. the additional note on 1 Kgs. 19:21)—Joshua also crossed the Jordan and entered the land of Israel near Jericho, "repeating" Moses' actions (Josh. 3). It is significant here that the names Elisha and Joshua are so similar in meaning ("God saves"; "the LORD saves"). We are meant to read the one story against the background of the other.

2:15–18 / A second puzzle now confronts us. Why is **the company** (lit. "sons," as in 1 Kgs. 20:35) **of the prophets** so intent on looking for Elijah? On the one hand these prophets seem to understand very well that the succession has taken place (**the spirit of Elijah is resting on Elisha,** v. 15). They offer Elisha due respect as a full-fledged prophet—they bow **to the ground.** Why, then, do they engage in what seems to the reader, as it does to Elisha, a futile search? If Elijah has been taken up into the heavens, why look for him on earth?

The text implies that the answer lies in their ignorance of what has really happened. We must remember that we, as readers, have a privileged position in respect of Elijah's fate—a position apparently shared (among those left behind) only by Elisha himself. We are told right from the beginning that Elijah has ascended into the heavens (Hb. *ʿlh haššāmayîm,* v. 1). It is, indeed, assumed by the authors that this is common knowledge—which is why this extraordinary event is introduced in verse 1 in such a matter-of-fact way. When it actually occurs, the reader is again told what is happening (Hb. *ʿlh haššāmayîm,* v. 11). Of the characters in the narrative, however, only Elisha "sees" that this is so (v. 12). The prophets are merely bystanders (cf. **at a distance,** v. 7). They are aware, no doubt, that **whirlwind** and **fire** are signs of the LORD's appearing (Exod. 3:2; 19:18; Ezek. 1:4ff.; Job 38:1; 40:6), but they are not privy to what is happening in the storm's midst. For all they know, the **Spirit** may simply have **picked** Elijah **up** and deposited him in a different place, as in the past

(v. 16; cf. 1 Kgs. 18:12). Their actions are on one level, therefore, quite comprehensible. Even Elisha is apparently uncertain enough of what he has seen as to be unwilling to tell them clearly what has happened and unable to withstand their pressure upon him to permit the search (v. 17).

There is, however, a further question to be asked of the prophets. If Elijah is **on some mountain or in some valley**—why seek him at all? They had themselves foreseen that Elisha would come out from under Elijah's shadow "today" (v. 5), and they have just greeted him as prophetic successor (v. 15). Why go looking now for the redundant old prophet? Are they simply confused? We could not blame them if they were. But there is another possibility. Do they, perhaps, think that Elijah is dead? Joshua did not, after all, succeed Moses until after Moses' death (Josh. 1:1–9), and they have seen Elisha tearing his own **clothes . . . apart** (lit. "in two pieces," v. 12)—actions that could be explained in terms of mourning ritual (cf. Gen. 37:34; 2 Sam. 13:31). Perhaps it is the retrieval of a body for burial (cf. 1 Sam. 31:11–13), rather than recovery of a living person, that they have in mind.

They do not find Elijah, of course, either living or dead. They are thus invited to draw the conclusion that we and Elisha have already reached: Elijah has indeed been taken up into the heavens. Whether that "taking up" is itself a kind of death or simply translation to a different sort of life is never resolved by the narrative. There are hints of death all around: the conversation about double portions in verses 9–10; the tearing of the clothes in verse 12; the search in verses 16–18. Yet in the final analysis these features of the text tell us only what the various actors may have believed about Elijah's departure. They do not tell us what the authors thought. The authorial "taken up" (Hb. *ʿlh*, vv. 1, 11) is distinctive language, never used by their characters ("taken" is Hb. *lqḥ* in vv. 3, 5, 9, 10), and never explained. It is language that guards the mystery at the heart of the event and does not allow us easy answers.

2:19–25 / With the two concluding stories of the chapter we leave behind uncertainties about the fate of Elijah (vv. 16–18) and concentrate upon what is clear (picking up vv. 13–15): that Elisha has indeed taken his place. He is an authentic prophet—a man able both to bless and to curse in the LORD's name (cf. Moses in Deut. 28). The first story concerns bad **water** in Jericho and its effects on the **land** (2:19–22). We are not told why Jericho is thus afflicted, but we recall that its rebuilding took place under the shadow of Joshua's curse (Josh. 6:26; 1 Kgs. 16:34). It is fitting that this new Joshua, having crossed the Jordan, should pronounce a blessing, his own prophetic word matching that of his illustrious predecessor. The second story concerns children from **Bethel** who jeer at Elisha. For the authors of Kings, **Bethel** is a city that provides the focal point for Israel's apostasy (cf. 1 Kgs. 12:25–13:34). It is no surprise to find its children adopting a disrespectful attitude towards a prophet. To treat a prophet with disrespect, however, is to treat *God* with disrespect and to risk immediate retribution—as various of the prophetic narratives thus far have told us (e.g., 1 Kgs. 13:1–4; 2 Kgs. 1:2–17). Elisha shows himself to be a true prophet as he **curses** the children and sees **two bears** come **out of the woods** and maul **forty-two** of them (v. 24; cf. 1 Kgs. 13:20–28 and 20:35–36 for divine judgment through animals in response to prophetic words).

The succession narrative ends with Elisha's trip to **Mount Carmel** (v. 25), the scene of Elijah's great victory over the priests of Baal. It is an appropriate ending since it reminds us of Elisha's place in the story of Israel taken as a whole. His prophetic credentials having been established, he is now ready to pick up where Elijah left off in the war against Baal. It is to pursue that war that he returns **to Samaria.**

Additional Notes §33

2:1 / **Gilgal:** It is not made clear if the LORD has any reason for sending Elijah from Gilgal to Bethel and then on to Jericho. All three cities appear in 2 Kings, however, as locations where there are prophetic communities ("sons of the prophets"; cf. 2:3, 5; 4:38); and it may be that Elijah is already exercising the kind of leadership role over these that Elisha exercises later (e.g., 4:1ff.; 6:1ff.). Note that the roots of the Jericho community's allegiance to Elisha lie in their conviction that he is Elijah's bona fide successor (2:15–22).

2:3 / **Do not speak of it:** No reason for this injunction is offered, but it may simply be a question of respect. It is disrespectful to speak of Elijah's passing while he is still around.

2:7 / **Fifty men:** As in other parts of 1 Kgs. 17–2 Kgs. 2, numbers are apparently functioning as a way of holding separate narratives together as a unity. Two companies of **fifty men** experience Elijah's ability to bring down fire from heaven in ch. 1, before a third escapes (1:9–15). Now one company of **fifty men** will witness (albeit not "see" in the way the Elisha will see) the prophet's departure in the midst of fire and storm, while another will search to see whether he has travelled to another spot (v. 16). In view of this and other examples of numerical linking, it seems noteworthy that the other larger number of this chapter—the "forty-two" of v. 24—also reappears, in 2 Kgs. 10:14.

2:10 / **A difficult thing . . . if you see me:** It is not easy for those who have read 1 Kgs. 19:15–18 to take these words seriously. We know that Elisha is destined to succeed Elijah as a Spirit-empowered prophet of the LORD. Can there really be any "difficulty" that faces God in transferring the Spirit from one to the other (cf. Num. 11:16ff.)? And is the contingency (*if* **you see**) a real one? If it is true that Elisha must **see,** then it is inconceivable that he will not succeed in doing so. Failure is in any case not to be expected from one who has aspirations to be a prophet; prophetic vision is simply part of the job (cf. Hb. *rʾh,* "to see," for example, in 1 Sam. 9:1–9). Elijah's words are curious indeed. Is he simply looking for problems?

2:11 / **A chariot of fire and horses of fire:** Hb. *reḵeḇ* is much better understood as a plural here, as it is in v. 12. The divine army, last encountered waging war on Ahab (1 Kgs. 22:1–38), has come for Elijah, and Elisha has seen it ("My father! My father! The chariots and horsemen of Israel!"). He will see it again in the famous story of the "battle" of Dothan in 2 Kgs. 6:8–23, and its noise will be heard by the Arameans (it is implied) in 7:5–7. It now becomes even clearer than before why the Arameans can never depend on having any advantage over Israel on the plains (1 Kgs. 20:23–25). Israel has chariots and horsemen after all—even if not the orthodox kind (cf. Exod. 14:9ff.; Deut. 20:1).

2:12 / **Tore them apart:** It may well be that at least part of the explanation for this action is to be found in mourning ritual. At the same time, when taken along with the picking up of Elijah's **cloak** that follows it (v. 13), this destroying of his old clothes is suggestive of a final transition from Elisha's old to his new life. The "mantle" has passed, quite literally, from Elijah to Elisha, and the cloak that was used in 1 Kgs. 19:19–21 to symbolize the prophetic call has now become his permanent possession. The ambiguity of the meaning of his actions is consonant with the ambiguity of Elijah's fate. Is Elijah to be thought of as deceased or not?

2:20 / **New bowl . . . salt:** The symbolism of the action is not made clear, as is so often the case in prophetic narratives of this kind (cf. 1 Kgs. 17:17–24). Characteristically, the emphasis falls not so much upon the actions of the prophet as upon his words—the channel for the divine word (vv. 21–22). The water becomes wholesome, not because of the actions in themselves, but because the LORD has said it will. We may note a similar instance in 1 Kgs. 11:29–31 (when Ahijah's **new** cloak is used as an illustration for what he says to Jeroboam).

2:23 / **Some youths:** The Hb. is *nᵉʿārîm qᵉṭannîm,* "children." The use of *naʿar* alone would allow the NIV's translation (cf. the additional note to 1 Kgs. 20:14), but the appearance of *qāṭān*, "small, young," precludes it. The NIV in fact translates *na'ar qāṭān* in 1 Kgs. 3:7 and 11:17 (correctly) as "little child" and "boy" respectively (cf. also *na'ᵃrâ qᵉṭannâ*, "young girl," in 2 Kgs. 5:2). The translator has apparently had more difficulty than the authors here in coming to terms with the idea that young persons as well as old should be subject to divine judgment for their sins. Whether there is something more specific to the taunt **you baldhead** is not clear. It is possible that some prophets, like later Christian monks, shaved their heads as a mark of their vocation. We certainly cannot cite verses like Lev. 21:5 (addressed to priests) and Deut. 14:1 (concerning actions "for the dead"), as some commentators have recently done, against this possibility.

§34 Excursus: Elijah in Canonical Context

Elijah was a mighty prophet of the LORD—a man for a crisis. He opposed Ahab and Jezebel and all their works, and played a pivotal role in the significant victory over Baal-worship that is described in 1 Kings 17–18. He was, as these stories illustrate, a man of great faith and courage. He was also, however, as all biblical heroes of the faith (bar one) are ultimately shown to be, a flawed character. Faced with unexpected opposition, he retreated from the conflict, casting faith aside and looking to lay down the prophetic mantle of his own accord (1 Kgs. 19:1–4). Frustrated in this quest and faced anew with the reality of God, he seems unwilling to listen as the divine voice seeks to place his life and mission in its proper context—to define him as one servant among many others (19:5–14). His life after Horeb continued to be one of service (1 Kgs. 21; 2 Kgs. 1), but at those points where he had to confront his own passing from the God's center stage, a definite reluctance, even disobedience, was displayed (1 Kgs. 19:19–21; 2 Kgs. 2:1–10). He did well when life went the way he expected. He was not so good at dealing with disappointment; he was certainly not prepared to smooth the way for others. In many ways he was similar to Moses (cf., for example, the commentary on 1 Kgs. 19; 2 Kgs. 2), even to the extent of "dying" on the other side of the Jordan (2 Kgs. 2:7–12; Deut. 34:1–8), but he was also somewhat like Jonah (1 Kgs. 19), the grudging, disobedient servant of God.

Unlike Solomon (cf. §18 above), Elijah appears "in person" in the NT, standing on the mount of transfiguration along with Moses and Jesus (Matt. 17:1–13; Mark 9:2–13; Luke 9:28–36). The significance of this is much debated, and the emphasis clearly falls in different places in the different Gospel versions of the story. The main point in all three, however, appears to be that Jesus is greater than both Moses and Elijah, those others privileged to meet with God on a mountain. The fact that Jesus is regarded as greater than Elijah, of course, does not prevent Elijah (like Solomon) from functioning typologically with respect to Jesus. He does so explicitly in Luke 4:24–26. Jesus' mission embraces the Gentiles, as Elijah's did: the greatest of prophets is to exercise his ministry in ways analogous to his predecessor. There are, of course, implicit connections as well. Angels minister to Jesus in the wilderness (1 Kgs. 19:5–8; Matt. 4:1–11); he opposes Baal(-Zebub), dealing firmly (albeit by radically different means) with the "possessed" (1 Kgs. 18:20–40; 2 Kgs. 1:2–17; Matt. 12:22–28; Luke 11:14–20); he works miracles of provision and healing (1 Kgs. 17:7–24; Matt. 14:13–21; 15:29–39; Luke 7:11–17); in the end he ascends into heaven (2 Kgs. 2:11; Acts 1:2). In all these ways and more, the NT portrait of Jesus is building on the portrait of Elijah in Kings.

For all that, however, it is not Jesus who is most often connected with Elijah in the Gospels; it is John the Baptist. Here it is Elijah's preparatory role that is in view (1 Kgs. 19:15–18, picked up in Mal. 4:1–6). He prepares the way for God's final victory over the powers of darkness. So it is that John the Baptist appears before the ministry of Jesus begins, dressed like Elijah (2 Kgs. 1:8; cf. Matt. 3:4; Mark 1:6) and warning of the coming kingdom of God. He is identified as the Elijah to come by an angel in Luke 1:11–17 and by Jesus in Matthew 11:1–19; 17:11–13 (cf. Mark 9:11–13). These passages show no agreement with the popular belief of the time that Elijah had not died, but had been translated into heaven or some intermediate place between earth and heaven, and that Elijah would therefore literally return to earth (cf. Matt. 16:13–16; 27:45–49; Mark 6:14–16; 8:27–30; 15:33–36; Luke 9:7–9, 18–20). It is, of course, natural that such a view should have arisen, given the ambiguities of Elijah's fate in 2 Kings 2:1–18 and the apparent similarity between his experience and that of Enoch, who was also "taken" (Hb. *lqḥ*) by God in Genesis 5:24 (cf. Heb. 11:5; *Gen. Rab.* 25:1). But the Gospels do not support this view and, by locating the "real" Elijah on the mountain, the transfiguration narrative in Matthew and Mark makes it quite clear that John is "Elijah" only in some figurative sense. This may explain John's own denial that he is Elijah (John 1:19–34). In one sense he is, in another he is not. He performs Elijah's task without "being" Elijah. The same is presumably true of the "witnesses" of Revelation 11:1–12, clearly patterned after Elijah (and Moses), who prepare the way for the final advent of God's kingdom but are not themselves "actually" Elijah (and Moses).

Like Solomon, Elijah not only functions in the NT as a type
of Jesus (and in this case, of John the Baptist as well) but also
appears as "someone just like us," one of the people of God.
Christians can learn valuable lessons from Elijah's life, the NT
writers affirm: whether about the way God works with "remnants" of his people (Rom. 11:1ff.; the remnant theme will remain
an important one throughout Kings); or about faith (Heb. 11:32–39);
or about prayer (Jas. 5:13–18). On the basis of my own reading of
the Elijah story, I may also suggest that there are things to be
learned from him regarding having a sense of perspective about
one's life of service; regarding the need for humility; regarding
willingness to be part of God's plan, rather than to be the plan
itself (cf. Matt. 3:11–15; 11:11; 20:20–27; John 3:27–30; 1 Cor.
3:1–9; Phil. 1:12–18). Both in his success and in his failure Elijah
is a helpful teacher.

§35 Elisha and the Conquest of Moab (2 Kgs. 3:1–27)

Elijah has gone, and Elisha has been authenticated as his successor. We expect, on the analogy of Elijah's own life (and because of God's words in 1 Kgs. 19:15–18), that succession means involvement in politics, and this is what we now find as Elisha is consulted about a military campaign. Echoes of 1 Kings 22:1–28 are everywhere to be heard, especially in Jehoshaphat's renewed alliance with the house of Ahab. We must listen to these words intently if we are to understand what is happening in this rather puzzling narrative.

3:1–3 / We expect that Jehoram (the NIV's **Joram**), as a **son of Ahab**, will be the one to see God's judgment falling at last upon Ahab's house (cf. 1 Kgs. 22:21–24). It is surprising, then, to find that the description of his reign distances him from the rest of his family. **He did evil . . . but not as his father and mother had done.** This distinguishes him, not only from his parents, but also from his brother Ahaziah (cf. 1 Kgs. 22:52). The implication is that he did not himself worship Baal: **he got rid of** (better "removed," i.e., "from the temple of Baal") **the sacred stone of Baal.** This is certainly an impression strengthened by the other narratives involving the king in 2 Kings 3–9, which never explicitly accuse him of Baal-worship, but make it clear that the Baal-cult is still very much alive (cf. 3:13; 9:22; 10:18–28). Indeed, the **sacred stone** survives until the reign of Jehu (cf. 10:26–27). Jehoram is presented, then, as tolerating the Baal cult while not himself necessarily participating in it. His own sins are of the less spectacular sort committed by the sons of Jeroboam and Baasha (1 Kgs. 15:25–26; 16:13), who worshiped, and encouraged others to worship, the calves of **Jeroboam** (cf. Hb. *dbq*, **clung,** of Solomon and his lovers in 1 Kgs. 11:2). His sins are still, of course, worthy of divine judgment.

3:4–8 / The surprises continue as the narrative unfolds. Jehoram's response to the rebellion of **Moab** (already mentioned in 2 Kgs. 1:1) is to seek help, like his father before him, from his southern neighbor **Jehoshaphat.** The Judean's initial response we recognize from 1 Kings 22:4: **I am as you are, my people as your people, my horses as your horses** (v. 7). Immediately, then, we are quite deliberately reminded of the earlier story and invited to make comparisons. This being so, we can hardly fail to notice that whereas, earlier, Jehoshaphat was very concerned to discover "the counsel of the LORD" before going off to war (22:5), he now moves directly from agreement to tactics (3:8, though it is not clear who is asking the question and who is answering it) and from tactics to action (v. 9). There is no prophet in sight. Is this the pious Jehoshaphat of earlier days? Why is he going off to war without consulting the LORD? Something seems amiss.

3:9–12 / It could be expected that a military venture undertaken without prophetic advice should face disaster in the desert without a blow being struck. Jehoram gives the impression of recognizing the LORD's hand in what has happened (v. 10), although how seriously we are meant to take such words on the lips of an idolater is open to question (cf. also 2 Kgs. 6:27). His is certainly not a "faith" that leads to pious behavior. It is left to Jehoshaphat—his memory suddenly restored—to suggest the appropriate action in such circumstances. It is action that should have been taken at the start: **Is there no prophet of the LORD here, that we may inquire of the LORD through him?** (v. 11; cf. the very close similarity to 1 Kgs. 22:7). Elisha's name is mentioned; and it is agreed to consult him.

3:13–19 / Elisha is certainly not about to acknowledge Jehoram as a true worshiper of the LORD. He advises him to consult **the prophets** of his **father** and **mother,** and ultimately agrees to help only because of righteous (albeit forgetful) Jehoshaphat's **presence.** A two-part prophecy is given; like previous prophecies, its contents are something of a surprise. Perhaps we had supposed that Ahab's son would fall like his father—that God had indeed **called** the **three kings together** to **hand** them **over to Moab** (v. 13). Apparently not. The prophecy that Elisha utters is not of woe (like Micaiah's oracle of 1 Kgs. 22), but of weal (like those in 1 Kgs. 20). The immediate crisis ("no more water," v. 9) is to be dealt with by miracle, the **valley filled with water** from an unspecified and unexpected source (**neither wind nor**

rain). As to the broader question, God will grant the alliance a comprehensive victory over Moab. They will **overthrow** (strictly "hit, attack," Hb. *nkh;* see the additional note to v. 19) **every fortified city** (Hb. *kol-ʿîr miḇṣār*) **and every major town** (Hb. *kol-ʿîr miḇḥôr*), devastating the land as they move through it. Victory, it seems, will be total.

3:20–27 / Events begin to unfold in line with the prophecy. Early in the morning, **about the time for offering the sacrifice** (we are not told when exactly this is), water mysteriously appears, **flowing from the direction of Edom** (Hb. *ʾeḏôm,* v. 20). This not only provides sustenance but also fools the Moabites (because the water appears **red,** Hb. *ʾaḏummîm,* **like blood,** Hb. *dam,* v. 22; note the play on words with *ʾeḏôm*) into thinking that the allies have slaughtered each other. Their reckless advance is met with force, as the Israelites drive them back and point by point act out Elisha's words (v. 25, cf. v. 19). They destroy the **towns** (Hb. *heʿārîm*), ruin the fields with **stones** taken from these towns, stop up **the springs,** and **cut down** the trees. But the greatest surprise has been kept until last. On the verge of the total victory that Elisha has apparently prophesied, the Israelites encounter unexpected difficulty. Child sacrifice in **Kir Haresheth** saves this city from the fate of all the others, as **fury** comes upon the Israelites and they withdraw. Weal has turned to woe after all, and Jehoram has apparently been proved right (vv. 10, 13). The LORD appears to have handed Israel over to Moab—in the end, if not in the beginning.

It is an amazing end to a story of many twists and turns. A wicked king, though unexpectedly better than his predecessors, faces disaster in war. He is comforted, unpredictably, by a prophet who foretells success. Then, once we have adjusted ourselves to this surprise, the disaster we first expected happens after all! What are we to make of all this? Did Elisha speak falsely when he described what would happen in Moab? To ask the question is to remind ourselves of the issues that were raised by 1 Kings 22. Micaiah's first word to Ahab, we recall, was not the true word (22:15). It was only when pressed by a suspicious king that he spoke truly.

Was Elisha's first (and only) word to the three kings similarly misleading? Strictly speaking, the answer is no. Everything that Elisha predicted actually happened: all the cities of Moab were attacked, all the good trees cut down, and so on (see the additional note to 3:19). Elisha did not lie. There is in his prophecy, nevertheless, a certain economy with the truth. All that he said about the Moabite campaign was true, but the whole truth was not spoken. Some crucial information (about its end) was withheld—information whose absence led the recipients of revelation (and the reader) to have quite mistaken expectations about what would happen. The LORD did hand Moab over to the kings (3:18)—but only up to a certain point. After that point, he handed the kings over to Moab. In the light of 1 Kings 22, we can scarcely doubt that this was his intention from the start. Total victory was never on the agenda, in spite of the way Elisha's words might have been construed. Once again a wicked Israelite king has been lured to disaster, this time not by a lying spirit speaking through false prophets, but by the Spirit of God revealing partial truth to a true prophet. Perhaps Jehoshaphat, who had seen it all before, should have probed more deeply— particularly when the prophecy so clearly raised questions in terms of Deuteronomy's rules of war (Deut. 20:19–20). But then, Jehoshaphat was apparently prone to forgetfulness where prophets were concerned.

A central lesson of the chapter is this: prophets do not control the prophetic word. It is something given to them by God (2 Pet. 1:21). They are simply channels through which it passes. We have been confronted with this lesson before (cf. 1 Kgs. 13:1–10; 14:1–18; 18:1–15). Nothing could make it clearer, however, than a story in which an indisputably true prophet is presented as unaware (fully) of God's plans (cf. further 2 Kgs. 4:27). God does not always reveal the entirety of the divine will, particularly when faced with wicked Israelite kings destined for judgment. Revelation cannot be taken for granted, just because it is the option that God so frequently chooses. This is a significant lesson to be reminded of at this point in our reading of Kings, when we have seen the regularity of God's self-revelation through the prophets. Like the other characters here—the pious Judean who fails to consult the LORD; the son of Ahab who takes the LORD's name upon his lips—God, too, can behave in ways that defy our expectations. God is not bound by conventions.

Additional Notes §35

3:1 / **Joram:** The NIV's substitution of **Joram** for MT's "Jehoram" here and in 2 Kgs. 1:17; 3:6; 9:15, 17, 21–24 is presumably due to a desire that this Israelite king should not be confused with the Judean whose reign is described in 2 Kgs. 8:16–24 (cf. 1 Kgs. 22:50), and whom the NIV consistently calls "Jehoram" even where the Hb. calls him **Joram** (2 Kgs. 8:21, 23–24; 11:2). This is to put asunder, however, what the Hb. has deliberately joined together. It is no coincidence that it is precisely at this point, when the southern monarchy has come to resemble the northern most closely in its worship (cf. further the commentary on 2 Kgs. 8:16–27), that its kings are called by the same name, be it Jehoram or Ahaziah. The latter also appears in two variants that are used of both the Israelite and Judean kings so named (cf. *ʾaḥazyâ* in 2 Kgs. 1:2; 9:16, 23, 27, 29; 11:2; *ʾaḥazyāhû* in 1 Kgs. 22:40, 49, 51; 2 Kgs. 1:18; etc.). On the date of Jehoram's accession, see the additional note on 2 Kgs. 1:17.

3:8 / **The Desert of Edom:** The idea is to attack Moab from the south, rather than from the north. This is possible because Edom is under Judean rule (1 Kgs. 22:47) and its "king" is Jehoshaphat's "deputy" rather than an independent monarch. That is why the king of Edom appears so suddenly in the narrative, without introduction (3:9). He is simply regarded as part of the "people" whom Jehoshaphat has committed to the campaign in v. 7.

3:11 / **An officer:** The Hb. is lit. "one of the servants." It is a pronounced feature of the Elisha stories in 2 Kgs. 3–8 that it is characteristically the politically powerless who are in touch with and open to what God is doing through Elisha, while the powerful (especially the kings) reveal only ignorance and arrogance, refusing to adopt a humble and respectful attitude towards him. Thus it is the maidservant of 2 Kgs. 5 who opens the way for Naaman to be healed; the king of Israel is unbelieving and Naaman himself (until persuaded by his servants) is unwilling to obey. The king of Aram is ignorant of reality in 6:11–12 until enlightened by his servants, and arrogant enough then to attempt to capture the prophet. His arrogance is matched by that of the king of Israel in 6:31ff. and by his ignorance in 8:1–6. It is not the armies of Israel who eventually relieve Samaria in 7:3ff. (the king of Israel again knows nothing of what is happening, v. 12), but four lepers. It is consistent with this general picture that it should be a servant of the king who in 2 Kgs. 3 is able to direct the king to the required prophet. See further U. Simon, "Minor Characters in Biblical Narrative," *JSOT* 46 (1990), pp. 11–19.

He used to pour water on the hands of Elijah: What this means is not clear. The NIV's guess that it has something to do with Elisha's role as Elijah's servant is plausible. The context in which Elisha's association with **water** is mentioned is, however, one of a water shortage. Is there perhaps an allusion here, therefore, to a water-miracle that Elisha is known to have performed but that remains unrecorded in Kings?

3:15 / **Bring me a harpist:** The implication is that music plays its part in Elisha's attainment of the prophetic "state" in which he utters his prophecy (cf. the discussion on 1 Kgs. 18:25–29; and note particularly the connection between prophecy and music in 1 Sam. 10:5–11).

3:16 / **Make this valley full of ditches:** The Hb. may not be so much an instruction to the kings to dig ditches (to catch the water?) as a part of the prophecy about what God will do: "I will make this valley full of pools."

3:19 / **You will overthrow:** This unfortunate rendering of Hb. *nkh* obscures the fact that the same verb appears in v. 25 (where we are told that the Israelites "attacked" Kir Haresheth). In obscuring this connection it creates the impression that Elisha's prophecy about the cities was not fulfilled (**every . . . city** was not "overthrown"). In fact, however, the authors choose their words in v. 25 very carefully in order to show that the prophecy *was* fulfilled, even if the eventual outcome of the battle was not quite what might have been expected. The comprehensiveness of the victory is plotted aspect by aspect at the beginning of the verse (**every good field . . . all the springs . . . every good tree**), reference to "every city" being omitted only because the "attack" (*nkh*) on the final city is still to be described. It is then described in the second part of the verse, and at this point everything promised by Elisha has, strictly speaking, come to pass.

3:27 / **The fury against Israel was great:** The nature of the fury (Hb. *qeṣep*) is left unspecified. It has been a common assumption that it is divine rather than human wrath. But it is very difficult to believe that this is right. To argue, on the one hand, that the authors had in mind the wrath of the Moabite god Chemosh—see most recently J. B. Burns, "Why Did the Besieging Army Withdraw? (2 Reg 3:27)," *ZAW* 102 (1990), pp. 187–94—is to ignore everything we have read up to this point about the LORD alone being God and the "gods" having no real existence. These are truths that will shortly be reinforced by the story of Naaman in 2 Kgs. 5. The LORD has no rivals in heaven, and Chemosh is no god but merely a "detestable thing" (1 Kgs. 11:7). To argue, on the other hand, that it is the LORD's **fury** that is meant (cf. *qeṣep* in Deut. 29:28; Josh. 22:20) is to accept that the authors are allowing for a link between child sacrifice and divine action—as if this practice, which other passages describe as abhorrent to the LORD (cf. 2 Kgs. 16:3; 17:17; 21:6), was in this one instance acceptable. This, too, seems unlikely. It is much more likely that the **fury** is thought of as in the first instance human (cf. both the other places in Kings where Hb. *qṣp*, "to be angry," appears, 2 Kgs. 5:11; 13:19). Having failed to "break through to the king of Edom" (v. 26, perhaps implying that this was the weakest point in the forces surrounding him and the only way out), Mesha sacrifices. His troops respond to this desperate act with a superhuman **fury** that carries them to victory. This is not to ignore the fact, of course, that at another level it is certainly the LORD whose hand must be seen in this reversal for Israel, for it is always he who gives other nations their victories in Kings (cf., e.g., 2 Kgs. 5:1; 23:26–27; 24:1–4, 10–17). The Moabites' anger would have counted for nothing, had God not ordained that it should count for something.

The Moabite affair has further established Elisha's credentials as a prophet in the line of Elijah. Both are now firmly associated with the God who provides water at will (cf. 1 Kgs. 18), whether by orthodox means (wind and rain, 1 Kgs. 18:45) or not (neither wind nor rain, 2 Kgs. 3:17). In this chapter we shall read of a number of further miracles, both of provision and healing, that remind us of Elijah in the same way.

4:1–7 / The first of these is occasioned by a crisis facing the widow of a member of the prophetic groups under Elisha's leadership (cf. 2 Kgs. 2:1 ff; 4:38ff.; 6:1ff.). Her sons are to be taken as **slaves** in payment of debt (cf. Isa. 50:1; Neh. 5:4–5). Like the widow of Zarephath (1 Kgs. 17:7–16), she possesses only a small amount of **oil** (Hb. *šemen*, 17:12 and 2 Kgs. 4:2). As in the Elijah story, this small amount is transformed into an abundance; it fills all the **empty jars** the widow can find. The proceeds from the sale of this oil will leave the family enough to live on, even after the **debts** have been settled.

4:8–37 / The major part of the chapter is taken up with a story reminiscent of the sequel to the "widow narrative" of 1 Kings 17:7–16 (cf. 1 Kgs. 17:17–24). The same basic elements— miraculous provision; unexpected death; prophetic intervention and restoration to life—are woven into a quite different story. The provision in this case is not food for the son, but the son himself, conceived when the **husband** of Elisha's **Shunammite** hostess is considered too **old** to father a child in any natural way (vv. 8–17; cf. Gen. 18:1–15, where both parties are too old). It is a great blessing, fallen upon a woman who has acted admirably in looking after the LORD's prophet (cf. Matt. 10:41). Unexpected life gives way, however, to unforeseen death (vv. 18–21; cf. the additional note to v. 27). The woman makes haste to **Mount Carmel** (vv. 22–26), brushing aside the questions of both her husband

and Elisha's servant **Gehazi** (v. 26) in her anxiety to confront Elisha with her grief. She did not **ask** him **for a son;** why has he done this? The sentiments seem similar to those of the widow of Zarephath (1 Kgs. 17:18). Those words were, however, only of accusation. Implicit in the Shunammite's words is a confidence that Elisha will be willing and able to act—as her persistence in seeking his attendance at the scene reveals (v. 30). She is not willing to accept his plan to resurrect the boy from a distance by means of his **staff** (cf. the power of Moses' staff in Exod. 14:15ff.; 17:8ff.). She wants his personal attention. His presence does, in fact, prove crucial. Gehazi fails to evoke any response from the corpse (v. 31), just as those on Carmel had failed to draw a response from the "corpse" of Baal (**there was no sound or response,** Hb. *ʾên qôl wᵉʾên qešeḇ;* cf. 1 Kgs. 18:29). It is only Elisha's own **prayer** and mysterious actions that succeed in bringing the boy back to life (cf. the commentary on 1 Kgs. 17:19–23, and the additional note on v. 21; cf. also Heb. 11:35).

4:38–41 / The third miracle of the chapter is reminiscent of the story in 2 Kings 2:19–22. This time it is food, rather than water, that is unsatisfactory—an important issue in time of **famine** (the same famine, perhaps, as is mentioned in 2 Kgs. 8:1ff.). We do not know whether the mixture is really deadly in a literal sense—that is only what the men who have tasted it say. What is indisputable is that Elisha knows, in his wisdom, what to add to the **pot** to make everything all right—even though no one else knows what the cook originally put in (v. 39). He has remarkable insight, even into the various properties of plants. It is this that makes him a better cook than his **servant**—as he was a greater healer in 4:8–37.

4:42–44 / The final miracle also concerns provision for the "sons of the prophets" and their families, although they appear here simply as **the people.** A limited amount of food is once again multiplied (cf. 4:1–7), in the face of the **servant**'s incomprehension (v. 43), so that it not only meets the immediate need but also produces a surplus (cf. 4:7). It is the chapter's concluding demonstration that the LORD is a God who heals and provides; a God who brings life from death. It is also the final proof that the God of Elijah is now the God of Elisha. Elisha is unusually endowed with spiritual power and insight—as the marked contrast between his and his servant's healing, cooking, and providing illustrates. We hear echoes of this story, of course, in the feeding narratives in the Gospels (Matt. 14:13–21; 15:29–39; Mark 6:30–44; 8:1–10; Luke 9:10–17; John 6:1–15); in the face of incomprehension, food is multiplied to provide more than enough for all to eat.

Additional Notes §36

4:10 / **A small room on the roof:** Lit. "a small, walled upper room," similar to that in the widow of Zarephath's house (1 Kgs. 17:17–24) but perhaps permanent ("walled"). The **roof** is not explicitly mentioned in the Hb., but that is in all probability where the **room** was, since the construction of accommodation on these flat expanses is known from elsewhere in the OT (e.g., 2 Sam. 16:22). The upper room is in this story, as in 1 Kgs. 17, both the location of the miracle and a private place of prayer (cf. Matt. 6:6; Acts 9:36–43).

4:12 / **She stood before him:** That is, she stood before Gehazi, outside the room where Elisha was, with Gehazi acting as intermediary. It is only when the oracle is to be delivered that she comes closer and stands in the doorway (v. 15). Elisha's unwillingness to deal directly with this woman is seen elsewhere (cf. vv. 26, 29). It is her single-mindedness and persistence that sways him (vv. 26–27, 30).

4:13 / **Can we speak on your behalf?:** Elisha offers the woman unspecified benefits, through his patronage, from **the king** or **the commander of the army**—two of the most powerful people in the land. She has no need of their help, since she is living among her own kinsfolk and has their support and protection. This will not always be the case (2 Kgs. 8:1–6).

4:23 / **It's not the New Moon or the Sabbath:** The implication is that it was customary to consult prophets on rest days (cf. Amos 8:5). A further implication is that the father either does not know that his son is dead or does not believe that a prophet can do anything about it. The mother takes all the initiative in the story, refusing to discuss what has happened with anyone other than the one man who can help ("All is well," vv. 23, 26).

4:27 / **The LORD has hidden it from me:** Elisha did not know this would happen, even though prophets commonly foresaw events (cf. 1 Sam. 9:15; 1 Kgs. 14:5). This is a most interesting statement in view of what has just occurred in 2 Kgs. 3, where Elisha's knowledge of the future is similarly incomplete. God is not a vending machine that pours out oracles when primed with prophetic pennies. Even more striking is the woman's complaint about being misled (see the additional note to v. 28). She is quite clear that a promise of blessing, when unqualified by any warning of trouble, should work out in an uncomplicated way. The implication of Elisha's words in v. 16 was not only that she would see a child born but also that she would see that child grow up. Now she is here to accuse him of deceit. Elisha does not take refuge in pedantic quibbling about words ("I didn't actually say that"), but appears to accept his responsibility in the matter.

4:28 / **Don't raise my hopes:** What she actually said was "Don't *mislead* your servant" (v. 16), and it is that injunction, obscured by the NIV, that she now recalls. Hb. *šlh,* "to deceive," is attested in Aramaic (cf. the Tg. to Ps. 119:10; Job 12:16).

4:29 / **Tuck your cloak into your belt:** As the woman had arrived in great haste (v. 24), so Elisha sends Gehazi back in similar haste. His **cloak** is to be hitched up so that he can run (1 Kgs. 18:46), and he is not to be distracted or delayed. Urgent attention, however, is not enough. Attention by the right person is what is required. A number of Gospel passages seem to echo this story in different ways. Jesus' disciples are sent out on a pressing mission to heal the sick in Luke 10:1–12, and they are told not to greet anyone on the road (10:4). They, like Gehazi, fail to fulfill their assigned tasks (e.g., Matt. 17:14–21; Luke 9:37–43) and require Jesus' own presence. Some of Jesus' followers invest great faith in his ability to heal—and even to raise from the dead—when present (e.g., John 11:17–37; cf. also Mark 5:21–24, 35–43; Luke 7:11–17 for resurrection stories that pick up elements from 2 Kgs. 4). Nevertheless, the highest commendation is reserved for those who believe that only his words are necessary (e.g., Luke 7:1–10).

4:38 / **In that region:** The Hb. is lit. "in the land," referring not just to the region of Gilgal but to the land of Israel as a whole. From here to ch. 8 (cf. 8:1), the whole narrative takes place in the context of famine—something that is not unexpected in view of the condition of Israel's religion during this period (cf. Deut. 28:15ff., esp. vv. 21–24; 1 Kgs. 8:35, 37; 18:2). A general state of famine does not, of course, imply an absolute absence of food (e.g., 2 Kgs. 4:42ff.), any more than a general state of drought implies an absolute absence of water (cf. the additional note to 1 Kgs. 18:35).

§37 An Aramean is Healed (2 Kgs. 5:1–27)

The account of Elisha's miracles continues with the story of Naaman the Aramean, who is healed as he bathes in the river Jordan. It is yet another narrative that picks up themes from the Elijah story; the LORD is seen to be God, not only of Israelites, but also of foreigners (1 Kgs. 17:17–24) and is acknowledged as the only real God (1 Kgs. 18:20–40).

5:1–8 / The sovereignty of Israel's God over the whole world is announced right at the beginning of the story, as we are told that—whatever Naaman himself may think—his success in life comes to him as the LORD's gift (v. 1). If **Aram** has been **given victory,** it is only because the LORD has ordained it so (cf. the commentary on 2 Kgs. 3). The vanquished are not specified, but it may be that we are intended to think of Israel's defeat at Ramoth Gilead (1 Kgs. 22:29–36). Certainly there appears to be an uneasy truce (however it has come about) between Aram and Israel. There is sufficient quiet for Naaman to travel to Israel with his various gifts and his **letter** (vv. 5–6). There is sufficient tension, however, for the king of Israel to be concerned that the king of Aram, in sending Naaman, **is trying to pick a quarrel** (v. 7). Perhaps he is, for although the Aramean king knows (since Naaman has told him what **the girl from Israel had said,** v. 4) that it is a **prophet** that Naaman seeks in **Samaria** (v. 3), he omits this fact in his letter. Instead of going to the prophet, he confronts the king of Israel himself with the problem. The king, of course, is powerless to help. It is an impossible demand for someone who is not **God,** for someone who cannot **kill and bring back to life** (v. 7; cf. Deut. 32:39; 1 Sam. 2:6; Hos. 6:1–2). This is a significant statement in the context of the story as a whole—as we shall see in a moment. It recalls 2 Kings 4:8–37, where God has indeed "killed and brought back to life" and reminds us that there is no need for the tearing of **robes** (vv. 7–8; a sign of despair, as in 2 Kgs. 18:37, rather than grief, as in 2 Kgs. 2:12—though the two emotions need not be far apart), for the LORD is indeed active in Israel. But it also calls to mind that it is the LORD, and not the servant-prophet, who is in control of human destiny. The king has already learned this second lesson—somewhat painfully (2 Kgs. 3). It is precisely this fact, perhaps, that causes his despair. Or does he really not know what appears to be such common knowledge (v. 3): that Elisha is well able to deal with this crisis? Perhaps not. Second Kings 8:1–6 suggests that the king is only belatedly enlightened about what has been happening outside the political sphere.

5:9–12 / Like so many other characters in Kings, Naaman seems to think that prophets are very much in control of their prophetic gift, able to say and do as they choose, and having a responsibility to please their superiors (e.g., 1 Kgs. 22:13). He has come to see someone who, he has been told (v. 3), has the power to **cure** him. He has prepared the ground carefully, using diplomacy and bringing great wealth. A great man (v. 1), sweeping up to Elisha's door with his **horses and chariots** (v. 9), he expects personal and immediate attention (v. 11)—a healing "on **the spot**"! He had not reckoned on being addressed only through an intermediary (a **messenger,** v. 10) and sent on somewhere else. This is surely no way to treat such an important person! What is worse, Elisha seems to be speaking, not about healing, but only about ritual cleansing (see the additional note on v. 12). He could have found that at home in the rivers **Abana and Pharpar.** Feeling let down, he goes off **in a rage** (v. 12). To Naaman, the LORD is only a local deity at the beck and call of the prophet. It is the prophet who is the healer, not the god. Why has he refused to do his job?

5:13–19 / **Naaman's servants,** more accustomed to being treated in such humbling ways, prevail upon him to do as he has been told, and he is miraculously cured. The humble have once again exhibited more insight than the exalted (cf. the additional note to 2 Kgs. 3:11). The healing is enough to convince Naaman that the LORD is not simply one god among many (v. 11), but is the only God: **Now I know that there is no God in all the world except in Israel** (v. 15; cf. Deut. 32:39 again for the connection between God's uniqueness and ability to kill and bring life, wound and heal). But why has Naaman come to believe this? He had been convinced all along that he would be healed; that is why he came to Israel. Why has the event, now that it has happened in the Jordan rather than outside Elisha's house, made such an impression on him? The point of the delay now becomes clear. He had looked to the *prophet* for a cure, based on the words of his Israelite informant (v. 3). The way the cure has been wrought, however, has made it clear to him that Elisha's god is not simply a convenient metaphor for unnatural prophetic powers but a living person. Healing has not come via a semi–magical wave of the prophetic hand (v. 11). It has been delivered by the living LORD, at a distance from the prophet. It is the directness of God's action that has convinced Naaman of God's reality—and it was necessary to take him to the Jordan if he was to experience that directness. Ambiguity would have remained, had Elisha been involved.

The lesson learned, Elisha is keen to drive it home. He refuses to accept any **gift;** for that is to trade in Naaman's old currency. It is the living **LORD,** and not Elisha, who must take center stage. Naaman's response reveals his grasp of what has happened. He will **never again make burnt offerings and sacrifices to any other god** (v. 17). He will instead worship the living God, focusing that worship (we deduce) upon an altar made of **earth** taken from God's special land (cf. Exod. 20:24 for earthen altars). The Syrian god **Rimmon** (another name for Hadad, the god of storm and thunder) is now clearly understood to be a mere idol, and Naaman's "worship" of Rimmon will be restricted to those unavoidable occasions when he is found in Rimmon's **temple** in the course of official duties (v. 18; cf. 2 Kgs. 7:2, 17).

5:20–27 / **Gehazi,** on the other hand, has not grasped the meaning of what has happened, or does not care. His "grasping" is of a baser sort. He pursues profit (vv. 20–21). He concocts a story that is designed to explain Elisha's change of heart (he has two new arrivals to provide for, v. 22). It is a clever ploy, for the amount requested is not excessive in relation to the massive sum Naaman was originally prepared to pay (v. 5)—**one talent of silver** and **two sets of clothing** out of ten. Refraining from asking too much (and particularly from asking for any gold), he is unlikely to arouse suspicion. And so it proves. Unsuspecting Naaman gladly divests himself of his goods. Presumably Gehazi has calculated that Elisha will not be aware of what has happened. He knows, after all, that the LORD sometimes conceals things from him (4:27). Unfortunately for him, however, Elisha has on this occasion "seen" only too clearly, and judgment is fierce, as Naaman's disease becomes Gehazi's and he turns **as white as snow** (v. 27). The fierceness is unsurprising, given the heinousness of the crime. Gehazi has sought to cash in on an act of God (cf. Josh. 7; Acts 8:18–24). He utters words that imply belief but does not have faith (as the LORD lives, v. 20; contrast v. 16, with its significant addition "whom I serve"). His aspirations to wealth and status (**olive groves, vineyards,** etc.; cf. the royal wealth of 1 Sam. 8:14–17, and particularly the verb *lqḥ,* **take,** as here) have led him to forget the LORD (Deut. 6:10–12). His initial "investment" for his future (**money, clothes**) has garnered only negative interest.

Additional Notes §37

5:1 / **Leprosy:** The Hb. is *meṣōrāʿ,* a participial form of the verb ṣrʿ, which appears also in vv. 11 and 27. The noun connected with this verb (*ṣāraʿat*) is found in vv. 3, 6, 7, and 27. Leviticus 13–14 indicates that the reference is to a wide range of patchy disfigurements of skin or material, which may or may not have included what is commonly called leprosy today (Hansen's disease). Given our ignorant state, "skin disease" is a much safer translation in 2 Kgs. 5 (cf. the NIV footnote). What kind of ṣāraʿat Naaman's disease actually was is, of course, inconsequential in terms of understanding the narrative. Much more important is knowing that ṣāraʿat signified to the Hb. reader ritual uncleanness (Lev. 13–14) and the judgment of God (Num. 12:1–15; 2 Sam. 3:28–29; 2 Kgs. 15:5). Naaman is one who is in every sense "outside the camp"—a foreigner and a leper as well. Yet God has been and will be gracious to him, and God's judgment will fall on the "insider" Gehazi (cf. also Ahaziah in 2 Kgs. 1, like Naaman, seeking help in a foreign land, but in the wrong place and of the wrong god). There is an inclusiveness here that is also found in Isa. 56:1–8 and throughout the NT. We may note in particular Luke 4:27, where Jesus provokes anger among his hearers by reminding them that, although there were many in Israel with "leprosy" (cf. 2 Kgs. 7:3ff.), only the foreigner Naaman was healed. The cleansing of lepers also appears as a NT theme in Matt. 8:1–4; 10:8; 11:5; Mark 1:40–45; Luke 5:12–16; 7:22; 17:11–19.

5:3 / **The prophet who is in Samaria:** There is the usual ambiguity here. Does **Samaria** mean the city or the region of which the city is capital (i.e., Israel; cf. the commentary on 1 Kgs. 16:23–28)? A curious numerical link (cf. the additional note on 1 Kgs. 22:30) suggests that it is the former. There are only two references in Kings to "two talents of silver." One such sum is carried by Gehazi to his home (2 Kgs. 5:23–24). The other is paid by Omri for "the hill of Samaria" (1 Kgs. 16:24). Since

Samaria was evidently built in conscious rivalry to Jerusalem, it is not surprising that it too should have an acropolis (Hb. *ʿōpel,* NIV's "hill," 2 Kgs. 5:24; cf. Isa. 32:14; Mic. 4:8; 2 Chron. 27:3; 33:14; Neh. 3:26–27; 11:21, for the only other uses of *ʿōpel* in regard to a city).

5:10 / **Wash yourself seven times:** Seven days is the period of quarantine prescribed for those with various skin diseases in Lev. 13–14 (cf. 13:4, 5, etc.), and such legislation may be influencing the choice of words in this verse. At the same time, there is another numerical link here, this time with the story of the Shunammite woman in 2 Kgs. 4:8–37, whose son, in the course of his "healing," sneezed seven times (Hb. *šebaʿ peʿāmîm,* 4:35). This is by no means the only link between these two narratives. Both involve Elisha, Gehazi and a "great" person in need (cf. "great [NIV's well-to-do] woman" in 4:8; "great man" in 5:1); in both, intermediaries interpose themselves between the prophet and the great person (4:11–16, 25–27; 5:9–12, 19–22), though with varying results; in both, we find question and answer concerning whether all is well, with the answer disguising the truth (4:26; 5:21–22); in both, the king and the commander of the army appear as the epitome of wealth and power (4:13; 5:4–12).

5:12 / **Couldn't I wash in them and be cleansed?:** These words distinctly evoke the cleansing ritual of Lev. 13–14, Hb. *rḥṣ* (**wash**) appearing in 14:8–9 and Hb. *ṭhr* (**be cleansed**) in 13:7, 35; 14:2, 23, 32. Naaman's complaint is that he came to have the leprosy removed and has been offered ritual cleansing instead. In his anger, he has failed to listen carefully to what the prophet has said: note the significant omission of "your flesh will be restored," when compared with v. 10. Fortunately for him, his servants have been more attentive and are able to persuade him to reconsider his hasty interpretation of Elisha's words (see the additional note to v. 13).

5:13 / **If the prophet had told you . . . :** The servants' words are much better rendered thus: "The prophet has spoken an impressive word/great thing. Will you not do it? Has he really said (Hb. *ʾap kî-ʾāmar*) to you, 'Wash and be cleansed'?" As in Gen. 3:1, the phrase *ʾap kî-ʾāmar* is designed to provoke discussion about what was really said. In this case, the servants seek to undermine a false interpretation of Elisha's words (he spoke only of ritual cleansing) in order that a true interpretation will prevail (he spoke of a cure, using the language of ritual cleansing; cf. the similar play on the notions of ritual cleansing and true "health" in Luke 17:11–19). The fulfillment of Elisha's promise in v. 10 ("your flesh will be restored") was put in jeopardy by the poor listening skills of a great, but impatient, man (v. 12); it is made possible again by the subtle, suggestive speech of the humble (appropriate to servants approaching a master in a rage, v. 13) and duly comes to pass in v. 14.

5:14 / **A young boy:** The Hb. is *naʿar qāṭōn,* and there is evidently a play on the phrase *naʿarâ qeṭannâ,* "young girl," in v. 2. The "great man" (v. 1) had a problem, to which the "young girl" had the solution, but it involved Naaman becoming, like her, "a little child." He is transformed, in the course of the story, from someone under the king of Aram's authority, standing on his own dignity, into someone under prophetic authority, humbly acknowledging his new faith. He, much more than Gehazi, is now a servant of Elisha (cf. *na ʿar* in v. 20) and of the LORD. See further R. D. Moore, *God Saves: Lessons from the Elisha Stories,* JSOTSup (Sheffield: JSOT Press, 1990), pp. 71–84. Various NT themes are evoked here, all clustering around the question of conversion. New birth is required to see the kingdom of God (John 3:1–8), which is inhabited by little children (those who humbly serve) and not by the great or the wealthy (Matt. 18:1–5; 19:13–15; Mark 9:33–37; 10:13–16; Luke 9:46–48; 18:15–17). The rite of passage into new life is a washing that makes one truly clean (Rom. 6:1–5; 1 Cor. 6:11; Col. 2:11–15; Titus 3:4–7). Naaman embodies new life, and Gehazi embodies the old, crying "LORD, LORD" (v. 20) while his actions reveal where his heart really lies (Matt. 6:19–24; 7:21–23). From this point of view, Jehoram's words about life and death in relation to Naaman (v. 7) begin to look prophetic.

5:18 / **May the LORD forgive:** The language is reminiscent of 1 Kgs. 8:22–53, the only other section of Kings thus far in which this Hb. verb *slḥ,* forgive, has been used (8:30, 34, 36, 39, 50; cf. 2 Kgs. 24:4 for the only other occurrence in the book). Of particular interest are 1 Kgs. 8:41–43, where Solomon, considering the case of the foreigner who prays towards the temple, asks God to do whatever the foreigner asks. Elisha's "Go in peace" (2 Kgs. 5:19) suggests a broad interpretation of the LORD's forgiveness. Naaman would find it even in the midst of sin, as he worshiped another god. Many later Jews and Christians have not found it so easy to accept this kind of compromise and have insisted that public and private life must be integrated if faith is to mean anything at all (cf. Jewish opposition to Hellenisation during the Maccabean period; Christian refusal to worship the Roman emperor in the early Christian centuries). It has never been easy to know exactly what the injunction "flee from idolatry" requires (cf. 1 Cor. 8:1–10:33), particularly when it is combined with commands such as "live at peace with everyone" (Rom. 12:18) and "submit to the governing authorities" (Rom. 13:1).

5:26 / **Is this the time to take money . . . ?:** A similar question is asked of his compatriots by Haggai (1:4), when they are found putting their own interests before those of the LORD. That is the point here as well. The servant of God must serve in a disinterested way, so that the observer is not hindered from giving glory to God.

§38 Miracles, Trivial and Significant (2 Kgs. 6:1–23)

Elisha's prophetic activity thus far has been of a relatively private character (2 Kgs. 2:19–25; 4:1–44). Prior to chapter 5, there was just that single excursion into the wider world in chapter 3. We know, however, that it is his destiny to be a pivotal figure in the drama of international politics between Israel and Aram (1 Kgs. 19:15–18). His contact with Aram began in chapter 5 and will now occupy most of our attention for the next two chapters, as we are prepared for the bloody events of 2 Kings 8–10. Second Kings 6:8–23 shows Elisha fully drawn into the politics of the region, yet always in control of events, as he mediates God's power in the midst of war. God's purposes are working out, even if Ahab's house has not quite met its end. Lest we forget that Elisha's ministry embraced the humble as well as the great, and so that we have a sense of the time that passed between 5:27 and 6:8, a short story about an iron tool is first interposed. "God saves" individual Israelites as well as Israel. God's purposes take in the "trivial" as well as the "significant."

6:1–7 / Of the "sons of the **prophets**" already mentioned, it is the Gilgal group that is assuredly in view here (2 Kgs. 4:38–41; cf. in particular their "meeting" with Elisha, Hb. *yšb lipnê*, in 4:38 and 6:1). A new meeting place is being built—the NIV's **place . . . to live** (for Hb. *māqôm lāšebet*) overstates the building's function (cf. Gen. 43:33; Ezek. 8:1)—and someone drops a **borrowed iron** implement (**axhead** is a plausible guess) in the **water**. Elisha has experience in manipulating waters, however (2 Kgs. 2:14), and he is able to make **the iron float** like the piece of wood he has thrown in beside it. It is an amazing event, though not in the least surprising to those who have read of the raising of the dead (4:8–37).

6:8–14 / Relations between Aram and Israel have deteriorated since 2 Kings 5:1ff., and the kings are once more **at war.** It seems at first sight (but see the additional note to 6:9) that relations between the Israelite king and the prophet have improved since 2 Kings 3 (cf. 3:13–15); Elisha is now voluntarily offering Jehoram the benefit of his prophetic gift. He is the "fly on the wall" of the Aramean king's own **bedroom** (v. 12), able to hear even his most intimate words. **Enraged,** the king orders his men to **find out where** Elisha **is** so that he can **capture him.** It is testimony to his plight, of course, that he does not know where Elisha is, whereas Elisha always knows where he is! It is also testimony to his befuddled thinking that he seeks to resolve his difficulty over troop movements by moving troops. Does he really think that Elisha will not "see" what is happening? Does he really think that he can constrain God's prophet by force? The reader knows otherwise (cf. 1 Kgs. 13:1–6; 18:9–14; 2 Kgs. 1:2–17).

6:15–23 / The king of Aram cannot see what Elisha can see. It is, nevertheless, the case that Elisha is found, when morning breaks, inside a city (Dothan, about 11 miles north of Samaria) surrounded by Aramean troops. Has his prophetic gift failed (cf. 4:27; and note the need for the question in 6:6)? He seems unperturbed, and it quickly becomes apparent why. Arameans may surround the city, as his anxious **servant** sees only too well (v. 15), but Elisha himself is surrounded by the army of the LORD (v. 17; cf. the additional note to 2:11). The Arameans, though they do not know it, are outnumbered (v. 16). Their blindness to the odds is quickly compounded by a **blindness** (Hb. *sanwērîm,* v. 18; cf. Gen. 19:11) to their surroundings, which puts them entirely at the mercy of the seer they had come to capture. Dependent upon him for guidance, they are led to the Israelite capital, where they too (like the **servant**) move from "blindness" to "sight," and discover they have been captured (v. 20, cf. v. 17). Jehoram wants to **kill them;** is this an attempt to avoid his father's mistake in 1 Kings 20? The circumstances, however, are not the same. Jehoram would not kill men **captured** with his own **sword or bow,** Elisha claims—and these are not even men like that. After a **great feast,** they are accordingly sent home, and there is a peace between Aram and Israel that transcends the uneasy peace described in 5:1ff. Arameans no longer venture into **Israel's territory** (cf. the **bands** of raiders in 5:2), not even in large groups sent by the king himself (6:14). When they come again it will be in the "safety" of overwhelming numbers (6:24ff.).

Additional Notes §38

6:9 / **The man of God sent word:** Are we meant to think that since Elisha offers Jehoram his help and the king adopts a respectful attitude in v. 21, something has altered in the king-prophet relationship since 2 Kgs. 3? The evidence does not support such an interpretation. Jehoram is quite prepared throughout his story to treat prophets properly when things are going well (as here). He is not quite so ready to do so when things are going badly (cf. 2 Kgs. 6:24–33). There is no evidence, on the other hand, that Elisha, or the authors, have changed their views about Jehoram since 2 Kgs. 3. He is an idolater throughout his reign, suffering those things that we expect wicked kings to suffer (reverses in war, 2 Kgs. 3; famine, 4:38; 8:1; siege, 6:24ff.; cf. Deut. 28:15ff.; 1 Kgs. 8:33–40), destined for the final judgment that Elisha will initiate in 2 Kgs. 9:1ff. If Elisha intervenes to help him, it is not because anything has changed. It is only because God has ordained that it is not yet the end.

6:17 / **The hills:** The Hb. is singular ("hill") and in the context must refer to the hill upon which the city is standing rather than the hills outside the city. The Arameans surround (Hb. *sbb*, v. 15) the city; but heavenly forces surround (Hb. *sᵉbîbōt*, v. 17) Elisha.

6:18 / **Blindness:** In view of vv. 19–20, this is probably not physical blindness, but rather a dazed condition. The Arameans are open to the suggestion and manipulation of the prophet, but they can still see well enough to follow him to Samaria.

§39 The Siege of Samaria (2 Kgs. 6:24–7:20)

The Aramean threat has been hanging over Israel for some time. The uneasy peace of 2 Kings 5 gave way in chapter 6 to sporadic Aramean raids into Israelite territory—themselves curtailed because of the events of 6:18ff. There has been an accumulating tension; it is no surprise to read of full-blown invasion, as the king of Aram, long anxious for a fight (5:7), encamps his army at the very gates of Samaria. Our only question is how long Elisha will continue to help doomed Jehoram. It is perfectly clear by this stage that Jehoram cannot help himself (5:7; 6:8–10). Is this siege, then, to be the context in which the house of Ahab finally meets its allotted end (1 Kgs. 21:21–24)? Or are we to wait yet longer for Elijah's prophecy about the end to be fulfilled?

6:24–33 / The second siege of Samaria by **Ben-Hadad, king of Aram,** is significantly more serious than the first (cf. the additional note on 1 Kgs. 20:1) and inflicts much greater hardship on the population. There is a **famine** so severe that one **woman** has been driven to the unthinkable. She has resorted to cannibalism—her own (already dead?) **son** the meal. Jehoram, as always, is powerless to **help** (Hb. *yšᶜ*, "to save," vv. 26–27), lacking both grain **from the threshing floor** and wine **from the winepress.** Only the LORD who provides such things can save, as Jehoram himself affirms at the reminding of the prophet whose name embodies this truth (Hb. *ᵓelîšāᶜ*, "God saves"). The only proper response in the face of **disaster . . . from the LORD** is to **wait** for deliverance (v. 33; cf. Lam. 3, esp. vv. 24–30). Jehoram has thus far adopted such an attitude, even wearing the **sackcloth** his father Ahab wore when humbling himself before the LORD (v. 30; cf. 1 Kgs. 21:27). Faced with the horror about which he has just been told, however, the king is unwilling to wait any longer—even to settle the dispute that has been presented to him by the woman. The humility of his father gives way to the bloodthirstiness of his mother, as he takes her kind of oath on his lips (v. 31; cf. 1 Kgs. 19:2) and sends a man "from his presence" (better than the NIV's **ahead,** v. 32) to remove Elisha's head from **his shoulders.** It is strange that he should invoke the name of God in threatening to make a donkey of God's prophet (cf. v. 25), just as it is curious that he thinks he has any other option than waiting (cf. his stated position in v. 27—only the LORD can help). Once again, we are made to wonder about the nature of Je-horam's "faith," already questioned by the authors in 2 Kings 3:2–3 and by Elisha in 2 Kings 3:13. Does he too believe that prophets are in control of their own and others' destinies (cf. Naaman in ch. 5)—in spite of his words in verse 27? Does he think that removing Elisha will remove the problem?

7:1–2 / Fortunately for Elisha, on this occasion his prophetic sight does forewarn him about events, and he is able to bar the door against the assassin. Communication ensues. The king, Elisha promises, will have to wait no longer: salvation is imminent. Normal business **at the gate of Samaria** will be resumed on the morrow. Produce worth eating will change hands at much lower prices (cf. the prices in 6:25). Jehoram's impatience is now matched by his officer's skepticism that such an economic recovery **could happen** overnight, in the aftermath of such a terrible siege. Where will the sudden abundance come from? What Elisha prophecies is inconceivable, yet his words seem to be sufficient to deflect the king's anger. His head remains on his shoulders (cf. 6:31). The king's **officer,** however, is not allowed to leave without a further word about his own fate (v. 2). What is possible for God cannot be measured in terms of what is conceivable to mortals. The officer will **see** the miracle happen, but he himself will not **eat.** Salvation for the people will involve judgment for this one man, for to mock the prophetic word is to mock the LORD.

7:3–11 / A leper had first brought the Arameans to Samaria during Jehoram's reign (2 Kgs. 5:1–7), and **four men with leprosy** (see the additional note on 5:1) now drive them away. Faced with certain death if they **go into the city** or **stay** where they are (v. 4), these men instead choose possible death in **the camp of the Arameans.** They are only four lepers; but seen in the half-light of **dusk,** with **the sound of chariots and horses and a great army** in the background (v. 6; cf. 6:17), they are perceived by the Arameans to be Hittite and Egyptian kings (note the play

on words between Hb. *miṣōrā'îm,* "lepers" and *miṣrayim,* "Egypt").
Supernaturally deceived into thinking that they are faced with a
mercenary army, the Arameans flee from the field, abandoning
their possessions where they lie (v. 7). The lepers simply walk
into their camp as unwitting victors. Their first thought is for
themselves (v. 8), but their second thought is more noble—or is,
at least, self-centered in a less damaging way. Mindful of the
likelihood of **punishment,** whether human or divine, if they keep
the **good news** to themselves until morning, they report to the
city gatekeepers.

7:12–20 / The news of the Aramean retreat is at first
greeted with suspicion; Jehoram suspects a trap. **Some men** are
sent out on what will be (if he is right) a suicide mission—though
their fate in this case will be no different to that of the other
doomed inhabitants of the city (v. 13). They are to **find out what
has happened** (v. 14). They follow the route of the retreating
army as far as the Jordan—a retreat in the direction of Ramoth
Gilead is perhaps presupposed—finding only **clothing and
equipment** (v. 15). This is no tactical withdrawal, but a true retreat. General plunder of the Aramean camp ensues (v. 16), with
the consequence that economic conditions in Samaria immediately improve. The skeptical officer—ironically stationed at the
very **gate** where he had anticipated seeing no trade (v. 2)—is
trampled in the scramble to acquire goods (vv. 17–20), fulfilling
Elisha's prophecy that he would not share in the bounty. He has
stood in the way of God's salvation, as kings and their officials
often do in these Elisha stories, and he has died in a rush of
judgment, a mocker of God's prophet (cf. 2 Kgs. 2:23–25). It is the
humble—in this case the lepers—who are the channels of God's
blessing to Israel.

Additional Notes §39

6:25 / **A donkey's head . . . seed pods:** The extremity of the
situation, confirmed by the woman's awful story in 6:26ff., is already
evident in the Hb. from the reference here to the "food" that was
available, although it is somewhat obscured by the NIV's **seed pods** for
Hb.'s "pigeon droppings." The point is that there was really nothing at
all worth speaking of to eat—thus the cannibalism, which is hinted at or

explicitly described as a consequence of siege in other places in the OT (Deut. 28:53–57; Lam. 2:20; 4:10; Ezek. 5:10).

6:26 / **Help me, my LORD the king:** The plea is directed to the king as the ultimate court of human justice, as in 1 Kgs. 3:16–28, where we also find two woman in dispute over a surviving son. We have travelled far in Israel's story, however, from the glorious era when a wise king could ensure justice. See further S. Lasine, "Jehoram and the Cannibal Mothers (2 Kings 6:24–33): Solomon's Judgment in an Inverted World," *JSOT* 50 (1991), pp. 27–53.

6:32 / **The elders were sitting with him:** As the sons of the prophets seem to have gathered to listen to the prophet, so here the elders of Samaria are gathered in Elisha's house (cf. the similar scene in Ezek. 8:1; 20:1).

6:33 / **The messenger . . . the king:** The NIV gives the impression that the king is present during this interchange. This interpretation may be influenced by 7:17–18, which says that the king "came down" to Elisha and that he spoke the prophecy "to the king." There is no **king** in the Hb. text of v. 33, however. The words are certainly his but they are spoken by the **messenger** he has sent. We are no doubt to understand that the king arrives shortly after his hit man (cf. "footsteps behind him" in v. 32), at which point the prophecy that Elisha has directed to him is reported to him by the messenger, and the conversation in 7:2 ensues.

7:2 / **The floodgates of the heavens:** The NIV unaccountably translates Hb. *ʾᵃrubbôt* as **floodgates** in this verse, but as "windows" in v. 19. The imagery is that of God handing out (through the windows) unexpected material blessings from his heavenly storehouse (cf. Mal. 3:10; Ps. 78:23). It will need a miracle of great proportions—similar to God's provision of manna in the wilderness (Exod. 16:4ff.)—if economic conditions are to stabilize in the way Elisha describes, and Jehoram's officer simply does not believe that it is possible. Ironically, the miracle does not come via "windows" in the heavens (*ʾᵃrubbôt*) but via four (Hb. *ʾarbāʿâ*) rather more mundane lepers.

7:3 / **At the entrance of the city gate:** We are never told why they found themselves at the **city gate,** but there is certainly no hint (as some commentators have claimed) that they are in some kind of quarantine because of their disease (cf. Lev. 13:11, 46). They consider the possibility of going into the city (v. 4), implying that they have the freedom to do so.

7:13 / **Five of the horses:** It is unclear whether **five** is an exact or a round number ("a few") and whether the action of v. 14 is to be taken as corresponding to the suggestion of v. 13 in every detail. If five is literally meant, and five horses actually went, then some of them were spares, whether the Hb. *šᵉnê rekeb sûsîm* in v. 14 is understood as "two chariots with their horses" (i.e., four horses) or as "two mounted men" (i.e., two horses).

§40 The End (of Ahab) is Nigh (2 Kgs. 8:1–29)

The tension has become almost unbearable. In spite of Ahijah's prophecy that Israel would be like a reed swaying in the water (1 Kgs. 14:15), the house of Omri has held the throne since 1 Kings 16:23. In spite of Elijah's prophecy about the end of this house (1 Kgs. 21:21–24), we are now reading of Ahab's second apostate son, who holds on to his kingdom with the help of Elijah's successor. Did Elijah sabotage God's plan by failing to anoint Hazael and Jehu (1 Kgs. 19:15–18)? Will Elisha continue forever to be a conduit for God's salvation to Jehoram, or will he at last show himself to be a "son of judgment" (cf. the Hb. root *špṭ*, "to judge," which lies behind his father's name, Shaphat)? The hints are increasing that the end is, in fact, nigh. The last story saw judgment in the midst of salvation, as Jehoram's officer died because he doubted whether prophecy could come to pass (7:2, 17ff.). Jehoram himself was found complaining about God's tardiness (6:33)—albeit in salvation, not in judgment. Chapter 8 now adds to this sense of imminence by (at last) introducing us to Hazael. We are on the edge of fulfillment. But there are loose ends to be tied up before we can go on. We must hear the end of the Shunammite's story, and we must catch up with happenings in Judah. Only then can we proceed with the story of Jehu, the destroyer of the house of Ahab.

8:1–6 / Throughout the Elisha story he has been portrayed as a channel of God's salvation, not only to Israel in general, but also to Israelite and foreign individuals (cf. 2 Kgs. 4–5; 6:1–7). Now, after the long narrative about the siege of Samaria but before we hear of Hazael, we are told again about the Shunammite woman of 4:8–37. The key to understanding this new story appears to be 4:13, where Elisha makes her an offer of help. The woman declines, for she has "a home among [her] own people." In 8:1–6, however, she no longer has such a home; she has followed Elisha's advice and avoided **famine** by sojourning in Philistia. While she has been away, someone seems to have taken her land. Perhaps it is even Jehoram himself, showing the same land-grabbing proclivities as his parents (cf. 1 Kgs. 21). Providentially, however, just at the moment she arrives at the royal court after **seven** long **years** to **beg for her house and land,** Gehazi is telling the king all about her. His words serve as the advocacy on her behalf that Elisha had had in mind in 4:13; and the king takes steps to ensure the return, not only of **everything that belonged to her,** but also of **all the income from her land** that she would have received had she stayed in the country. God looks after those who look after his prophets (Matt. 10:40–42).

8:7–15 / Elisha first became involved with Aram when an Aramean ventured into Samaria. His dealings with them now come to an end, as he himself ventures into the Aramean capital of **Damascus. Ben-Hadad** is **ill** and more concerned to gain a prognosis about his future than to get revenge for the past. There is evident irony in the fact that a foreign king knows well enough to **consult the LORD** (v. 8) in such circumstances, whereas the Israelite Ahaziah had sought the opinion of Baal-Zebub (2 Kgs. 1:2). **Hazael** is sent with an extravagant **gift** (**forty camel-loads** of **wares**) to smooth his way. His approach is respectful, like a **son** to his father (v. 9; cf. 2 Kgs. 6:21). The answer he receives is puzzling (see the additional note to v. 10), but the general thrust is that Ben-Hadad is going to **die** (v. 10). Hazael receives more information than he expects, however, for Elisha sees beyond Ben-Hadad's death into Aram's future—a future in which Hazael will be **king** and will inflict great suffering on Israel (vv. 12–13) as he ravages the land and brutalizes the people (cf. Amos 1:13; Hos. 13:16; 2 Kgs. 15:16). Elijah's failure to anoint Hazael will not thwart the LORD's purposes after all (cf. 1 Kgs. 19:15–18). Elijah was not even crucial to God's plans in *this* respect, for Hazael succeeds to the throne without his help. Hazael smothers his master with a wet **cloth** (if that is what the unique Hb. word in v. 15 means) and somehow (we are not given the details) takes power.

8:16–24 / We last heard of Judah in 2 Kings 3, when Jehoshaphat was involved in the ill-fated campaign against Moab. We now return to Judah to learn of **Jehoram son of Jehoshaphat**—first introduced briefly in 1 Kings 22:50 and then mentioned again in 2 Kings 1:17. After two relatively righteous kings (Asa and Jehoshaphat), Judah has a monarch who shares with his Israelite counterpart not only a name (see the additional note to 2 Kgs. 3:1) but also a liking for idolatry. Indeed, Jehoram (and his successor) are apparently worse than their northern neighbor, if the phrase **walked in the ways of the kings of Israel, as the house of Ahab had done** is intended to refer (as 2 Kgs. 11:17–18 implies) not only to idolatry of Jeroboam's kind, the worship of golden calves, but to the worship of Baal (contrast 2 Kgs. 3:2–3). The disease of Ahab's household, carried south by **his daughter** (v. 18), has proved infectious. Intermarriage has again wreaked its havoc (1 Kgs. 11:1ff.; 16:31–33).

Judah is in a very different position than is Israel, nevertheless. We do not expect to find a prophet springing into a narrative about a Judean king and uttering dire threats against David's house. God has promised David a **lamp** (1 Kgs. 11:36; 15:4). Sins are to be punished by the "rod of men" rather than by rejection (2 Sam. 7:14–16)—all the kings of Judah are suffering because of Solomon's sins in this period of "humbling" for David (cf. 1 Kgs. 11:39; 15:16–22; 22:48–49). In this context, it is no surprise to find that **the LORD was not willing to destroy Judah** because of Jehoram's sins. Nor is it any surprise, however, to find Jehoram facing, and failing to subdue, rebellion by **Edom** (vv. 20–22)—a country hitherto ruled by a Judean appointee (1 Kgs. 22:47; 2 Kgs. 3:8ff.) but now seeking self-determination. Not even righteous Judean kings can in these days emulate Solomon in his grand imperial designs (1 Kgs. 15:16–22; 22:48–49); how much less can this wicked monarch expect to do so? His fate is exactly that of his northern namesake, who was ultimately unable to subdue Moab (2 Kgs. 3). It is worse, in fact; his only "victory" is to escape **by night** from an Edomite ambush (see the additional note on verse 21). The "empire" that remains to Israel is gradually contracting. Even cities within Judah itself are showing signs of unrest (cf. **Libnah**, v. 22—a city southwest of Jerusalem, near the Philistine border).

8:25–29 / **Ahaziah**—like his father, Jehoram—has habits of religion that match those of his family **by marriage.** The influence on this occasion comes from his mother **Athaliah**—the daughter of Ahab (though lit. "daughter of Omri," which must mean **granddaughter,** in v. 26), we assume, who is mentioned in verse 18. We anticipate that the Davidic promise will hold good for Jehoram's son as well as for his father. It is not explicitly repeated, however, and it is somewhat disconcerting to read in verse 26 that Ahaziah **reigned** only **one year**. Did he die without an heir, we begin to ask? What of the Davidic line after him? It is particularly troubling when we read in verse 25 that he came to the throne in Jehoram of Israel's **twelfth year,** for we know from 2 Kings 3:1 that Jehoram ruled for only twelve years. We are in the last moments of the house of Ahab. Is the house of David, mixed up with Ahab's house through marriage, to be caught up in the coming judgment after all? Or will the promise to David hold? The answer is difficult to determine throughout 2 Kings 9–10, as Ahaziah, visiting Jehoram in **Jezreel** in the aftermath of another joint campaign against **Ramoth Gilead** (vv. 28–29), is caught up in Jehoram's troubles.

Additional Notes §40

8:1 / **The Lord has decreed a famine:** We have already heard of a general state of **famine** in the land in 4:38, and we are presumably to understand, therefore, that the warning cited here was given to the woman around the same time that Elisha restored her son to life. We should distinguish this general state of famine from the **famine** in the city of Samaria (6:25 and 7:4), which seems to be a result of, rather than a circumstance preceding, the siege. The implication is that before the seige the city itself had not been suffering from hunger to the same extent as the rest of the country.

8:4 / **Gehazi:** Why Gehazi is to be found talking with the king is never made apparent. Nor is it clear whether, in spite of the events of ch. 5, he is still **the servant of the man of God** or whether the title is being used loosely of his previous employment. There is absolutely no indication that he has recovered from his "leprosy," as some commentators have argued.

8:8 / **Hazael:** Hazael's entrance into the narrative is a little mysterious. We are not told his lineage or even his role (servant? officer?). He comes from nowhere, a "mere dog" as he puts it, the "son of nobody" according to an Assyrian source (cf. *ANET,* p. 280).

8:10 / **Go and say to him, "You will certainly recover":** As the NIV rightly points out in its footnote, it is possible to read the Hb. here in such a way as to transform Elisha's message to Ben-Hadad into its opposite: "You will certainly not recover." The ambiguity is caused by the Hb. word *lōʾ,* which is normally a negative of some kind, but which sometimes appears in the OT as a variant for *lô,* "to him" (e.g. Isa. 9:13)—the reading that the Masoretic scribes wish us to read here (cf. further GKC §103g) and that a number of Hb. MSS contain. It is therefore not entirely evident whether or not Elisha is once again speaking less than the whole truth (cf. the commentary on 2 Kgs. 3; and note in particular the similarity in this case with Micaiah, who in 1 Kgs. 22:14–17 first speaks what is not true, and then what is true). The motivation for such a deception (**You will certainly recover**) would presumably be to lull Ben-Hadad into a false sense of security so that Hazael can strike—a ploy that Hazael fully understands and acts out (vv. 14–15). If, however, Elisha does intend to tell Ben-Hadad the truth ("You will certainly not recover"), then credit for the ploy must go to Hazael himself, who lies to his master about what Elisha has said (v. 14) and then kills him.

8:11 / **He stared at him with a fixed gaze until Hazael felt ashamed:** The Hb. is lit. "he made his face stand, he set (it), until he was ashamed/embarrassed." The syntax of the sentence makes it unlikely that the subject of "he made . . ." is Elisha. It is Hazael, rather, who stares at Elisha, perhaps somewhat dazed by what he has heard, until Elisha's weeping breaks into his reverie. A better paraphrase than the NIV's is thus: "Hazael stared at him impassively, to the point of embarrassment. Then the man of God began to weep . . ."

8:20 / **Set up its own king:** The Hb. is lit. "they made a king rule over them." It is often stated that there is a degree of tension between this verse and either 1 Kgs. 22:47 ("there was no king in Edom; a deputy was king") or 2 Kgs. 3:9 ("the king of Israel set out with . . . the king of Edom"). It is difficult to see the problem. First Kings 22:47 already makes it clear that "king" can be used with reference to Edom in two senses—their own Edomite king, and a king appointed by Judah. In 2 Kgs. 3:9 "king" has the latter sense and in 2 Kgs. 8:20 the former (as the NIV recognizes).

8:21 / **The Edomites surrounded him . . . :** The Hb. is lit. "He arose in the night and attacked the Edomites who surrounded him and the chariot commanders, and the people fled to their tents." We are not explicitly told which "people" fled to their tents, but in the context it can hardly have been any other than the Judean army. Jehoram has gone to subdue Edom and has found himself in an ambush. Facing disaster, he chooses to break through enemy lines and run for home. No contrast between king and chariot commanders, on the one hand, and people, on the other, is intended (cf. the NIV's imaginative **however,** which is most unlikely in terms of the Hb. syntax).

§41 The Axe Falls (at Last) on Ahab (2 Kgs. 9:1–37)

The twelve years of Jehoram, son of Ahab, are completed (2 Kgs. 3:1; 8:25); and the time for judgment has come (1 Kgs. 21:21–29). Elisha is still with us, and Hazael—though not in the way first planned—is king of Aram. Ahab's drama is approaching its final curtain. Of the players mentioned in 1 Kings 19:15–18, we await only Jehu. Right on cue, he now makes his entrance. Israel will be purged at last of Ahab's house and the worship of Baal it has introduced. Judah, too, will be cleansed. Even the Davidic line will seem under threat. God's quiet ways are, for the moment, at an end. Earthquake is the order of the day.

9:1–13 / Elijah had been commanded to **anoint** Jehu **king over Israel** (1 Kgs. 19:16) but had failed to do so. It is left to Elisha now to fulfill his mission. Although Jehoram himself has retired wounded to Jezreel (2 Kgs. 8:28–29), his army is still at **Ramoth Gilead.** It is thither that Elisha sends a subordinate prophet at speed (**tuck your cloak into your belt;** cf. 1 Kgs. 18:46; 2 Kgs. 4:29) to find Jehu, who is one of the army commanders. A secret anointing takes place, reminiscent of the anointing of Saul (vv. 2, 6; cf. 1 Sam. 9:27—10:1, esp. the **flask** of oil, Hb. *pak,* poured on the head, which appears in the OT only in 10:1 and 2 Kgs. 9:1, 3). Jehu's reaction is also similar to Saul's; he is reluctant to respond to questions (1 Sam. 10:15–16; 2 Kgs. 9:11). His reticence is overcome, however, by the persistence of his companions, perhaps aware of his oily head: **that's not true!** (v. 12). The prophet may be a **madman** (cf. the commentary on 18:25–29 and the additional note on 18:29), but that is not to say that his words are of no account. When Jehu tells them what has been said, they immediately proclaim him king (v. 13; cf. 1 Kgs. 1:34, 39; Matt. 21:8; Mark 11:8; Luke 19:36). They seem most eager to do so. Perhaps Jehoram's lack of military success had already caused unrest in the army.

9:14–29 / The terms of the prophecy are broadly in line with those of Elijah's prophecy to Ahab in 1 Kings 21:21–24 (cf. also 1 Kgs. 14:6–11; 16:1–4; see the additional note to 2 Kgs. 9:7 and the commentary on 9:30–37 for a few distinctive features): Ahab's house is to be destroyed, especially Jezebel. Jehu now sets about his task. Leaving instructions about security in Ramoth Gilead (**don't let anyone slip out of the city to go and tell the news in Jezreel**), he himself rides to Jezreel with an army (vv. 14–16). As he approaches, those within the city are confused. The **lookout** at first sees only **troops** (lit. "a multitude," v. 17). After the two messengers he sent out fail to return, he observes that the driving of the lead chariot is like that of Jehu (vv. 17–20). At this point, Jehoram himself, accompanied by Ahaziah, goes to find out what is going on. He is unaware that he is approaching a man secretly anointed to be his successor (cf. the parallel in 1 Sam. 16, which is interesting in view of the manner of Jehu's own anointing and the characterization of Ahab in 1 Kgs. 17ff.— see the commentary on 1 Kgs. 22:37–40). The two kings meet Jehu outside the city, at a **plot of ground that had belonged to Naboth the Jezreelite** (vv. 21–22). The name has fateful connotations, for it was an incident involving a piece of ground belonging to Naboth (the same piece?—it is not clear) that elicited Elijah's oracle against Ahab in the first place (1 Kgs. 21, esp. vv. 1–2; 16–24) and precipitated that king's death (1 Kgs. 22, esp. v. 38). Echoes of Ahab's death resound throughout this passage. As Jehoram, suddenly made aware by Jehu's words of his intentions, turns to flee, he is struck by an **arrow** and killed (1 Kgs. 22:34). His death, like his father's, is portrayed as divine retribution for **the blood of Naboth** (and now also **of his sons,** whose death has not been reported before) and as fulfillment of prophecy (vv. 25–26; 1 Kgs. 21:19; 22:38). Even Ahaziah, linked with Ahab in marriage and at one with him in religion, shares in his fate. He is **wounded . . . in his chariot,** dies, and is later transported to his capital for burial (v. 27–28; 1 Kgs. 22:34–37). Judgment, at this point, has exceeded expectations. Ahaziah's choice of location in this crucial hour has proved as unfortunate as his choice of gods.

9:30–37 / Jehu now approaches Jezreel in search of Jezebel. He discovers her sitting at a window, adorned as a prostitute (v. 30; cf. Ezek. 23:36–49)—as befits the greatest of all the patrons of the fertility cult (cf. the commentary on 1 Kgs. 22:37–40). She is unrepentant and taunts Jehu as one unlikely to survive his own revolution. All may be well now, but his reign will be a "seven-day wonder" (cf. "you **Zimri,**" v. 31—an allusion to the events described in 1 Kgs. 16:8–20). She meets her end, fittingly enough, at the hands of those least able to benefit from the cult that she has introduced (**two or three eunuchs**—a common condition of officials of royal courts in the ancient Near East; cf. the "official" in 2 Kgs. 8:6). She is thrown down onto **the plot of ground** beneath (v. 36)—the most natural reading of the phrase is to understand it as Naboth's land by the royal palace (1 Kgs. 21:1)—and **trampled underfoot** by Jehu's chariot **horses** (v. 33). Unmindful of prophecy (cf. 2 Kgs. 9:10), or perhaps simply aware of the stereotypical nature of much prophetic utterance (cf. 1 Kgs. 14:11; 16:4) and not taking this part quite literally, Jehu (some time later) orders her burial. While he has been eating and drinking, however, the **dogs** have also been at their dinner (vv. 34–36; cf. the link with Ahab's end in 1 Kgs. 22:38). Most of Jezebel is gone. Prophecy has again been fulfilled; it is just as **Elijah** said (1 Kgs. 21:23; cf. 2 Kgs. 9:10).

Yet the end of the chapter throws up a particularly difficult problem, even as it is claiming such fulfillment. The majority of Hebrew MSS at 1 Kings 21:23 have Elijah saying that Jezebel would be eaten by dogs "by the *wall* (Hb. *ḥēl*) of Jezreel." The MT at 2 Kings 9:36 (and also v. 10) has her eaten **on the plot of ground** (Hb. *ḥēleq*) **at Jezreel.** This is most puzzling, when so much is being made here of the link between the two texts. An easy way out of the difficulty would be to argue that 1 Kings 21:23 has suffered textual corruption. Although a few Hebrew MSS do read *ḥēleq* there, however, the accidental omission of a *q* is very difficult to understand in the context. Did the authors mean us to understand, then, that Elijah used *both* words in talking of Jezebel? It is certainly possible to read 2 Kings 9 as telling us that she was eaten up *both* on Naboth's plot *and* by the wall. We need only surmise that the royal palace was built into the city wall (and Jezebel fell from a window set in this wall; cf. the window of Rahab the prostitute in Josh. 2:15) and that Naboth's vineyard, while outside the city (as 9:21ff. might imply and as is certainly likely in terms of general probability), partly adjoined that wall. A difficulty here is that the Hebrew word for **plot of ground** in verses 21–26 is slightly different (*ḥelqâ*) from the one in verses 10 and 36–37, which is a little surprising if the same place is meant.

Additional Notes §41

9:2 / **Jehu son of Jehoshaphat, the son of Nimshi:** Jehu has hitherto been referred to only as "Jehu son of Nimshi" (1 Kgs. 19:16; cf. also 2 Kgs. 9:20), but it is now clear that "son" in these places must mean "grandson." **Jehoshaphat** is not, of course, the Judean king of that name, but someone else. Although this use of Hb. *bēn,* "son," is not unprecedented in the OT (e.g., Gen. 29:5; 31:28), and there may be other places where it was intended to have this meaning, it is unusual. Perhaps Jehu's grandfather was a particularly well-known person.

9:3 / **I anoint you . . . run; don't delay!:** Two features of the instructions are of interest. In the first place, the oracle we find on Elisha's lips here is much shorter than the one passed on by his messenger in vv. 6–10. The gist of the message is described, but the full substance is delayed until later—presumably so that repetition should not unnecessarily hold up the narrative (cf. 1 Kgs. 14:5, where the entire message is subsumed under Hb. *kāzōh wᵉkāzeh,* "such and such"; and note further Judg. 18:4; 2 Sam. 11:25). For the same reason, it is the condensed message that is later communicated by Jehu to his fellows (v. 12), the details being subsumed under his "Thus and thus he said to me" (Hb. *kāzōʾṯ wᵉkāzōʾṯ,* the NIV's unhelpful "Here is what he told me"; cf. Judg. 8:8; 2 Sam. 17:15; 2 Kgs. 5:4).

Why, secondly, is the man to **run**? The reasons are not spelled out; but perhaps Jehu's reputation as something of a "madman" (v. 20) has been earned in other ways than simply by chariot driving. Who knows how one madman will react to the words of another (v. 11)? Who knows, and perhaps this is the reason for the secrecy, how the other officers will react to the idea that Jehu should be king? It is better just to do the job and leave quickly.

9:7 / **I will avenge the blood of my servants the prophets:** It is not explicitly stated in 1 Kgs. 21:21–24 that the LORD's action against Ahab's house is partly a matter of vengeance for the blood of the prophets. It is, however, implicit that this is so in 1 Kgs. 19:14–18, where the LORD responds to Elijah's complaint about the murder of the prophets (cf. 18:4, 13) by sending him to anoint Jehu (among others). Similarly, it is not stated explicitly in 1 Kgs. 21:23 that "no one will bury" Jezebel (2 Kgs. 9:10), or that "her body will be like refuse . . . so that no one will be able to say 'This is Jezebel' " (9:37), but these things are implicit in the statement that "dogs will devour Jezebel" (1 Kgs. 21:23; 2 Kgs. 9:10, 36).

9:14 / **Defending Ramoth Gilead:** The preceding narrative has not told us about an Israelite recovery of the city. Perhaps we are meant to think that it was abandoned in the course of the general Aramean retreat in 7:3ff. Such "gaps," which the reader must fill in order fully to grasp the story line, are a pronounced feature of Hb. narrative, as of other kinds of narrative. We were never told in the first place, it must be remembered, of the Aramean capture of Ramoth Gilead, an Israelite city in 1 Kgs. 4:13.

9:22 / **Have you come in peace, Jehu?:** It is possible that Hb. *hᵃšālôm* has this sense in 9:17–18 (and that *šālôm* has the same sense in 9:19), since it is conceivable that Jehoram does not at this point know the identity of the people who have appeared on the horizon. It seems improbable, however, once Jehu has been recognized and the people with him therefore identified, that Jehoram and Ahaziah would have left Jezreel to meet him if there had been any doubt in their mind about his intentions. The Hb. *hᵃšālôm* has, in fact, appeared several times already in 2 Kgs. (4:26; 5:21; 9:11), where it has always had the sense "Is everything all right?" That must be its sense in 9:22, and given its appearance so recently in 9:11 it is much better to take it this way also in 9:17–18 (and, uttered sarcastically, in v. 31; the NIV's footnote is a most unlikely rendering of the Hb. in view of the earlier use of *hᵃšālôm*). Jehoram is well aware that these are his soldiers. He is not fearful for his own safety, only anxious to discover what is going on. Has disaster overtaken Ramoth Gilead? Is this "multitude" ("rabble"?—*šip̄ᶜâ* in v. 17 is not the normal Hb. word for troops) all that remains of his army?

Jehu's response reveals the superficiality of Jehoram's grasp of reality. The NIV's **idolatry** is lit. "prostitution" (Hb. *zᵉnûnîm*, also linked with **witchcraft,** Hb. *kᵉšāp̄îm*, in Nah. 3:4), a term associated with fertility religion in Hosea (1:2; 2:2, 4; 4:12; 5:4) and derived from the root *znh* found in 1 Kgs. 22:38 (cf. also 1 Kgs. 3:16). All cannot truly be well in Israel while the worship of Baal continues, for all is not well between Israel and the LORD. Jehoram is thus the first character in Kings to receive a negative answer (*mâ haššālôm*) to this question (*hᵃšālôm*); for it is *his* father's house that must be removed if there truly to be "well-being" in Israel (cf. the word play in v. 26, Hb. *šillamtî lᵉk̄ā*, "I will make you pay for it").

9:25 / **This prophecy about him:** It is not exactly clear whether we are to understand Jehu as offering an interpretation of Elijah's prophecy of 1 Kgs. 21:19 (thought by the authors of Kings, but not necessarily by Jehu, as having been fulfilled in 1 Kgs. 22:38) or as referring to another incident entirely. Certainly he *claims* prophetic justification for his actions.

9:29 / **The eleventh year of Joram:** The conflict between this date for Ahaziah's accession and the date given in 2 Kgs. 8:25 ("the twelfth year") can be resolved easily at one level by accepting that such dates could be reckoned in different ways, particularly in terms of the way that partial years were handled. The interesting question, nevertheless, is why the authors of Kings should have included two different dates in their text and why they should have chosen to include the information about **the eleventh year** at this point in particular. The answer is probably that we have only just been told that Ahaziah and Jehoram died at the same time, something that was not clear from 8:25–26. It is only at this point, therefore, that the possibility of confusion arises for the reader: how can both men have died at the same time if Jehoram reigned for twelve years (3:1), yet Ahaziah, who came to the throne in Jehoram's twelfth year, reigned for one? Second Kings 9:29 is intended to clarify this point.

§42 The Destruction Continues (2 Kgs. 10:1–36)

Elijah had prophesied that the LORD would consume Ahab's descendants and cut off from him every last male in Israel (1 Kgs. 21:21; cf. the previous prophecies against Jeroboam and Baasha in 1 Kgs. 14:10; 16:3). It comes as little surprise, in view of the literal fulfillment of such prophecy in 1 Kings 15:29 and 16:11–12, to find that Jehu is not content with the deaths of Jehoram and Jezebel but now looks to wipe out Ahab's family in toto (2 Kgs. 10:1–17). Nor is it any surprise to find him taking decisive action against the worship of Baal (10:18–28), for it is towards final victory over Baal-worship that 1 Kings 19:15–18 points in naming Jehu (along with Hazael; cf. 2 Kgs. 10:32–33) as the LORD's instrument of judgment. What continues to puzzle, however, is the way the Judean royal family keeps being drawn into these events: first Ahaziah, and now his relatives (10:12–14). This we were not forewarned about. Is the house of David to suffer the same fate as the house of Ahab?

10:1–11 / The first to be dealt with are the **seventy sons** (i.e., male members; cf. commentary on v. 13) **of the house of Ahab,** living in the capital, **Samaria,** under the tutelage and care of the **leading men of the city** (v. 6). These are the people from whom a successor to Jehoram would normally be chosen, and Jehu confronts this threat head on. By writing letters to the leading citizens (note the echoes of Jezebel's plot against Naboth in 1 Kgs. 21:8ff.), challenging them to place one of these "**sons**" on the **throne** and **fight** for their **master's house,** he makes them choose sides. Their reply reveals their decision: they are no longer Ahab's or Jehoram's, but are now Jehu's **servants** (v. 5). Forced to prove their loyalty to him (note Jehu's insinuation of insincerity in v. 6; Ahab, he implies, is still their **master,** in spite of their words in v. 5), they murder the **princes** and deliver their **heads** to Jezreel (while choosing themselves to remain at a distance; contrast **come to me** in v. 6 and **sent them** in v. 7). Jehu himself then goes on to deal with the remaining members of the house of Ahab in Jezreel, as well as those closely associated with Ahab there (v. 11; cf. 1 Kgs. 16:11). The prophetic word has and will come to pass (2 Kgs. 10).

10:12–17 / His work in Jezreel complete, Jehu leaves for Samaria. On the way, he meets **some relatives of Ahaziah** (v. 13), who claim to be on the way **to greet the families** (lit. "sons") in Samaria that have just been wiped out. Like Ahaziah himself, these men find themselves in the wrong place at the wrong time (cf. the analogous Jer. 41:4–9), and with an unconvincing story at that. Why are they north of Samaria, on the Jezreel road, if (as we suppose) they have come from Judah? They are captured and, perhaps after questioning (cf. **Take them alive!**), duly **slaughtered,** just like the sons of Ahab in v. 7 (note the connection between vv. 11 and 14: **he left,** Hb. *hišʾîr,* no survivor). This is no time to be offering members of Ahab's house "greetings" (Hb. *šālôm*). This is not a time of well-being (Hb. *šālôm;* cf. 2 Kgs. 9:11, 17–22), but a time of judgment. The only people to find blessing in such a time are those, like **Jehonadab son of Recab** (cf. Jer. 35, where he appears as the founder of a purist religious group committed to Israel's older ways), who are of one mind with zealous Jehu (cf. 1 Kgs. 19:10, 14) and will **ride** with him on his crusade (vv. 15–16). **Jehonadab** becomes a witness to events in Samaria, as **all who** are **left there** (Hb. *hannišʾārîm*) of the house of Ahab are **destroyed** (v. 17).

10:18–28 / Samaria had been the focal point for the Baal cult (cf. 1 Kgs. 16:32–33), and it is that cult to which Jehu now gives his attention. He pretends enthusiasm while preparing for slaughter. The dynasty may have changed, he tells the **people** of Samaria, but the religious policy will remain the same. **Ahab served Baal a little; Jehu will serve him much** (v. 18). A religious festival is organized (**a great sacrifice,** its true nature as yet unrevealed), and all the servants of Baal are gathered together under one roof (vv. 19–21). They are lulled into a false sense of security, provided with proper worship **robes** by the king and assured by him that no **servants of the LORD** are anywhere at hand (vv. 22–23). The king himself (not explicit in the Hb., but clearly implied) actually makes the **burnt offering** in their temple (v. 25). It is all deception. The servants of Baal are massacred as a "sacrifice" to the god they worship, the **sacred stone** of Baal is emphatically destroyed, and the **temple of Baal** is demolished (vv. 26–27; cf. 1 Kgs. 16:32–33; 2 Kgs. 3:2). Baal-worship in Israel is officially at an end. It has neither royal patronage nor royal tolerance.

10:29–31 / The narrative has concentrated upon the worship of Baal since 1 Kings 16:29ff. Had we not been reminded by 1 Kings 22:52 and 2 Kings 3:3, it would have been easy to forget that this kind of idolatry represents for the authors only a particularly bad form of the general idolatry practiced in Israel since Jeroboam's time (1 Kgs. 12:25ff.). Jehu has decisively dealt with Baal-worship, and yet, it turns out, he does nothing at all about **the worship of the golden calves** (vv. 29, 31). It is somewhat surprising, then, to find him addressed in verse 30 as one who has **done what is right** in the **eyes** of the LORD (Hb. *yāšār*, "right"; cf. the additional notes to vv. 3 and 15 for Jehu's own claims in this regard). Apart from 2 Kings 10:30, the authors of Kings use *yāšār* positively only when speaking of David (1 Kgs. 15:5) and of the relatively good (i.e., non-idolatrous) kings of Judah (1 Kgs. 15:11; 22:43; 2 Kgs. 12:2; 14:3; 15:3, 34; 16:2; 18:3; 22:2). It is even more surprising to find Jehu receiving a David-like dynastic promise. His descendants will **sit on the throne of Israel to the fourth generation.** This is not the same thing as a promise of eternal dynasty. It is, nevertheless, extraordinary. Jeroboam, it will be recalled, was promised a dynasty like David's if he "did what was right" in the LORD's eyes (1 Kgs. 11:38). He did not do so (1 Kgs. 14:8), and his son was overthrown (15:25ff.). The same fate befell Baasha (15:33–16:14). All this happened because of participation in the **sins of Jeroboam**—the very sins of which Jehu stands accused in 2 Kings 10:29, 31 (cf. 1 Kgs. 15:29–30, 34; 16:7). Yet now the idolater is promised a dynasty stretching to the fourth generation. Evidently the eradication of Baal-worship is so significant that, for the moment, participation in the sins of Jeroboam pales into insignificance. What Jehu has done that is **right** (v. 30) far outweighs what he continues to do that is wrong (vv. 29, 31).

10:32–36 / First Kings 19:15–18 told us that when God's judgment fell, Jehu would deal with those who escaped Hazael, and Elisha with those who escaped Jehu (cf. Hb. *mlṭ*, "to escape"). It is implied in such ordering that Hazael would turn out to be the greatest destroyer of the three; 2 Kings 8:12, with its emphasis upon his brutality, also points towards this. It is no surprise, therefore, to read now of Hazael's aggression. Through him **the**

LORD began to reduce the size of Israel (v. 32), conquering Transjordan as far south as the Arnon Gorge, the southern limit of Israelite territory there (Josh. 12:2). We shall hear more of his conquests later (12:17–18; 13:3–7, 22–23). Will Israel survive the assault? There has been a pronounced emphasis throughout the chapter, after all, on the thoroughness of Jehu's campaign. "No one was left" after the sword of Jehu had done its work (cf. the Hb. root *š'r*, "to remain," in vv. 11, 14, 17, 21), no one of the house of Ahab, of the relatives of Ahaziah, of the servants of Baal. No one escaped (Hb. *mlṭ*, v. 24) to meet Elisha. If Hazael is to be as thorough, what hope can there be for Israel? Yet the language of nonsurvival itself reminds us of another aspect of God's word to Elijah—that he would ensure the survival of a remnant (Hb. *š'r*, 1 Kgs. 19:18) in the midst of all the destruction: 7,000 who had not bowed the knee to Baal (cf. the additional note to 1 Kgs. 20:15 on the symbolic significance of the figure). Hazael, we know, will not be the king to uproot Israel from the good land (1 Kgs. 14:15). His will not be the final assault, however destructive his campaign proves to be.

Additional Notes §42

10:1 / **The officials of Jezreel . . . the guardians:** We assume that the **officials** are the two men whose titles appear in v. 5: the "palace administrator" and the "city governor." The impression there, however, is that these are officials based in (rather than simply visiting or having fled to) Samaria. Why they should be called **officials of Jezreel** is a mystery, unless the idea is that Jezreel, while having its own elders and nobles (1 Kgs. 21:8), was ultimately governed from Samaria ("officials responsible for Jezreel"). **The guardians** (Hb. *'ōmenîm 'ah'āb*) are probably not **guardians** at all (since the NIV's **children** does not appear in the Hb. text of v. 1, but represents the interpretation of the NIV translator). They are in all likelihood simply "pillars, stalwarts" of Ahab, those *in general* (rather than **officials** and **elders** in particular) who were loyal to him and to his house.

10:3 / **Choose the best and most worthy:** The Hb. is *haṭṭôb wehayyāšār*, a phrase that is picked up in v. 30, where Jehu is described as one who has "done well in accomplishing what is right" (Hb. *heṭîbōtâ la'ašôt hayyāšār*) in the eyes of the LORD. A contest is being proposed, in which the outcome will determine who is truly in the right with God. The leading officials deduce from what has happened so far (two kings have not resisted him, v. 4) what the authors will later tell the reader—that Jehu is in the right, and God is with him. They do not, therefore, allow the contest to proceed.

10:9 / Who killed all these?: Jehu knows, of course, who killed them; but the people, asleep when the heads arrived, do not. All they know is that, when they awoke there were two piles of heads lying "at the entrance of the city gate" (v. 8). The point of the exercise is to convince them that it is truly the LORD who is at work in overthrowing the house of Ahab. The revolution is bigger than Jehu; greater powers, seventy times more lethal than he (he only **killed** his **master**), are at work in Israel. You people are fair minded (better in context than the NIV's **innocent**), he says, able to judge what is right and wrong; judge for yourselves whether this is of God or not.

10:15 / Are you in accord with me, as I am with you?: The Hb. is lit. "is your heart right, as my heart with your heart?" Given the usage of both *yāšār*, "right," and *lēbāb*, "heart," in v. 30 (lit. "accomplishing what is right in my eyes . . . done . . . all that was in my heart) and elsewhere in Kings (e.g., 1 Kgs. 14:8), it is most unlikely that this is meant to be a question only about Jehonadab's agreement with Jehu. A better translation would be: "is your heart right? As (it is) with my heart, (is it) with your heart?" The theme throughout the chapter is essentially "who is on the LORD's side, who is in the right?" The leading men of Samaria (who do not side with one of Ahab's "sons," claiming him to be "right," v. 3) and Jehonadab (**on his way to meet** Jehu, rather than to visit the apostate royal families) are on the right side, and they live; Ahaziah's relatives and the servants of Baal are not, and they die.

10:25 / The inner shrine: The Hb. is *ʿîr*, which normally means "city." In this context, it presumably refers to some "citylike" aspect of the temple, and that is how we come to have **inner shrine**. We might equally well understand *ʿîr* as a walled courtyard of some kind, however, where the bodies were dumped and the "sacred stone" demolished/burned.

The destruction of the house of Ahab has impinged to an unsettling extent upon the house of David (2 Kgs. 9:27; 10:12–14). We recall the ominous lack of any restatement of the Davidic promise in 8:25–27. Have the two houses become so identified in intermarriage (8:18, 27) that a distinction is no longer to be maintained between them? Second Kings 11 begins by bringing us almost to the point of believing that this is so. There is a Jezebel in Judah, intent on doing there what Jehu has done in Israel. By the chapter's end, however, it is indisputable that Judah is very different from Israel and the house of David is in a very different position from that of the royal houses of the north. Ahab has died, but "David" survives "Jezebel" and lives on.

11:1–3 / **Athaliah** could well have been a daughter of Jezebel (cf. 2 Kgs. 8:26); she certainly displays the same ruthless streak. Her son dead, she proceeds **to destroy the whole royal family** (lit. "the seed of the kingdom"). Family ties mean nothing if power is at stake. This comes as something of a shock to the reader, the *whole* royal family? Surely David has not been left without a descendant? Happily, Hebrew *kōl*, "all," is not always to be taken quite literally. We find out immediately that at least one royal prince has been saved. Smuggled away by his aunt **Jehosheba**, baby **Joash** is hidden with **his nurse** in **the temple of the LORD.** He survives, perhaps unrecognized rather than undetected, since the palace and temple are in such close proximity, for the **six years** of Athaliah's rule. He is apparently all that remains to shield David's "lamp" (8:19) from the winds of irreversible change.

11:4–16 / It is not immediately clear who the **Jehoiada** is who organizes the coup that eventually unseats Athaliah, but in the course of the narrative we learn that he is the chief priest (vv. 9, 15 etc.). Choosing his moment (**in the seventh year**), he conspires with the **commanders** of the various military units in Jerusalem (**Carites, guards**) and manages to create a secure environment in which the young prince can be made king. The details of these arrangements remain obscure, largely due to our ignorance of how the troops involved were organized. It is by no means as plain in the Hebrew as in the NIV, for example, that the "thirds" (Hb. *šelišît*) of verses 5–6 are **three companies** in the same sense that the "two parts" (Hb. *štê hayyāḏôt*) of v. 7 are **two companies**. Nor is it certain that all three "thirds" are going on duty on the Sabbath. Only the first (**guarding the royal palace**) is explicitly described as doing so. It is, finally, most unlikely that we are to read the text as saying that all personnel are to abandon normal duties and congregate at the **temple** to protect the king. It is much more likely that the three "thirds" are being assigned to the temple of Baal (see the additional note on 11:5–6). The details, then, are obscure. What quite clear is that sufficient security is provided for the ceremony to take place within the temple precincts. Troops surround the entrance, as Joash is **brought out,** is crowned, is presented with a list of divinely-ordained laws (Hb. *ʿēḏût;* the NIV's **a copy of the covenant;** cf. 1 Kgs. 2:3; 2 Kgs. 17:15; 23:3; and note Deut. 17:18–20), is **anointed,** and is acclaimed (v. 12). Athaliah, rushing from her unguarded palace to the temple precincts to find out what is happening, discovers the conspiracy (Hb. *qešer,* the NIV's **Treason!,** v. 14) much too late and, having unwisely drawn attention to herself, is taken away from holy ground to be executed (vv. 15–16).

11:17–21 / There follows a **covenant** renewal ceremony, in which **the king and the people** once more identify themselves, after the idolatrous interlude represented by the reigns of Jehoram and Ahaziah, as the LORD's **people** (cf. Josh. 24:1–27; 2 Kgs. 23:1–3). At the same time, a **covenant** is made between the **king** and **the people** (cf. 2 Sam. 5:1–3). It is important to redefine kingship in distinctively Israelite terms (cf. Deut. 17:18–20 again) after a period dominated by foreign ideas (cf. the kingship described in 1 Sam. 8:11–18). The identity of Judah and the principles upon which she will be governed have thus been re-established, and steps are taken to remove Baal-worship from the city (v. 18). The king subsequently takes **his place on the royal throne** unopposed, since the focal point for opposition is dead (vv. 19–20). A chapter that began by appearing to tell us that the "seed" (Hb. *zeraʿ,* v. 1) of David was at an end has concluded on a more positive note. It has become clear, in fact, that what has happened here is nothing more than another example of the humbling of that "seed" (Hb. *zeraʿ*, 1 Kgs. 11:39). The house of David has survived, even if only by the skin of its teeth. Peace has been restored to David and his seed, his house and his throne (cf. 1 Kgs. 2:33), whereas Ahab has known only destruction (cf. 2 Kgs. 9:22).

Additional Notes §43

11:1 / **She proceeded to destroy:** This is not the only time in the Bible when God's promises hang by the slender thread of a baby boy whose life is threatened by wicked rulers. Moses is hidden away in the midst of Egyptian genocide, growing up unrecognized for who he is, under Pharaoh's very nose (Exod. 2:1–10). Jesus, himself a "son" of David, is removed from Herod's dominion in the face of a similar threat (Matt. 2:13–18). He, too, grows up, his true identity concealed, under the gaze of other "kings of the Jews."

11:2 / **She put him and his nurse in a bedroom:** The Hb. is simply "him and his nurse in the bedroom," the governing verb being the earlier "she stole away." The **bedroom,** in other words, is the place from which the child was taken. The only "hiding" that occurs takes place in the temple. The nurse contrasts sharply, of course—in her willingness to share danger with the child whose care she has—with those spineless men in 2 Kgs. 10:1–7. Not for the first time in 2 Kgs., the lowly come out very well when compared with the great.

11:4 / **The Carites:** These have appeared so far only in the consonantal Hb. text of 2 Sam. 20:23, where they form part of the elite royal bodyguard. They may well be the same body as the Kerethites (cf. the additional note on 1 Kgs. 1:38), the name the Masoretic scribes wish us to read in 2 Sam. 20:23.

11:5–6 / **You who are in the three companies . . . :** The NIV paraphrases here to an unhelpful and misleading extent. A more literal rendering of the instructions would be: "The third of you coming for Sabbath duty (that is, those who guard the palace), and the third at the Sur Gate, and the third at the gate behind the guards, you shall guard the house *massāḥ.*" This last word is admittedly difficult, but that is no reason for leaving it out entirely. The root *nsḥ,* "to tear down, away," from which it probably derives, is always found in contexts where divine judgment of the wicked is in view (Deut. 28:63; Prov. 2:22; 15:25; Ps. 52:5), and in Prov. 15:25 it is explicitly the proud man's "house" that is destroyed (Hb. *bayit*). Its attachment to Hb. *habbayit* here makes it most unlikely that the reference is to the same "house" as in v. 7 (explicitly called "the temple of the LORD"). Nor is it likely to be to the royal palace. Athaliah leaves the palace unhindered in v. 13, and it suffers no damage in the course of the narrative. It is probably the temple of Baal that is meant, the same temple that is destined for destruction in v. 18. Troops are sent to both temples. Those who would normally be off-duty are to protect the king in the one temple ("two parts," v. 7), while those who would normally be on duty are to leave their normal tasks and go to the other temple, in order (we presume) to discourage interference by the worshipers of Baal and detain the priest Mattan (three "thirds," vv. 5–6; cf. v. 18). We may render *habbayit massāḥ* as "the temple (called) Destruction."

11:10 / **The spears and shields:** Hb. *šelāṭîm* (the NIV's **shields**), sometimes rendered here (somewhat obscurely in a context where we expect a weapon) as "quivers," is probably better translated as "bows" (cf. Jer. 51:11; for David's acquisition of these, cf. 2 Sam. 8:7). The MT has "spear" in the singular, rather than **spears** in the plural. Thus "the spear and the bows." Why does Jehoiada hand these over to the **commanders**? It is difficult to believe that their soldiers needed to be armed by the priest. Is it, then, a matter of symbolism, of making it clear that the commanders have allied themselves with David's cause? Or are these articles given so that they may be handed over to the new king as symbols of his royal power? The spear is a prominent royal weapon in the books of Sam. (e.g., 1 Sam. 18:10–11; 22:6; 26:7ff.). It is interesting that the root *šlṭ* (cf. *šelāṭîm* above) can mean "to rule over" (e.g., Gen. 42:6), and that the more common Hb. word for "bow" (*qešet*) is sometimes used figuratively of "might" or "dominion" (Hos. 1:5; Jer. 49:35).

11:14 / **The pillar:** Hb. *ʿammûd* has hitherto appeared only in 1 Kgs. 7, of the pillars of the Solomonic palace (7:2–3, 6) and temple (7:15–22, 41–42). Given the context, most likely either Jakin or Boaz are in view here (cf. 7:21). The emphasis on **custom** is interesting, for it is clearly one of the purposes of the authors throughout the chapter to stress the legitimacy of Joash's claim to the throne. He is the rightful heir (vv. 2–3) and is regarded as king by Jehoiada (and the authors) even before the coronation (vv. 7–8, 11), which takes place in line with law (vv. 12, 17) and custom (vv. 12, 14; cf. the parallels with the accession of Solomon, 1 Kgs. 1:38–40), and in full view of the people of the land (v. 14, 19–20; contrast Jehu's "coronation" in 2 Kgs. 9:12–13). So anomalous is Athaliah's "reign" that she does not receive the opening and closing regnal formulas that are attached elsewhere to the reigns of even wicked (but legitimate) rulers (e.g., 2 Kgs. 8:16–17, 23–26). So far as the authors of Kings are concerned, she did not really "reign" at all.

§44 Joash (2 Kgs. 12:1–21)

Joash sits on his throne, but until now the main actor in his story has been the priest Jehoiada. Now we begin to hear of his own activities, as the "highlights" of his forty-year long reign over Judah are described to us. They do not make particularly inspiring reading.

12:1–3 / The introductory regnal formulas for Joash correspond to those found elsewhere for Judean kings who have eschewed idolatry (cf. Asa in 1 Kgs. 15:9ff.; Jehoshaphat in 1 Kgs. 22:41ff.; also the early Solomon, 1 Kgs. 3:3). There is the usual commendation (he **did what was right;** contrast the verdict on Jehoram and Ahaziah, 2 Kgs. 8:18, 27), accompanied by the usual qualification (**the high places were not removed,** cf. 1 Kgs. 15:14; 22:43).

12:4–16 / The temple of the LORD, we assume, had suffered from some neglect (though it was not entirely abandoned, cf. v. 18) during the years in which the worship of Baal was encouraged. Joash now undertakes its repair. His initial plan is to leave it to the priests (vv. 4–5), but the **priests** (it is implied) are not anxious to spend good money on mere buildings (vv. 6–8). Joash therefore takes control of the project, ensuring that money is truly set aside for it (cf. the **chest** of v. 9, beside the **altar** of uncertain identity) and that all this money goes to the **men appointed to supervise the work** (vv. 9–12). The repairs are duly carried out, but it is a sorry episode that reflects well on neither king nor priests.

The priests are represented as being more concerned about their own benefit than that of the temple. They divert funds to themselves (vv. 7–8), even though they are well provided for under the normal laws of sacrifice (v. 16; cf. 1 Sam. 2:12–17, 27–29, for a similar situation). Even Jehoiada's zeal for the LORD does not, apparently, extend as far as his pocket (v. 7). He is to be trusted only so far as the **royal secretary** can see him (v. 10). The priests needed to be watched, we are told—thus the **chest,** perhaps a secure box (with a **hole** in it for deposits) that could not be raided, out in the open where it could be seen. They stand in stark contrast to the supervisers, who **acted,** we are explicitly told, **with complete honesty** (v. 15).

The king, however, does not come out of the story any better. We are not told exactly when his building plan was initiated. It either takes him a long time to begin to think about the temple (cf. **the twenty-third year** of v. 6), or an incredibly long time to "discover" that nothing is being done about his instructions for its repair. This, too, speaks of no great zeal for the LORD nor of great wisdom; his achievements are, indeed, somewhat mediocre. Although Joash resembles Solomon in reigning for forty years (1 Kgs. 11:42) and in (re)building the temple (compare vv. 11–12 and 1 Kgs. 5:15–18), his temple is but a poor reflection of its former glory (contrast v. 13 with 1 Kgs. 7:50). Once again we are reminded of that "humbling of David" theme (1 Kgs. 11:39) that has surfaced in the description of even the best of the post-Solomonic Judean kings (cf. the commentary on 1 Kgs. 15:18–24; 22:47–50).

12:17–18 / This theme continues as we turn to consider Joash as a military figure. For Judah, too, is oppressed by **Hazael** in this period (cf. 2 Kgs. 10:32–33 for his assault on Israel), as he turns east from the Philistine city of **Gath** to **attack Jerusalem.** Like Asa, Joash knows no Solomonic peace during his rule. Like Asa, he sees tribute flowing north from Israel to Aram, instead of south from Aram to Israel (cf. the commentary on 1 Kgs. 15:18–24). Both kings empty **the treasuries of temple** and **palace** of all that has accumulated there, particularly those items **dedicated** by the various kings since the last time they were emptied (v. 18; cf. 1 Kgs. 15:15, 18), in order to save Jerusalem. But we are very far from the days when the king of Israel had "peace on every side" (1 Kgs. 5:4).

12:19–21 / Just how far we have travelled is evident now in the report of Joash's death. We have become accustomed to the idea of northern kings meeting a violent end. The only Judean king to suffer this fate thus far, however, is wicked Ahaziah. Is there a suggestion here (as there may be in the case of Asa; cf. the commentary on 1 Kgs. 15:18–24) that Joash, later in his reign, turned to wickedness? Second Kings 12:2 might imply, if it is indeed to be translated with the NIV as "he did right . . . all the years Jehoiada the priest instructed him," that he did not do quite so well after priestly instruction had ceased (but see the additional note). The Chronicler picks up this theme in 2 Chronicles 24:15ff., telling us of apostasy that preceded both the Aramean assault on Jerusalem and Joash's murder.

Additional Notes §44

12:2 / All the years Jehoiada the priest instructed him: We might just as legitimately translate this as: "all his days, because Jehoiada the priest instructed him." That is, he was brought up well and later continued on the right path.

12:4 / All the money: Three sources of income are specified under the general heading **money . . . as sacred offerings.** Two of these appear to represent regular temple income: payments made in relation to the periodic **census** of male Israelites (Exod. 30:11–16), and payments connected with **personal vows** (monetary equivalents for things dedicated to God, Lev. 27:1–25). The wording of the Hb. with regard to the third sort of payment, however (which we may render "all the money that it is laid upon someone's heart to bring"), strongly suggests that this is a special fund-raising campaign similar to that initiated by Moses, at God's command, in Exod. 35—note there the great emphasis upon the willingness of the people to give "from the heart" (Hb. *lēḇ* in vv. 5, 21–22, 26, 29). Both the **voluntary payments** and **the money collected in the census** are intended in Exod. 35 and 30, as here in 2 Kgs. 12, to be put towards building-work on the central place of worship (tabernacle/ temple; cf. Exod. 30:16; 35:21; 36:1, 3, 5).

12:5 / One of the treasurers: Hb. *makkārô* is not clear, but the wording of the verse suggests that it refers to those bringing the money to the temple in v. 4 rather than to some other group not yet mentioned. There is a Hb. verb *mkr*, "to sell," that can be used more generally in the sense of "give over into the power of" (e.g., Deut. 32:30). It may be, then, that we should translate the phrase "each from his donor." For the view that *makkār* is priestly income from the sale of portions of the sin and guilt offerings (cf. v. 16) see L. S. Wright, "*Mkr* in 2 Kings 12:5–17 and Deuteronomy 18:8," *VT* 39 (1989), pp. 438–48.

12:10 / Counted the money . . . put it into bags: The Hb. is *wayyāṣurû wayyimnû*, which can only give the sense of the NIV translation if the second verb is read before the first. The Hb. actually tells us that they "tied it up" first (presumably in **bags** or bundles; cf. *ṣrr* in 2 Kgs. 5:23) and then counted the groups of items organized in this way to gain a total. It is a well-known strategy in counting, multiplication of tens in the decimal system (for example) being much easier than the addition of single units.

12:16 / **The money from the guilt offerings . . . :** There is a possible ambiguity in the Hb. phrase *napšôṯ ʿerkô* in v. 4 that, in referring to the payment of monetary equivalents, might lead the reader to think that Joash's instructions embraced **guilt offerings** (cf. Hb. *ʿerek* in Lev. 5:5, 18; 6:6). Verse 16 makes it clear that they did not and that the closely associated **sin offerings** (Lev. 4:1–5:13) were not involved either. The implication is that it was proper for the priests to benefit from these offerings (cf. Num. 5:5–10). But it was not proper in the case of the offerings of v. 4, which they ought to have handled (as the supervisers did, v. 15) "with complete honesty," using them for their intended purpose.

§45 Jehoahaz and Jehoash (2 Kgs. 13:1–25)

The crisis of 2 Kings 9–11 is past. A descendant of David once more sits on the throne of Judah, and a new house governs Israel, with security of tenure until the fourth generation (10:30). We anticipate a period of relative calm within the two countries, even if not in their relations with other countries (cf. 8:12; 10:32–33; 12:17–18). Chapter 13 unfolds much as expected, updating us on events in Israel during the reigns of the two Israelite kings who acceded during the reign of Joash in Judah (cf. the analogous situation in 1 Kings, where the account of Asa's reign in 15:9–24 is followed by all the happenings of 15:25–22:40). Both kings hold on to their thrones all their days, and both survive (if only just) the Aramean onslaught. Yet there are hints now of a darker future, a future in which Israel will have to do without their great protector Elisha; a future of defeat and exile in a foreign land. It is the end of an era in which two mighty prophets have walked the land. What will happen now?

13:1–9 / The first of Jehu's descendants was **Jehoahaz**— a wicked king who indulged, as his predecessors had done, in **the sins of Jeroboam.** Under normal circumstances we might expect the appearance of a prophet to announce the end of Jehu's house (cf. 1 Kgs. 14:6ff.; 16:1ff.; 21:21ff.). These are not normal circumstances, however. The divine promise to Jehu (2 Kgs. 10:30) is functioning like the earlier promise to David (2 Sam. 7:1–17), and the Israelite royal house is, for the moment, being treated like the Judean. There still is divine punishment, in the form of Armaean oppression (**the LORD**'s anger burned against Israel, v. 3). It is so severe that it reduces **the army of Jehoahaz** to little more than a remnant (cf. Hb. *š'r* in v. 7, as in 1 Kgs. 19:18; 2 Kgs. 7:13, 10:11, 14, 17, 21), as insubstantial as the **dust at threshing time** that is caught by the wind and blown away. But there is no rejection (2 Sam. 7:14–15). Although he is an idolater, God responds to

Jehoahaz's plea for **favor** (v. 4), and Israel is saved from complete destruction (v. 5).

The precise means by which salvation occurs remains obscure. Who is the **deliverer**? It is a strange way of referring to Elisha, if that is who is meant. Is it perhaps a gifted Israelite general? Or a foreign king, distracting Aram from its war with Israel? We are not told. But we are told that God's gracious intervention makes no difference to Israel's religious outlook (v. 6). They continue in their sins, and compound them with the re-introduction of a symbol of the fertility cult so recently attacked by Jehu (**the Asherah pole**).

13:10–19 / Next in line is another king named Joash/ **Jehoash** (cf. the same variation in name for the Judean king of 2 Kgs. 11–12). His reign is, for the most part, devoid of much interest (he became king, he sinned, he died, vv. 10–13, although we shall later hear more of the **war against Amaziah,** v. 12; cf. 14:8–14). Its importance lies mainly in the context it provides for the death of Elisha. The prophet falls ill in a period when **the chariots and horsemen of Israel** have been decimated by the Arameans (v. 14; cf. v. 7). The king, in distress about his reduced resources, arrives to consult him. It is divine intervention through the prophets, after all, that has from the beginning ensured Israelite survival in the face of superior Aramean forces (cf. 1 Kgs. 20:1–34; 2 Kgs. 6:8–7:20). Elisha is able to offer Jehoash words of some comfort (vv. 15–19); however, they are qualified, apparently because the king's response to prophetic commands is not unreserved. He begins well, doing exactly as he is told (cf. the emphasis on the complete match between the four instructions and their corresponding actions in vv. 15–17), and the LORD's arrow of victory flies **east** to meet the Aramean threat. At this point Elisha's promise is that Jehoash will **completely destroy** (Hb. *nkh ʿad-kallēh*) **the Arameans at Aphek.** But because Jehoash chooses, in response to Elisha's next command to **strike** (Hb. *nkh*) the ground with the arrows, to **strike** only **three times** instead of **five or six,** the promise is revised. The destruction will not be complete after all; his **defeat** (Hb. *nkh* again) of Aram will be of a more limited kind (vv. 18–19). It is not (it is implied) that the king did not obey the prophetic word. It is that he did not obey it enthusiastically enough. The importance of wholehearted obedience to prophetic words has already been seen in the story of 1 Kings 13:1–32.

13:20–25 / The chapter closes with two seemingly unrelated sections. We may best understand the connection between these passages if we begin with the second of the two: a review of what has happened in Israel during the reigns of Jehoahaz and Jehoash (vv. 22–25). There was indeed oppression (vv. 4, 22) **throughout the reign of Jehoahaz,** but God was gracious and compassionate **because of his covenant with Abraham, Isaac and Jacob.** This reason for Israel's survival during Jehoahaz's reign is a deeper one than that given in 2 Kings 10:30. Long before making promises to Jehu about kingship, long before making a covenant with David (2 Sam. 7:1–17), God was dealing with Israel's ancestors (Gen. 15:1–21; 17:1–27; etc.), committing to Israel as a people and promising it a land. It is this everlasting **covenant** that is now mentioned as the fundamental reason for God's help in the midst of oppression. That is why Aram was kept at bay during the reign of Jehoahaz, in spite of sin, and that is why the equally sinful Jehoash was able to lead Israel to recovery during the reign of **Ben-Hadad son of Hazael** (but not at the beginning, cf. v. 3), recapture **towns** earlier lost to Aram, and defeat the Arameans (as Elisha had promised) **three times.** It was a matter of grace.

This is a new idea in Kings, so far as the northern kingdom is concerned (though note the hint in 1 Kgs. 18:36) and one that changes considerably the reader's perspective on the narrative. From very early on in the story, we have been faced with a tension regarding God's dealings with Judah and its kings precisely because at one level there seems to be an unconditionality about these (David will always reign over Judah; cf. 1 Kgs. 11:36; 15:4; 2 Kgs. 8:19), while at another there is an undeniable conditionality (David's sons must obey or face dire consequences; cf. 1 Kgs. 2:4; 8:25; 9:4–9). We have not hitherto faced this problem with regard to the northern kingdom. Here, conditionality has apparently always been the rule, the promise to Jehu bringing about only a temporary change (four generations) in God's practice. Second Kings 13:23 now presents the Abraham promise as analogous to the David promise and introduces a tension between law and grace with respect to Israel that is similar to what we have found regarding Judah. God was **unwilling to destroy** Israel because of Abraham and was "unwilling to destroy" Judah because of David (cf. Hb. *lō˒ ˒āḇâ hašḥît* in both in 2 Kgs. 8:19 and 13:23). The two kingdoms are ultimately being treated by God in the same way, whatever the apparent differences we have perceived thus far between them.

This raises a question about God's dealings with Israel that we have addressed before with regard to Judah: how will this tension between law and grace ultimately be resolved? Since 1 Kings 14:15–16, we have expected to read of Israel's exile from the land. Second Kings 13:5 describes exile for the first time as an event (after which the people were able to live in **their own homes** again, v. 5) rather than as an idea—an ominous happening that presages the definitive "banishment" of Israel **from his presence** in 2 Kings 17:1–23 (Hb. *šlk mippānāyw*, 2 Kgs. 17:20). Will this be the end for Israel? Second Kings 13:23 suggests not. God has always been unwilling to **banish them from his presence** (Hb. *šlk mēʿal-pānāyw*), and that is the case **to this day** (Hb. *ʿad-ʿattâ*, cf. 2 Kgs. 8:6) in this postexilic period for Israel. There is, therefore, hope for Israel in Abraham, as there is for Judah in David. Grace will triumph over law in the end.

With this understanding of 2 Kings 13:22–25 in mind, we may now return to the story in verses 20–21. It is a curious little tale that presupposes the presence of a now independent Moab (cf. 2 Kgs. 3) waging limited warfare on Israel from the south (cf. the **raiders** of Aram in 2 Kgs. 5:2; 6:23; and **spring** as the time for war, though expressed by a different phrase, in 1 Kgs. 20:22). Surprised by Moabite troops, **some Israelites** in a burial party hurriedly throw a corpse into **Elisha's tomb**, and there is a resurrection! Evidently, Elisha's powers live on (cf. 2 Kgs. 4:8–37). But why should we be told this here? What is the point?

The connection between this story and the verses that follow seems to lie in the use in verse 21 of that same verb *šlk* that is found in verse 23 and in 2 Kings 17:20. The Israelites "throw" the body (presumably unwillingly) into the tomb; God unwillingly "throws" Israel into exile. The point appears to be this: Elisha, the great protector of Israel, is dead. His was an age when "God saved" Israel (cf. the Hb. root *yšʿ* underlying the name "Elisha" and the words "deliverer" in v. 5 and "victory" in v. 17), even in the midst of great sin (cf. 13:1–7, 14–19). With the passing of that era, Israel has entered a time in which devastating judgment will not long be held at bay. They are shortly to enter the **tomb** of exile, to be cast out of God's presence with not so much as a remnant left (cf. Ps. 88:3–12, and see the additional note on 1 Kgs. 13:33 for another place where death appears to be a metaphor for exile). Yet even in exile, there is hope. If contact with the great prophets of the past is maintained, through obedience to their teachings (we presume), death may yet be followed by unexpected resurrection (cf. Ezek. 37:1–14), defeat by victory. For God's love is ultimately strong enough to overcome death. It is no coincidence that the first allusion in Kings to exile as an aspect of Israelite experience appears in a chapter that contains the first mention of the covenant with the patriarchs. Only a promise like that can offer Israel any comfort in the midst of the devastation that it is shortly to endure.

Additional Notes §45

13:3 / **The LORD's anger burned:** The language here and throughout vv. 3–5 is reminiscent of the book of Judges, where Israel's idolatry was followed by divine **anger** (cf. Hb. *wayiḥar-ʾap YHWH* in 2 Kgs. 13:3 and Judg. 2:14; 3:8; 10:7), expressing itself in oppression by foreigners (Hb. *lḥṣ,* "to oppress," in 2 Kgs. 13:4 and Judg. 2:18; 4:3; 10:12). When Israel cried out (Hb. *zʿq* in Judg. 3:9, 15; 6:6–7; 10:10) under this oppression, God sent them a deliverer (Hb. *môšîʿa* in 2 Kgs. 13:5 and Judg. 3:9, 15) or "judge" to rescue them. Judges suggests, then, that the process of turning to God involves "crying out" and also turning away from idolatry (Judg. 2:11–19; 10:10–16). Second Kings 13:2–6 emphasizes that there was no such "turning away" (vv. 2, 6); the sins of Jeroboam prevailed throughout. Equally significant is that Jehoahaz does not "cry out" to the LORD. We are told only that he "sought the LORD's favor" (v. 4). The verb is *ḥlh,* which is otherwise used in Kings only in 1 Kgs. 13:6, where an equally unrepentant Jeroboam asks for healing. The language has been chosen to emphasize the extraordinary graciousness of God, which will be the theme of v. 23. He listens to, and acts on behalf of, even the most apostate people—out of grace.

13:6 / **The Asherah pole remained standing in Samaria:** The Hb. is lit. "the Asherah pole stood in Samaria." The NIV translation implies that this is the pole of 1 Kgs. 16:33, which has survived **in Samaria** throughout the period from Ahab to Jehoahaz, untouched by Jehu's reformation. Asherim are elsewhere associated with the golden calves as well as with Baal (1 Kgs. 14:15), and since Jehu did not remove the calves (2 Kgs. 10:29) it is possible that this pole remained too. It must be remembered, however, that the definite article in Hb. need not necessarily imply that the item to which it is attached has already appeared in the narrative (GKC §126 q—s; cf. "the oak tree" in 1 Kgs. 13:14; "the lion will kill you" in 1 Kgs. 20:36; "the day" in 2 Kgs. 4:8, 11, 18). We could translate the line, therefore: "an Asherah pole (once again) stood in Samaria."

13:14 / **Wept over him:** The NIV gives the impression that Elisha is the *cause* of the king's distress. The Hb., however, is *wayyēbk ʿal-pānāyw*, which must mean that he wept *before/in the sight of* the prophet (cf. Lev. 10:3; Jer. 6:7 etc.). He weeps because he thinks he is on the point of defeat. Elisha, however, knows that the real **chariots and horsemen of Israel** are not of flesh and blood (cf. 2 Kgs. 2:11–12; 6:8–17). He is therefore able to promise Jehoahaz—whose repetition of Elisha's words from 2 Kgs. 2:12 only reveals his lack of perception—victories of the kind won by Ahab (1 Kgs. 20:13–34). Ahab had also been reduced to a remnant (20:15) and had also faced Aramean forces vastly superior in horses and chariotry (20:13, 21, 23–25, 28–30). Given that Elisha has in mind a series of victories in 2 Kgs. 13:18–19, it may well be that his use of "Aphek" (v. 17; cf. 1 Kgs. 20:26, 30) is not meant to signify the location of Jehoahaz's victories but to inform him of the sort of victories he can expect.

13:21 / **Elisha's tomb:** Since tombs in ancient Israel were characteristically dug out of soft rock or located in caves (e.g., Gen. 23), they did not present the difficulties of access to people in a hurry that more modern Western forms of burial might have done.

13:23 / **To this day:** The interpretation of this kind of statement requires caution (cf. the additional note to 1 Kgs. 8:8 on the phrase *ʿaḏ-hayyôm hazzeh,* "until this day"). Yet in a context where an everlasting promise is being cited, it seems likely that we are being told about God's continuing attitude to Israel in the postexilic period in which Kings was coming into its final shape. Such an understanding helps to make sense of the chapter and the book as a whole. Israel is still the people of the exodus (cf. 1 Kgs. 8:22ff.). It may be punished, but it will not be destroyed or "blotted out" now (2 Kgs. 14:27), any more than it was then (Deut. 9:14).

§46 Excursus: Elisha in Canonical Context

The ministry of Elisha was in many respects similar to that of Elijah. This is not surprising, since he was Joshua to Elijah's Moses (cf. 2 Kgs. 2:1–18). Like Elijah, he brought life in the midst of death (1 Kgs. 17:17–24; 2 Kgs. 4). Like him, he mediated salvation even to foreigners (1 Kgs. 17:17–24; 2 Kgs. 5). Having asked of Elijah a double portion of his spirit, he went on to perform many more miracles than his predecessor. As a true prophet of God, however, he brought with him not only blessing but also curse, not only salvation but also judgment (cf. the significance of his name, Elisha ["God saves"] son of Shaphat ["judgment"], and of his first two prophetic actions in 2 Kgs. 2:19–25). Though he could function as a mediator of salvation to Jehoram (2 Kgs. 5:7–8; 6:8–7:20), as the unnamed prophet of 1 Kings 20:13–34 had done for Jehoram's father Ahab, his ultimate destiny (as also Elijah's and Micaiah's in 1 Kgs. 21:17–24; 22:1–28) was as a mediator of judgment (2 Kgs. 9:1ff.). Thus, in God's own time, the process of judgment that Elijah had initiated came to completion in the destruction of the house of Ahab and the conclusion of the war against Baal-worship. That for which Elijah had prepared the way was, in Elisha's time, made a reality.

Elisha is mentioned only once in the NT, in Luke 4:27, where he functions typologically in respect of Jesus. Jesus' mission embraces the Gentiles, as the mission of Elisha did; what Jesus will do is analogous to what Elisha did when healing Naaman. Implicit connections between the two, however, are frequent in the Gospels. Jesus heals lepers, just like Elisha (2 Kgs. 5; Matt. 8:1–4; 10:8; 11:5; Mark 1:40–45; Luke 5:12–16; 7:22; 17:11–19; cf. also John 9:1–12 for a different kind of healing story that has analogies to the Naaman narrative). He transforms water (2 Kgs. 2:19–22; John 2:1–11) and suspends the laws of gravity in relation to it (2 Kgs. 6:1–7; Matt. 14:22–33; Mark 6:45–51; John 6:16–21). He raises the dead (2 Kgs. 4:8–37; Mark 5:21–24, 35–43; Luke

7:11–17; John 11:17–37) and multiplies food (2 Kgs. 4:1–7, 42–44; Matt. 14:13–21; 15:29–39; Mark 6:30–44; 8:1–10; Luke 9:10–17; John 6:1–15). He does all this especially for the benefit of the humble, who are generally more open to God's salvation than are the great. He mediates salvation, but he also brings judgment. He utters prophetic curses (2 Kgs. 2:23–25 and Matt. 21:18–22; Mark 11:12–14, 20–21, noting also Matt. 25:41). He comes so that those who see will become blind, even as those who are blind gain their sight (2 Kgs. 6:8–23; John 9:35–41; 12:37–41). He is the initiator of the coming of God's kingdom, when all will know divine justice (Matt. 13:36–43 etc.).

Given the many links between the two, including the fact that the names "Joshua," "Elisha," and "Jesus" have essentially the same meaning ("God saves"), and that John the Baptist is so clearly identified in the Gospels with Elijah (cf. §34 above), it is intriguing that more is not explicitly made in the NT of the Jesus-Elisha connection. Yet it may be that it is precisely because both Joshua and Elisha are successors to more famous men that this kind of thinking was inhibited. There would have been a natural desire within the church to avoid the suggestion that Jesus was John's successor in any sense that detracted from his pre-eminence—particularly since this was apparently a live issue in some quarters (note the careful way in which John 1:1–42 addresses the issue). Thus it is not surprising that the typological significance of Elisha in relation to Jesus has been downplayed.

Solomon and Elijah are presented in the NT as those from whom Christian believers can learn. Whether Elisha is presented in this way is less clear. Hebrews 11:34–35 (and possibly v. 36, if the boys from Bethel are in mind) may be taken as referring to him, and the early church certainly exercised faith of the kind being exhorted in Hebrews 11, in their mediation of both salvation and judgment in the manner of Elisha and Jesus (cf. Acts 5:1–11; 9:36–43).

§47 Amaziah, Jeroboam, and Azariah (2 Kgs. 14:1–15:7)

Second Kings 13 has ended with the description of a modest upturn in Israel's fortunes. The LORD has saved them, even in the midst of idolatry, because of both his covenant with the patriarchs (2 Kgs. 13:23) and—remembering the context in which the chapter is narrated—his promise to Jehu (2 Kgs. 10:30). The impetus of that recovery continues now into chapter 14, as the house of Jehu brings Israel relief, not only from Aram, but also from a foolishly hostile Judah.

14:1–6 / The introductory regnal formulas for Amaziah are the standard ones for relatively good (non-idolatrous) kings of Judah: he **did what was right** (v. 3) but failed to centralize the worship of the LORD in Jerusalem (**the high places . . . were not removed,** v. 4). In Amaziah's case, however, we find an additional criticism: in his "doing right" he was not like **David,** but like **his father Joash** (v. 3). This is a curious statement, whose meaning is never explicitly unpacked in the text. It is difficult to see any real difference in religious policy between the early Solomon, Asa, and Jehoshaphat, on the one hand ("like David" explicitly, 1 Kgs. 3:3; 15:11, or implicitly, 1 Kgs. 22:43), and Joash and Amaziah ("not like David" implicitly, 2 Kgs. 12:2, or explicitly, 2 Kgs. 14:3), on the other. The piety of Amaziah is, indeed, emphasized by verse 6, which tells us of adherence to the **Law of Moses** (rather than to custom) in dealing with the families of those who had murdered his father (cf. Deut. 24:16). Yet we shall not read of another Judean king who is "like David" until we read of Hezekiah (2 Kgs. 18:3; contrast 15:3, 34). There seems to be some doubt in the authors' minds about the wholeheartedness of the Davidic kings' commitment to the LORD throughout the period from Joash to Jotham, but they have not revealed to us their reasons for holding this opinion.

14:7–14 / Amaziah's military exploits included a successful campaign against the **Edomites** in northern Edom (v. 7; cf. the **Valley of Salt** in 2 Sam. 8:13 and the link back to 2 Kgs. 13:7 provided by the number **ten thousand;** cf. the additional note to 1 Kgs. 22:30) and a disastrous one against Israel (vv. 8–14). His arrogant challenge to Jehoash (**meet me face to face;** cf. the same phrase in v. 11) resulted in defeat at **Beth Shemesh,** about 20 miles west of Jerusalem (vv. 11–12) and an inevitable assault on the capital itself (vv. 13–14). A section of **the wall** was broken down (cf. Jer. 31:38; Neh. 8:16 for the gates mentioned) and plunder taken from the apparently refurbished **temple** and **palace** (cf. 2 Kgs. 12:17–18 for the most recent removal of treasures). On this occasion **hostages** were also taken away, to ensure future good behavior. Jerusalem has fallen for the first time, and Judah has now had its first experience of an "exile" to match Israel's experience under Jehoahaz (cf. 2 Kgs. 13:5).

14:15–22 / Why are the concluding formulas for Jehoash repeated (vv. 15–16; cf. 13:12–13), albeit not in identical wording, just before the information about Amaziah's demise (vv. 17–20)? The answer may lie partly in the contrast between the two kings in their deaths. Jehoash came to a natural and peaceful end; Amaziah met a violent death, the victim (like his father) of a conspiracy. The effect of placing the information about the two together is to emphasize this difference and to suggest that there is a connection between their fates and their roles in the war of 14:8ff. The innocent party dies in peace; the aggressor, acting as Rehoboam had been forbidden to act (1 Kgs. 12:22–24), is murdered.

Yet there is probably more to it than that. Although we are told of Amaziah's capture in verse 13, we are never told of his release—only of additional prisoners being taken (v. 14). Even more interesting is the wording of verse 17, which informs us that Amaziah "lived" (rather than "reigned") for fifteen years after the death of Jehoash. The "misplaced" formulas for Jehoash begin, in light of these two verses, to take on a new significance. Are we perhaps being told that the defeat at Beth-Shemesh was even more traumatic than we at first supposed? Has Judah been brought under Israelite rule, its own king a prisoner in Samaria? This first account in Kings of foreign capture of Jerusalem is very reminiscent of the second from last (2 Kgs. 24:8ff.) where we also read of a king (Jehoiachin) taken captive with hostages and of temple and palace being plundered. That king, of course, went on living (Hb. *ḥyh*, as in 2 Kgs. 14:17) in Babylon for many years afterwards, still called "king" by the authors of Kings even though it was the king of Babylon who effectively ruled over Judah (2 Kgs. 25:27–30; note the analogous use of "king of Edom" in 2 Kgs. 3:9, 26, cf. 1 Kgs. 22:47). Most significantly, it is precisely in that context of the deportation of Judean kings that we begin to find the regnal years of a foreign king being cited (the king of Babylon: 2 Kgs. 24:12; 25:8), indicating that he was the ruler who was really in control. Chronology is an aspect of political power. Are the events of 2 Kings 14:13–20 being presented, then, as a foreshadowing of those of the closing chapters of the book?

If the formulas for Jehoash are indeed placed as they are because he is the real "king" of 2 Kings 14:13–20, this would certainly explain one other curious feature of the Amaziah ac-count. The Hebrew of verse 22 is literally "He was the one who rebuilt Elath and restored it to Judah after the king rested with his fathers" (Hb. *škb ʿim-ʾaḇōṭāyw*). The NIV interprets "king" as "Amaziah," but it is Jehoash, and not Amaziah, who has just been described as "resting with his fathers" (Hb. *škb ʿim-ʾaḇōṭāyw*, v. 16). It is after the passing of Jehoash—the real power in the land—that **Azariah** is able to consolidate Amaziah's gains in Edom by claiming the port of **Elath** (cf. 1 Kgs. 9:26). The fact that he is called simply "the king," with no further indentification made, bears out our interpretation of the whole passage.

The "humbling" of the house of David thus continues (cf. 1 Kgs. 11:39; 15:16–22; 22:48–49; 2 Kgs. 11–12). There is limited success of the kind enjoyed in the old days of empire (cf. the defeat of Edom). Amaziah is unable to be a Solomon. He is unable to exploit his Edomite success and fails to exert power over the north of Israel. Judah "falls" (v. 10), in fact, under Israelite domin-ion, and it is Jeroboam II of Israel, rather than Amaziah of Judah, who ends up as the Solomon figure of the chapter—as we shall now see.

14:23–29 / The account of Jehoash's reign in 2 Kings 13 concluded in an upbeat way, with the recapture of some Israelite towns from the Arameans (13:25). It has now finally come to an end with an even more positive sign of Israelite recovery (14:8ff.). His son **Jeroboam** now carries the recovery still further. He is able to restore **the boundaries of Israel from Lebo Hamath** (see the additional note on 14:25) **to the Sea of the Arabah** (i.e., the Dead

Sea; cf. Josh. 3:16; 12:3). This represents, not merely the restoration of all the territory in Transjordan captured by Hazael in 2 Kings 10:32–33, but the wholesale incorporation of Aram into his kingdom (cf. also **Damascus and Hamath** in v. 28), the re-establishment of the ideal borders of northern Israel as they had existed under Solomon (cf. 1 Kgs. 8:65). This is not because he is a good king (v. 24). It is, rather, because in this period immediately after Elisha's death there is still deliverance to be found, in spite of idolatry. The promise to Jehu stands (2 Kgs. 10:30); the compassion of God is still active (13:23). When God sees, therefore, **how bitterly everyone is suffering** (v. 26; on **slave or free** see the additional note on 1 Kgs. 14:10), a **prophet** like Elisha is sent to announce deliverance and salvation (Hb. *yšʿ*; v. 27; cf. the commentary on 2 Kgs. 13:5, 20–25). But Israel's respite from foreign oppression is as temporary as its domination of Judah—as we shall shortly discover. The son of this second "Solomon" will fall even more spectacularly than the son of the first.

15:1–7 / The reign of **Azariah** (also called Uzziah; cf. 15:13, 30, 32, 34) is now picked up in more detail, though the information offered is sparse. The silence about his achievements is striking when we consider how much information is given about Jeroboam within a similar space. **He did what was right; but at some point he was afflicted . . . with leprosy,** and became unable to govern. Is there a suggestion (as in the case of Asa, cf. 1 Kgs. 15:23) that Azariah at some point departed from God's ways, like Gehazi before him (2 Kgs. 5:20–27)? It is Azariah's reign that sees the beginning of Isaiah's prophetic ministry (Isa. 1:1; 6:1).

Additional Notes §47

14:9 / **A thistle in Lebanon:** The point is that a puny **thistle** (i.e., Amaziah), easily trampled upon by any **wild beast,** should not think too highly of itself in relation to the mighty **cedar of Lebanon** (Jehoash). It is a mistake to take the detail about the **marriage** as suggesting that Amaziah had proposed a marriage-alliance with Jehoash (as some commentators do) because nothing else in the narrative suggests this interpretation. It is the **wild beast** after all, and not the **cedar,** that tramples the **thistle;** yet this does not imply that it was some third party, rather than Jehoash, who later attacked Amaziah. It is the general thrust of the fable that is important and not the detail (as in Judg. 9:7–15). For an interesting discussion of the possible connection between 14:6 and 14:9 (via Gen. 34), see C. M. Carmichael, *Law and Narrative in the Bible* (Ithaca: Cornell University Press, 1985), pp. 270–76.

14:19 / **They conspired against him in Jerusalem:** It is not clear who **they** are, although it is interesting that we hear nothing later of any reprisals by Amaziah's son (15:1–7; contrast 14:5–6). Was Azariah perhaps implicated? Nor are the circumstances in which the coup took place clear. It seems that Amaziah has, by this stage at least, returned to Jerusalem. He was bound to be unpopular there, given the consequences for the city of his military folly.

14:22 / **He was the one . . . :** For a recent discussion of Israel-Judah relations during the reigns of Azariah and Jeroboam that lends support to aspects of my reading of 14:15–22, see N. Na'aman, "Azariah of Judah and Jeroboam II of Israel," *VT* 43 (1993), pp. 227–34.

14:25 / **From Lebo Hamath to the Sea of the Arabah:** If the Hb. *lᵉḇô' ḥᵃmāṯ* is indeed intended as the name of a city, then the question arises as to its location. It is commonly supposed to be located to the southwest of Hamath itself. The difficulty with this view, however, is that in 1 Kgs. 8:65 the phrase "from Lebo Hamath to the Wadi of Egypt" seems intended as a designation of the whole Solomonic empire, analogous to the phrases "from the River to the land of Philistines, as far as the border of Egypt" and "from Tiphsah to Gaza" in 1 Kgs. 4:21, 24 (contrast the designation of Israel proper in 4:25—"from Dan to Beersheba"). In 2 Kgs. 14:28, Hamath itself is mentioned as part of Jeroboam's reconstituted empire, and in 15:16 it is implied that Tiphsah, well to the northeast of Hamath, was also brought back under Israelite control at this time. It is evident from these texts that the authors of Kings thought *lᵉḇô' ḥᵃmāṯ* lay much further north than most modern commentators do.

Jonah son of Amittai: That Jonah was a prophet of salvation similar to Elisha is crucial to the understanding of the book of Jonah, where he is presented as somewhat reluctant to understand his role in its broadest terms—as mediating salvation to the nations, as well as to Israel (contrast 2 Kgs. 5). He was not, of course, the only prophet active during this period, and his was not the only message for Israel (cf. Hos. 1:1; Amos 1:1).

14:26 / **Bitterly:** It does seem likely in the context that Hb. *mōreh* is to be derived from the verb *mrr*, "to be bitter," although it is then a word that occurs only here in the entire OT (cf. the closely related *mōrâ* of Gen. 26:35). *Mōreh* is usually the Hiphᶜil participle of the verb *yrh*, "to teach" (found also in 2 Kgs. 17:28; cf. the same verb in 1 Kgs. 8:36; 2 Kgs. 12:2; 17:27), and 1 Kgs. 8:35–36 makes a connection between affliction and teaching, using the same verbal roots that we find in 2 Kgs. 14:26 (ᶜnh, "to suffer"; *yrh*, "to teach"; cf. Lam. 3:25–39 for the idea that God instructs people through divinely-imposed suffering). Has the choice of *mōreh* in 2 Kgs. 14:26 perhaps been dictated by a desire to suggest that Israel has benefited from its experience?

14:27 / **The** LORD **had not said . . . :** To **blot out the name of Israel from under heaven** would be to destroy it utterly (Deut. 9:14), making forgiveness and restoration impossible (Deut. 29:20). This is something that the LORD **had not said** he would do; and when there was a danger of it happening, during the time of Jehu's dynasty, he took steps to prevent it. This statement must be understood in the context of what the LORD *has* said about judgment upon Israel in the book of Kings Israel will go into exile for its sins (1 Kgs. 14:15–16), but this will not be the end of Israel (1 Kgs. 8:33–51). God's covenant promises are still in force (2 Kgs. 13:23).

14:28 / **He recovered for Israel . . . belonged to Yaudi:** The Hb. is lit. "he restored Damascus and Hamath to Judah in Israel." It is a difficult line, but it is better to leave the difficulty unresolved than to seek to "clarify" the meaning, as the NIV does, by ignoring both text (which plainly has "Judah") and context (cf. Hb. *šûb lîhûdâ*, "restore to Judah," in both v. 22 and v. 28), and by introducing a place name (**Yaudi**) of which the OT elsewhere knows nothing. The gaps in our knowledge about Israel-Judah relations during Jeroboam's reign are certainly large enough to make space for different scenarios in which he might have "restored" territory to his southern neighbor (under treaty? for administrative purposes?). The perplexing "Judah in Israel," for all we know, could have been an Israelite designation for Judah during Jeroboam's reign (representing a claim to overlordship?), if indeed the Hb. phrase *lîhûdâ bᵉyiśrāʾēl* does not simply mean "to Judah at Israel's cost" (cf. Hb. *bᵉ* in 1 Kgs. 2:23; 16:34).

15:5 / **In a separate house:** The Hb. is lit. "in the house of freedom" (*bᵉbêt ḥopšît*), the meaning of which is debatable. We certainly cannot assume that Azariah's **leprosy** was a contagious disease and that the reference is to long-term quarantine (see the additional note to 2 Kgs. 5:1). The NIV footnote is probably on the right track, taking the phrase as a metaphor for being relieved of (set free from) responsibility in government. It may be that the king was seriously incapacitated, regarded as effectively "dead" (cf. Hb. *ḥopšî* in Job 3:19; Ps. 88:5).

§48 Israel's Last Days (2 Kgs. 15:8–31)

With the death of Jeroboam II, we have reached the "fourth generation" of the divine promise to Jehu (2 Kgs. 10:30). We expect a return to the unstable government, implied by 1 Kings 14:15 and illustrated in 1 Kings 14–16, that preceded the houses of Omri and Jehu. That is what we now find. Reigns change in quick succession, as Israel plunges speedily towards its doom. All deliverance has ceased, and judgment lies just around the corner.

15:8–12 / Scarcely has Jeroboam's son **Zechariah** sat on his throne and repeated the **evil** of **his fathers** when he is **assassinated**. The promise has run its course (v. 12; cf. 2 Kgs. 10:30), and before even one more regnal year has passed, the LORD removes Jehu's house from government. We have the impression of accumulated wrath, ready to burst in upon Jehu the moment the blockage to the normal flow of events is removed.

15:13–16 / Shallum, however, survives for an even briefer time. He holds on to power for a mere **month** before losing both crown and life to **Menahem**, whose power base is apparently in the old Israelite capital of **Tirzah** (vv. 14, 16; cf. 1 Kgs. 15:33; 16:8, 15, 23). In what will be the last action of an Israelite king claiming control of a Solomon-like empire, Menahem then attacks **Tiphsah** on the Euphrates river at the northernmost extent of Solomon's empire (1 Kgs. 4:24; cf. the commentary on 2 Kgs. 14:25, 28 and the additional note on 14:25), forcing the city's capitulation and brutalizing its population (cf. 2 Kgs. 8:12).

15:17–22 / **Menahem** reigns for **ten years,** but in a flash the recently reconstituted empire of Jeroboam disappears, as the **king of Assyria** invades ("comes against," as in Gen. 34:25) the land. It is uncertain whether Samaria itself is under any threat, since it is uncertain how far into "the land" **Pul** (another name for the Tiglath-Pileser of v. 29) has come. Comparison with 15:29 might suggest that it is only the reclaimed territories to the north of Israel proper that the first part of verse 19 has in view. Menahem nevertheless desires to have Pul as a friend rather than an enemy, particularly in view of the apparently unstable internal situation in Israel (he needed **to strengthen his own hold on the kingdom,** v. 19). He pays, therefore, to turn an enemy into a friend, just as Asa had once bought Ben-Hadad's support against his enemy Baasha (1 Kgs. 15:16–20). No details are given about the deal that leads to Pul's departure. It is an ominous development, however, for it is the king of Assyria who will eventually attack Samaria and take the Israelites into exile (2 Kgs. 17:1–6). He may not stand **in the land** for the moment (v. 20), but he does stand as a threat on the horizon. Aram has given way to Assyria as the great northern enemy, and the deliverance of the past, represented by Elisha ("God saves"), has given way to the very temporary comfort of the present, represented by Menahem (meaning "comforter") and his money.

15:23–26 / Menahem's son **Pekahiah** lasts only **two years,** until **one of his chief officers, Pekah,** launches an attack on the **royal palace.** Pekahiah is **assassinated,** along with **Argob and Arieh** ("the lion," a nickname perhaps). It is not clear who these people were, but we may be meant to think of the king's sons (cf. the fate of the families in 1 Kgs. 15:25–32; 16:8–14, other occasions when kings reigned for two years).

15:27–31 / Pekah's reign is longer (**twenty years**) than those of his four predecessors put together, though this is not to his great benefit. The main consequence of his lengthy reign is that he sees **Tiglath-Pileser** demonstrate that **Assyria** has indeed replaced Aram as the great foe, when he annexes much of Israel's northern (cf. 1 Kgs. 15:20) and eastern territory and deports a significant percentage of its population. First the empire has disappeared, now much of Israel—and all in the space of a few years. Worse is to come, as Pekah is assassinated by **Hoshea,** the king who will see the fall of Samaria and the final end of the kingdom. Before we hear of that, however, we must first catch up on events in Judah.

Additional Notes §48

15:10 / **In front of the people:** The "Ibleam" of the LXX MSS referred to in the NIV footnote is probably a guess, indicating that the syntactical difficulty in the Hb. was already felt by the translators. The general sense is clear enough: the assassination was in public.

15:13 / **One month:** It is noteworthy that Shallum receives no evaluation from the authors of Kings ("he did evil" etc.). This is not, as some have suggested, because his reign is so short (compare 1 Kgs. 16:15–20); but it is unlikely, either, to be because the authors considered him alone of all the northern kings to be blameless. The omission is a mystery.

15:16 / **Because they refused to open their gates . . . :** The NIV appears to be offering a paraphrase of the Hb., which is lit. "for he did not open and he smote all its pregnant women, he cut open." The general direction of the translation is probably correct, although the subject of "did not open" must strictly, in the context, be Menahem. The thought is perhaps that he failed to persuade them to open the gates (i.e., surrender).

§49 Jotham and Ahaz of Judah
(2 Kgs. 15:32–16:20)

The kingdom of Judah has been going through hard times. Its royal house has seen three of the last four kings assassinated, and the fourth lay aside power because of illness. Things are not about to improve.

15:32–38 / **Jotham** has already been exercising power in Judah because of his father's illness (15:5), but now he becomes king in his own right. He is a relatively good (non-idolatrous) king, doing **right in the eyes of the LORD**, though like his father rather than like David (cf. the commentary on 14:3) and still failing to centralize worship of the LORD in Jerusalem. It is he who rebuilds **the Upper Gate of the temple** (cf. Ezek. 9:2), presumably damaged in the course of Jehoash's incursion into Jerusalem in 14:13–14. He is no stranger to trouble on his northern border, suffering combined assault by **Rezin king of Aram and Pekah son of Remaliah**. This is the beginning of the so-called Syro-Ephraimite war, which features so prominently in the early chapters of Isaiah (7–9). It is during Jotham's reign that Micah's prophetic ministry begins (Mic. 1:1).

16:1–4 / With **Ahaz** we return to a period of officially sanctioned idolatry in Judah (**he did not do what was right**), as the king walks **in the ways of the kings of Israel** and the **high places** become centers, not of the worship of the LORD, but of the fertility cult. The language is largely that of 1 Kings 14:23–24, where Judah's adherence to the fertility cult was first described (cf. v. 3b with 14:24b and v. 4b with 14:23b). The new element is the child sacrifice **in the fire** (v. 3a)—an unmistakable allusion to participation in the cult of Molech, which is mentioned in 1 Kings 11:7 (cf. the additional note to v. 3). Ahaz is a particularly wicked king. It is surprising, then, that there is such a notable absence here of any reference to the promise to David (cf., by contrast,

1 Kgs. 15:4 and 2 Kgs. 8:19). It has been some time, in fact, since we have heard this promise cited in relation to Judah. This is disconcerting. The last time it was absent from the account of a wicked king's reign (Ahaziah's) we saw the Davidic house brought to the brink of extinction. What are we to expect now, when a Judean once more follows **the detestable ways of the nations** and when we are reminded, not of the LORD's promise to David, but of his "driving out" of the nations **before the Israelites** because of their sins? Is the Davidic promise no longer in force? Is Judah is to be "driven out" of the land for *its* sins?

16:5–9 / The Syro-Ephraimite alliance now puts great pressure on the Judean king, besieging him in Jerusalem and depriving him of **Elath** (only recently won back for Judah by Azariah, 2 Kgs. 14:22). Ahaz's response is to send **messengers** to the **king of Assyria** with yet more treasure from temple and palace (cf. 12:17–18). He accepts vassal status and requests his help (vv. 7–8). It is a strategy that succeeds well; Tiglath-Pileser descends upon **Damascus** and captures it and removes both **Rezin** and **its inhabitants,** though by different means (cf. the reverse "exodus" implied by deportation to **Kir,** the original Aramean homeland according to Amos 9:7). The effect of this invasion on Israel has already been described in 15:29. Jerusalem has been saved, though at the cost of its independence. The reader of Isaiah, to whose book we are directed by 16:5 (note the similarity to Isa. 7:1), knows that the decision to involve Assyria in this way will not be to Judah's long-term benefit.

16:10–20 / The intervention of Assyria into Judean affairs is fateful, not only in its political but also in its religious consequences. Ahaz travels to **Damascus** (v. 10) to meet his new overlord. The result is a new **altar** for the temple of the LORD. The new **altar** displaces the old (cf. 1 Kgs. 8:64), which will now be used only **for seeking guidance,** perhaps for sacrifice in relation to divination (the reading of entrails, etc.; cf. 2 Kgs. 17:17, and the use of the verb *bqr* in Lev. 13:27, 34, of ritual examination). There are also various other innovations (vv. 17–18); Ahaz takes apart the **movable stands** (1 Kgs. 7:27–36; 2 Kgs. 25:13; 2 Chron. 28:24), disposing of their **side panels** and **basins,** and he exchanges the twelve **bronze bulls** under the **Sea** (1 Kgs. 7:23–26) for a **stone base.** Finally, he takes two actions of uncertain nature (cf. the additional note to v. 18).

The motivation for all these innovations is not evident. Our first suspicion, given the close relationship between religion and politics in the ancient world, might be that there is some connection between his actions and his new vassal-status. Yet there is no suggestion in the text that any of the changes were specifically required of him as a vassal. The implication of verse 10 (**he saw . . . and sent**) is that, at least in the case of the altar, it was simply a matter of aesthetics—he liked what he found in Damascus. The removal of the basins and the bulls may have been dictated by similar considerations. It has sometimes been suggested that it was a matter of financial necessity. There is certainly no evidence for this in the text; the "gift" described in verses 7–8 includes no bronze, and its giving obviously precedes, in narrative time, the actions of verse 17. It is simply that travel has broadened Ahaz's mind. He has gained some new ideas. Only in the case of the last two innovations is it said that the motive was **deference to** (or fear of) **the king of Assyria;** again, there is no hint here of requirement, only of a desire to remove a possible source of offence. Ahaz is presented as a king who is open to foreign *influence* in his religious policy (as in 16:2–4). He is not presented as one who is under foreign *control.* These are dark days, nonetheless. Never before has a Judean king taken it upon himself to redesign the Solomonic temple in such a way. The days of Solomon's glory seem farther and farther behind us.

Additional Notes §49

16:3 / **Sacrificed . . . in the fire:** The Hb. is *he ᶜebîr bā᾽ēš*. The NIV footnote implies that there is some doubt about the meaning of the phrase. This is true only if one does not allow texts from elsewhere in the OT to inform our understanding of it (e.g., Ezek. 16:20–21; 20:26–31; with Lev. 18:21; Jer. 32:35). See further Day, *Molech,* esp. pp. 15–28.

16:18 / **He took away . . . :** The Hb. is difficult: "The screen [a unique word in Hb., related to the verb *skk,* "to screen, cover"] of the sabbath that they built in the house and the outer entranceway of the king he caused to go around the house of the LORD . . ." Both the architectural details and the nature of the king's actions are beyond our grasp. All that is assured is that he is motivated by a desire not to offend (for whatever reason offence might have been taken) the king of Assyria. Perhaps the two aspects of the temple mentioned here symbolized in a particularly obvious way the claims of the Davidic kings to preeminence.

§50 The End of Israel (2 Kgs. 17:1–41)

The "uprooting" and "scattering" of Israel (1 Kgs. 14:15) has long been delayed because of God's promises and character (2 Kgs. 10:30; 13; 14:23–29). God has continually saved (Hb. $yš^c$) it from its enemies: through Elisha, through Jeroboam (2 Kgs. 14:27), through other unnamed saviors (2 Kgs. 13:5). There have been signs in the preceding chapters, however, that deliverance is now at an end, that the "exile" of 2 Kings 13:5 was a dry run for a now imminent main event. The most recent act of "salvation," in fact (16:7–9, cf. "save me," $yš^c$, in 16:7) was in reality an act of judgment upon Israel that brought the Assyrian king to within striking distance of Samaria (15:29). The third siege of the city (cf. 1 Kgs. 20:1ff.; 2 Kgs. 6:24ff.) will be the last. There will be no prophet like Elisha to announce God's intervention. The king will stand alone. And though his name promises much (Hoshea, "salvation"), he—unlike the prophet—will have no power to fulfill its promise.

17:1–6 / The story of the last days of Israel provides us with one surprise. **Hoshea,** like most of his predecessors, is said to have done **evil;** however, he was not as bad as they were (v. 2). As in the case of the kings of Judah who were "not like David" (2 Kgs. 12:2; 14:3; 15:3, 34), we are left to surmise what exactly this might mean. Is there some hint at a lack of wholeheartedness in his pursuit of Jeroboam's sins (significantly not mentioned here), a hint at the beginnings, perhaps, of religious reform? If so, it was too late. Hoshea's political maneuvering between Assyria and Egypt brought down upon his head the full wrath of the Assyrian **Shalmaneser.** Hoshea was imprisoned, Samaria eventually **captured,** and the **Israelites** carried off to **Assyria** and dispersed throughout the empire.

17:7–17 / A number of explanations might be and have been given for the way the northern kingdom came to the end it did. The authors of Kings are interested only in the explanation that underlies all others: **the Israelites had sinned against the LORD their God, who had brought them out of Egypt.** The line echoes the prolog to the Ten Commandments in Exodus 20:2 and Deuteronomy 5:6, where the LORD reminds the people who *God* is, before going on to tell them who *they* must be, in response to God. The basic requirement is that they must have "no other gods before him" (Exod. 20:3; Deut. 5:7). It is this most central commandment that Israel forgot, as they **worshiped other gods** and became involved in the many religious **practices** we have read of thus far (vv. 7–8). Across the whole land, **from watchtower to fortified city,** they built themselves **high places** and participated in the fertility cult, provoking **the LORD to anger** (Hb. *kᶜs;* cf. 1 Kgs. 14:9; 15:30; 16:2, 7, 13, 26, 33; 21:22; 22:53). They worshiped **idols** (Hb. *gillulîm,* v. 12—cf. 1 Kgs. 21:26; *hebel,* v. 15—cf. 1 Kgs. 16:13, 26), in disobedience to the divine command (cf. Exod. 20:4–5 for the prohibition, if not these precise words), and were fashioned in their image (**became worthless,** v. 15). In particular, they built themselves **two calves** and an **Asherah pole,** and **worshiped Baal** (v. 16; cf. 1 Kgs. 12:25ff.; 16:31ff.). All of this was done in flagrant disregard for God's **Law** and **covenant** (vv. 13, 15) and in defiance of God's **prophets** (v. 13). It was done with the stubbornness and pride of those who had come out of Egypt in the first place (v. 14; cf. the **stiff-necked** people of Deut. 9–10, esp. 9:6, 13; 10:16). It was done in imitation of **the nations around them** (v. 15), whom **the LORD had ordered them** not to imitate (v. 15; cf. Deut. 7; 18:9–12), and whom **the LORD had driven out before them** (v. 8). In doing as they did, Israel has now met the same fate. The Israelites have been driven out of the promised land.

So much for Israel. The alert reader will have noticed something strange, however, while reading through this catalog of sins. Several of the references appear to be to religion, not in the northern kingdom, but in Judah. The combination **high places . . . sacred stones and Asherah poles** (vv. 9–10) has appeared thus far only in 1 Kings 14:23 and the phrase **under every high hill and under every spreading tree** (v. 10) only in the same verse. An almost identical phrase appears in relation to Ahaz (2 Kgs. 16:4), and it is only in that passage that we have hitherto read of fire-sacrifice (v. 17). The reference to **divination** in v. 17, if meant specifically rather than generally, can also refer only to him (cf. 16:15).

These links back to 1 Kings 14 and 2 Kings 16 are significant. It was right at the beginning of the account of the divided monarchy that hints were first given that Judah, in imitating the practices of the nations, might ultimately share in their (and Israel's) fate. Nonetheless, for much of the succeeding history Judah and its monarchy have been treated quite differently than Israel by God, because of David. Yet the account of the reign of Ahaz has once again raised a question about whether this state of affairs will continue forever, and 2 Kings 17:7–17 now sharpens the question still further. Both kingdoms have sinned, and both have received prophetic warnings (v. 13). The implication is that, in the absence of any response, Judah will indeed go the same way as Israel. The Davidic promise will not in the end protect it (cf. the threat of 1 Kgs. 9:1–9). Its determination to *act* like Israel (1 Kgs. 14:21–24; 2 Kgs. 8:16ff.; 16:1–4) will at last earn it the distinction of being *treated* like Israel.

17:18–23 / This is also the implication of verses 18–23. We are again mainly concerned with the sins and fate of the northern kingdom. As verses 7–17 have offered us a general catalog of sins, so verses 21–23 remind us of the specific sin that lay at the heart of Israel's apostasy: the **great sin** (cf. Exod. 32:21, 30–31) of **Jeroboam . . . who enticed Israel away** (1 Kgs. 12:25ff.). They failed to **turn away** (Hb. *swr*) from the cult he introduced, although they sometimes supplemented it, and so the LORD eventually **removed them** (Hb. *swr*) to **Assyria** (vv. 22–23). The way that **Judah . . . followed the practices Israel had introduced** is, however, highlighted (vv. 18–19), raising the specter of future doom for Judah as well. The phrase **all the people of Israel** in verse 20 is, indeed, highly ambiguous. Does it refer only to the "Israel" of verses 18 and 21 (the northern kingdom)? Or does it reach forward in the story to embrace **Judah**—"rejecting" God's decrees (Hb. *mʾs*, v. 15) and in the end being **rejected** by him (Hb. *mʾs*, v. 20)? Are **plunderers** (Hb. *šōsîm*, v. 20) to be given free reign throughout the land, with no savior to bring rescue as of old (Judg. 2:11–16)?

17:24–41 / We shall have to wait for an answer to this last question. For the moment the narrative continues with its main concern—the fate of the north. The Israelites have been exiled; however, the land of Israel was not left empty. The **king of Assyria** settled various other peoples there, from places both close at hand (e.g., **Hamath;** cf. 2 Kgs. 14:28) and further away (e.g., **Babylon**), and these peoples **took over Samaria and lived in its towns.** It is their religion that is the subject of interest in this last section of the chapter. It is a difficult passage, which can be understood only if we assume that it does not necessarily present the authors' own point of view. Only thus can we understand the sharp contradiction between verses 25–33 and verses 34–39, summed up in the adjacent verses 33–34: **they worshiped the LORD, but they also served their own gods . . . they neither worship the LORD nor adhere to the decrees. . . .**

The first passage makes certain claims about northern worship in this period. It is true, it tells us, that when these peoples first settled in Israel, **they did not worship the LORD** (v. 25). When the **lions** struck, however, they realized that the god of the land was against them, and they contacted the king of Assyria. He sent an exiled Israelite priest to **Bethel,** who **taught them how to worship the LORD** (v. 28). The LORD was thus truly worshiped alongside all the various other foreign gods of the peoples concerned (vv. 29–33).

Merely to state what the passage claims is to see how at variance it is with the whole thrust of the story of Kings thus far. Its fundamental assumption is that the LORD is simply a local god. This god must be appeased, certainly, by the new residents in the land, by being worshiped correctly alongside all their other gods. But this is the extent of their religious obligation to the LORD. The God of whom the remainder of Kings knows, on the other hand, is the LORD of all peoples and all history. This God does sometimes use lions as emissaries (1 Kgs. 13:24ff.; 20:35–36) but is not confined to a single territory. As the only God, the LORD claims exclusive worship. It is impossible that the authors who have told us all this should now be telling us that a broad pantheon of gods is acceptable—that this new use of the **high places,** with its new priesthood (vv. 29, 32; cf. 1 Kgs. 13:33), is any less reprehensible than the old Jeroboam cult it has replaced. The kind of worship of the LORD that is taught by the exiled Israelite priest is evidently and predictably just as flawed as the worship that led to Israel's exile in the first place.

We must reckon, then, with the presence of irony in 2 Kings 17:25–33. It is not a passage meant to be taken at face value. The authors are simply setting up a particular point of view in order to demolish it—rather in the manner of a participant in a debating competition. The tone of the passage is best caught, in fact, if the reader mentally supplies quotation marks to the words "wor-

ship" and "worshiped" in the NIV translation of verses 28 and
32–33. For we are certainly not to regard the "worship" described
in these verses as true worship—as verses 34–39 make clear. An
intrinsic feature of true worship, they tell us, is its exclusivity.
Mixed worship is not true worship of the God who has from the
beginning demanded **Do not worship any other gods** (vv. 35,
37–38). What is clear by the end of the chapter, then, is that the
exile of Israel has not led to any improvement in the religion of the
people who dwell in the land. They pursue their path of **"worshiping" the** LORD while **serving their idols.** Nothing has changed.

Additional Notes §50

17:4 / **So king of Egypt:** It is much more likely, given the form
of the Hb. and the normal practice of the authors elsewhere in Kings of
referring to foreign kings by their personal name, that such a name is
intended here, rather than the place-name of the NIV footnote. Whether
So is intended as an abbreviation for Osorkon is another matter. For a
good discussion of the issues, see J. Day, "The Problem of 'So, King of
Egypt' in 2 Kings 17:4," *VT* 42 (1992), pp. 289–301.

17:9 / **Secretly did things:** The Hb. verb is *ḥpʾ*, which occurs
only here in the OT. It is usually regarded as a synonym for *ḥph*, "to
cover"; as the NIV translation reflects. It has to be asked, however,
whether such a translation fits the context. There has been no suggestion so far that Israel's apostasy was meant to be, or succeeded in being,
a secret from anyone. If the connection with *ḥph* is correct, then it might
be better to understand the verb in the sense of "to overlay" that *ḥph* has
in 2 Chron. 3:5–9. That is also a context in which preparations for
worship are described; various parts of the Solomonic temple are overlaid with gold. 2 Kgs. 17:9 would refer, then, to the construction of
illegitimate items for worship—including the golden calves of Jeroboam
themselves (v. 16). We may translate: "the Israelites overlaid things that
were not right so far as the LORD their God was concerned."
From watchtower to fortified city: That is, all over the land, from
the smallest to the largest place where people lived. The phrase in this
particular context may also carry connotations of the Israelites, through
idolatry, undermining their own defences from within.

17:16 / **All the starry hosts:** It is interesting that neither this sin,
nor that of **sorcery** (v. 17), has been introduced to us so far in the narrative.
These sins will not be mentioned again until the account of Manasseh's
reign in 2 Kgs. 21 (cf. 21:3–6). The passage embraces not only the sins of
Judah in the preceding narrative, then, but also those yet to come.

§51 Hezekiah (2 Kgs. 18:1–12)

Second Kings 16 and 17 have suggested that Judah, like Israel, may be heading for exile unless it heeds the prophetic warnings and turns away from its sins. It is at this point in the narrative—after reading of several kings who were not quite like David (Joash to Jotham) and one who was utterly different from him (Ahaz)—that we are now presented with a king who is not merely similar to David in the way that Asa (explicitly, 1 Kgs. 15:11) and Jehoshaphat (by implication, 1 Kgs. 22:43) were, but resembles him more closely than any Davidic king so far. This is the king for whom we have been waiting, the second David who reforms Judean worship and makes it what it should be.

18:1–4 / Even the most righteous of the Judean kings thus far have failed to act against the shrines outside Jerusalem. The recurrent complaint has been that the **high places** "were not removed" (Hb. *habbāmôt lōʾ sārû,* 1 Kgs. 15:14; 22:43; 2 Kgs. 12:3; 14:4; 15:4, 35). The possibility has always existed, therefore, that they would become focal points for the kind of slide from authentic worship into apostasy that happened during the reign of Solomon (compare 1 Kgs. 3:2–3 with 11:7–8, noting the continuing effects in 14:22–24). This is precisely what has occurred during the reign of Ahaz (2 Kgs. 16:4; the "he" indicates royal promotion of the fertility cult, of course, rather than personal visitation of all the shrines). **Hezekiah** now appears as the one who at last addresses this issue: **he removed the high places** (Hb. *hûʾ hēsîr ʾet-habbāmôt,* 2 Kgs. 18:4). He also took action in relation to other aspects of the cult introduced by his father, the **sacred stones** (cf. 1 Kgs. 14:23; 2 Kgs. 17:10) and the **Asherah** pole (MT; NIV's **poles;** cf. the additional note to v. 4). Finally, **he broke into pieces the bronze snake** of the wilderness story (Num. 21:4–9; cf. 1 Kgs. 8:1–9 for other religious items from the Mosaic age that had been deposited in the temple). The OT tradition does not present **Nehushtan** as having originally been made for worship.

It is unlikely that the authors of Kings mean us to understand that it was worshiped continually, even in the monarchic period (cf. the additional note). It is most unlikely, then, that the name is meant to echo uncleanness (NIV footnote c, perhaps thinking of Hb. *šiqquṣ*, "detested thing," or *štn*, "to urinate") unless we are intended to think of it only as a nickname given to the snake by Hezekiah himself (cf. NIV footnote b). The name plays simply on Hb. *nāḥāš*, "snake," and *nᵉḥōšeṯ*, "bronze."

18:5–8 / Thus Hezekiah was not merely one in a line of kings, as these verses go on to emphasize. In at least one respect, the way in which he **trusted in the LORD** (v. 5), there was **no one like him among all the kings of Judah**. This evidenced itself in the way that he **held fast** to God (Hb. *dbq*) and kept the law of **Moses** throughout his life, in contrast to Solomon, who in his old age "held fast" to foreign wives (Hb. *dbq*, 1 Kgs. 11:2; cf. also Jehoram in 2 Kgs. 3:3) and broke the law. The consequence of this religious faithfulness was that Hezekiah's military exploits paralleled David's in a way that was not true of any of the rest of his descendants. Only of David and Hezekiah among the Davidic kings is it said that **the LORD was with him** (v. 7; cf. 1 Sam. 16:18; 18:12, 14; 2 Sam. 5:10) and that the king **was successful** in war (Hb. *śkl*, v. 7; cf. 1 Sam. 18:5, 14, 15). Only David and Hezekiah, furthermore, are said to have **defeated** the Philistines (Hb. *nkh*, v. 8; cf. 1 Sam. 18:27; 19:8; etc.). As similar to David as he was, he was by the same token utterly dissimilar to Ahaz, for he would not continue to **serve** the king of Assyria (Hb. *ʿbd*; contrast Ahaz's description of himself as "servant" in 2 Kgs. 16:7) but **rebelled** against him. Foreign influence or domination, of whatever kind, was rejected.

18:9–12 / To remind us of the kind of environment in which Hezekiah pursued this bold policy and to prepare us for the story in 18:13–19:37, the fate of the northern kingdom is now reiterated (cf. 2 Kgs. 17:1–6). This was a time when rebellion against the Assyrian king evoked an aggressive, devastating response (vv. 9–11). We can hardly doubt that in such an environment, Judah, too, will soon be attacked. What will be the outcome then? The reminder in verse 12 that the people of the north, unlike the people of Judah under Hezekiah, had departed from **all that Moses . . . commanded** (cf. 2 Kgs. 17:7–23) is suggestive of a different fate for Judah, whose king clearly kept these same commands (v. 6). The Assyrian victory over the north was itself possible only because it was the will of God that Assyria should execute judgment on a sinful people. Yet we cannot forget that it was under the best of the northern kings that judgment fell (2 Kgs. 17:2). Is it possible that Hezekiah's reforms have come too late to make any difference? Are we now to read of the end of Judah?

Additional Notes §51

18:4 / **Asherah poles:** The MT has the singular here; only one Hb. MS contains what may be a plural (Hb. ᵃˣᵉrôt̠, as in Judg. 3:7), although it is not the form of the plural found elsewhere in Kings (Hb. ᵃˣērîm, as in 1 Kgs. 14:15, 23; 2 Kgs. 17:10). It seems that a particular Asherah pole is in mind, as in the earlier reformation of Asa (cf. 1 Kgs. 15:13). The implication is perhaps that Ahaz had placed one of these in the Jerusalem temple itself—as Ahab may have done before him, in his temple for Baal (1 Kgs. 16:32–33; cf. its reappearance in 2 Kgs. 13:6), and as Manasseh certainly did later (cf. 2 Kgs. 23:6, referring back to 21:3).

The bronze snake: It comes as something of a surprise to find **Nehushtan,** hitherto unmentioned in the narrative of Kings, making an appearance as the object of idolatrous worship, not least because of the implicit claim of the verse that it has been a feature of Judean worship for some time (**up to that time,** implying customary practice). The authors of Kings have, of course, gone out of their way to make a distinction between Judean kings who were apostate ("did evil"), leading the people into false worship, and those who were faithful to the LORD ("did right"), acting against idolatry. It is precisely in the accounts of the reigns of the righteous kings (and only there) that we have hitherto met the Piᶜel participle mᵉqaṭṭᵉrîm, **burning incense** (1 Kgs. 22:43; 2 Kgs. 12:3; 14:4; 15:4, 35), used there of acceptable worship of the LORD. It is thus apparent that **up to that time** (Hb. ᶜad-hayyāmîm hāhēmmâ) is not to be interpreted as implying that they venerated the snake continually throughout the preceding period, but rather that they did so in that period and never thereafter. As with other artefacts in the temple (cf. the additional note to 1 Kgs. 6:18), the symbolism of the snake (a fertility symbol associated elsewhere with the goddess Asherah) was open to misconstrual in periods when the fertility cult was resurgent (the reigns of the later Solomon; Rehoboam and Abijam; Jehoram and Ahaziah; Ahaz). Like the high places, then—equally capable in principle of finding their proper place within authentic worship, but often becoming in practice focal points for idolatry—even this relic of the Mosaic age had to go so that Moses' law should not be broken (Deut. 4:15ff.). For similarly general language about the past, which must be regarded in the same nuanced way when its context within the book of Kings as a whole is appreciated, see 2 Kgs. 22:13, 17; 23:5, 11–13.

§52 The Assyrian Assault on Judah (2 Kgs. 18:13–19:37)

The second David has arrived. He has reformed Judean worship according to Mosaic law, casting off foreign influence and domination. We wait to see what will happen when the king of Assyria tries to take the kind of vengeance on Judah that he has just inflicted upon Israel.

18:13–16 / The beginning of the Assyrian assault is reported in verses 13–16, as a new king (**Sennacherib**) attacks **all the fortified cities** and captures them. This is not a very promising beginning. It seems that Hezekiah may indeed be about to suffer the same fate as Hoshea, regardless of his trust in God (v. 5). For all that Hezekiah has been lauded as a king quite unlike anyone who preceded him, his first reaction to foreign attack is a familiar one; he raids the royal **treasuries** and **the temple,** even stripping the **gold** from its **doors and doorposts** (cf. 1 Kgs. 15:18ff.; 2 Kgs. 12:17–18; 16:7ff.). The opening verses of the chapter did not lead us to expect this response, with its accompanying confession of sin against a foreign king (v. 14). We are presumably to regard it as a regrettable lapse—a disappointing prolog to what will turn out to be Hezekiah's finest hour.

18:17–25 / The rules of the game, as they have been followed thus far, are that kings who accept silver and gold should keep their side of the bargain. For the first time these rules are broken. **The king of Assyria** has decided (for reasons undisclosed in the narrative) that, on this occasion, payment is not enough. While Jerusalem's gates remain closed to him, he will regard Hezekiah as a rebel. Far from withdrawing from Judah (v. 14), therefore, he now sends an **army** from **Lachish** to Jerusalem, and his commanders try to talk Hezekiah into surrender. The issue at the heart of the **field commander**'s speech is precisely that of "trust" (Hb. *bṭḥ* in v. 5 and in vv. 19, 20, 21, 22, 24, where the NIV translates it as "basing confidence" and "depending"). Does Hezekiah depend on human help from **Egypt,** as Hoshea did (2 Kgs. 17:4)? Pharaoh is only the **splintered reed of a staff,** unable to offer genuine support (v. 21). There is no evidence in Kings, of course, that Hezekiah does look to Egypt, but the Assyrian is covering all the possibilities. His next assault is right on the mark. Do Hezekiah and his officials depend on the LORD? Well then, what of the fact that it is *his* **high places and altars** that have been **removed** (v. 22)? Is he likely to help under such circumstances? Is it not much more likely that he has sent the Assyrians to **destroy** Jerusalem (v. 25)? It is an argument designed to sow seeds of doubt. It is undoubtedly true that the high places were, throughout much of the preceding period, places where worship of the LORD took place. It is equally the case that the LORD has just used the Assyrians to bring judgment upon his people (17:1–23; 18:9–12). Are the Judeans wise, the commander questions, to trust in the unseen LORD, when the all too visible Assyrian army stands at the gates with overwhelmingly superior numbers (v. 23)?

18:26–37 / Hezekiah's officials (see the commentary on 1 Kgs. 4:1–6 for a brief discussion of their offices as listed in v. 18) evidently feel the force of these arguments, for they are anxious that **the people on the wall** should not hear them. They request the **commander** to speak in Aramaic, the language of international diplomacy, rather than in Hebrew (strictly "Judean," v. 26). But it is not in the commander's interest that the people, shortly to know the horrors of a long siege (they will **eat their own filth and drink their own urine,** v. 27; cf. 2 Kgs. 6:24ff.), should be deprived of the opportunity to hear his words. He therefore now addresses them directly (vv. 28ff.). They should not listen to Hezekiah, with all his talk of **trust** (Hb. *bṭḥ* again) and deliverance. The realities are quite different. If they **make peace** with Assyria and surrender the city, they will at least know life. They will escape the misery of siege (they will **eat** proper food instead of filth and **drink water** instead of urine, v. 31). Although they will be taken into exile, their exile will not be harsh; they will dwell in a new "promised land" like their own (v. 32; cf. Deut. 8:7–9). If rebellion persists, however, they will know only death. For no **god** has been able to deliver **his land from the hand of the king of Assyria** (vv. 33–35), and it will be no different with the LORD.

19:1–7 / With these last words the Assyrian has clearly overreached himself. It is one thing to claim that the LORD *will* not deliver Jerusalem because Assyria is the LORD's instrument of judgment (v. 25). It is quite another thing to claim that the LORD is simply one of many powerless gods and *cannot* deliver Jerusalem (vv. 33–35), and to offer oneself in the LORD's place as the true provider of material blessings and life itself (vv. 31–32). It is the Assyrian, and not Hezekiah, who thus reveals himself to be out of touch with reality. We are reminded of the similar misconception of the Arameans in 1 Kings 20:23ff., and the divine response in 20:28ff., when another vast army was given into Israel's hand; now we understand better what the outcome of the siege is likely to be.

Our suspicions are confirmed in 19:1–7. Hezekiah, attired in a suitable way for one who faces disaster (v. 1; cf. 2 Kgs. 6:30), consults Isaiah. He graphically describes the situation to the prophet as a day of great humiliation and powerlessness (v. 3). The only hope for **the remnant** of the people of Judah **that still survives** in the city is that the LORD—truly **the living God,** and not simply one false god among many—will act to repulse the foreign king who has sent his servant to **ridicule** God (v. 4). The prophetic word is duly delivered (vv. 5–7), and this is the word of the LORD, in contrast to the word of the "great king" (18:19, 28). The LORD will so influence Sennacherib's thinking (**put such a spirit in him;** cf. 1 Sam. 16:14–16; 1 Kgs. 22:21–23; 2 Kgs. 7:6; Isa. 19:14) that **when he hears a certain report** he will abandon his campaign and **return to his own country** to meet his death. The LORD will thus engineer the "return" (Hb. *šwb̠*) that Hezekiah could not secure through monetary payments (cf. *šwb̠* in 18:14, translated by the NIV as "withdraw").

19:8–13 / The prophecy is reassuring, but somewhat vague about the circumstances of its fulfillment. What will be heard (Hb. *šmᶜ*)? When will the king return (Hb. *šwb̠*)? There is a suggestion of reprieve for the city as early as verse 8, as the **field commander** "hears" (Hb. *šmᶜ*) that Sennacherib has **left Lachish** and "returns" (Hb. *šwb̠*; the NIV's **withdrew**) to find him, now **fighting against Libnah.** Nothing comes of this, however. Sennacherib stays firmly rooted in the land, and the "great army" evidently remains outside Jerusalem, under the supreme commander (18:17). A second false dawn follows close behind. The Assyrian king "hears" (Hb. *šmᶜ*) about the advance of **Tirhakah,**

king of Cush (v. 9). This time he himself "returns" (Hb. *šwb*), but only to his verbal assault on Hezekiah (cf. the Hb. idiom "he returned and he sent," meaning **he again sent**). It seems that the prophecy is not to be fulfilled immediately. Far from being sent to his death in Assyria, Sennacherib remains to compound his sin of blasphemy by committing it a second time (vv. 10–13). The argument is subtly different on this occasion. In 18:28ff. it was Hezekiah who was deceiving (Hb. *šnʾ*, v. 29) the people about what would happen if they trusted the LORD (*bṭḥ*, v. 30). In 19:10ff. it is Hezekiah himself who is deceived by the God in whom he trusts (*nšʾ*, *bṭḥ*, v. 10). This is a god, says Sennacherib, who is not only weak, but duplicitous. Thus, he implies, this is a god who will be destroyed just like the deities of so many other lands (he amplifies the list in 18:34 to emphasize just how many kings and gods were destroyed; vv. 12–13). Here is a much more direct attack on the LORD than the one in chapter 18, and one that displays monumental arrogance.

19:14–19 / Hezekiah's response is, this time, not to ask *Isaiah* to pray (v. 4), but rather to pray *himself*. It is a memorable prayer, in which self-interest is for the moment left behind, and concern for the LORD's reputation, so besmirched by Sennacherib's slander, takes over. The God **enthroned between the cherubim** (cf. the commentary on 1 Kgs. 6:14–35), who has taken Israel for God's special people, is not merely one among many gods. Hezekiah prays to God **alone**, creator of **heaven and earth—God over all the kingdoms of the earth** (v. 15; cf. Deut. 4:32–40, and the beginning of the similarly memorable prayer in Acts 4:24ff.). It is undeniable that the Assyrians have known success and have destroyed the gods of the nations they have conquered. These were not truly **gods**, however, **but only wood and stone** (Deut. 4:28). That all the **kingdoms on earth** should know the difference between God and the gods, Hezekiah now asks that Jerusalem be delivered from the Assyrian's hand (cf. 1 Sam. 17:45–47; 1 Kgs. 18:36–37, where the issue is also represented in this way).

19:20–34 / A second Isaianic prophecy, in three parts, brings God's response to Hezekiah's prayer. The first part (vv. 20–28) opens with general indications about the consequences of Sennacherib's blasphemy and **pride** in terms of his future downfall, when he will be despised and mocked by **Jerusalem** as he flees (vv. 21–22). His mistake has been to imagine that his military accomplishments have been achieved in his own strength (vv. 23–24). In reality, however, the LORD **ordained** and **planned** it all (vv. 25–26). Assyria was merely the rod of his anger (to use another Isaianic phrase; cf. Isa. 10:5–11), something already implied, unwittingly, in Sennacherib's use of the verb *ḥrm*, "destroy," in 19:11 (cf. 1 Kgs. 9:21 and 20:42 for the characteristic use of *ḥrm* in relation to the LORD). Now the judgment of the all-knowing God (v. 27) will come upon Assyria instead, and Sennacherib will be forced to **return by the way** he **came** (v. 28).

The second part of the prophecy looks beyond the withdrawal of the Assyrians from Judah, addressing the question of what will happen then. Recovery will be slow, but the **remnant** remaining in Jerusalem will survive (cf. 19:4) and go on to **take root** in the land and prosper (vv. 30–31). The **sign** that this human recovery will take place in the long term is to be found in the way the remnant will be provided for in the short term. In the aftermath of the Assyrian assault, life will be bleak. But the people will be able to survive because of the crops that spring up from what is already in the ground, and **in the third year** it will be possible to resume normal agricultural practice. The initial fragility of both human and economic conditions, in other words, should not be a reason for despair. This is not a people under God's judgment, like those in verse 26—**grass sprouting on the roof,** withering in the sun for lack of deep roots. This is a people under God's providential care, guaranteed to **bear fruit** (cf. Matt. 13:1–30, 36–43; Mark 4:1–20; Luke 8:1–15).

The third part of the prophecy makes explicit the circumstances in which Sennacherib will **return** home **by the way that he came** (vv. 28, 33). He will do so before the army encamped outside the city, playing its waiting game, takes military action—before an **arrow** is fired, a **shield** raised, a **siege ramp** built (v. 32). The LORD will protect Jerusalem completely, saving the city (Hb. *yšʿ*) from the Assyrians just as Hezekiah had requested (19:19, 34). God will do so to protect the reputation that Sennacherib's words have called into question (cf. 19:9–19, 34). God will also do so **for the sake of David** his **servant** (v. 34). This allusion to the Davidic promise (cf. 1 Kgs. 11:13, 32; 2 Kgs. 8:19) illustrates well the position in which Judah finds herself in these latter days. Hitherto in Kings this promise has been invoked only to explain why the Davidic line continued to rule over Judah even though a particular king was apostate (1 Kgs. 11:9–13, 32–39; 15:4; 2 Kgs. 8:19). Now we find it mentioned in a narrative featuring the very best of kings. Even *his* survival must now be explained explicitly in terms of divine grace, for in these days when Judah is herself moving towards final judgment (2 Kgs. 17:7–20), the piety of even the most faithful offers no guarantee of deliverance.

19:35–37 / Isaiah's first prophecy had promised that Sennacherib would hear a report and return to his own country (19:7); but the only report he heard actually resulted in a different "returning" altogether (19:9). The second prophecy has now re-emphasized the theme of return (vv. 28, 33), and we read immediately of the event that precipitated Sennacherib's flight. The "great army" outside Jerusalem's gates (18:17) sustains enormous casualties as **the angel of the LORD** moves among them (v. 35; cf. Acts 12:21–23), and Sennacherib returns (Hb. *šwḇ*), with his remaining forces, to his capital **Niniveh** (v. 36). The connection between the two events is not explicitly made, but we cannot doubt that these are connected—particularly when we read the sequel in verse 37. Having failed to understand from his experience that the LORD is God, Sennacherib finds himself one day **in the temple of his god.** He had thought that Hezekiah's God could not protect the Judean; now he finds that it is he who lacks protection, as he is murdered by **his sons.** The prophecies of Isaiah have been fulfilled. Jerusalem has been saved. "David" has once more overcome "Goliath."

Additional Notes §52

18:17 / **The aqueduct of the Upper Pool:** This aqueduct, of uncertain location, but evidently regarded here as just outside the city wall, has interesting associations for the reader of Isaiah. Here Isaiah had earlier called on Ahaz to exercise faith in the midst of the Syro-Ephraimite crisis (Isa. 7:3ff.). It is one of several differences between Ahaz and his son that Ahaz chose to ask for help from the Assyrian king, while Hezekiah chose to resist him.

18:20 / **You have strategy and military strength:** The Hb. is lit. "surely word of lips is counsel and power for war," implying that Hezekiah thinks that mere talk (cf. "word of lips" in Prov. 14:23) is sufficient preparation for the confrontation. The NIV translation is thus unfortunate. Hezekiah is not claiming any sort of **military strength,** and quite evidently does not have sufficient troops to be able to take advantage of military hardware if he possessed it (vv. 23–24). He depends on "the word"; and the word *is*, of course, sufficient for the crisis, if it is the word of a prophet (19:6, 20–21) sent by the LORD who is the ultimate possessor of "counsel and power" (Job 12:13ff.). See further the additional note on 19:35.

18:24 / **How can you repulse one officer of the least of my master's officials?:** It is not likely that Hb. *šwḇ ʾeṯ penê*, which appears in 1 Kgs. 2:16–17, 20 meaning "refuse," is to be taken as meaning here (uniquely) **repulse**, or that Hb. *peḥâ*, which is used in 1 Kgs. 10:15; 20:24 (and elsewhere in the OT) of high officials, should be translated here (uniquely) as **officer**. The reference is clearly to the bargain of v. 23. Hezekiah is asked not to refuse this man who is strictly speaking a high official, but describes himself (with what is no doubt false humility) as one of the least of his master's servants (Hb. *ʿeḇeḏ*). The king must avail himself of the Assyrian's excellent (if insincere) offer, even while looking to Egypt for **chariots and horsemen.** The fact that both *peḥâ* and *ʿeḇeḏ* are in the construct state does not imply that we need the NIV's **of,** since it is by no means unknown for two words in the construct to appear in apposition to one another (GKC §130e).

18:29 / **From my hand:** The MT has "his hand," marking out the latter part of the verse through to the beginning of v. 31 as the words, not of the king, but of the commander. This slide from the one to the other is, in fact, a feature of the speech as a whole (compare, for example, vv. 19–20 with vv. 23–24).

18:34 / **Hamath and Arpad . . . : Hamath** has been mentioned already in 17:24, along with **Sepharvaim,** and **Ivva** may well be the "Avva" of that verse. **Arpad** and **Hena** are new to us. This fact alone makes it unlikely that the Assyrian is asking whether the gods of these cities had **rescued Samaria** from his hand, for there is no mention of the people of **Arpad and Hena** being resettled in Israel in 17:24ff. The emphasis is in any case upon what has happened to the *home* cities of the gods, as it is in 19:12–13, where the kings of these cities are mentioned. We should understand by **they,** then (**have they rescued Samaria?**), the original gods of Samaria in general, not the particular ones mentioned just beforehand.

19:1 / **He tore his clothes:** We have grown accustomed to monarchs tearing their clothes, signifying deep emotion (1 Kgs. 21:27; 2 Kgs. 5:7–8; 6:30; 11:14). The contrast between wicked Jehoram and pious Hezekiah, in their reaction to enemies at their gates, is particularly interesting. Jehoram tears his clothes and, unwilling to wait for God, looks to kill God's prophet (2 Kgs. 6:30–31). Hezekiah tears his clothes and humbly requests prophetic prayer.

19:4 / **The remnant that still survives:** Remnants have been much in evidence when the story of the northern kingdom has been told (cf. Hb. *šʾr* in 1 Kgs. 19:18; 2 Kgs. 7:13; 13:7). Now only Judah remains (2 Kgs. 17:18). The remnant will on this occasion be saved (19:31), and Jerusalem escape Samaria's fate, but this will not always be the case (21:14).

19:24 / **All the streams of Egypt:** Much ink has been wasted debating whether Hb. *māṣôr* can really be **Egypt** (as in Isa. 19:6) when Sennacherib never literally conquered Egypt. The absurdity of the discussion becomes evident as soon as we ask whether we are meant to think that he "literally" ascended the heights of the mountains and cut down Lebanon's tallest trees (v. 23), or "literally," once in Egypt, **dried up** all her streams **with the soles of** his **feet** (v. 24). Did he measure all the trees? How did his feet come to have such absorbent qualities? The passage is not *meant* to be taken literally. It is the very point that Sennacherib has an exaggerated view of his own accomplishments, as Assyrian kings often did. He thinks of himself as a god. He claims to have brought judgment—as only the LORD can do—upon the cedars of Lebanon (cf. Ps. 29:5; Isa. 2:12–13; Amos 2:9; Zech. 11:1–3) and upon Egypt (Isa. 19:1–15). He ascends the heights so that he can look God straight in the face (Hb. *mārôm*, "height" in both v. 22 and v. 23; cf. Pss. 73:8; 75:4–5; Isa. 14:13–15). It is he, and not the LORD, who brings or withholds fertility, creating springs (not digging **wells**) and drying up rivers (Ps. 36:8–9; Jer. 2:13; 17:13; 51:36; Ezek. 31; Hos. 13:15).

19:28 / **My hook . . . my bit:** The metaphor may reflect actual Assyrian practice, if their own pictographic representations of conquest are to be taken as referring literally to the past. The LORD will lead the Assyrian, like an animal, back to his own land (cf. Ps. 32:9; Prov. 26:3; Ezek. 19:1–9).

19:35 / **The angel of the LORD:** There is a play on the Hb. word *malʾāk* ("angel, messenger") similar to that in 1 Kgs. 19:1–8. Sennacherib's messengers speak many words against the LORD (2 Kgs. 19:9, 14, 23), but neither Sennacherib nor his messengers have any power to act. The LORD has power of both speech and action and a messenger who is terribly effective.

§53 Deliverance and Exile (2 Kgs. 20:1–21)

It seems that the veiled threats in 2 Kings 16–17 with regard to Judah have come to nothing. Jerusalem has not suffered the same fate as Samaria. Yet the Davidic promise has been cited in 2 Kings 16–19, not in relation to a wicked king, but in relation to the most pious king Judah has had (19:34). This creates the impression that in these days of accumulated sin, even a good king requires God's special grace if the kingdom is to survive. It brings into question, therefore, whether Judah may expect in the future, under *apostate* kings, the kind of special treatment it has received in the past (1 Kgs. 15:4; 2 Kgs. 8:19). Is the protection of Jerusalem to go on for ever? Second Kings 20 hints that it will not.

20:1–7 / The chapter opens with an account of an illness that Hezekiah contracted around the time of the Assyrian assault on Judah, in his fourteenth year (cf. the promise of v. 6, taking into account the figures in 18:2 and 18:13). It is unclear how the illness relates to the events described in 18:13–19:36, although the ordering of the material implies that it happened after Sennacherib withdrew from Judah. Nor is the nature of the illness specified. It was evidently life-threatening (v. 1), but all we hear of the specifics is that it involved an inflammation or **boil** (Hb. *šeḥîn*, v. 7, as in Exod. 9:9–11; Lev. 13:18–20, 23; Deut. 28:35; Job 2:7). Its importance lies more in Hezekiah's response to it than in its nature. As in the midst of the Assyrian crisis, he turns to prayer (vv. 2–3; cf. 19:4, 15–19). The prayer is somewhat more self-centered than in 19:15–19, stressing the king's own righteousness. There is for the first time a suggestion that Hezekiah has an attitude problem. He turns **his face to the wall** (cf. Hb. *sbb ʾet-pānāyw* in 1 Kgs. 21:4, where the NIV translates "sulking") and weeps over his fate. Nevertheless, God answers him. The king will be well enough by **the third day** to **go up** and worship in **the temple** (v. 5), and he will live for another **fifteen years** (v. 6). Throughout that period (it is implied), God will continue in the ways of chapters 18–19. God will **deliver** the king and the **city,** not because of Hezekiah's **wholehearted devotion** (v. 3), but for God's own sake and the sake of **David** (v. 6). The message of 19:34 is thus reinforced. Even a king who has **done what is good** survives now only because of grace.

20:8–11 / The application of the fig poultice (v. 7) produces the complete cure promised in verse 5 (cf. the NIV's "he recovered," strictly "he lived"), or is simply a first step, rescuing Hezekiah from immediate death. Consequently, it is ambiguous whether verses 8–11 represent a flashback to some undescribed moment before Isaiah's action (cf. the NIV's **Hezekiah** *had* **asked Isaiah**), or—more naturally—a description of what happened next. If the latter interpretation is correct, then the king appears unwilling to believe that temporary remission will indeed lead to complete recovery; he asks for a further **sign.** What he is given is, in fact, analogous to the sign of recovery that Isaiah had offered in 19:29–31. Something in the natural world offers a pointer to something that will happen in the human sphere. Here it is the movement of a **shadow** on some **steps** (Hb. *ma‛ᵃlôṯ*) associated with the name of his father. As the sun (implied in v. 11, rather than stated) has **gone down,** the shadow has lengthened (Hb. *nṭh,* as in Judg. 19:8; Jer. 6:4), and under normal circumstances, it will continue to do so. This is just like Hezekiah, sinking towards death, destined for darkness. He is miraculously to recover, however, and **go up** (Hb. *‛ālâ*) to the temple, so the shadow itself miraculously recovers ground (goes back up). God has intervened in the normal processes of the world. The clock (metaphorically, or perhaps literally, if the "steps" are intended for this purpose) has been turned back.

20:12–21 / Verse 6 implied no more than that Jerusalem would be protected for another fifteen years. This closing narrative about Hezekiah addresses the question: What then? Its answer concerns, not Assyria, but **Babylon.** In a scene reminiscent of the Solomon story, Hezekiah shows some Babylonian visitors arriving in Jerusalem with their **gift** (Hb. *minḥâ,* v. 12; cf. 1 Kgs. 4:21; 10:25), everything in his **storehouses** and the **armory** and throughout the **kingdom** (v. 13; cf. 1 Kgs. 10:1ff.). As we have frequently been reminded, however, these are no longer the days of Solomon (cf. the earlier contrasts between Solomon and the Judean kings in 1 Kgs. 15:16ff.; 22:48–49; etc.). The clock has not been turned back that far, not even for David's greatest successor. In these days foreigners surveying Jerusalem's splendor do not simply marvel. Now we expect them to return with hostile intent. What Hezekiah's Babylonian visitors *saw*, Isaiah tells the king, they will one day *take away* to the **distant land** from which they have come (vv. 14, 16–18; cf. 1 Kgs. 8:46), along with some of the king's **descendants.** Hezekiah is surprisingly unmoved by this news. A man recently rescued from death, he is content simply to have **peace and security in** his **lifetime** (v. 19), a Solomon-like existence for a little while longer (cf. 1 Kgs. 5:4). Not for the first time in the chapter, there is a suspicion of self-centeredness about this righteous king. Second Kings 20 does not explicitly announce Judah's exile. Like chapters 16 and 17, it gives us only hints. Treasure has been carried off before; hostages have been taken before (cf. 2 Kgs. 14:14). But the hints are accumulating. References to plunder (v. 17) have an air of finality about them when read in the light of 2 Kings 17:20, and references to royal **eunuchs** (v. 18) do not encourage confidence in the enduring nature of the Davidic line.

Additional Notes §53

20:4 / **The middle court:** The NIV follows the Qere (the text the Masoretic scribes wished us to read) and many Hb. MSS in reading *ḥāṣēr hattîkōnâ*, perhaps a court between the temple and the palace. The Hb. as written is *hāʿîr hattîkōnâ*, which would normally be rendered as "the middle city." The word *ʿîr* can refer to part of a temple-complex, perhaps even to a courtyard (cf. the additional note to 2 Kgs. 10:25).

20:5 / **I will heal you:** As Hezekiah's response to the crisis of 18:7ff. recalled by way of contrast the response of Jehoram under siege (cf. the additional note on 19:1), so this story brings to mind others that have featured kings and prophets. Both Jeroboam and Ahaziah, in the midst of illness (1 Kgs. 14:1ff.; 2 Kgs. 1:2ff.; cf. also 2 Kgs. 8:7ff.), also received negative prophetic oracles of the kind received by Hezekiah in v. 1. But these were two kings under God's judgment; Ahaziah had even consulted another god. Hezekiah simply prays to the LORD, and the prophet is sent back with a different message entirely.

20:9 / **Shall the shadow go forward?:** This is an unlikely translation, which creates difficulties in v. 10—it is patently no more **simple** to accelerate the shadow's lengthening than to reverse it. The verb is better read as referring to the past: "The shadow has gone forward ten steps; shall it go back ten steps?" The contrast in v. 10 is between what is natural and has already happened (cf. v. 11), and what is unnatural and still to happen.

§54 Manasseh and Amon (2 Kgs. 21:1–26)

First there was a good king who went bad and lost most of his kingdom (Solomon). The remainder of the kingdom (Judah) was ruled by good kings mixed with bad (Rehoboam to Jehoshaphat). The LORD kept faith with the Davidic house through the bad times, because of the Davidic promise. He continued to do so even through the very bad times when that house was allied with the house of Ahab (Jehoram, Ahaziah). By the time of Ahaz, however, divine patience was wearing thin. Hints that Judah would ultimately share Israel's fate abound in 2 Kings 16–20, the deliverance of Jerusalem under Hezekiah notwithstanding. With Manasseh, God's patience breaks, and hints of disaster give way to explicit prophetic announcements. Fifty-five years of the worst apostasy Judah has seen are just too much to bear.

21:1–9 / **Manasseh** is the very worst of the Judean kings, indulging in and adding to all that has been most reprehensible in the religion of Israel in the preceding chapters. His father's reforms are reversed; **the high places** are **rebuilt** so that idolatry can resume there, and a new **Asherah pole** replaces the one Hezekiah removed (v. 3; cf. 18:4). It is his grandfather Ahaz who is the new king's role-model, as he sacrifices **his own son in the fire** and practices **divination** (v. 6; cf. 16:3, and possibly 16:15), **following the detestable practices of the nations** (v. 2; cf. 16:3). Manasseh also imitates the arch-apostate **Ahab,** by building **altars to Baal** (v. 3; cf. also the Asherah pole in 1 Kgs. 16:33) and worshiping **idols** (v. 11; cf. 1 Kgs. 21:26); he emulates Jeroboam and the other Israelite kings who **caused** Israel **to commit** sin (v. 16; cf. 1 Kgs. 14:16; 15:26, 30, 34; 16:2, 13; etc.). Manasseh does not simply follow the example of others, however. He himself is the supreme innovator in religious practice. He practices **sorcery** and consults **mediums** and **spiritists** (v. 6; cf. Deut. 18:9–13), and he takes it upon himself to install **the starry hosts**

(sun, moon, stars) as objects fit for worship alongside the LORD (and the Asherah pole) in the **temple** (vv. 4–5, 7). The LORD *of* hosts (1 Kgs. 18:15; 19:10; etc.) has thus become merely a god *among* hosts, with a consort goddess for company, open to manipulation by occult means. It is the religion of a man who has entirely ceased to believe in the one true God—the creator of heaven and earth, transcendent in respect of the natural world (Gen. 1, esp. vv. 14–19; 2:1; cf. Deut. 4:19; 17:3), and beyond all human control.

21:10–18 / Twice in the first nine verses we have been reminded of the nations "driven out" or "destroyed" by the LORD for the same sins that Manasseh and Judah have now committed (vv. 2, 9). We have also been reminded that Israel's possession of the land is contingent upon obedience to the law of Moses (v. 8). The implicit threats of these verses and of chapters 16–17 (cf. 16:1–4; 17:7–23) are now explicitly worked out. As Manasseh and the people have done **evil** (Hb. *raʿ*, vv. 9–11), so now the LORD will bring **disaster** (Hb. *rāʿâ*, v. 12) upon **Jerusalem and Judah.** The city will be assessed by the divine building inspector (cf. the use of the **measuring line** in Isa. 34:11; Lam. 2:8) and, like a dangerous building, condemned. It will be emptied, wiped clean like a **dish** after a meal is finished (v. 13). Judah, **the remnant of** the LORD's **inheritance,** will be handed over to her enemies, for the sins of Israel, much in evidence throughout her history since the exodus, have now reached their full measure (vv. 14–15; cf. 17:18, 20; 19:4, 31). Judgment will be analogous to that which earlier fell upon **Samaria** (v. 13; cf. 2 Kgs. 17; Amos 7:7–9). Worse than this, it will be analogous to what happened to the **house of Ahab.** That judgment, we should recall, completely destroyed the royal house (1 Kgs. 21:21–22; 2 Kgs. 9–10; cf. 1 Kgs. 14:10 and 21:21 for the only occurrences of **I am going to bring . . . disaster** found prior to 2 Kgs. 21:12). It seems that the Davidic line is to end after all, as 1 Kings 2:1–4; 8:25; 9:4 had implied it might. There will be no narrow escape like that of 2 Kings 11:1ff. This time, identification with Ahab will lead the house of David to Ahab's fate.

21:19–26 / In the shadow of such spectacular apostasy, the reign of Manasseh's son Amon has the appearance of a relatively unimportant footnote. He continues in the ways of his father, worshiping his **idols** (vv. 11, 21) and forsaking the LORD. He reigns, like other (northern) kings whose fathers received oracles about the destruction of their house, for only **two years** (1 Kgs. 15:25; 16:8; 22:51), and like the first two of these kings (Nadab, Elah), he is **assassinated**. As with Ahab's son Ahaziah, however, Amon's death does not immediately lead to the end of the royal house. It seems that we are to see the kind of delay in judgment we saw in 2 Kings 2–8. We await Josiah (1 Kgs. 13:2), and beyond him, Babylon (2 Kgs. 20:12ff.).

Additional Notes §54

21:5 / **Both courts of the temple:** First Kings 6:36 mentions an inner court, and 2 Kgs. 20:4 a middle court. Presumably it is these courts that the authors have in mind; however, the precise model of the temple with which they are working is unknown, since "middle court" implies the existence of an outer court (a feature of the new temple in Ezek. 40:17–19).

21:6 / **Mediums and spiritists:** As Ahab and Jeroboam function as models for Manasseh, so too does their model, Saul, stand in the far distance behind them (see the commentary on 1 Kgs. 11–13, 17–21, for the detailed comparison here). Saul, the very first king, was found towards the end of his reign consulting a medium (1 Sam. 28:3–25), having supposedly expelled **mediums and spiritists** from the land. It was shortly afterward that final judgment fell upon his house (1 Sam. 31–2 Sam. 4). It seems that the house of David is to suffer the same fate, in spite of the promise of 2 Sam. 7 (7:14–15).

21:12 / **Ears . . . will tingle:** The expression appears in 1 Sam 3:11 and Jer. 19:3, which also describe human reaction to bad news. The verb (Hb. *zll*) is rare, and translation requires educated guesswork. It is difficult to defend **tingle**, however, for all that its history is older than the NIV (cf., e.g., the RSV). If a physiological reaction is in mind, Hab. 3:16 (where *zll* appears alongside *rgz*, "be agitated, quiver, quake") suggests that "quiver" would be better. It is more likely, however, that the ears, as the organs by which news enters the body, are simply being used by extension for the whole body. People who hear what God has done will shake with terror (cf. *rgz* in Exod. 15:14; Deut. 2:25; Isa. 32:11; 64:2).

21:16 / **Much innocent blood:** It is no surprise to find Manasseh, who was "like Ahab," accused of the shedding of blood. The judgment that fell upon Ahab's house was explicitly said in 2 Kgs. 9:7 to have represented the LORD's vengeance upon him for the blood of his "servants the prophets" and all his other servants, including (we assume) Naboth (cf. 1 Kgs. 21:19; 22:35, 38; 2 Kgs. 9:26, 33). The blood shed by Manasseh is to be seen likewise as including that of God's "servants the prophets," who have announced the LORD's judgment against him (v. 10; cf. Heb. 11:37 for NT reflection of a Jewish tradition that Isaiah met his death at this time, sawed in two), and those other loyal worshipers who have, like Naboth, suffered the injustice that naturally follows on from apostasy (see the commentary on 1 Kgs. 21). Judah has failed to listen to the prophets (2 Kgs. 17:12–13) and now faces the same judgment as Israel, as the LORD visits their blood-guilt upon them (1 Kgs. 2:32; cf. Deut. 19:10, 13; 21:8–9). A story that began with the house of David claiming freedom from such blood-guilt (1 Kgs. 2:5–9, 31–33, 37) is to end with guilt fully imputed. David's descendants are not going to know "the LORD's peace forever" (1 Kgs. 2:33).

21:18 / **The garden of Uzza:** Hitherto we have read in the regnal formulas for Judean kings only of burials "in the city of David." From Hezekiah onwards the notices are more varied, and there is no reference to the city of David. That this indicates a change in burial practice is disputable. On the general point, see further Provan, *Hezekiah*, pp. 134–38. All that can safely be said is that we are given considerably more detail about the burial places of Manasseh and Amon than about any other king. The interesting question is, as always, "Why?" The answer probably lies in the associations of the name **Uzza.** This was the name of the man struck down by God in 2 Sam. 6:1–8 for his irreverent act in taking hold of the ark. The LORD's wrath broke out against him (6:8). Manasseh was, of course, the epitome of the irreverent person, "taking hold of" and perverting Judean worship and provoking the LORD to great anger. It is fitting that the name of the burial place of Manasseh, and of the son who walked in his ways, should carry connotations of spectacular judgment upon impiety.

§55 Josiah (2 Kgs. 22:1–23:30)

Judgment has been announced. It is now simply a matter of timing. At this juncture in Judean history, strangely enough, Judah finds herself with yet another righteous king—a second Moses to match her second David (Hezekiah). Josiah is a king long-awaited (1 Kgs. 13:2). He is the best of all kings, but he is a king come too late.

22:1–2 / The verses that introduce **Josiah** alert us to the kind of king he is going to be. There is reference to **David**—as we would expect. More significantly, however, there is an unmistakable allusion to Deuteronomy 17:20, where the ideal king is one who does not "turn" (Hb. *swr*, as in 2 Kgs. 22:2) from the law **to the right or to the left.** This is only the first of many references in 2 Kings 22–23 that link Josiah with the law of Moses in general and the figure of Moses in particular. For the authors of Kings, Josiah was the best of all kings, transcending even David and Hezekiah in his faithfulness to God (cf. 23:21–25). Never had anyone turned to the LORD as Josiah did, in accordance with all the law.

22:3–13 / It is nevertheless not until the **eighteenth year of his reign,** apparently, that the new king begins to take action concerning the apostate condition of Judean worship. His initial concern is simply to repair the temple, like Joash in 2 Kings 12:1–16 (compare 12:9–16 with 23:3–7), not to reform its cult. It is not until **Shaphan,** returning with his report of diligence in financial matters (v. 9), presents him with **the Book of the Law** (v. 11), that Josiah really becomes worried (v. 11). Only then does he comprehend just how far short of divine acceptance Judean worship falls (v. 13). It is, of course, quite understandable that a child brought up in a royal court that was apostate for fifty-seven years and subjected all opposition to a reign of terror should not be aware of the LORD's demands, and he is not blamed for it. As soon as he was aware of the contents of the book, our authors insist, he acted as a pious king should. He tore his **robes** in grief and despair and sent various of his officials to **inquire of the LORD**. A couple (at least) of interesting questions are raised by this passage. The first of these is: Which "book" has been found? This seems a straightforward question to answer; the phrase **book of the law** is used in the Pentateuch only of Deuteronomy (Deut. 28:61; 29:21; 30:10; 31:26; cf. also Josh. 1:8; 8:30–35; 23:6; 24:26). It is Deuteronomy that is read to the king and that provides the basis for his actions in the remainder of the narrative.

A more difficult question is this: How long is the book envisaged as having been out of the public domain? We are not explicitly told, but the impression throughout Kings has been that it was available to the various rulers of Israel and Judah. They did not conform themselves to its laws by chance, nor did they fail to do so through ignorance. Their success and failure in keeping the law had to do, rather, with their will. Thus Solomon is charged with keeping the law of Moses (1 Kgs. 2:3); Jehu criticized for not keeping it with all his heart (2 Kgs. 10:31); Amaziah commended for acting in accordance with it (14:6); and the Israelites in general condemned for ignoring it (17:13–14; cf. also 17:34, 37). As recently as 2 Kings 18 Hezekiah has been commended for keeping this law (v. 6), after a description of religious reform that clearly recalls Deuteronomy 12:1–7. There is no reason to think, then, that the loss or concealment of the book is being presented as anything other than a recent event, occurring during the long reign of the apostate Manasseh. It is easy to imagine (though again we are not told) why it may have been removed from its proper position beside the ark of the covenant (Deut. 31:26) during his reign. It is a book whose laws Manasseh systematically infringed—whose authority over him he refuses, as king, to acknowledge (Deut. 17:18–20). It is not a book that he would want to have in the temple. Nor would the priests have wished to provoke him by leaving it there. Whether Hilkiah really **found** it, of course, or whether his choice of words is dictated by a desire to remain distanced from it until he discovers how Manasseh's grandson will react, must remain open to question. The circumstances in which it "comes to light" are entirely veiled in mystery.

22:14–20 / The prophet chosen by Josiah's officials for consultation was not Jeremiah, whose ministry had begun five years earlier (according to Jer. 1:2), nor Zephaniah (Zeph. 1:1), but **Huldah,** a resident of Jerusalem's **Second District** (wherever that might have been) and the **wife** of the **keeper of the wardrobe** (v. 14—perhaps a temple official, cf. 2 Kgs. 10:22). Her words confirm what we already know from the unnamed prophets of 2 Kings 21. The LORD is **going to bring disaster** on Jerusalem and its people (v. 16; cf. 21:12) because the Judeans have **forsaken** the LORD (Hb. ʿzḇ, v. 17; cf. 1 Kgs. 9:9; 11:33; 2 Kgs. 21:22; etc.), **burned incense to other gods** (cf. 2 Kgs. 16:4), and **provoked** him **to anger** in countless other ways (Hb. kʿs, 2 Kgs. 21:6, 15; cf. the NIV footnote). God has noted Josiah's reaction to the reading of the book of the law, however. Because he has **humbled** himself **before the LORD** (Hb. knʿ, v. 19), he will not personally **see all the disaster** that is to fall on Jerusalem (v. 20). There is to be a further delay (cf. 21:19–26) of the kind that we saw with Ahab, whose house was also spared for a while because he tore his clothes and "humbled himself" (Hb. knʿ, 1 Kgs. 21:27–28). Manasseh's grandson is now being treated, as his grandfather was, like Ahab. Josiah's reaction makes a difference—but only to himself. The judgment that has been announced will still surely fall.

23:1–3 / Since Josiah is a pious king, Huldah's oracle about the future does not deflect Josiah from the path of reform. Reformation in the light of the law-book is still the right thing to do, and Josiah is one who above all others does what is right (22:2). His first move, therefore, is to gather all the people together and to read to them **all the words of the book** (v. 2; cf. Deut. 31:9–13). It is now referred to as the **book of the covenant,** for the purpose of the reading is to prepare for a renewal of the covenant between the LORD and the people, to which Deuteronomy is the supreme witness (cf. Deut. 5:2–3; 29:1–28). A similar covenant-renewal ceremony after a period of apostasy in Judah took place in 2 Kings 11:12–14, when the king also **stood by the pillar** (v. 3; 11:14). The essence of the ceremony is the royal promise to **follow the LORD** and to **keep his commands, regulations and decrees** wholeheartedly (cf. Deut. 6:17; 1 Kgs. 2:3). The people then follow suit (v. 3; cf. 2 Kgs. 11:17, noting the implication there that the commitment *of* both parties to God involves also a similar degree of commitment *between* the parties under God; cf. 1 John 4:20 etc.).

23:4–14 / Joash's renewal of the covenant was followed by the destruction of Baal-worship in Jerusalem; those truly in covenant with the LORD cannot also be in covenant with God's

enemies (cf. Deut. 7:1–6). Josiah now proceeds, likewise, to remove all trace of apostasy from Jerusalem and Judah. Everything
to do with **Baal** and **Asherah** and the worship of the **starry hosts**
is subject to radical treatment: **articles** are removed from the
temple and **burned** (v. 4); **priests** are deported from their **high
places** and the high places are **desecrated** and destroyed (vv. 5,
8–9; cf. the additional note to v. 5); the **Asherah pole** is partially
burned and then **ground . . . to powder** (v. 6); the **quarters** of the
shrine prostitutes are destroyed (v. 7; cf. the additional note to
1 Kgs. 14:23–24); the **horses** and **chariots dedicated to the sun** are
removed (v. 11); and the **altars** erected by Ahaz and Manasseh
are **pulled down** and hastily **smashed to pieces** (v. 12, where the
MT has "he ran," rather than the NIV's **he removed them**). It is
clear that the **kings of Judah** who are in mind as the authors
generalize about the past (vv. 5, 11–12) are mainly these two
arch-idolaters, Ahaz and Manasseh, although some of the specific features of the cult that they are said here to have introduced
are not, in fact, explicitly mentioned in the accounts of their
reigns (compare 16:1–4 and 21:1–16 with 23:4–14). Mention of the
worship of **Molech** (v. 10), however, reminds us also of **Solomon;**
it is interesting that the reform embraces also the worship of
those other deities who have had their devotees since his day
(v. 13; cf. 1 Kgs. 11:5, 7). It is comprehensive and thorough.

    23:15–20 / A marked feature of the Josianic reform is
that he not only destroys but also desecrates (vv. 8, 10, 13), particularly by placing items considered to be holy in proximity with
graves and human bones (vv. 6, 14; cf. Num. 19:1–22 for the idea
of death as a pollutant, esp. v. 18). It has already been hinted in
verse 4 that this procedure is to be extended to **Bethel**, where
Josiah takes the **ashes** of the idolatrous vessels brought out from
the temple, but it is only in verse 15 that this line of narrative is
picked up. **Jeroboam**, it will be recalled, had started out as a new
Moses and finished up instead as a second Aaron, fashioning
calves for the people and instituting a new cult focused on Bethel
(see the commentary on 1 Kgs. 12–13). Josiah now takes action
against this cult, which has lived on in the activities of the new
settlers in the land of Israel (cf. 2 Kgs. 17:24ff.). He does so in a
way that recalls Moses's own action against the first golden calf.
He burns **the high place** (along with **the Asherah pole**) and
grinds it **to powder** (cf. Hb. *šrp*, "to burn," and *dqq leʿāpār*, "to
grind to powder," in v. 15 and Deut. 9:21, noting also 23:6). He

then defiles the altar with **bones** taken from the surrounding **tombs, in accordance with** the prophecy of the **man of God** in 1 Kings 13:2 (cf. also 13:11–32 for the background to vv. 17–18). The other part of the prophecy—that Josiah would sacrifice the priests of Bethel upon the altar—is not explicitly cited as fulfilled, but verses 19–20 presuppose fulfillment, in telling us that Josiah did to all the shrines **in the towns of Samaria** just what he did at Bethel (cf. **slaughtered all the priests,** v. 20). For the first time since Solomon a king has been able to treat the northern area of Israel as if it were part of the same kingdom as the south. His reform affects the whole country. One might almost believe that the days of humbling for the house of David were over (1 Kgs. 11:39) were it not for the prophecy of Huldah in 2 Kings 22:15–20.

23:21–25 / Josiah's reform is already far more all-encompassing than Hezekiah's; but there is more to come. After purification of worship comes the command to **celebrate the Passover,** according to the stipulations of Deuteronomy (Deut. 16:1–8, noting esp. v. 6). In celebrating this festival Josiah not only outstrips Hezekiah in faithfulness to God, the authors tell us, but even David himself, for a Passover like this had not been observed since before **the days of the judges who led Israel** (cf. Josh. 5:10–12 for the last mention of Passover in the narrative). Little wonder, then, that having reported the removal of **mediums and spiritists** (2 Kgs. 21:6), **household gods** (lit. "teraphim"; cf. Judg. 17:5; 18:14, 17), **idols** (2 Kgs. 21:11, 21), and **detestable things** in general (1 Kgs. 11:5, 7; 2 Kgs. 23:13) from Judah and its capital, the authors should conclude their account of Josiah's reforms by telling us that there was no **king like him** when it came to "turning to the LORD" (vv. 24–25). He did so, in fact, **with all his heart and with all his soul and with all his strength, in accordance with all the Law of Moses** (cf. Deut. 6:5).

23:26–30 / Yet Judah's fate was already settled. The LORD had decided to **remove Judah** and to **reject Jerusalem** and its **temple.** Josiah's reforms changed none of that, even though Deuteronomy 17:14–20 had promised a long-lasting dynasty to the king who turned from the law neither to the right nor the left (cf. 2 Kgs. 22:2). Even Josiah himself did not come to a happy end. Unwisely interposing himself between **Egypt** and **Assyria,** he was killed at **Megiddo,** suffering the same ignominious exit from the stage as his apostate ancestor Ahaziah (cf. 2 Kgs. 9:27–28): carried by **chariot** from **Megiddo** to **Jerusalem** and **buried . . . in**

his own tomb (v. 30; cf. 22:20). That the best king of Judah should end his days in the same way as one of the worst indicates the way things are now going. The delay of judgment for Jerusalem and its kings is utterly at an end.

Additional Notes §55

22:4 / **Go up to Hilkiah:** 22:3–7 presupposes the reforms introduced by Joash in 12:9–16. It is still the task of the doorkeepers to collect the money for temple repairs; but it is the task of the secretary to oversee, with the high priest, its counting and distribution to the (still trustworthy) men in charge of the work.

22:13 / **Our fathers have not obeyed:** The statement is akin to the one in 21:15, which characterizes the past generally as one of sinfulness. This does not mean that there were no periods when people did obey, any more than the reference to Solomon's high places in 23:13 means that no king had ever acted against these before, or the reference to "kings of Judah" in 23:5, 11–12 means that all Judean kings had indulged in idolatry. Second Kings 23:12, in particular, shows how we must always reckon with hyperbole when reading Hb. narrative; for taken literally, it would have some kings of Judah building altars near an upper room that had not yet been constructed.

22:20 / **You will be buried in peace:** It has sometimes been argued that this is a reference to the manner of Josiah's death and that as such it stands in conflict with 23:29, where Josiah's death is violent rather than peaceful. It is not the *manner* of Josiah's death that is in view here, however, but its *timing*. He will die before the terrible events prophesied in 21:12–14 and 22:15–17 come to pass—while Judah and Jerusalem still know **peace,** rather than the sword. See further Provan, *Hezekiah,* p. 149.

23:5 / **The pagan priests:** The NIV wishes us to distinguish between the **priests** of this verse (Hb. *kemārîm*), who are **pagan,** and the priests of vv. 8–9 (*kōhanîm*), who are priests of the LORD, whether serving in the towns of Judah or in the capital itself ("at the entrance to the Gate of Joshua"). The latter "did not serve at the altar of the LORD," as Deut. 18:6–8 had said they might, but they did "share equally in the benefits" by sharing their fellow-priests' bread (18:8). But there are several difficulties with the NIV's interpretation of the material. In the first place, vv. 8–9 are placed right in the middle of an account that is otherwise entirely concerned with Josiah's action against idolatrous worship. They employ verbs that are elsewhere in the passage used of idolatrous worship (Hb. *qṭr,* "to burn incense," vv. 5, 8—appearing alone *only* of such worship in the rest of Kings; cf. 1 Kgs. 12:33; 13:1–2; 2 Kgs. 17:11) or of Josiah's action against it (Hb. *ṭmʾ,* "to desecrate," vv. 8, 10, 13, 16).

If the authors of Kings mean us to think these are not idolatrous priests, they have not gone out of their way to make that apparent. In the second place, the NIV's interpretation also requires that we take the passage as telling us of both orthodox and idolatrous high places functioning in the towns of Judah and in Jerusalem throughout Manasseh's reign. It is difficult to see Manasseh as an advocate of consumer choice throughout his dominion, much less at one of his own city gates (v. 8). In the third place, it would be strange if v. 9 were saying that the king who kept "all the law of Moses" (22:2; 23:25) actually ignored it in the matter of these loyal (and brave) orthodox priests, failing to apply Deut. 18:6–8.

All in all, then, it is better to take vv. 5 and 8–9 as using different words to refer to the same idolatrous priests (cf. *kōhᵃnîm* in 1 Kgs. 12:31–32; 2 Kgs. 10:11, 19; etc., esp. 23:20). They are removed from office (rather than "done away with") by Josiah, but permitted to live on among their kinsfolk (lit. "brothers"). The point of v. 9 (where "although" is better translated "but") is to stress that these so-called "priests" were not allowed near the temple in Jerusalem. The concern is that they should not compromise its restored purity. The verse therefore has nothing to do with Deut. 18.

23:7 / **Weaving for Asherah:** The Hb. is lit. "weaving (in) quarters for Asherah." It probably refers to the manufacture of ritual garments for worship (cf. 2 Kgs. 10:22).

23:11 / **The horses . . . the chariots:** Extrabiblical evidence suggests a particularly close connection between **horses** and **chariots** and religion in which heavenly bodies feature prominently. It is no surprise to find them mentioned, therefore, in a passage where worship of the starry hosts has such a high profile. See further M. S. Smith, "The Near Eastern Background of Solar Language for Yahweh," *JBL* 109 (1990), pp. 29–39. We are no doubt meant to regard the roof-altars in v. 12 as associated with such a cult, the roof being a particularly appropriate place to worship heavenly bodies. It is tempting, although it is only a guess, to link the "upper room of Ahaz" here with the "stairway of Ahaz" in 20:11.

23:13 / **The Hill of Corruption:** It seems likely that this is a deliberate corruption of the name of this hill, analogous to the kind of corruption we find elsewhere in personal names (cf. the discussion in the introduction, note 21). "Mount of Olives" (Hb. *har hammišḥâ*) has been altered to **Hill of Corruption** (Hb. *har hammašḥît*) to express the authors' distaste for what went on there. "Topheth" in 23:10 (taking the vowels of *bōšet*, "shame") is probably another example of the same phenomenon.

23:18 / **The prophet . . . from Samaria:** The choice of words is noteworthy. He is not from *Bethel* (the city, 1 Kgs. 13:11), but **from** *Samaria* (the region). The phrase has been quite deliberately chosen in tandem with **man of God . . . from Judah** earlier in the verse. The two prophets lie united in their grave. Is there just a hint that lasting union between the two kingdoms from which they have come will likewise now be found only in death? Josiah's efforts at "reunion," like all his other efforts at reform, will be to no avail (cf. 2 Kgs. 13:21 for another occasion where individual death becomes a metaphor for national demise).

§56 The End of Judah (2 Kgs. 23:31–25:30)

Josiah, like Ahab, humbled himself before the LORD, and judgment, as in Ahab's case, did not fall during Josiah's reign. The implication of the analogy is that we may expect it to fall during the reign of Josiah's son (cf. 1 Kgs. 21:28–29). This is exactly what we find now, as the story of Kings comes to its end. It is not, however, the first of Josiah's sons to sit on his throne (Jehoahaz) who experiences the full force of God's wrath (cf. 1 Kgs. 22:51–2 Kgs. 1:18), or even the second, Jehoiakim (cf. 2 Kgs. 3–9). It is the third, Zedekiah. Even though the story is almost over and the distinctions between Israel and Judah are all but obliterated, God still differentiates between them. But gradually the glory of Solomon is dismantled, as imperial power passes to Babylon, temple and palace are destroyed, and Jerusalem's treasures are carried off to a foreign land. It is left to Josiah's grandson, Jehoiachin, to offer us such hope as we can find for the future of the Davidic "lamp," as the lights go out all over Judah.

23:31–35 / The first of Josiah's successors is **Jehoahaz.** He is not the eldest son, for Eliakim/Jehoiakim, at least, is older than he (compare vv. 31 and 36). He is thus something of a Solomon to Eliakim's Adonijah (cf. the commentary on 1 Kgs. 1:5–6 and the additional note to 2:22). These are not the days of Solomon, however, as the authors of Kings have often been at pains to point out, and Jehoahaz, doing **evil in the eyes of the LORD** like his **fathers** before him (note the same general term in 2 Kgs. 22:13), reigns for only **three months** (vv. 31–32; contrast 1 Kgs. 11:42). The circumstances in which he is first imprisoned at **Riblah** on the river Orontes south of **Hamath,** then taken south to **Egypt,** are not described. What is evident, however, is that Jehoahaz is not a ruler acceptable to the Pharaoh of Egypt, and Pharaoh is (temporarily) Judah's new overlord, in the aftermath of Josiah's death at Megiddo. Jehoahaz is replaced with his brother (v. 34), and **the people of the land,** responsible for installing Jehoahaz as king (v. 30), pay for their actions (v. 35). We are far away from the time when Solomon was thought worthy of Pharaoh's daughter (1 Kgs. 3:1).

23:36–24:7 / **Jehoiakim** is no better than Jehoahaz in terms of his religious commitments (23:37), and now we hear of **Babylon,** the ultimate agent of divine judgment on Judah (cf. 2 Kgs. 20:12ff.). "Off-stage" it is the **king of Babylon** who has been taking the Assyrian empire apart (cf. the book of Nahum for a graphic treatment of its fall), in spite of Egyptian support (23:29). Now he comes at the head of the army sent by the LORD **to destroy Judah . . . because of the sins of Manasseh** (24:2–4; cf. 17:20; Dan. 1:1–2). He subdues **Egypt** and comes into possession of the whole Solomonic empire, **from the Wadi of Egypt to the Euphrates River** (cf. 1 Kgs. 4:21, 24; 8:65). Jehoiakim first becomes **his vassal** (24:1), but inevitably—for the story must end with disaster—he rebels.

24:8–17 / It is his son **Jehoiachin** who succeeds him and pays the price for his rebellion. The armies of Babylon march on **Jerusalem** and besiege the city, as the Assyrians had done before them (2 Kgs. 18–19). Jehoiachin is no Hezekiah (v. 8). He surrenders (v. 12) and is carried off into exile, along with **all the treasures** from the **temple** and the **palace** (v. 13; cf. 20:17–18 and the additional note to 1 Kgs. 14:26). Solomon's **gold,** which once flowed into his empire in fabulous quantities (1 Kgs. 9–10), now flows into the coffers of the new imperial power in Babylon. As people used to come from all over the world to Solomon's court, so now all the notables of Jerusalem journey on enforced pilgrimage abroad (vv. 14–16; cf. 1 Kgs. 10:23–25). A remnant still remains—but only **the poorest** in the land (v. 14; cf. 2 Kgs. 19:4, 30). Among the exiles, although Kings does not tell us this, is the prophet Ezekiel, whose prophetic ministry begins a few years later in Babylon (Ezek. 1:2–3).

24:18–25:7 / As the history of the kings draws to a close, independent rulers govern for hardly any time at all ("three months," 23:31; 24:8). The kings with whom foreign powers replace them rule for only a little longer (**eleven years,** 23:36; 24:18), before they rebel (Hb. *mrd,* vv. 1, 20) and bring disaster. Jehoiachin, having held on to power no longer than his uncle Jehoahaz, is now replaced by another uncle, Mattaniah (v. 17); Mattaniah, as **Zedekiah,** duly rebels (v. 20). The result is a third

siege of Jerusalem that, like the third siege of Samaria (2 Kgs. 17:5), is also the last. Zedekiah's new conscripts flee when faced with a breach in the city wall, and the king flees with them, only to be overtaken near **Jericho** (vv. 4–5). The site of Israel's first military victory in their new land (Josh. 6) thus becomes a place associated with their final defeat in it, as Zedekiah is **captured** and taken to **Riblah** (cf. 23:33). The last thing he sees before he is blinded is the execution of his **sons**.

25:8–21 / A few weeks later (cf. vv. 3, 8) full vengeance is visited upon the city. **Every important building** is **burned down,** including Solomon's **temple** and **palace** (v. 9), and the **walls around Jerusalem** are broken down (v. 10). More people are deported, both those who had resisted and those who had collaborated, again leaving only the **poorest** (vv. 11–12). On this occasion, some are executed (vv. 18–21). More of the temple's contents are removed: **the bronze pillars;** parts of **the movable stands; the bronze Sea;** and various other items (vv. 13–17; cf. 1 Kgs. 7:15–45). The threats of 1 Kings 9:6–9 have become reality. **Judah,** like Israel, has gone **into captivity, away from her land** (v. 21; cf. 2 Kgs. 17:23). The book of Obadiah appears to reflect the distress of this period.

25:22–26 / **Gedaliah,** the grandson of Josiah's secretary **Shaphan** (22:12), is now appointed to govern what is left, under the watchful eye of some **Babylonian officials** (vv. 22, 24), and the remnants of the scattered army (v. 5) gather to him at the new administrative center of **Mizpah** (v. 23). He does not survive long. **Ishmael son of Nethaniah,** who apparently has ambitions to be the next king (he is **of royal blood,** v. 25), takes it upon himself to slaughter everyone at Mizpah, Judean and Babylonian alike. The final exile of the book of Kings is a voluntary one, as the remaining people flee to **Egypt** (v. 26; cf. Jer. 40:7–43:7). The epic saga that began with the exodus from that land has turned into a horror story of sin and judgment (21:15), and Israel now returns whence it came.

25:27–30 / There is, however, an epilog. It concerns Jehoiachin, carried off to Babylon in 24:15, and now, many years later, **released . . . from prison** and given **a seat of honor . . . at the king's table.** It is a tailpiece that has provoked some debate. It might be taken simply as the final nail in the coffin that the authors have so skilfully been preparing for Israel throughout the preceding chapters. Solomon's glory has departed to Babylon. The empire has dissolved. The Babylonian king has destroyed Solomon's city, his palace and his temple; he controls Solomon's empire, and he possesses all Solomon's wealth. Now Solomon's last-surviving successor (so far as we know) sits, amply provided for, at the Babylonian **table:** the great symbol of imperial power (1 Kgs. 4:27). He sits; he eats; and then (it is implied) he dies. The exiles (it is implied) ought to behave in the same way, accepting the advice of Gedaliah to the people in Judah: "Settle down . . . serve the king . . . and it will go well with you" (v. 24).

Yet it is difficult to believe that this is all there is to it. The fact is that the authors of Kings have chosen to tell us that Jehoiachin lived on (in contrast to Jehoahaz, 23:34), when they could have allowed him to dwell (with Zedekiah) in obscurity. They have also chosen to contrast the fate of Jehoiachin's family (exile, 24:15) very clearly with that of Zedekiah's (death, 25:7). It is Zedekiah, and not Jehoiachin, who ends up effectively as "a eunuch in Babylon" (20:18), a mutilated man deprived of heirs who might later claim the throne. These distinctions between the two must be significant; the parallels drawn between the house of David and the house of Ahab in 2 Kings 21–23 distinctly implied that the destruction of David's house would be total. There would be no escape of the kind that occurred in Athaliah's day (2 Kgs. 11:1ff.). Yet Jehoiachin lives, and his reappearance in the narrative is strikingly reminiscent of the reappearance of Joash after that earlier destruction of the "whole royal family." He survives, unexpectedly, in the midst of carnage, and he represents, like Joash during Athaliah's "reign," at least the *potential* for the continuation of the Davidic line. All is not yet necessarily lost after all; the destruction of the family of the "last king of Judah" does not mean that there is no member of the house of David left. As the prayer of Solomon in 1 Kings 8:22–53 looks beyond the disaster of exile, grounding its hope for the restoration of Israel to the land in God's gracious and unconditional election of Abraham, Isaac, and Jacob (cf. also 1 Kgs. 18:36–37; 2 Kgs. 13:23; 14:27); as it refuses to accept that God's words about the rejection of people, city and temple (e.g., 2 Kgs. 21:14; 23:27) are God's final words; so too 2 Kings 25:27–30 hints that the unconditional aspects of the Davidic promise may even still, after awful judgment has fallen, remain in force. These verses express the hope that grace may, in the end, triumph over law; that, God's wrath having been poured out upon good Josiah's sons, his (admittedly wicked) grandson might still produce a further "lamp for Jerusalem," as his (equally wicked) forefathers did (1 Kgs. 11:36; 15:4; 2 Kgs. 8:19). These verses look back beyond Kings, in fact, to Samuel, and they hang on tenaciously to the words of 2 Samuel 7:15–16: "my love will never be taken away from him . . . your throne will be established forever."

Additional Notes §56

23:34 / **Pharaoh . . . changed Eliakim's name:** To give someone a new name is to make clear that one has power over the other person. In both 23:34 and 24:18, loss of name symbolizes loss of power. Judah no longer controls its own destiny. It is dictated to by others.

24:2 / **Raiders:** The verse recalls those earlier **raiders** (Hb. *geḏûḏîm*) from Aram who afflicted Israel in the period before the full-scale Aramean assault on Israel and the siege of Samaria (2 Kgs. 5:2; 6:23; 6:24ff.). The storm clouds are gathering. Possession of Solomon's empire has passed to Babylon, and Solomon's erstwhile vassals (**Aramean, Moabite and Ammonite**) have joined the opposition (contrast 1 Kgs. 5:4).

24:16 / **Seven thousand fighting men:** It is interesting to find the figure **seven thousand** occurring yet again, since that is the number of "the remnant" in 1 Kgs. 19:18 (cf. also the additional note to 1 Kgs. 20:15). One wonders whether its appearance has to do with a desire on the part of the authors to tell us (2 Kgs. 24:14 notwithstanding) that those days when Israel had a significant remnant are past. "Ten thousand" (24:14) is the number of soldiers left to Jehoahaz in the desperate days described in 13:1–7; there it is the number of the remnant, here, the number of the exiles. The LORD's anger is burning even more fiercely now than it was then (13:3; 23:26; 24:20).

§57 Excursus: Hezekiah and Josiah in Canonical Context

Josiah was the perfect king, conforming himself in all respects to the law of Moses. Hezekiah was a second David. He was (like David) not without flaws, as his first reaction to the Assyrian invasion revealed (18:13–16) and as his later reaction to illness confirmed (20:1–11). His trust in the LORD was, nevertheless, impressive. Yet Hezekiah and Josiah were good kings living in bad times. With the death of Jeroboam II in 2 Kings 14:29, all restraint upon the wrath of God against Israel was lifted and exile for the northern kingdom quickly followed (2 Kgs. 17). It also began to be clear that Judah, in becoming increasingly like Israel, was risking Israel's fate, that the promise to David might in the end not protect the south for very much longer than the promise to Jehu had protected the north. Hezekiah escaped the fate of Hoshea, in spite of Ahaz, and Josiah was spared the worst of what was to come, in spite of Manasseh; but neither was able to prevent Judah's ultimate demise. Thus all Israel went into exile from their land, apostasy triumphant over reform.

That is almost the end of the story in Kings. Yet as we have seen, there are hints in the book's closing that the Davidic line still has a future, and these hints become full-blown expectation in other parts of the OT. For example, Jeremiah 30:1–11 looks forward to a time when a descendant of David will once again sit on the throne of a united kingdom of Israel (cf. 1 Kgs. 11:39), and in Haggai 2:20–23 Jehoiachin's grandson Zerubbabel becomes the focus of messianic hope. It is not surprising that when such thinking about the future messiah was being done, the figures of righteous Hezekiah and Josiah should have sprung to mind as models.

In Jeremiah, for example, Josiah is the model (22:15–16) for the Davidic king of the future who will rule over Israel and Judah in righteousness (23:1–8)—an anti-type of the wicked Jehoiakim, who burns scrolls rather than obeying their words (Jer. 36; contrast 2 Kgs. 22:11ff.). The description in Zechariah 12:10–14:2 of the shepherd who is "pierced" and the fall of Jerusalem and the exile that follow this are also reminiscent of the later events of Josiah's reign (cf. "Megiddo" in 2 Kgs. 23:29 and Zech. 12:11; and the description of Josiah's death in 2 Chron. 35:23–24). The suggestion of vicarious suffering in Zechariah 13:1 reminds us of Isaiah 52:13–53:12; and some have wondered whether this Isaiah passage, too, does not also reflect those events.

For the Chronicler (2 Chron. 29–32), Hezekiah was the first king since the division of the united kingdom to reunite all Israel under one king and around one temple—a kingly model for the future and a focus of expectation in relation to the time when God would reestablish his kingdom. This move from present to future is even more manifest in the book of Isaiah, which contains in chapters 36–39 much of the material found in 2 Kings 18–20 (with additions). These chapters function within the book as a counterpart to Isaiah 6:1–9:6, describing the reign of the first person (Hezekiah) who might have been seen as the Davidic child of Isaiah 9:1ff., the one in whom the promises to David would be realized. Seen in the context of the book as a canonical whole, they appear now, not so much as records of the past, but as prophecies about the future; they point the reader to a Hezekiah-like figure who will usher in the period of deliverance and restoration for God's people that is described in Isaiah 40–55.

It is therefore not surprising that, although Hezekiah and Josiah do not appear by name in the NT except in the genealogy of Jesus in Matthew 1:1–17 (cf. vv. 10–11), we should hear so many echoes of the OT narratives about their reigns when we read the NT authors. For Jesus' reflection upon his own identity, and the thinking of the early Christians about the one they regarded as the Root and Offspring of David (Rev. 22:16), was bound to be influenced—as the thinking of the Jewish rabbis about the Messiah in the early centuries A.D. was clearly influenced (cf., for example, b. *Sanh.* 94; 98b; 99a; b. *Ber.* 28b)—by the reading of these narratives in their canonical context. Thus it is that we find, for example, in Jesus' attitude to the ritually "unclean" and in his healing of people after assuring them of divine forgiveness (Mark 2:1–12; 7:1–23), echoes of Hezekiah's attitude to the "unclean" Israelites during his Passover celebration in 2 Chronicles 30:18–20. Jesus cleanses the temple, like both Hezekiah and Josiah (Matt. 21:12–13 and parallels; John 2:13–17), looking for a truly reformed religion. He himself is one who, like

Josiah, keeps the whole law of Moses and actively promotes its keeping (e.g., Matt. 5:17–20; 8:4). There is to be no lasting reform, however, and no immediate deliverance for Jerusalem from her foreign oppressor (Rome). Jesus does not function as a Hezekiah in this respect, at least not at this time. The city will fall again, the temple will know desecration of Manasseh-like proportions, and there will once more be exile (e.g., Matt. 23:37–24:21). Jesus' own fate in the midst of all this judgment is to die, like righteous Josiah (cf. John 19:37), at the hands of a foreign power, a suffering servant to his people. His fate is also to be "restored to health" after three days (like Hezekiah; cf. b. *Ber.* 10b for the rabbinic view that Hezekiah's recovery was a near-resurrection from the dead, comparable to the Elisha miracle in 2 Kgs. 4:18–37). There will be a second coming, when Jerusalem and her remnant will once again know salvation. Victory, rather than defeat, will be experienced at Megiddo (=Armageddon, Rev. 16:16), as the nations are defeated and Babylon is brought low by the Davidic King (Rev. 16–19). The kingdom of God will have fully arrived. The Lamb will sit forever upon his throne (Rev. 21–22).

Like Solomon, then, both Hezekiah and Josiah function typologically within the whole canon of Scripture, preparing the way for the one who is ultimately to sit upon David's throne and usher in God's kingdom. Like Solomon, however, they can also serve as models for behavior for those called to follow Jesus with their cross. They remind us of how the believer should trust and pray in a crisis, even when besieged by a great army of enemies or troubles (2 Kgs. 18:17–20:7; Matt. 26:36–46 and parallels; Luke 21:34–36; John 14:13–14; Acts 4:23–31; 16:25–34; Rom. 15:30–33; Eph. 6:10–18; Phil. 4:6–7; Jas. 5:13–16). They remind us of the importance of ongoing reform in worship, of the importance of ensuring that God alone is the focus of our attention and that what we do is in complete conformity to God's will (2 Kgs. 18:1–8; 23:1–25; Matt. 6:1–34; 19:16–24; Luke 18:9–14; Rom. 12:1–2; 1 Cor. 10–14). They remind us, finally, of the necessity of obedience to God's Word, as it addresses us in the present through the inspired writings of the past (2 Kgs. 22:11ff.; Matt. 5:17–20; 2 Tim. 3:14–17), of the necessity of such obedience even where it goes against the grain of the surrounding culture, and even where it offers no immediate prospect of reward. This is a fitting note upon which to end our reading of Kings, as we turn from the text and seek to apply Scripture to life.

For Further Reading

It is always difficult to know how to construct a select bibliography—precisely because it is select, and not comprehensive. This compilation contains a fairly full listing of recent commentaries on Kings. It also contains a selection of books and articles that will aid, firstly, further reflection upon the matters discussed in the introduction, and, secondly, further study of various sections of the text in terms of narrative and theology. Readers should also consult the commentary itself for additional, very recent books and articles on individual passages. Those wishing to supplement the suggested reading here, and in particular to think further about aspects of the book of Kings that this commentary has not highlighted, should consult the much fuller bibliographies in the FOTL and WBC volumes.

Commentaries

Auld, A. G. *Kings*. DSB. Edinburgh: Saint Andrew, 1986.

Cogan, M., and H. Tadmor. *2 Kings*. AB. Garden City: Doubleday, 1988.

DeVries, S. J. *1 Kings*. WBC. Waco: Word, 1985.

Hobbs, T. R. *2 Kings*. WBC. Waco: Word, 1985.

Hubbard, R. L., Jr. *First and Second Kings*. EBC. Chicago: Moody, 1991.

Jones, G. H. *1 and 2 Kings*. NCB. 2 volumes. Grand Rapids: Eerdmans, 1984.

Long, B. O. *1 Kings, with an Introduction to Historical Literature*. FOTL. Grand Rapids: Eerdmans, 1984.

_____. *2 Kings*. FOTL. Grand Rapids: Eerdmans, 1991.

Nelson, R. D. *First and Second Kings*. IBC. Louisville: John Knox, 1987.

Rice, G. *1 Kings: Nations under God*. ITC. Grand Rapids: Eerdmans, 1990.

Wiseman, D. J. *1 and 2 Kings*. TC. Downers Grove, Leicester: InterVarsity, 1993.

On Introductory Matters

Kings as Narrative Literature

Alter, R. *The Art of Biblical Narrative.* London: Allen & Unwin, 1981.

Bar-Efrat, S. *Narrative Art in the Bible.* B&L. Sheffield: Almond, 1989.

Berlin, A. *Poetics and Interpretation of Biblical Narrative.* Sheffield: Almond, 1983.

Frei, H. W. *The Eclipse of Biblical Narrative: A Study in Eighteenth and Nineteenth Century Hermeneutics.* New Haven: Yale University Press, 1974.

Gunn, D. M., and D. N. Fewell. *Narrative in the Hebrew Bible.* OBS. Oxford: Oxford University Press, 1993.

Haynes, S., and S. L. McKenzie. *To Each Its Own Meaning: An Introduction to Biblical Interpretations and Their Applications.* Louisville: Westminster/John Knox, 1993.

Licht, J. *Storytelling in the Bible.* Jerusalem: Magnes, 1978.

Longman, T., III. *Literary Approaches to Biblical Interpretation.* FCI. Grand Rapids: Zondervan, 1987.

Nelson, R. D. "The Anatomy of the Books of Kings." *JSOT* 40 (1988), pp. 39–48.

Sternberg, M. *The Poetics of Biblical Narrative: Ideological Literature and the Drama of Reading.* Bloomington: Indiana University Press, 1985.

Kings as Historiographical Literature

Bebbington, D. *Patterns in History.* Downers Grove, Leicester: InterVarsity, 1979.

Clive, J. *Not By Fact Alone: Essays on the Writing and Reading of History.* New York: Knopf; London: Collins, 1989.

Goldingay, J. *Approaches to Old Testament Interpretation.* ICT. Updated ed. Downers Grove, Leicester: InterVarsity, 1990. Pages 66–96.

Halpern, B. *The First Historians: The Hebrew Bible and History.* San Francisco: Harper & Row, 1988.

Long, V. P. *The Art of Biblical History.* FCI. Grand Rapids: Zondervan, 1994.

Nash, R. H. *Christian Faith and Historical Understanding.* Grand Rapids: Zondervan, 1984. Pages 93–109.

Van Seters, J. *In Search of History: Historiography in the Ancient World and the Origins of Biblical History.* New Haven: Yale University Press, 1983.

Younger, K. L., Jr. *Ancient Conquest Accounts: A Study in Ancient Near Eastern and Biblical History Writing.* JSOTSup. Sheffield: JSOT Press, 1990. Pages 1–58.

Kings as Didactic Literature

Baker, D. L. *Two Testaments, One Bible: A Study of the Theological Relationship between the Old and New Testaments.* Rev. ed. Leicester: Apollos, 1991.

Carson, D. A., and H. G. M. Williamson, eds. *It Is Written: Scripture Citing Scripture. Essays in Honour of Barnabas Lindars.* Cambridge: Cambridge University Press, 1988.

Childs, B. S. *Biblical Theology of the Old and New Testaments: Theological Reflection on the Christian Bible.* Minneapolis: Fortress, 1993.

_____. *Introduction to the Old Testament as Scripture.* Philadelphia: Fortress; London: SCM, 1979. Pages 27–106, 229–38, 281–301.

Fishbane, M. *Biblical Interpretation in Ancient Israel.* New York: Oxford University Press; Oxford: Clarendon, 1985.

Goldingay, J. *Approaches to Old Testament Interpretation.* ICT. Downers Grove, Leicester: InterVarsity, 1990. Updated ed. Pages 97–122.

Goppelt, L. *Typos: The Typological Interpretation of the Old Testament in the New.* Grand Rapids: Eerdmans, 1982.

Hobbs, T. R. *1, 2 Kings.* WBT. Dallas: Word, 1989.

McConville, J. G. *Grace in the End: A Study in Deuteronomic Theology.* Grand Rapids: Zondervan, 1993.

_____. "Narrative and Meaning in the Books of Kings." *Bib* 70 (1989), pp. 31–49.

Von Rad, G. *Old Testament Theology.* Vol. 1. Edinburgh: Oliver & Boyd, 1962. Pages 334–47.

Weinfeld, M. *Deuteronomy and the Deuteronomic School.* Oxford: Oxford University Press, 1972. Pages 191–319.

Wolff, H. W. "The Kerygma of the Deuteronomic Historical Work." In *The Vitality of Old Testament Traditions.* Edited by W. Brueggemann and H. W. Wolff. Pages 83–100. Atlanta: John Knox, 1975.

On 1 Kings 1–11

Brettler, M. "The Structure of 1 Kings 1–11." *JSOT* 49 (1991), pp. 87–97.

Frisch, A. "The Narrative of Solomon's Reign: A Rejoinder." *JSOT* 51 (1991), pp. 22–24.

_____. "Structure and its Significance: The Narrative of Solomon's Reign (1 Kings 1–12:24)." *JSOT* 51 (1991), pp. 3–14.

Jobling, D. " 'Forced Labor': Solomon's Golden Age and the Question of Literary Representation." *Semeia* 54 (1992), pp. 57–76.

Parker, K. I. "The Limits to Solomon's Reign: A Response to Amos Frisch." *JSOT* 51 (1991), pp. 15–21.

_____. "Repetition as a Structuring Device in 1 Kings 1–11." *JSOT* 42 (1988), pp. 19–27.

_____. "Solomon as Philosopher King?: The Nexus of Law and Wisdom in 1 Kings 1–11." *JSOT* 53 (1992), pp. 75–91.

Younger, K. L. "The Figurative Aspect and the Contextual Method in the Evaluation of the Solomonic Empire (1 Kings 1–11)." In *The Bible in Three Dimensions: Essays in Celebration of Forty Years of Biblical Studies in the University of Sheffield.* Edited by D. J. A. Clines, et al. Pages 157–75. JSOTSup. Sheffield: JSOT Press, 1990.

On 1 Kings 12–2 Kings 2

Carroll, R. P. "The Elijah-Elisha Sagas: Some Remarks on Prophetic Succession in Ancient Israel." *VT* 19 (1969), pp. 400–415.

Cohn, R. L. "The Literary Logic of 1 Kings 17–19." *JBL* 101 (1982), pp. 333–50.

_____. "Literary Technique in the Jeroboam Narrative." *ZAW* 97 (1985), pp. 23–35.

Hauser, A. J., and R. Gregory. *From Carmel to Horeb: Elijah in Crisis.* JSOTSup. Sheffield: Almond, 1990.

Herr, D. D. "Variations of a Pattern: 1 Kings 19." *JBL* 104 (1985), pp. 292–94.

Wallace, R. S. *Elijah and Elisha: Expositions from the Book of Kings.* Edinburgh: Oliver & Boyd, 1957.

On 2 Kings 3–13

Bostock, D. G. "Jesus as the New Elisha." *ExpT* 92 (1980), pp. 39–41.

Brodie, T. L. "Jesus as the New Elisha: Cracking the Code." *ExpT* 92 (1981), pp. 39–42.

Cohn, R. L. "Form and Perspective in 2 Kings 5." *VT* 33 (1983), pp. 171–84.

Ellul, J. *The Politics of God and the Politics of Man.* Grand Rapids: Eerdmans, 1972.

LaBarbera, R. "The Man of War and the Man of God: Social Satire in 2 Kings 6:8–7:20." *CBQ* 46 (1984), pp. 637–51.

Moore, R. D. *God Saves: Lessons from the Elisha Stories.* JSOTSup. Sheffield: JSOT Press, 1990.

Olyan, S. "*Hašālôm:* Some Literary Considerations of 2 Kings 9." *CBQ* 46 (1984), pp. 652–68.

On 2 Kings 14–25

Ackroyd, P. R. "An Interpretation of the Babylonian Exile: A Study of 2 Kings 20, Isaiah 38–39." *SJT* 27 (1974), pp. 329–52.

Daube, D. *He that Cometh.* The St. Paul's Lecture, 1966. London: n. p., 1966.

Fewell, D. N. "Sennacherib's Defeat: Words at War in 2 Kings 18:13–19:37." *JSOT* 34 (1986), pp. 79–90.

Gerbrandt, G. E. *Kingship According to the Deuteronomistic History.* SBLDS. Atlanta: Scholars, 1986.

Laato, A. *Josiah and David Redivivus: The Historical Josiah and the Messianic Expectations of Exilic and Postexilic Times.* ConB. Stockholm: Almqvist & Wiksell, 1992. Esp. pp. 356–63.

_____. *Who is Immanuel?: The Rise and the Foundering of Isaiah's Messianic Expectations.* Åbo: Åbo Academy Press, 1988. Esp. pp. 313–26.

Subject Index

Scripture Index

OTHER EARLY WRITINGS